Practical Applications in Business Aviation Management

James R. Cannon and Franklin D. Richey

Government Institutes
An imprint of
THE SCARECROW PRESS, INC.
Lanham • Toronto • Plymouth, UK
2012

Published by Government Institutes
An imprint of The Scarecrow Press, Inc.
A wholly owned subsidiary of The Rowman & Littlefield Publishing Group, Inc.
4501 Forbes Boulevard, Suite 200, Lanham, Maryland 20706
http://www.govinstpress.com

Estover Road, Plymouth PL6 7PY, United Kingdom

British Library Cataloguing in Publication Information Available

Library of Congress Cataloging-in-Publication Data

Cannon, James R.
Practical applications in business aviation management / James R. Cannon and Franklin D. Richey.
p. cm.
Includes index.
ISBN 978-1-60590-763-5 (cloth : alk. paper) — ISBN 978-1-60590-770-3 (pbk. : alk. paper) — ISBN 978-1-60590-764-2 (electronic)
1. Local service airlines--Management. 2. Airlines—Management. 3. Aeronautics—Flights—Management. 4. Business travel—Management. 5. Private flying. 6. Executives—Transportation. I. Richey, Franklin D., 1938- II. Title.
HE9785.C36 2012
387.7'42—dc23 2011038530

∞™ The paper used in this publication meets the minimum requirements of American National Standard for Information Sciences—Permanence of Paper for Printed Library Materials, ANSI/NISO Z39.48-1992.

Printed in the United States of America

To my wife, Lin Cannon, whose love, support and motivation has made our journey through life such a meaningful one.

To my wife, Manous Richey, whose understanding and support made my contribution to the writing of this book possible.

Contents

Foreword

Business Aviation: A Proud Legacy, A Promising Future

By Ed Bolen, President and CEO, National Business Aviation Association

Business aviation is one of America's most important yet least understood industries.

Contrary to popular misconception, the vast majority (85%) of the companies that operate business aircraft are small and medium-size enterprises. Fortune 500 companies fly only about 3% of U.S. business aircraft. In fact, operators include a broad cross-section of organizations, such as state governments, universities, and charitable organizations, as well as all types of businesses.

Many of the smaller U.S. businesses that rely on business aviation are located in the dozens of markets across the country where the airlines have reduced or eliminated service. Thus, business aviation provides an essential transportation link—a lifeline—between these smaller companies and communities and the rest of the world. While the organizations that rely on business aviation are varied, they all have one thing in common: the need for fast, flexible, safe, and secure access to destinations worldwide.

Most business aviation missions involve time-critical trips by sales, technical, and middle-management employees, not flights by top executives, who account for less than one quarter of all business aircraft trips. It's also worth noting that a jet is not the typical business airplane. While the business aviation fleet includes a variety of aircraft—from light, single-engine airplanes to helicopters and long-range jets—there are far more piston-powered aircraft registered in the United States than there are jets. And three quarters of all business aircraft operators fly only one aircraft, not a fleet of airplanes.

Why do companies use business aircraft? Business aviation helps them compete in an intensely competitive global marketplace by fostering efficiency and productivity. The business airplane is the closest thing to a flying office or conference room, so it can truly turn travel time into productive work time. Employees can prepare presentations or openly discuss proprietary information without fear of eavesdropping.

People who fly on business aircraft can be in more places in less time, often visiting three sites in one day, rather than one site in three days. And because many business aircraft are equipped with the latest communications technologies, passengers can stay connected to their associates on the ground.

In fact, studies have consistently shown that companies that operate business aircraft are more competitive, productive, and profitable than those that do not. Companies that utilize business aircraft outperform non–aviation users in several important financial measures, including annual earnings growth, stock and dividend growth, total share price, and market capitalization.

Surveys also have shown that companies using business aircraft are among the most innovative, most admired, best brands, and best places to work. In addition, operators dominate the list of companies strongest in corporate governance and responsibility.

Business aviation also is a fundamental part of our nation's humanitarian delivery system. Companies that rely on business aircraft often give back by transporting cancer patients to treatment, reuniting combat veterans with their families, flying organs for transplants, or assisting in times of natural disasters.

Perhaps the most often-overlooked fact is that business aviation is a critical engine for the U.S. economy. Besides being a vital link in our nation's transportation system, providing access and economic development in thousands of communities with little or no commercial airline service, business aviation employs more than 1.2 million Americans, generates over $150 billion in economic activity, and contributes positively to our nation's balance of trade.

The vast majority of business aircraft are manufactured, operated, serviced, and maintained in the United States. Even the few airplanes that are manufactured overseas often are outfitted in the United States with American-made engines, avionics, electronics, systems, interiors, and other aircraft components. Consequently, business aviation is a source of good jobs. Besides the many people who build business aircraft, tens of thousands of others—pilots, maintenance technicians, schedulers, dispatchers, flight attendants, training professionals, airport employees, and other support personnel—are employed in business aviation.

For individuals considering a career in business aviation, the future is bright. Today's business airplanes are among the most sophisticated in all of aviation, the potential destinations are almost limitless, and the career opportunities are diverse.

This textbook, *Practical Applications in Business Aviation Management,* systematically examines business aviation and provides you with a comprehensive understanding of and appreciation for one of America's most dynamic industries.

Preface

I was cruising along at FL410 in December of 2005 when Memphis Center broadcast a second call to a business jet in our area to switch frequencies. Immediately the pilot apologized, saying that he had missed the first call and repeated the frequency change along with his "N" number. That was followed by an anonymous comment, "Little airplanes"; another voice, "Yeah there are too many of them up here," and yet another, "You can say that again." The second voice repeated, "There are too many of them up here." I looked at my flying partner and said, "If the airlines weren't in so much trouble, maybe there wouldn't be as many business and fractional jets in the air today." He suggested that I repeat that on the air, but I declined to do so. Just because they were being unprofessional on center frequency, didn't mean that we had to be. That brief exchange on the air did stimulate some discussion in our cockpit as to what has transpired over the past 20 years to cause several professional airline crews to feel compelled to violate the sterile integrity of a center frequency.

When I stepped out of the navy and into civilian aviation back in the early 1970s, Southern Airlines was still in existence. Hughes Air West was going strong. PSA Airlines was dominating the west coast. Eastern Airlines was competing head to head with Delta and Western Airlines appeared to own the Eastern Pacific. Braniff was a great airline based in Dallas with all those wild paint schemes on their birds. There was also a start-up, based at Love Field, called Southwest Airlines, that began operations the year before I separated from the navy. Bill Lightstone, a fellow LSO from the Ranger and Midway cruises, had joined Southwest that year. Bill retired from Southwest in 2004.

During the fall of 1973, driving back to east Tennessee from South Texas, my last duty assignment, I interviewed with Federal Express in Little Rock. They were operating Falcon 20s with large cargo doors and the pilots wore leather jackets to keep the chill off during those evening deliveries. The recruiter with FedEx offered me an opportunity to train in Memphis and gain a type rating and 10 hours in the Falcon 20. Once that was completed, he said, I would go into a pool of pilots waiting for a slot with the company. All it would cost me was my GI benefits and $1,500 cash. I've often reflected back to that decision and wondered how different my life would have been if I had accepted that opportunity instead of declining. Certainly FedEx has become a very successful company and thousands of pilots have had very rewarding careers there. The fall of that year was highlighted by the oil embargo, long lines at gas stations and the cessation of all airline hiring. Delta, having never furloughed a pilot in their history, placed several hundred junior pilots in baggage handling jobs with the company to keep them actively employed. John Manstrom, a squadron mate of mine who got out of the navy about the same time Bill did, was one of those Delta pilots who smashed bags until a seat opened back up several years later. John turned 60 in 2003 and by the strangest of coincidences, my wife happened to be on his last flight from Phoenix to Atlanta.

John and Bill were able to enjoy great careers with two stable commercial aviation companies during their golden years. Many others, just as talented in the cockpit and just as deserving as my two friends, languished through takeover after takeover, through consolidation and furlough, as the route structures and fare wars continued to be managed and often mismanaged by executives who ran our nation's airlines and the organized labor forces that opposed them. The employees of those less fortunate carriers suffered financially and emotionally. Timing being what it is, John and Bill were very lucky. In retrospect, I think I was very lucky as well. Not being able to land an airline job when I was eligible, the maximum age back then was 30, I ventured into the strange world of business aviation.

It truly was a different aviation world back then as compared to today. Business aviation was considered a "perk" for the elite upper crust of Wall Street. You could buy a new G-II for under $5 million, but seating was limited to senior officers only. I was often asked by friends and relatives if I was ever going to get a real job and give up this career that obviously was never going to amount to anything. How times have changed. Owning a business jet is almost a necessity in today's corporate environment. I can't imagine a senior executive of a progressive corporation using the airlines as a means of transport, given the inconvenience, uncertainty of schedule, and relative lack of security as compared to what business aviation offers. We have evolved from small groups to large fleets. From the standard company-operated departments, to management companies, and on to fractional programs. All three of these methods of providing lift for companies and individuals have proven to be successful, even in the competitive environment that exists. We do, after all, compete with one another. When Executive Air Fleet first emerged over 30 years ago, many a traditional aviation manager cried "foul." Matt Weisman, Bill Watt, and others had found a way to share risks, costs, and assets in order to make a business out of business aviation. Richard Santuli came along years later and refined the art of business aviation management from a financial perspective. Fractional ownership is a viable and important portion of our industry.

All of this has driven traditional corporate aviation departments over the years to offer better and better customer service to their parent companies. In turn, we have become better and better at doing our jobs. National and local associations have formed to support and promote "best practices." Our industry has much to be proud of in a time when the airline industry has much to be ashamed of. While we worked to serve the companies that paid our salaries, airline pilots, mechanics, and flight attendants have struggled with the difficult task of whether they should support or defy the companies that paid theirs. It's certainly not all their fault. The sad state of commercial aviation today is due to the lack of legislative, executive, and labor representatives not being able to look into the future that was fraught with excessive fuel costs, intense capital pressures, and extremely high labor costs. I really do feel for those folks who have been caught up in this mess. Something will have to be done soon.

The next time I hear complaints on the air about how many "little" airplanes are up there, I wonder what the big boys would think if they knew about the number of VLJs (very light jets) that will be joining us over the next few years. It's also time for all of us in business aviation to look back at the mistakes that others have made in commercial aviation. We need to study these errors in judgment in order to prevent making similar mistakes. The recent recession hit our industry very hard, but it is on the mend. Over the past twenty years business aviation has witnessed tremendous growth, but we cannot afford to rest on our laurels. Make your voice heard through the NBAA and local associations. Volunteer to make a difference in your future. Our airline brethren thought the golden goose would always be there for them. There is no guarantee that it will be there for us.

Jim Cannon

Acknowledgments

This book was written by Dr. Frank Richey, Assistant Dean of Aviation at Embry-Riddle Aeronautical University and Jim Cannon, a retired business aviation manager. Jim and Frank met in January 2010 in Daytona Beach during the residency week of the first PhD in aviation cohort. Frank is a professor in the program and Jim was fortunate to be one of the eleven members of that first class.

Many friends and colleagues made contributions to this book through their insight, encouragement, and review of material. The authors would like to express their gratitude to Drew Callen, Bill McBride, Mike Lederer, Suzanne Dempsey, Dr. Joanna Cannon, Dr. Alan Stolzer, Dr. David Esser, Dr. Tim Brady, Susie Bencsik, Sean Glynn, Larry Fletcher, Alan King, Jay Evans, Bill Garvey, Amy Stalzer, Heidi Fedak, Abby Soley, and John Sheehan.

1

Description and History

Learning Objectives: After reading this chapter you should be able to:

- Define the various aspects of business aviation
- Explain the similarities and differences of non-scheduled and GA business aviation
- Describe the U.S. aviation structure as defined by the FAA
- Explain the role of corporate aviation in the overall U.S. air transportation system
- Discuss the early development and history of corporate aviation

The Federal Aviation Administration (FAA) breaks civil aviation into two distinct categories: commercial air transport (CAT) and general aviation (GA). GA is a catchall category used by the FAA to classify all aviation except CAT and military aviation. Business aviation is defined by the National Business Aviation Association (NBAA) as the use of any general aviation aircraft for a business aviation purpose (nbaa.org). Business aviation is further categorized into employee-flown and corporate aviation (Sheehan 2003, p. 1, 2). Commercial air transport is also separated by the FAA into three specific operational types: scheduled airlines (FAR Part 121), scheduled commuter, and on-demand charter. Both scheduled commuter and on-demand charter are regulated by FAR Part 135.

This text is offered as a guidebook for students and business aviation professionals into the complexities involved in the management of a business aviation flight department to include: corporate (Part 91) employee-flown (Part 91), and commercial business use (Part 135). In order to standardize terminology, and for the remainder of this text, the term business aviation will serve as the generic description of both Part 91 categories and the subcategory of on-demand charter (FAR 135). The purpose of business aviation is to provide safe, efficient, and convenient air transportation to support the mission and goals of the corporation. Corporate aviation is defined by the National Business Aviation Association (NBAA) as the use of an aircraft that is owned, partially owned, or leased and operated by a corporation for the transportation of people or cargo in the furtherance of a firm's business, flown by professional pilots who receive a direct salary or compensation from the corporation for that service. This definition applies to companies that have travel needs sufficient to support the operation of a company aircraft and pay for the services of professional pilots. Some of the larger corporations operate a fleet of turbine-powered aircraft to meet their corporate travel needs. Business aircraft range in size from small single and multi-engine piston/turboprops to business jets capable of traveling more than 6,000 miles nonstop. At the upper end of this spectrum are the very large (>170,000 lb max takeoff gross weight) ultra-long-range business jets manufactured by Boeing and Airbus.

Employee-flown GA has a slightly different definition: the use of an aircraft for the furtherance of the company's business, but flown by a pilot who is not compensated for services as a pilot. Typically, this is the smaller one-aircraft operator, where the company owner is also a pilot and uses a four- to five-passenger single or multiengine piston aircraft to meet the travel needs of his company. The introduction of the very light jet (VLJ) category of aircraft will offer employee-flown GA the opportunity to fly at the same flight levels as the current commercial and business jets do. The NBAA represents the full spectrum of business aircraft operators and has almost 9,000 members, about 70% of the total whom are single aircraft flight departments. These definitions are not found in the Federal Air Regulations (FAR) Part 1, definitions and abbreviations, or elsewhere in the federal rules and regulations, but are in common use, and most importantly, the FAA statistical reports separate corporate and business flight activities into two separate categories.

U.S. AVIATION STRUCTURE

The Federal Aviation Administration (FAA) has divided the U.S. aviation industry into the three broad categories for reporting and data collection purposes. The three categories are: (1) commercial, (2) military, and (3) general aviation. The term "commercial operator" is defined in FAR Part 1 as anyone who uses an aircraft in air commerce for compensation or hire. Air commerce is defined as operating an aircraft in the federal airways system. In other words, if you use an aircraft to make money and fly it in the federal airway system within the United States, you must obtain a special FAA certificate to do so. The type of certificate needed to conduct commercial operations depends upon the size of the aircraft. Small aircraft weighting 12,500 pounds or less (certified takeoff weight), with less than 10 seats, need an FAR Part 135 certificate to conduct commuter or on-demand service. The FAR Part 135 certificate covers both scheduled commuter airline operations and on-demand (charter) operations; however non-scheduled charter operations may operate aircraft up to 30 seats in size. A charter is defined as a flight where both the aircraft and crew are hired to perform an on-demand flight to a specified number of destinations. These types of flights are sometimes referred to as air taxi operations because of the on-demand nature and the fact that they are very similar in operation to a ground taxi service. Airlines fall under the commercial category and normally operate on a scheduled basis. When engaging in scheduled air transportation and operating aircraft of 10 seats or more, a commercial carrier is required to possess an FAR Part 121 certificate to operate. Scheduled commercial helicopter air carriers must obtain an FAR Part 127 certificate. The term "air transportation" is defined as flying between states, flying external to the United States, or engaging in the transportation of mail by aircraft. All commercial operators are grouped under the commercial category for FAA record keeping and statistical reporting purposes and must hold an FAR Part 135, 121, or 127 certificate to conduct business.

The U.S. military have their own set of rules and regulations, which are separate and independent from civil aviation. This category includes all active-duty, reserve, and National Guard flying activities under the control of the U.S. Department of Defense (DOD). The GA category includes all aviation activities, except the scheduled airlines and military. The FAA definition is more precise in that it defines general aviation as "all civil aviation activity except air carriers certified under FAR Parts 121, 123, 127, and 135." General aviation plays a very important role in U.S. national air transportation system. On the average, general aviation aircraft fly over 26 million hours each year, transporting around 166 million passengers to various destinations (GAMA 2008). Table 1.1 contains a list of major GA activities, grouped in a manner similar to the way the FAA gathers statistics. As can be seen from this table, corporate/business (including GA corporate; GA employee-flown; Part 135 business) aircraft are listed as part of the general aviation activities area. It is the largest component in terms of dollar value of equipment and percentage of hours flown each year.

Rules governing the operation of all aircraft are contained in FAR Part 91 of the federal air regulations. These regulations are generally less stringent than the additional regulatory requirements imposed on commercial operators who use the aircraft for "compensation or hire." Additional rules and

Table 1.1 General Aviation Activities

Aerial Application—agriculture crop dusting, firefighting, cloud seeding, mosquito control, and forest service.

Air Ambulance (med)—medical evacuation by helicopter or aircraft.

Aerial Observation—mapping, photography, survey, pipeline patrol, fish spotting, traffic advisory, search and rescue, sightseeing, and sports events.

Air Travel Clubs—not classified as commercial operators, however a FAR Part 125 certificate is required if the aircraft has a seating capacity of 20 or more passengers, or a maximum payload capacity of 6,000 pounds or more.

Business/Corporate Aviation—use of aircraft to meet corporate travel needs, usually non-commercial in nature. Some corporations elect to use their aircraft for "compensation or hire," and in this case are required to obtain a FAR Part 135 certificate.

Fixed Base Operator (FBO)—conducts aircraft and fuel sales, on-demand charter, flight instruction, aircraft maintenance, aircraft rentals, and sightseeing tours. Usually located at an airport and have a contract with the local airport authority detailing their scope of work.

Law Enforcement—use of aircraft by local, state, and federal governments to enforce laws; includes federal homeland security and drug enforcement agencies.

Personal/Recreational—non-commercial, personal use of aircraft by individual aircraft owners.

Other—air shows, parachuting, glider towing, banner towing, air racing, helicopter hoisting, and aerial advertising.

requirements for operation of civil aircraft are contained in Subpart K of FAR Part 91. This subpart applies to aircraft that are owned on a fractional basis. Assuming the aircraft are not used commercially, corporate/business flight operations are regulated solely by the requirements contained in FAR Part 91. Corporations who wish to use their aircraft for "compensation or hire" must obtain an FAR Part 135 certificate in addition to meeting the FAR Part 91 requirements. Some corporations choose to obtain an FAR Part 135 certificate because they can use the revenue from commercial use of the aircraft to offset the cost of owning and operating the aircraft. The downside of this is that there are additional operational restrictions, costs, and recordkeeping requirements for FAR Part 135 operations. As an example, crew duty requirements are not required under FAR Part 91, but are very restrictive under FAR Part 135. There are also additional training requirements, equipment requirements, and maintenance requirements under FAR Part 135, which will add additional costs to the operating budget. These additional expenses can be greater than the revenue generated by operating the aircraft commercially. For this reason, most business aviation flight operations that have the flexibility to do so prefer to operate under FAR Part 91 as a corporate flight department. This gives more freedom and allows the department to operate their aircraft in such a manner as to maximize the ability to meet air travel needs without the additional costs incurred by maintaining an FAR Part 135 certificate.

BUSINESS AIRCRAFT OPERATIONS

A business aviation flight department when managed efficiently provides the corporation it serves with both tangible and intangible benefits—tangible in the sense of measurable offsets of airline travel costs, savings in executive time, the flexibility to respond to any request with minimum notice, and the added benefit of access to more than 5,000 airports throughout the United States. Intangible benefits include increased levels of security, the ability to conduct important business meetings while aboard the aircraft, and departures when the passengers wish to leave, not when the schedule dictates. The term "corporate aircraft" is often used to describe a business aviation department's aircraft that is used exclusively for company business and operates under the guidelines of FAR Part 91. This term also applies to the vast majority of private aircraft that are owned by high-net-worth individuals, but are managed and flown by professional aviators. The use of corporate/business aircraft greatly enhances the productivity of company executives and managers by reducing the non-productive time spent traveling on the airlines and the inability of commercial aviation's schedule and city pairs to be able to accommodate the requisite business itineraries in a reasonable amount of time. Time is a critical asset for a busy corporate executive and anything that can be done to help manage time, or allow them to be more efficient in the use of time, is very valuable. A corporate aircraft is sometimes called a "time machine" because of its capability to reduce non-productive time when traveling, especially when traveling direct to remote geographical areas and international locations.

Security requirements imposed by the Transportation Security Administration (TSA) since the events surrounding September 11, 2001, have greatly increased non-productive time when traveling on the commercial airlines. As the airlines struggle with profit margins, reduce the number of flights between cities, and continue to manipulate pricing programs, business travel via commercial aviation has declined. The increased load factors on individual aircraft and have dramatically increased profit margins for the airlines and at the same time increased the inconvenience of air travel for business flyers. The decrease in service levels by the major airlines has also made business aviation travel more attractive. The flexibility offered by the use of a business aircraft allows a scheduled series of trips to be accomplished in one day without the need to stay overnight. The growth of multi-national corporations in recent decades has greatly increased the need for corporate executives to travel globally. There is no faster and more convenient way to do this than on a large ultra-long-range business jet. Helicopters can also be great time-savers when traveling over short distances and between destinations without the use of an airport. As a general rule, the helicopter is the most efficient means available for portal-to-portal travel within a radius of less than 200 miles. For this reason, many corporations have included a helicopter among the aircraft used to meet their corporate travel needs.

Another very important benefit offered by the use of business aircraft is the increased level of safety and security available to corporate passengers. In many parts of the world executives have become targets for criminal activity. The use of business aviation aircraft allows for a secure working environment while traveling between international destinations. If a business aviation flight department is large enough to have the capability to travel internationally it will have a scheduling function (Chapters 6 and 9) that takes care of making arrangements for executive travel. These normally include reservations at a secure hotel near the point of meeting and arrangements for secure ground transportation to and from the airport. Business aviation pilots also take precaution to guard against terrorist or criminal activity by parking the aircraft in a secure and well-lighted area at the destination airport. Many corporate aircraft are equipped with sensing devices to protect against sabotage where the aircraft are parked or secured in a hangar overnight. Pre-departure planning and on-site awareness on the part of business aviation crews has resulted in an excellent record of safety and security for corporate executives around the world (see Chapter 13).

Most modern business aviation aircraft are equipped with the capability for secure and private communications, similar to those in the corporate offices at company headquarters. Larger cabin aircraft are equipped with folding desks and office support equipment including wireless networking capability, satellite telephone communications, document scanners, and satellite television, as well as teleconferencing capability. Every effort is made to replicate the working environment that is available on the ground, so that the passengers can feel at ease and be productive during the duration of the flight. Many airline-class business jets contain sleeping quarters and shower facilities, so that the executive will arrive rested and refreshed after a long flight.

Business aviation, in the early years, was reserved for the use of the president/chief executive officer of the corporation. It was, and in many ways still is the ultimate "perk." The industry has evolved to the point that the business aircraft is used to support the total travel needs of the company. The goal of business aviation is to serve all levels of the corporate structure as needed to sustain the company's mission. A business aviation aircraft should be looked upon as just another tool in the toolbox of company managers to make the organization more competitive.

"The corporate aviation department should be viewed as an integral and strategic element in the corporate structure, regardless of the company's primary functions. A manufacturing firm depends upon its production facilities and personnel, but would not be able to function without its administration, sales, research and other essential departments." The *NBAA Management Guide* goes on to say, "In the same manner, the aviation department provides a variety of transportation and communication functions, which, once instituted, become indispensable to the company's operations."

From a business perspective, one of the greatest advantages offered by owning a company aircraft is the flexibility that it gives to management when scheduling travel. The on-demand nature of corporate flight means that the company has the capability to respond rapidly to business opportunities that arise. The company jet provides the capability to meet face-to-face with a potential partner in a matter of hours, even when great distances are involved. Many business opportunities must be responded to in a rapid manner, or they will disappear. With the aid of a business aircraft an executive team can be dispatched anywhere within the United States in a matter of hours. The corporate branch of business aviation has a safety record that for decades has been as good as or better than the major commercial carriers.

Available for review since 1979, a series of studies have been conducted by Aviation Data Service, Inc. (AvData), of Wichita, Kansas, concerning the benefits of using corporate aircraft. Similar studies have been undertaken by the Arthur Anderson accounting firm and NEXA Advisors, LLC. The results of these studies have been published in various magazines such as *Fortune* magazine, *Business & Commercial Aviation* (*B/CA*), or *Professional Pilot* magazine each year. In the beginning, the AvData studies focused on use of corporate aircraft in the Fortune 1000 service and manufacturing companies, but recently they have concentrated upon the use of corporate aircraft in the Fortune 500 industrial companies. The results of these studies have been remarkably consistent over time. According to AvData, approximately 63% of the corporations in the study own and operate business aircraft, yet they account for 89% of total sales, and have 92% of the total assets and 99% of total net income within their respective industry sectors. The annual AvData study includes an efficiency comparison between aircraft owners and non-owners. The results of these assessments indicate that aircraft owners as a group outperformed non-owners, often by significant margins. A compilation of efficiency comparisons, over a number of years, show that aircraft owners had sales that were 11% higher than those companies that do not own aircraft. Even more impressive is the fact that net income per employee was around 17% higher for aircraft owners than non-owners. The accounting firm Arthur Andersen produced a landmark study in 2001 providing evidence that business aviation has contributed to America's corporate drive for greater shareholder and enterprise value. This landmark accounting study was later updated by another series of studies, beginning in 2003, by NEXA Advisors, LLC, of Washington, DC. Both the Arthur Andersen and the NEXA studies examined the benefits of aircraft use among Fortune 500 companies. The latest NEXA data was published in 2009 and compiled all of the previous studies into a single report titled *Business Aviation—An Enterprise Value Perspective.* The format of the NEXA report was slightly different from the AvData studies, but strongly supports the idea that use of a company-owned aircraft can greatly contribute to the efficiency and productivity of a large corporation. Surprisingly, the NEXA report also concluded that business aircraft users had a dominant presence as being among the most innovative, most admired, best brands, and best places to work (NEXA Advisors 2009). These studies also postulated that companies that owned a business aircraft dominated the list of Fortune 500 companies in the areas of corporate governance and responsibility. These series of studies by three independent companies offer the best scientific-based evidence of the cost-effective use of the aircraft as a business tool to help a corporation gain a competitive advantage over rivals.

THE ROLE OF BUSINESS AVIATION

Business aviation plays a significant role in the U.S. air transportation system. The FAA breaks out corporate and business aircraft as separate use categories as shown on Table 1.2. According to the FAA, there were 32,943 corporate and business aircraft in the U.S. general aviation fleet in 2009, the latest year for which statistics are available. As a group, the corporate and business aircraft are very active, flying more hours each year than any other category. Even though the numbers of business/corporate aircraft constituted only 14.7% of the total number of general aviation aircraft in CY 2009, roughly 25% of all hours flown are for business purposes. Aircraft numbers as contained in this table were derived from the general aviation and air taxi survey information conducted by the Statistics and Forecast Branch of the FAA Office of Aviation Policy and Plans. These statistics are collected annually and historically have been published in the *FAA Statistical Handbook of Aviation,* but the FAA stopped publishing hard copies of this handbook in 1996. The data are now available on-line at URL: http://www.faa.gov/data_research/aviation_data_statistics/general_aviation/

Table 1.2 Number of General Aviation Aircraft by Primary Use in U.S. Fleet

Use Category	*2005*	*2006*	*2007*	*2008*	*2009*
Corporate (professional pilot)	10,553	11,054	10,864	11,715	10,498
Business (employee-flown)	25,524	24,413	24,993	22,432	22,445
Personal	151,408	149,026	152,514	154,417	152,272
Instructional	13,399	14,316	14,650	14,975	14,130
Aerial Application	3,548	3,430	4,164	3,106	3,161
Aerial Observation	4,663	4,407	5,188	5,304	5,288
Aerial Other	811	831	1,358	1,036	849
External Load	226	212	188	374	157
Other Work	732	729	936	934	1,177
Sightseeing	945	906	1,276	673	849
Air Med	418	357	222	411	486
Other	3,612	3,179	5,776	4,786	4,005
Total	224,353	221,943	231,607	228,663	223,877

Source: FAA *General Aviation and Air Taxi Surveys*, available online at URL: www.faa.gov/data_research/aviation_data_statistics/general_aviation/

As seen in the above table, aircraft that are privately owned and used by the owners for personal use constitutes the largest number of aircraft in the general aviation fleet. The second largest numbers of aircraft are aircraft that are used for corporate and business purposes. Approximately 26,000 of the corporate/business aircraft shown in Table 1.2 for CY 2009 were turbine-powered. These corporate/business aircraft conduct thousands of aircraft flights on a typical day, a count that includes many flights to airports without scheduled commercial airline service and to international destinations. Within the United States, more than 5,000 airports are available to corporate/business aircraft. Commercial carriers are limited to approximately 500 airports in the same geographic area. On a worldwide scale, general aviation is also very important. The worldwide general aviation fleet number over 320,000 aircraft spread all over the world and range from two-seat training aircraft to the intercontinental ultra-long-range business jets. They make similar contributions to transportation needs and economies of other countries as they do in the United States.

The General Aviation Manufacturers Association (GAMA) represents 65 of the world's leading manufacturers of fixed-wing general aviation airplanes, engines, avionics, and components. In addition to building most of the corporate and business airplanes flying worldwide today, GAMA member companies also operate aircraft, fixed-based operations, pilot/technician training centers, and maintenance facilities throughout the world. Over two-thirds of all hours flown by general aviation aircraft are for business purposes according to the GAMA annual *Statistical Databook and Industry Outlook report* (GAMA 2009). Table 1.3 shows the number of

Table 1.3 Corporate/Business Aircraft Shipments (Calendar Years 2005–2009)

	Number of Aircraft Shipped by Type				
Aircraft	*2005*	*2006*	*2007*	*2008*	*2009*
Ultra-long-range Jets	43	90	65	66	66
Jets (>20,000 lb MTOW)	421	480	508	515	427
Jets (<20,000 lb MTOW)	240	343	536	630	353
Multi-engine Turboprops	134	140	157	172	119
Single-engine Turboprops	247	253	281	331	322
Multi-engine Pistons	109	200	217	136	48
Total	1194	1506	1764	1850	1335

Source: GAMA, 2009 *General Aviation Statistical Databook & Industry Outlook*

aircraft delivered each year for the years of 2005–2009. This list is representative of most aircraft normally used for corporate/business aviation, except for helicopters.

General aviation contributes more than $150 billion to the U.S. economy each year and employs more than 1,265,000 people. It also contributes to the U.S. balance of payments, with $9.1 billion of U.S. manufactured aircraft sold overseas in CY 2009. This was a significant portion of the total U.S. exports, constituting 46.1% of the total dollar value of exports shipped in that year (GAMA 2009).

HISTORY OF CORPORATE/BUSINESS AVIATION

The history of corporate/business aviation goes back to September 16, 1905, when Lincoln Beachey, an 18-year-old aeronaut, made an advertising flight for business purposes over Portland, Oregon, in the Knox airship Gelatine to advertise the world's first pre-granulated gelatine (see Figure 1.1). The Gelatine was a semi-rigid motorized balloon shaped like a football used by Charles Knox to commercially advertise his company's products. Beachey's primary qualifications for this flight were that he was light in weight and brave enough to go up in the balloon. The pilot of the balloon was called an aeronaut and rode in an open-frame cockpit hanging from webbing below the balloon. The aeronaut guided the motorized balloon in flight and made a spectacular sight for crowds on the ground, because he could be seen walking around on the open frame as he balanced the balloon. One could argue that business aviation began with the invention of the flying machine by the Wright brothers in 1903, but historians generally credit the Lincoln Beachey flight in the Gelatine as being the first use of aviation to promote business. Charles Knox took Lincoln Beachey and the Gelatine on a tour in 1906, visiting air shows coast-to-coast and making

Figure 1.1 Semi-rigid motorized balloon flown by Lincoln Beachey. Photo courtesy of Corbis Images.

headlines in all of the local newspapers at each stop. As a result, he became known as the "Napoleon of advertising" and was able to increase sales of his gelatine product dramatically by use of this unique advertising method (Whempner 1982).

Whempner emphasized in his book that nations have developed through commerce and trade. Transportation and communications systems are necessary for this to happen. He noted that as we look back on the history of the development of this country we see that development started first in seaport towns, and then moved up rivers where ships served as the primary mode of transportation and communications. As the U.S. road system was developed, towns grew up where major roads crossed. Later, some of these towns lost out in the competition as canals and railroads were developed and new towns developed along these transportation centers. The common thread in this development was an efficient means of transportation and communications. Improvements in different modes of transportation and better communications devices that made business activity happen were such things as riverboats, diesel locomotives, automobiles, large fuel-efficient trucks; telegraph, telephone, radio, television, and finally the aircraft. The same general pattern has emerged as business has grown, evolved internationally, and gone global. The difference is that distances are much greater and there are large oceans to cross. Fortunately, aircraft have been developed to meet this emerging worldwide transportation need. A testament to how successful the aircraft has been at meeting worldwide transportation needs is the fact that large freighter aircraft transport 40% of the world's manufactured goods to market each year and large wide-bodied passenger aircraft move billions of international travelers around the world each year (Rhoades 2008).

From the time of the Knox Gelatine balloon flight until WWI, limited use was made of the aircraft for personal or business purposes. A few early aircraft were used for advertising or special purposes, but for the most part, the open-cockpit biplane aircraft of the day were not yet reliable enough for general business transportation use. In addition, exposure to the elements in these open cockpit aircraft necessitated the wearing of goggles and appropriate clothing, which was impractical for executive travel. Use of the company airplane for executive and passenger travel did not materialize until an enclosed cabin airplane was developed. The end of WWI made available a large number of military surplus aircraft and trained pilots, but it was not until the early 1920s that enclosed cabin aircraft became available (see Figure 1.2). One of the first such aircraft was the Bellanca CF, manufactured by the Bellanca Aircraft Company in Wilmington, Delaware, in 1921. This aircraft was unique in that the pilot sat in an open cockpit behind and offset to the left side of the four-passenger compartment. The four passengers sat in an enclosed cabin in front of the pilot. Only one CF was built, because it was too expensive for general use, but the design served as the prototype for a line of successful cabin aircraft, including the Pacemaker and Aircruiser that later made the enclosed cabin design successful.

The first practical enclosed cabin aircraft to appear, however, was the Stinson SM-1 Detroiter, which first flew in 1926. The SM-1 was a four-seat enclosed cabin biplane that had such novel features such as cabin heating, individual wheel brakes and electric starter. It was made available for sale shortly after passage of the Air Mail Act of 1925, commonly called the Kelly Act. The Kelly Act set up the competitive bidding process for the carriage of airmail and authorized the awarding of government mail contracts to private carriers (see Figure 1.3). It also set airmail rates and the level of cash subsidies to be paid to companies that carried the mail. The idea was to permit the expansion of the airmail service without placing a burden upon the taxpayers by transferring airmail operations to private companies. By virtue of this act, the government effectively helped create the commercial aviation industry because it provided an incentive for the aircraft manufacturers to manufacture aircraft that met U.S. postal specifications for carrying the mail. In the beginning, the carriers were paid by the piece, but this proved to be unworkable because each piece of

Figure 1.2 Bellanca CF: First aircraft designed for corporate use. Photo courtesy of the Smithsonian Institute.

mail would have to be logged and accounted for. The payment was then changed to weight, which provided an incentive for the manufacturers to produce aircraft that could carry more weight. The payment was later changed to volume, which provided an incentive for the manufacturers to produce larger aircraft. There was also a requirement to haul the mail in all weather conditions. This provided the incentive for aircraft manufacturers to instrument their aircraft so they could fly at nighttime and in bad weather conditions. Over time, these incentives resulted in larger and more capable aircraft.

Stinson Aircraft Corporation sold 10 SM-1 Detroiters in 1926, and started refining the basic design. The Stinson SM-2 Junior, a three- or four-seat high-wing cabin monoplane designed for both business and personal flight, soon followed. Business steadily increased, and Stinson delivered 121 aircraft in 1929. This early success led to the development of the Reliant, a high-wing four- or five-place monoplane which first flew in 1933 (see Figure 1.4). Many new advances were incorporated into this aircraft; the conventional landing gear was equipped with hydraulically-operated

Figure 1.3 Stinson SM-1 Detroiter: First enclosed cabin aircraft. Photo courtesy of the Smithsonian Institute.

brakes and the wing flaps were vacuum-operated. Most importantly, it had markedly increased performance over other aircraft that had been developed up to this point; it could carry four to five passengers at speeds close to 165 miles per hour and could fly about 815 miles on a tank of fuel. This increased range and speed made the aircraft much more useful over other modes of transportation for saving time when traveling over long distances. The Reliant's high price tag—new models sold for between $10,000 and $18,000—prevented its wide acceptance among private owners, but corporations and commuter airlines eagerly purchased the plane because of its speed, amenities, and styling. Gulf Oil, Shell Oil, and Pepsi-Cola were among the first corporations to use Stinson Reliants to ferry their executives and clients around the country, while future military leaders Dwight Eisenhower and Jimmy Doolittle used the airplane as a versatile transport in remote areas such as the Philippines. The reliant had a very long production run with a total of 1,327 built at the Wayne, Michigan, factory from 1933 to 1941. There were other aircraft of similar design manufactured during this time period, but the Reliant did more than any other to establish the market for business/corporate use.

Figure 1.4 Stinson Reliant. Photo used by permission of Doug Anderson.

The first aircraft specifically built for business/corporate use was the Beechcraft Model 17, popularly known as the "Staggerwing." At the height of the Great Depression in 1932, Walter H. Beech and airplane designer T. A. "Ted" Wells joined forces to collaborate on a project many considered foolhardy—a large, powerful, and fast biplane designed for a yet to be established market. After a slow start, the aircraft proved to be very successful and set the standard for private passenger airplanes for many years to come. It was considered, during its time, to be the premier executive aircraft, much as the Gulfstream executive jets are considered in contemporary times. Each Staggerwing was custom-built by hand with a luxurious cabin, trimmed in leather and mohair, holding up to five passengers. A total of 785 Staggerwings were manufactured between 1933 and 1949 at the Wichita, Kansas, factory (see Figure 1.5). In 1937 Beechcraft also developed a 6–11 seat light twin aircraft with the official name of "Model 18," commonly called the "Twin Beech." Due to additional safety offered by two engines and its all-weather capability, this aircraft became one of the most popular light twins ever produced, with over 9,000 manufactured between 1937 and 1970. Many of the military versions of this aircraft were available at very low prices after WWII, along with military trained pilots, and as a result, many business aviation flight departments were started using this aircraft. At that time, it was the most used light twin for business travel, in much the same way that the King Air is today. The Twin Beech was so successful that Beechcraft continued its manufacture exclusively for corporate use for 25 years after the war ended. In 1955 the E18S was introduced, this model featured a fuselage that was extended 6 inches higher for more headroom in the passenger cabin. All later Beech 18s (sometimes called Super 18s) featured this taller fuselage and some of the earlier models were modified to this larger fuselage. The Model H18, introduced in 1963, also featured optional tricycle undercarriage. As a matter of fact, the King Air was initially developed using the basic Twin Beech airframe upgraded to tricycle gear and using turboprops as the propulsion system.

Before WWII, a few companies found that they could save travel time and money by using the aircraft to transport their executives. Shell Oil Company was one of these; they acquired a Fokker tri-motor to transport their executives on business trips and hired James H. Doolittle, who later became famous for leading the raid on Tokyo, as their chief pilot. Other oil companies followed suit to meet the competition, but use of

Figure 1.5 Beech Staggerwing. Photo courtesy of the Smithsonian Institute.

the aircraft prior to WWII was mainly limited to a few forward-thinking wealthier companies. Even though the capability was there, and the use of the aircraft could be justified, change was slow in coming; it took WWII to bring about the change necessary to see a dramatic growth in corporate/ business aviation. During WWII many things happened that set favorable conditions for growth after the war. First of all many new airports were built to support the war effort. Even though civilian business travel by air was restricted during the war, people became accustomed to travel by air for military purposes and after the war they served as the nucleus that saw the benefits of air travel. A large number of pilots were trained which provided a pool of professionally trained crews to operate the aircraft. Probably the most important item resulting from the war to spur the postwar growth of corporate/business aviation is the fact that a large number surplus aircraft became available after the war at a fraction of what it cost to manufacture them. When business aviation started its rapid growth after WWII, the fleet was dominated by war-surplus aircraft. The C-47 military transports became DC-3 civilian aircraft, each with a corporate logo on the tail, with a very comfortable interior custom designed to accommodate 10 to 18 passengers. Right after the war ended a war surplus C-47 could be bought for less than $10,000. Three or four times this amount was usually spent on refurbishment and so these newly designated DC-3s became the queen of the corporate fleet. In a few years after the war, the market price of a DC-3 rose to as much as $200,000, because of the increase in demand caused by the growth of business aviation. A few bombers such as the Martin B-26 and North American B-25s were converted for corporate passenger service, but the Beech D-18 and Douglas DC-3 became the most prominent aircraft in the business/corporate fleet for a good number of years after the war.

Following Beechcraft's lead with its successful B-18 series after the war, Cessna, Piper, and general aviation manufacturers saw the potential for a growing corporate/business market need for a new and more capable light twin aircraft. This led to the post-war development of new more fuel efficient engines and inspired the design of a new breed of corporate/business aircraft. The small silhouette of these horizontally opposed engines allowed the manufacture of four- to six-passenger aircraft that were as fast, if not faster, than the DC-3s and a lot more economical to operate. They also had a range of sufficient length to allow transcontinental flights with only one stop. These light twins increased the efficiency of the corporate fleet allowing the transport of small groups of company staff in all weather conditions to thousands of smaller airports that had previously been inaccessible. These less-expensive aircraft allowed the benefits of air travel to be extended to hundreds of smaller companies that could not afford the bigger and more expensive aircraft. The availability of these small multi-engine aircraft led to a dramatic and explosive growth of business aviation in the years immediately after WWII.

NBAA

On May 17, 1946, thirteen men met in New York City at the Wings Club, to discuss the possibility of forming an organization that would serve the future interests of business aviation. Initially called the Corporation Aircraft Owners Association (CAOA) and with members representing corporations such as Bristol-Myers, Corning Glass Works, General Electric, B.F. Goodrich, Goodyear, Republic Steel and Sinclair Refining, this fledgling group has grown to almost 9,000 members in 2011. CAOA became the National Business Aircraft Association in 1953 and the present day National Business Aviation Association (NBAA) in 1997. The purpose of this dynamic organization has not wavered since its inception: "to protect [business aviation] interests from discriminatory legislation by federal, state and municipal agencies...to enable corporation aircraft owners to be represented as a united front...[to foster] improvements in aircraft, equipment and service...and to further the cause of safety and economy of operation" (Searles and Parke 1997).

THE JET AGE

The first commercial jet was the de Havilland Comet, introduced into service in 1952. After the U.S. airlines moved into turboprop and turbojet pressurized aircraft in the late 1950s, the business flight departments, who were still using unpressurized WWII aircraft, suffered from a poor comparison by their passengers. Despite the convenience of a flexible flight schedule and recovery of work time enroute, the corporate traveler preferred the three hour smooth airline trip on the airlines to the sometimes bumpy six hour flight in the corporate aircraft. As a result, the corporate aircraft were flying fewer long-range flights, because the available corporate aircraft at the time were short-range machines. They were relegated to taking passengers from the local airport to the nearest airport where airline connections could be made for the longer flights.

In 1958 the Timken Roller Bearing Company accepted delivery of a French manufactured Morane-Sauliner. This side-by-side seating four-place aircraft is considered to be the first business jet. The four-engine aircraft cruised close to 400 mph and was marketed by Beechcraft. The Morane-Sauliner did not prove to be popular and the program was discontinued several years later. In 1960 Grumman introduced the Gulfstream G-1 turboprop and the Dee Howard Company responded with the piston-powered

Howard 500. The first flight of the G-I occurred on August 14, 1958 and 200 of the aircraft were built during the ensuing 11 years. The GI could sit 12 passengers comfortably, had a maximum speed of 350 mph at 25,000 feet and a range of 2,200 miles. This aircraft provided a good replacement for the DC-3 in that it had a comparable cabin size, but much better capabilities when it comes to range and speed. Concurrently, during the same time frame, two military jets became available for corporate use. North American had just won the navy contract for a small jet transport with the T-39 in 1958 and eventually decided to make the aircraft available for the corporate market. The T-39 became available under the civilian name of the Model 40 Sabreliner. The Lockheed Aircraft Company, who lost the navy contract, found itself with a jet design and no orders. Lockheed decided to redesign the prototype as a four-engine aircraft for the corporate market, and called it the JetStar (see Figure 1.6).

The JetStar became the first passenger cabin jet aircraft used in corporate aviation. It was introduced for civilian use shortly before the Sabreliner. Lockheed later entered the JetStar design into the air force competition for a small pure-jet military transport and won this competition. These aircraft

Figure 1.6 Jetstar. Photo courtesy of the NBAA.

filled the increasing demand for business jets until 1964 when Bill Lear introduced the first jet aircraft, built in the United States, specifically designed for the business aviation market. Consciously aware of the upcoming corporate need for a small jet to provide competitive travel with the airlines, Bill Lear founded the Swiss American Aviation Corporation in the early 1950s with the purpose of developing and certifying a 6 to 8 passenger business jet. It took him over 10 years to accomplish his goal because of setbacks, including a crash of one of the prototypes, but the Learjet 23 finally flew on October 7, 1963. The first production model delivered in October 1964. The Learjet began its life as a Swiss ground-attack fighter aircraft. The basic structure of this fighter aircraft was seen by Bill Lear and his team as a good starting point for the development of a business jet and they used the proven Swiss military fighter aircraft structural design as the pattern for the Learjet. The basic wing design with its distinctive tip fuel tanks and landing gear were little changed from those used by the fighter prototypes. Shortly before beginning production on the Learjet 23, Lear changed the name of his company to the Lear Jet Corporation. The Learjet series went on to have one of the longest production runs of any corporate jet in history and is still in production today. The design marketing slogan of the day offered "magic carpet" service for small groups of people traveling over relative long distances in a short period of time. The Learjet was the fastest means available, when traveling between developed airports over distances of between 500 and 1500 nautical miles.

The 1960s led to a change in the use of the company logo on corporate aircraft. Up until this time, many corporations proudly displayed a very visible copy of the company logo on the tail of the aircraft. It was during this time period that stockholders began to be concerned about the efficient use of corporate capital funds when they saw images on television of business aircraft, with the company logo prominently displayed on the tail, pulling up to the air terminal and deplaning one or two passengers. This concern for public image led to the removal of company logos from most corporate aircraft. The public's negative perception of business aircraft became and in many ways is still today a symbol of corporate waste and excess on the part of senior executives. Trade associations, GAMA, NBAA, Aircraft Owners and Pilot Association (AOPA) and others have worked diligently to counter the unfounded negative public perception of business aviation and to promote the positive aspects of this vital industry.

The 1960s was a very dynamic era in business aviation aircraft development. The BAe 125 Jet Dragon was under development by de Havilland in the United Kingdom, with its first flight in August of 1961. Across the English Channel, Marcel Dassault authorized the production of the Dassault-Burget Mystère 20, later renamed the Falcon 20, in December of 1961. Delivery of the first BAe 125 occurred in September, 1964, followed closely by the U.S. certification of the Mystère 20 in June of 1965. Both of these aircraft accommodated six to eight passengers, depending on the interior configuration, and had 3 hours of range at 400 mph, with proper reserves upon landing.

The King Air 90 (see Figure 1.7), first introduced by Beechcraft Corporation in the early 1960s, was a derivative of the earlier piston powered Queen Air. In order to compete with the faster and higher flying jet aircraft, the Model 200 was first conceived in 1969 and introduced to the marketplace in the early 1970s. This was a much faster aircraft with a large cabin that could operate in and out of short runways. It was, and is today, an efficient medium range turboprop capable of providing excellent value to its customers.

The King Air aircraft has been in continuous production since 1964, becoming the most popular turboprop by a wide margin, selling more models than all of its competitors combined. It is still in production today with over 3,100 built to date. Piper Aircraft Corporation also entered the corporate market with several turboprop models. Rockwell International produced a turboprop version of its Jet Commander using the Garrett TPE-331 engines. Swearingen also powered its Merlin models with the Garrett engine. At the peak of its development, there were 15 manufacturers competing in the U.S. turboprop market. The number of manufacturers has been reduced

Figure 1.7 King Air 200. Photo courtesy of the NBAA.

today; however the turboprop remains a viable means of aircraft propulsion for the shorter-leg niche and when runway length is a factor.

In 1971 Cessna (see Figure 1.8) introduced the Citation; having originally flown in September of 1969 under the original designation of FanJet 500. Markedly slower than its jet competitors, the Citation jet offered turbojet service into a wide variety of airports at an efficiency that rivaled the King Air 200. The ability to operate in and out of smaller runways, its advertised ease of maintenance, and smooth handling characteristics that offered a less hectic transition from piston powered aircraft made the Citation a very popular business option. This versatile aircraft was improved in 1976 with an added wingspan and higher gross weight as well as a new name, the Citation I. From that date forward, Cessna has produced a series of small- to medium-range business jets that have become the stalwart of the business aviation industry. From the improved Citation II, to the Encore, from the Citation III to the Excell (one of the most popular business jets to be introduced in the history of the business aviation industry) Cessna Aircraft Company has consistently developed and introduced innovative jet aircraft for the business aviation market. In June of 1996, the Citation X won FAA Certification. The following month Arnold Palmer became the first owner/operator of the fastest production passenger jet, with a top end speed of slightly under .92 Mach and a cruise speed of .90.

Grumman Aircraft followed up the success of its Gulfstream I turboprop with the development of the Gulfstream II turbojet in 1969. Gulfstream

Figure 1.8 Cessna Citation. Photo courtesy of the NBAA.

produced 256 of this popular model before transitioning production to the Gulfstream III in 1979, under new ownership and leadership from the legendary Allan Paulson. The company name was changed to Gulfstream Aerospace and the manufacturer continued to build the largest business jets during this era, with little competition at the high end of the marketplace. The increased range offered by the Gulfstream II and III made long distance international travel possible. All four branches of the U.S. military flew Gulfstream aircraft. International sales increased dramatically, as many foreign nations purchased Gulfstream IIs and IIIs.

Several years prior to the introduction of the G-III, Bill Lear, always the innovator, designed the LearStar 600. Canadair, a former subsidiary of General Dynamics, was sold to the Canadian government in 1976. The new venture, meant to bolster the Canadian aerospace industry, concurrently purchased the rights to produce and develop the LearStar from Bill Lear. The aircraft was renamed the Challenger 600 (see Figure 1.9). This was the first wide body business jet in history. Although fraught with reliability issues from the beginning, the Challenger design incorporated the first supercritical wing and a stand-up height cabin. From 1978 to 1983, 83 Challenger 600s were built and delivered to business aviation customers. In 1986, the company was purchased by Bombardier Corporation.

A redesigned Challenger 601, powered by General Electric CF-34 engines replaced the 600s in 1984. Six years later, in 1990, Bombardier purchased the bankrupt Learjet Company. Bombardier Aerospace became one of the world's largest aircraft manufacturers. Bombardier greatly expanded its manufacturing base by stretching the Challenger cabin and producing the Canadair Regional Jet, one of the most popular commuter airline aircraft in the world. In the early 1990s the company's design teams later mated the Regional Jet's basic fuselage with a supercritical wing to develop the Global Express, in order to compete with Gulfstream for a large segment of the rapidly expanding global business aviation market.

Another vital aircraft manufacturer, Dassault Falcon Jet, developed the Falcon 50, tri-engine business jet in 1979, on the heels of its very successful Falcon 20 program. The Falcon 50 has continued to be produced with enhancements in technology to the present day. Dassault made the strategic decision in the spring of 1983 to announce the development of the Falcon 900 (see Figure 1.10) and joined the competitive long distance marketplace. The 900 was also a three-engine jet with an entirely new fuselage, wider than the Gulfstream's, and longer than the Challenger's.

During the 1980s with the competition heating up in the upper end of the market, Beech Aircraft Corporation became a subsidiary of the Raytheon Corporation. British Aerospace introduced a new version of its popular mid-size cabin BAe 125 series, the Hawker 800, in 1983. Raytheon purchased the corporate jet division of British Aerospace ten years later and

Figure 1.9 Challenger 601. Photo courtesy of the NBAA.

Figure 1.10 Falcon 900. Photo courtesy of the NBAA.

continued the advancement of technological innovation within its family of aircraft offerings. In 1986, the Beechcraft division of Raytheon purchased the manufacturing rights to the Mitsubishi MU-300 Diamond. This jet competed with the smaller Citation series and was renamed the Beechjet 400.

During the same year, 1986, the company that would eventually become NetJets was launched by Richard Santulli. No longer relegated to the burden of owning a complete aircraft, NetJets sold fractional shares to its customers, typically in blocks of 200 hours of flight time. These quarter-shares proved to be extremely popular with companies and individuals who were new to the business aviation community. NetJets not only introduced innovation in ownership, it offered new concepts in scheduling, maintenance, crewing, and operational control. The aircraft mix ranged from Citation IIs, Hawker 700s, to the newest version of the Gulfstream series, the G-IV. The G-IV (see Figure 1.11) was to become the most popular large cabin business jet, with 500 aircraft produced from 1987 to 2002. NetJets also operated a fleet of Dassault Falcon 2000s, the twin engine version of the Falcon 900, beginning in 1991.

The later part of the 1990s saw the introduction of the Lear 45, the ultra-long-range G-V, the first flight of the Boeing Business Jet series, the debut of the Challenger 300, and the purchase of Gulfstream by the General Dynamics Corporation. With the new millennia, business aviation continued to

Figure 1.11 Gulfstream G-IV. Photo courtesy of the NBAA.

grow at a rapid pace. Galaxy Aerospace was added to the Gulfstream family in 2001. Embraer developed the Legacy 600 from its regional jet production program with a first flight in 2001.

Bombardier introduced the Global 5000 in 2003 with a shorter range version of the popular ultra-long-range Global Express (see figure 1.12).

At the mid-point of the first decade in the 21st century, the very light jet market was under development. Speculation that every aircraft enthusiast who could afford it, would purchase a single-pilot lightweight jet aircraft, led a variety of start-up manufacturers to enter the business aviation field. Two of the most serious contenders for this marketplace, Cessna and HondaJet, have surfaced as the leaders of this market segment. The Citation Mustang (see Figure 1.13) was FAA certified during the later part of 2006 and more than 300 aircraft are currently in service. The HondaJet is anticipated to gain its certification in 2011.

The Hawker 4000 and 850XP were introduced to potential buyers in 2006. The 4000 was the latest entry into the super-midsize class which includes the Challenger 300 and the Gulfstream 250 (former Galaxy). The following year Dassault began deliveries of the Falcon 7X (see Figure 1.14),

Figure 1.12 Global Express. Photo courtesy of the NBAA.

Figure 1.13 Citation Mustang. Photo courtesy of the NBAA.

the French manufacturer's entry into the ultra-long-range market. This aircraft was so popular with Falcon customers that the 100th 7X was delivered in November of 2010. This aircraft is the first business jet to incorporate a fly-by-wire flight control system.

BUSINESS AVIATION HELICOPTER DEVELOPMENT

Although Bell Helicopter produced the first certified helicopter in 1946, and the helicopter was proven as a medical evacuation platform during the Korean War, it wasn't until the late 1950s that the helicopter began to be used by the business aviation flight departments (see Figure 1.15). The first use was by the oil companies for the highly specialized purpose of flying personnel and supplies to the remote offshore oil rigs located in the Gulf of Mexico. The reason for the delay in adopting this versatile tool was that the early helicopters' range was limited and travel comfort left a lot to be desired. The early model helicopters had a disturbing vibration due to the use of piston engines and the fact that the rotor vibration mechanism had not yet been developed. These aircraft had not yet been approved for instrument conditions, which resulted in frequent weather cancellations. Requirements to meet military specifications for use in the

Figure 1.14 Falcon 7X. Photo courtesy of the NBAA.

Vietnam War would lead to continued improvement in helicopter design providing much greater range, greater speed, and the ability to fly in an all-weather environment. Today, most helicopters use gas-turbine engines and are smooth and sophisticated, with the ability to fly passengers from a company heliport to any destination within a matter of minutes, under most weather conditions.

Business aviation helicopters have gained great popularity in major metropolitan areas with multi-national corporations. One of the most widely used executive helicopters is the Sikorsky SK-76 (see Figure 1.16), first introduced in 1977.

Bell/Agusta helicopters became workhorses in the energy/minerals exploration field and eventually joined forces in 1998 to develop the new tilt-rotor technology aircraft.

THE FUTURE

As large multinational corporations began to form in the late 1980s, there developed a need for a larger and more capable aircraft that could travel nonstop over a distance greater than 6,000 miles. Both Gulfstream and Bombardier were offering future options in this market with their

Figure 1.15 Bell Helicopter. Photo courtesy of the NBAA.

ultra-long-range aircraft, but there was a limited demand for a very large cabin where a large numbers of executives could travel in total comfort, and sleep if necessary, to arrive refreshed and ready to work. This market need prompted both Boeing and Airbus to modify two of their existing air transport passenger aircraft to meet corporate needs. Boeing modified the B737 commercial airliner into an aircraft called Boeing Business Jet (BBJ) which seats between 25 and 50 passengers in a luxurious configuration to include a master bedroom, a washroom with showers, a conference/dining area, and a living area. After the successful launch of the BBJ, Airbus followed suit with the launch of their Airbus Corporate Jet (ACJ), which was derived from their A319 commercial airframe. They have also launched the larger A320 and A321 Prestige and the smaller A318 Elite to compete in this market. Boeing responded by introducing other versions of the BBJs including configurations based on the Boeing 777, Boeing 787 and the Boeing 747-8 Intercontinental.

Looking forward the business aviation headlines will continue to be filled with bigger, faster, and longer-range options. Bombardier recently

Figure 1.16 Skorsky SK-76. Photo courtesy of the NBAA.

announced the Global 7000 and 8000 series that are planned for 2016 and 2017 respectfully. Gulfstream has more than 200 firm orders for the newly designed G-650 (see Figure 1.17) that is currently involved in certification testing with an anticipated first delivery in 2012. Aviation futurists predict a supersonic business jet before 2020 in addition to transonic options on the not too distant horizon. All these glamorous predictions aside, it is important to remember that the vast majority of business aviation operations will never purchase or operate these beautiful, but very expensive, options. The workhorse aircraft that will continue to produce the product that was first postulated by members of the Wings Club in 1946, "the safe and efficient transportation of company personnel aboard leased or wholly owned business aviation assets," will be the small- to medium-range turboprops,

Figure 1.17 Gulfstream 650. Photo courtesy of the NBAA.

helicopters, and business jets flown and maintained by dedicated industry professionals.

REFERENCES

Bill Lear Sr., father of the RJ, among other things . . . (2006, Aug 1). *Air Transport World 43*(8): 92.

Dassault Aviation and Dassault Systemes make industry history—Falcon 7X jet becomes first aircraft entirely developed on virtual platform. (2004, May 24). *Business Wire*: 1.

Dassault reaches Falcon milestone. (2009, Jul 21–Jul 27). *Flight International 176*(5198): 18.

FAA Office of Aviation Policy and Plans. (2008). *General Aviation and Air Taxi Survey*. Washington, DC: U.S. Government Printing Office.

General Aviation Manufacturers Association (GAMA). (2009). *Statistical Databook and Industry Outlook*. Washington, DC.

George, F. (2011, Mar). Dassault Falcon 7X. *Business & Commercial Aviation* 107 (3): 46.

______. (2011, Jan). Dassault Falcon 900LX. *Business & Commercial Aviation* 107 (1): 24.

______. (2010, Nov). Falcon 2000. *Business & Commercial Aviation* 106 (11): 84.

Hughes, Graham. (2006, Feb). Challenger 600 touches down on place in history. *The Ottawa Citizen*.

National Business Aviation Association. (published annually). *NBAA Management Guide*, Washington, DC.

NEXA Advisors, LLC. (2009). *Business Aviation: An Enterprise Value Perspective: The S& P 500 from 2003–2009.* Washington, DC.

Rhoades, Dawna L. (2008). *Evolution of International Aviation: Phoenix Rising (2nd ed.).* Burlington, VT: Ashgate Publishing.

Ruvinsky, Maxine. (1992, Jun 14). Author convinced that Challenger was story of success, not failure. *The Ottawa Citizen.*

Sarsfield, K. (2011, Jan 4–Jan 10). Forecasts 2011: Business aviation—New beginnings. *Flight International* 179 (5272): 28.

Searles, R.A. and Parke, R.B. (1997). *NBAA's Tribute to Business Aviation.* Washington, DC: National Business Aviation Association.

Sheehan, John J. (2003). *Business and Corporate Aviation Management: On-Demand Air Travel.* New York: McGraw Hill.

Whempner, R. J. (1982). *Corporate Aviation.* New York: McGraw-Hill Publishing Company.

2

Regulatory Compliance

Learning Objectives: After reading this chapter you should be able to:

- Identify important regulations governing corporate aviation
- Understand how aviation regulations developed under the U.S. republican form of government
- Be familiar with the underlying reasons and impact of deregulation of the U.S. airline industry
- Be able to recite the process for implementing a Federal Aviation Regulation
- Understand the impact of safety regulations on the operation of a corporate flight department

HISTORY OF THE DEVELOPMENT OF AVIATION REGULATION

The source of all aviation law in the United States is the U.S. Constitution. Although the aircraft was not yet invented at the time of the time of the writing of the U.S. Constitution, provisions were included in this document for the later enactment of federal laws governing all aviation activities in the United States. The basis of the federal laws governing aviation is contained in Article I, Section 8 of the Constitution, which addresses the powers of Congress. This article states

> The Congress shall have power to lay and collect taxes, duties, imposts and excises, to pay the debts and provide for the common defense and general wel-

> fare of the United States; but all duties, imposts and excises shall be uniform throughout the United States; to borrow money on the credit of the United States; to regulate commerce with foreign nations, and among the several States, and with the Indian Tribes.

The underlined portion of this article is commonly known as the commerce clause. This clause, along with the necessary and proper clause (clause 18), are the two clauses in the Constitution that allowed the federal government to step in and take over the regulation of aviation, starting in the mid-1920s, even though the aircraft had not yet been invented and the aviation industry had not yet been developed at the time the Constitution was written. Clause 18 is a general purpose clause that authorizes Congress to pass laws to execute all of the powers given to the federal government. This clause states that the federal government has the right "to make all laws which shall be necessary and proper for carrying into execution the foregoing powers, and all other powers vested by this Constitution in the government of the United States, or in any department or officer thereof." The U.S. Constitution also contains a provision allowing the federal government to establish post offices and transport the mail over roads. This is the basis for the Air Mail Act of 1925 (Kelly Act). This was the first major piece of federal legislation created by Congress directly affecting the aviation industry. This act authorized the awarding of government mail contracts to private carriers. It established the rates for transporting the mail by any method and it also set the airmail rates. Contracts were awarded through the United States Postal Service and were awarded through a bidding process. As airmail began crossing the country in the mid-1920s, railroad owners started complaining that this government-sponsored enterprise was cutting into their business. They found a friendly ear in Congressman Clyde Kelly of Pennsylvania, chairman of the House Post Office Committee, who represented railroad interests. Kelly reasoned that by passing this act and transferring airmail operations to private companies, it would permit the expansion of the airmail service without placing a burden upon the taxpayers and would also protect the railroads from subsidized competition. This act, along with later modifications and follow-on airmail acts would help create and develop the commercial aviation industry in the United States, because they provided the incentive for the manufacturers to produce larger, faster and more capable aircraft.

The first act to directly regulate the aviation industry was the Air Commerce Act of 1926. This act gave the federal government responsibility for fostering air commerce, establishing airways and other aids to air navigation, and making and enforcing safety rules. This act also established federal regulations regarding aircraft, airmen, navigational facilities and the establishment of air traffic regulations. Under this act, aircraft were required to be inspected for airworthiness and were required to have markings placed on the outside of the aircraft for identification. Airmen were required to be tested for aeronautical knowledge and required to have a physical completed to insure their physical fitness. Both pilots and planes had to be licensed and registered by the federal government and to be in compliance with civil air regulations. This act is the reason that all pilots must now get a federally issued license to fly in any state today. No such federal law was passed concerning automobiles and is the reason vehicle drivers are licensed by each state, rather than by the federal government. Under this act, the federal government was also required to build new airports, develop and maintain airways, and institute regulations that would address aircraft altitude separation and set rules of the air. The driving force for passage of this act was safety; during the five year period starting in 1920 over four hundred people were killed in aircraft accidents. News about these accidents was making the headlines in newspapers across the country most every day. By the end of the period, there was a nationwide outcry for Congress to do something. This outcry was responsible for passage of the Air Commerce Act of 1926. Both the Air Mail Act of 1925 and the Air Commerce Act of 1926 provided the foundation for all federal aviation laws to follow, which regulate every aspect of aviation today, including corporate aviation.

A very important result of the Air Commerce Act of 1926 was development of an embryonic system by which aviation regulations are instituted into law. This system involves an administrator writing proposed safety rules, usually after passage of a congressional act, and seeking input from the public before they incorporated into permanent rules that have the effect of law. After the proposed rules have been posted in the Federal Register for the required length of time for public comment, the administrator was authorized by Congress to publish the proposed rule/s as what was called Civil Air Regulations (CARs), at the time. This was later changed to what is now known as Federal Air Regulations (FARs). Today, the familiar FAR Parts 61, 91, 135, and 121 are permanent rules that have gone through the process of being published in the Federal Register for comment and later published as a permanent regulation by the FAA Administrator. An FAR is a permanent rule that all aviation operators must be familiar with in order to engage in flight within the United States. The reason for this is that once they are published as an FAR, they have the effect of law and are binding on all persons who engage in flight within the United States. Violators of these regulations may be punished by fines and, in some cases, sentenced to jail time. New aviation rules are usually proposed after a series of aviation accidents, or action by Congress resulting from public concern for safety. In the beginning, aviation regulations were promulgated by the Department of Commerce, but later acts of Congress set up agencies that were purely devoted to aviation and staffed by aviation professionals.

The Civil Aeronautics Board (CAB) and Civil Aeronautics Authority (CAA) were created as a result of the passage of the Civil Aeronautics Act of 1938 (as modified by President Roosevelt in 1940). This act amended and replaced the Air Commerce Act of 1926 and completed the process whereby the federal government took over economic and non-economic control of aviation in the United States. This act authorized the CAB to set air fares, establish civil aviation regulations, and control most all economic aspects of air travel in the United States. This act remained in effect for a period of roughly 20 years, until it was amended and replaced by the Federal Aviation Act of 1958. The Federal Aviation Act of 1958 was the result of a series of midair collisions by large commercial passenger carrying aircrafts, which resulted in a high number of fatalities. These accidents were brought about by introduction of large jet air transport aircraft into the commercial air carrier fleet and the lack of an effective air traffic control system to maintain separation between these faster moving aircraft. In particular, it was the 1956 Grand Canyon midair collision between a United Airlines passenger airliner and a Trans World Airlines passenger airliner, resulting in 128 fatalities, that received widespread public attention. This accident was, at the time, the deadliest aviation disaster in history, and would be a catalyst for sweeping changes in the regulation of flight operations over the United States. This spectacular crash between these two large transport aircraft was so great that the impact spread small pieces of aircraft and bodies over the bottom to the Grand Canyon for several miles. It is possible to fly over certain parts of the Grand Canyon today and see tiny shiny slivers of metal reflecting in the sunlight that are left over from the accident. This is because the terrain is so rugged and the collision so horrific that it is impossible to collect all of the debris. Along with two other midair accidents the next year, these accidents caused a large public outcry that forced Congress to take action and pass the Federal Aviation Act of 1958. The Federal Aviation Act of 1958 terminated the Civil Aeronautics Administration and established the Federal Aviation Agency (FAA) in its place. In addition, the Act transferred the authority to establish civil aviation regulations from the Civil Aeronautics Board to the FAA. This act granted the FAA sole responsibility for the nation's civil-military system of air navigation and air traffic control. The act empowered the FAA to oversee and regulate safety in the airline industry and the use of American airspace by both civilian aircraft and military aircraft. Today, the original civil aviation regulations are known as the FARs (Federal Aviation Regulations) as the result of passage of this act.

The Department of Transportation Act of 1966 was a significant act that reorganized the federal regulation of all modes of transportation under one huge department. At that time the Federal Aviation Authority was renamed the Federal Aviation Administration to better reflect its function, and it was re-organized under the secretary of transportation. An important feature of the act was to establish the National Transportation Safety Board (NTSB), whose mission was to investigate all transportation accidents (regardless of mode) and determine probable cause. The NTSB was later removed from the Department of Transportation (DOT) by the Transportation Safety Act of 1974, and now reports directly to Congress.

An important act that does not directly regulate aviation, but has had a large impact on airports and navigation facilities, is the Airport and Airway Development Act of 1970. This act set up the Airport and Airway Federal Trust Fund and authorized the FAA to administer disbursements from this fund. Monies from the trust fund are used to repair and upgrade aviation airports and navigation facilities. The trust fund receives its money from federal taxes on aviation fuel and other federal taxes that are placed on all aviation users. There has been much controversy over the use of this trust fund because it was used by several administrations to help balance the federal budget, rather than to upgrade aviation facilities. The Airport and Airway Development Act of 1970 was replaced by the Airport and Airway Improvement Act of 1982, which set up the Airport and Airway Improvement Program, placed restrictions on how monies could be used from the Airport and Airway Trust Fund. It also provided the funds for a study with the objective of reforming of the Air Traffic Control System to provide better service to users.

A trend toward deregulation was started when Congress passed the Airline Deregulation Act of 1978. The main purpose of the act was to remove government control over fares, routes, and market entry (of new airlines) from commercial aviation. Under the act, the Civil Aeronautics Board's powers of regulation were to be phased out allowing the airlines to be exposed to free market forces in the U.S. commercial air transportation industry. This phase-out actually happened and U.S. airlines have been operating in a competitive free market environment since around 1983. Over the years since deregulation, there has been a drop in long-haul airline fares, as predicted, but surprisingly there has been a rise in the average short-haul fares. On the economic side there have been a few bankruptcies since passage of this act, but the airline industry has continued to function safely and improve its service to customers. There has also been a long-term trend toward consolidation of the industry with many mergers as predicted by classical economic theory. The act, however, did not remove or diminish the FAA's regulatory powers over all aspects of airline and general aviation safety and there have been no drastic changes in the overall long-term statistical aviation accident rates as was predicted by some.

AVIATION REGULATIONS APPLICABLE TO CORPORATE AVIATION

Commercial air transportation is more regulated than any of the other four modes of transportation. In addition to the normal FAA safety regulations,

Corporate Aviation and most all other forms of aviation are subjected to many other federal and state rules and regulations. Starting with the Air Quality Act of 1967, Congress has passed many federal acts that have had an impact on emissions, noise, or other pollutants stemming from the operation of any type of internal combustion engine, or emissions from any other source such as a manufacturing company. This was the first federal legislation aimed at reducing air pollution. Without setting standards, imposing hard deadlines, and providing enforcement, it failed to accomplish its goals; however, it was a good first step that provided a framework for more effective later legislation. The Clean Air Act of 1970 was the first act that had teeth. This act set up the Environmental Protection Agency (EPA) and established *National Ambient Air Quality Standards* (NAAQS) to serve as a standard for enforcement. Over the years, many amendments have been passed to the Clean Air Act which have tightened standards on emissions and set new tougher milestones for cleaner air.

The Noise Control Act of 1972 is another act that has had a large impact on the operation of corporate aircraft. This act established a national policy to promote an environment for all Americans free from noise that jeopardizes their health and welfare. This act has had a very large impact on aircraft engine noise, especially during takeoff and landing. As a result, engine manufacturers have had to design quieter engines and many older aircraft have become obsolete because they could not meet the new noise standards for operation in the National Airspace. This has meant that corporate operators have had to trade up to more modern aircraft that meet the new standards. Also, the FAA has issued noise reduction regulations governing how aircraft are to be operated in order to reduce noise in and around airports.

In addition to the above federal acts concerning pollution and noise for aircraft operation, there are a myriad of international, federal, state, and local laws that govern ownership and operation of a corporate aircraft. These laws deal with such issues as aircraft registration, accident reporting, financial responsibility, aircraft maintenance, taxation, aircraft leasing, labor relations, how the aircraft are manufactured, and the qualifications of pilots and mechanics. The flight department manager must be familiar with these laws to assure that the corporate aircraft is operated safely and legally. Table 2.1 contains a tabulation of the more important federal, state, local, and international topics of concern to the operator of a corporate aircraft; there are many others.

The Federal Aviation Regulations, or FARs, are rules prescribed by the Federal Aviation Administration (FAA) governing all aviation activities in the United States. The Federal Aviation Regulations are under Title 14 of the Code of Federal Regulations (CFR). The subject of Title 14 is Aeronautics and Space. The Federal Aviation Regulations are located under Chapter I

Table 2.1. Regulatory Topics of Concern for Operation of a Corporate Aircraft

	Regulatory Topics and Regulating Agency		
Topic	*Applicable FAR*	*State/Local*	*International*
Aircraft		Many states require aircraft registration, others require special insurance, and most all have labor laws that affect corporate flight departments.	IBAC/NBAA/EBAA, etc. set standards by issuing Recommended Practices and Procedures for Air Navigation (PANS).
Certification	Parts 23 & 25		
Airworthiness	Parts 23, 25 & 33		
Maintenance	Parts 43 & 91		
Registration	Parts 45 & 47		
Ownership	Part 47		
Economic	Parts 200–1199		
Airmen		Each state has rules for environmental protection from noise and other pollutants.	International agreements between countries cover the mutual recognition of certificates.
Certification	Part 61		
Medical	Part 67		
Type Ratings	Part 61		
Responsibilities	Part 61		
Flight Rules		Federal flight rules cover flights between states, landings, etc.; no need for state approval.	ICAO rules govern filing flight plans between countries and exchange of data, but individual states require prior approval for over flights, landings, etc. within the country.
General Rules	Part 91		
Airspace Control	Parts 71 & 73		
IFR Rules	Parts 91 & 97		
Approaches	Part 97		
Airports	Part 139		
Accidents	NTSB 830		
Taxes	IRS Rules	State and local taxes apply	

of Volume 1-3 of the Code of Federal Regulations. The Regulatory entity for this chapter is the Office of the Federal Aviation Administration, Department of Transportation. The responsibility for maintaining the FARs is a primary responsibility of the FAA Administrator. The Federal Aviation Regulations were originally published in paper form, but now the government has switched over to an electronic format for publishing all regulations. These regulations are available and may be viewed by anyone at any time on the FAA website at URL: www.faa.gov/regulations_policies/faa_regulations/. The FARs are organized into sections called *parts* due to their organization within the CFR. Each part deals with a specific type of activity. The parts are further divided into *subparts* that deal with a smaller segment of the activity; each subpart is given a letter designation. As an example, subpart K of Part 91 (General Operating and Flight Rules) deals with fractional ownership operations. Under Title 14, a wide variety of activities are regulated, such as airplane design, typical airline flights, pilot certification, and training activities. The rules are designed to promote safety and to protect pilots, passengers, and the general public from unnecessary risk.

They are also intended to protect the national security of the United States, especially in light of the September 11, 2001, attacks.

The parts of the Federal Aviation Regulations that set airworthiness standards for aircraft are Parts 23 and 25. Part 23 contains airworthiness standards for airplanes in the normal, utility, aerobatic, and commuter categories. It dictates the standards required for issuance and change of type certificates for airplanes in these categories. This part has a large number of rules to ensure airworthiness in the areas of performance, stability, controllability, and safety mechanisms, how the seats must be constructed, oxygen and air pressurization systems, fire prevention, escape hatches, flight management procedures, flight control communications, emergency landing procedures, and other limitations, as well as testing of all the systems of the aircraft. It also determines special aspects of aircraft performance such as stall speed and rate of climb. This part contains airworthiness standards for airplanes in the transport category in a similar manner to Part 23. Transport category airplanes are either: (1) Jets with 10 or more seats or a maximum takeoff weight (MTOW) greater than 12,500 lb; or (2) propeller-driven airplanes with greater than 19 seats or a MTOW greater than 19,000 lb. Part 33 of the Federal Aviation Regulations sets airworthiness standards for aircraft engines, to include noise emissions.

Part 43 contains standards of how maintenance technicians conduct aircraft maintenance, to include preventive maintenance, rebuilding, and alterations that may be made to an approved aircraft design. This part also contains the recordkeeping requirements for maintenance work on aircraft. Part 91 also contains rules pertaining to how aircraft will be operated in order to maintain continued airworthiness. Aircraft maintenance checks are periodic checks that have to be done on all aircraft after a certain amount of time or usage. Under the maintenance rules, prescribed on part 91, an aircraft must have an annual inspection by a certified mechanic holding Inspection Authorization (AI). In addition, a periodic inspection is required for each 100 hours of flight time to be performed by a certified mechanic. Large gas turbine–powered and turbojet multi-engine aircraft require a more stringent continuous maintenance inspection program approved by the FAA. The way the system works is that each operator prepares a Continuous Airworthiness Maintenance Program (CAMP) for approval by the FAA. Once approved the operator must follow this program for both routine and detailed inspections. The detailed inspections are referred to as "checks," commonly one of the following: A check, B check, C check, or D check. The A and B checks are lighter checks, while C and D are considered heavier checks. In this way the aircraft are continually checked to maintain their airworthiness.

Part 45 sets standards for identification and required registration marking to be displayed on the aircraft in accordance with international agreements.

Aircraft fly all over the world and must display markings that identify which country they are from. Part 47 covers how aircraft that are manufactured in the U.S. are registered with the federal government.

Part 61 sets the requirements for issuing pilot, flight instructor, and ground instructor certificates and ratings. The part also defines the conditions under which those certificates and ratings are necessary and the privileges and limitations of those certificates and ratings. This part also sets proficiency check ride standards, pilot-in-command requirements, second-in-command requirements, type rating requirements, requirement and duration of medical certificates, duration of category II and III authorizations, and recent flight experience requirements for instrument and night flight. Part 67 sets medical standards and certification for the three classes of airman medical certificates. It is legally possible under the FAR regulations to act as pilot-in-command of large turbojet aircraft with only a commercial pilot's certificate, but the NBAA-recommended standard is to require the Airline Transport Certificate (ATP). The First Class Medical is also required to exercise ATP privileges. Part 71 designates the different classes of airspace including Class A, Class B, Class C, Class D, and Class E Airspace Areas. It also defines the airways over which IFR (instrument flight rules) traffic flows, sets IFR routes and reporting points within the controlled airspace. Part 73 defines Special Use Airspace such as Restricted Areas, Warning Areas, etc. Part 139 sets the standards for certification of airports. Most large commercial hub airports are certified under this part.

Part 91 is a very important regulation to corporate aircraft operators, because it contains the operating rules for all non-commercial aircraft operating in the United States, and in some cases outside the U.S. This regulation applies to all aircraft that are not operated for compensation or hire, including corporate owned aircraft. Operators who desire to use their aircraft for compensation or hire must obtain an FAR 135 certificate, unless they desire to run a scheduled airline. In this case they will need an FAR 121 certificate. There are 12 subparts to part 91 as follows:

1. Subpart A—General
2. Subpart B—Flight Rules
3. Subpart C—Equipment Instrument and Certificate Requirements
4. Subpart D—Special Flight Operations
5. Subpart E—Maintenance, Preventative Maintenance, and Alteration
6. Subpart F—Large and Turbine Powered Multi-engine Airplanes and Fractional Ownership Aircraft
7. Subpart G—Additional Equipment and Operating Requirements for Large and Transport Category Aircraft
8. Subpart H—Foreign Aircraft Operations and Operations of U.S. Registered Civil Aircraft Outside the United States

9. Subpart I—Operating Noise Limitations
10. Subpart J—Waivers
11. Subpart K—Fractional Ownership Operations
12. Subpart L—Airworthiness and Safety Improvements</nl>

In addition to the subparts, Part 91 also contains seven Appendices which contain important rules applicable to the operation of corporate aircraft. These Appendices are:

1. Appendix A to Part 91—Category II Operations: Manual, Instruments, Equipment, and Maintenance
2. Appendix B to Part 91—Authorizations To Exceed Mach 1 (91.817)
3. Appendix C to Part 91—Operations in the North Atlantic (NAT) Minimum Navigation Performance Specifications (MNPS) Airspace
4. Appendix D to Part 91—Airports/Locations: Special Operating Restrictions
5. Appendix E to Part 91—Airplane Flight Recorder Specifications
6. Appendix F to Part 91—Helicopter Flight Recorder Specifications and
7. Appendix G to Part 91—Operations in Reduced Vertical Separation Minimum (RVSM) Airspace.

The basic rules contained in Part 91 are very important because they apply to everyone. These rules are especially important to corporate flight departments because of the type aircraft they operate and where they operate. The rules contained in this part are particularly important to corporate flight departments because they cover operation of large turbine powered aircraft, noise reduction, foreign operations, Category II operations, operations over the North Atlantic, and in Reduced Vertical Separation Minimum (RVSM) Airspace. These issues are unique to corporate flight. Each of the above issues will be discussed in simple terms so that they are easily understood.

Turbine powered means that the aircraft is powered by a gas-turbine engine, whether it is a turboprop, turbojet or turbofan. A large aircraft is defined by the FAA as an aircraft of more than 12,500 pounds, maximum certified takeoff weight. Under Subpart F, these type aircraft are required to have additional equipment and operator qualifications, over and above that required for the smaller aircraft that operate at lower attitudes because of the additional risk for loss of life, they carry more passengers and fly at higher altitudes and speeds which increases the risk. As an example, the pilot-in-command of large turbojet aircraft is required to have a Type Rating in the aircraft. This is a special pilot rating that requires additional training specific to the aircraft and requires administration of a specified check ride to show that the pilot is qualified in this type aircraft. There is also a requirement for flight attendants and second-in-command under this subpart. The same rationale concerning risk is applied to Subpart G for the large transport category aircraft. As an example, these large transport aircraft have additional safety requirements for takeoff weight, emergency exits, and a requirement for flight recorders and cockpit voice recorders, which is not normally required for the smaller aircraft. Operating noise limits are required under Subpart I for aircraft operating from airports in the United States. These limits are most applicable to large turbojet aircraft that produce a lot of noise on takeoff. This subpart prescribes operational procedures for takeoff and landing needed to meet the noise standards specified in Part 36. This subpart also contains restrictions on the operation of supersonic aircraft over the continental United States. As a general rule civil aircraft cannot be operated at a flight Mach number greater than 1 because of the noise created on the ground by trailing edge sonic booms.

Understanding Minimum Navigation Performance Specifications (MNPS) is very important to corporate flight operations because it would be impossible to fly back and forth across the Atlantic Ocean without this knowledge and qualification. Under FAR Part 91 operations in the North Atlantic (NAT) are not permitted by a civil aircraft of U.S. registry in airspace designated as Minimum Navigation Performance Specifications airspace, unless both the aircraft and crew are MNPS-qualified. Historically, aircraft navigation specifications have been specified directly in terms of sensors (navigation beacons and/or waypoints). A navigation specification that includes an additional requirement for onboard navigation performance monitoring and alerting is referred to as a required navigation performance (RNP) specification. The International Civil Aviation Organization (ICAO) sets the standards for flights across the heavily traveled North Atlantic and has designated this area as Minimum Navigation Performance Specifications (MNPS) airspace. The ICAO performance-based navigation (PBN) represents a shift from sensor-based to performance-based navigation. PBN specifies that aircraft systems performance requirements be defined in terms of accuracy, integrity, availability, continuity, and functionality required for operations in MNPS airspace. In simple terms, this means that all aircraft must have the required equipment and the crew must be trained and certified in MNPS procedures before they can fly across the Atlantic along the preferred navigation route.

Reduced Vertical Separation Minimum (RVSM) is another item of concern for those corporate aircraft with a need to fly above FL 290. FAR Part 91 states that "Except as provided in paragraph (b) of this section, no person may operate a civil aircraft of U.S. registry in airspace designated as Reduced Vertical Separation Minimum (RVSM) airspace." RVSM is a term used to describe the reduction of the standard vertical separation required between aircraft flying at levels between FL290 (29,000 ft.) and FL410 (41,000 ft.) from 2,000 feet to 1,000 feet. This increases the number of aircraft that can safely fly in a particular volume of airspace. Historically, standard vertical separation was 1,000 feet from the surface to FL290, 2,000 feet from FL290 to FL410 and 4,000 feet above this. This was because the accuracy of the pressure altimeter decreases with height. Over time, air data computers (ADCs), combined with altimeters, have become more accurate and autopilots have become more adept at maintaining a set level. Therefore, it became apparent that for many modern aircraft, the 2,000-foot separation was too cautious, and consequently, it was proposed by ICAO that this separation standard be reduced to 1,000 feet. A gradual phase in to RVSM was begun in 1997 and the entire Western Hemisphere implemented RVSM FL290-FL410 on January 20, 2005. Africa implemented it on September 25, 2008. Now that most of the world is on this standard, it is necessary that corporate operators with aircraft that have the capability to operate at this altitude have an authorization. Authority for an operator to conduct flight in airspace where RVSM is applied is issued in operations specifications, a letter of authorization, or management specifications issued under Subpart K.

Part 91 also covers general rules for instrument flight (including Category I, II, and III operations). Rules for conduction of a standard instrument approach are contained in Part 97. These two parts are important to a corporate flight department because most all corporate flights involve the filing of an IFR flight plan. Depending on the weather, many flights also involve making actual instrument approaches down to Category II minimums. Instrument flight rules govern a flight when weather conditions are less than that required for visual flight, or when an IFR flight plan is filed. Category I approaches and landings are necessary when weather conditions are very low at the point of intended landing, in terms of ceiling and visibility. When weather conditions are such that Category II operations are required, the aircraft and the crew must be certified to conduct Category II approaches; the aircraft may continue the approach down to Category II minimums, using published procedures, at large airfields that are properly equipped. This allows flight operations to continue in extremely marginal weather conditions. Normal minimums for a precision approach are around 200 feet above the landing surface and one-half mile visibility. A Category II approach is allowed to go down to a decision height of no less than 100 feet above the landing surface, depending on equipment on the aircraft, pilot qualifications, and equipment on the ground. All three must meet Category II requirements and the airfield must be conducting Category II approaches, before a Category II approach can be started. Many modern business jets are equipped to conduct Category II operations.

ETOPS is another item of interest to the manager of a corporate flight department. The original meaning of the ETOPS acronym was Extended-range Twin-engine Operational Performance Standards; it has since been simplified to just Extended Operations. The ICAO sets Standard and Recommended Practice (SARP) for operations outside the jurisdiction of sovereign nations. Due to the unreliability of piston engines in the early 1950s, ICAO set the standard for transoceanic flights as four engines to mitigate the risk. Using twin-engine aircraft for this type of flights was considered too risky at the time. In 1953, the FAA, in a compromise recognizing piston engine limitations, and to allow two-engine aircraft to conduct such flights, introduced the "60-minute rule" for two-engine aircraft. This rule stated that the flight path of twin-engine aircraft should not be farther than 60 minutes of flying time from an adequate airport. This forced these aircraft to fly a dogleg path to stay within regulations and they were totally excluded from certain routes due to lack of en-route airports. After the introduction of the more reliable jet-powered transport aircraft in the late 1950s, the FAA and the ICAO concluded that it was safe for a properly designed twin-engine airliner to conduct intercontinental transoceanic flights. The U.S. guidelines were issued in letter form by the FAA as ETOPS regulations in 1985. These guidelines spelled out conditions that need to be fulfilled for a grant of 120 minutes' diversion period, which is sufficient for direct transatlantic flights. The North Atlantic airways are the most heavily used oceanic routes in the world. Most North Atlantic airways are covered by ETOPS 120-minute rules, removing the necessity of using 180-minute rules. ETOPS 240 and beyond have been permitted on a case-by-case basis by some countries. In this case, authority was only granted to operators of two-engine airplanes between specific city pairs. The ETOPS regulation is still on the books, but the trend has been to remove ETOPS restrictions from some very dependable aircraft on a case-by-case basis. On February 15, 2007 the FAA began allowing properly equipped and approved twin-engine aircraft to fly oceanic and polar routes that are indefinitely out of range of emergency airports along the way (Chiles 2007).

Another FAA regulation that could be very important to a flight department manager, depending on the circumstances, is FAR Part 135. Part 135 regulates scheduled commuter and on-demand commercial operations. Most large corporate flight departments elect to not make the company aircraft available for commercial use; however, if they do, they must obtain an FAR 135 certificate. As a general rule flight operations under a FAR 135 certificate are less flexible and more expensive than operating under FAR Part 91. As an example, the crew duty time/rest requirements under FAR 135 are mandatory, whereas Part 91 does not contain a mandatory requirement for crew rest periods, except for certain fractional ownership operations under subpart K. The NBAA recommends that operators abide by the Part 35 crew duty rest period, and most do, but it is not mandatory. FAR part 135 also requires an FAA-approved training manual with a training curriculum detailing how the pilots and other crewmembers will be trained. There is also a requirement for mandatory pilot check rides at short intervals (each six months for IFR check rides), whereas part 91 only sets pilot currency standards with pilot check rides at less frequent intervals. The biggest expense of operating under Part 135 vs. Part 91; however, has to do with maintenance. Part 135 operators must have an FAA approved aircraft maintenance program detailing how the aircraft will be maintained with standards somewhat higher than for a FAR 91 operation. The FAR 135 maintenance standards call for a Continuous Maintenance Program for aircraft with ten or more seats. Part 91 has no such requirement, except for large, turbo jet, or turbine-powered multi-engine airplanes. These additional maintenance requirements mean that it is much more expensive to maintain an aircraft operating under FAR 135, and there is less flexibility scheduling the aircraft for periodic maintenance and scheduling it for flight. There is also a requirement for part 135 operations to have an FAA-approved operations manual. The FAR 135 operations certificate also contains strict operations specifications which detail a specific area and the type of approaches that may be conducted. Depending on the wording of the Operations Specifications, this could be a severe limitation on a corporate operator, since many operate on a worldwide basis. For all of these reasons, many corporate flight departments elect to operate their aircraft under FAR part 91 rather than FAR part 135.

REFERENCES

Chiles, Patrick. (2007). ETOPS redefined: A new name and sweeping new rules for extended operations. Retrieved from http://flightsafety.org/asw/mar07/asw_mar07_p12-16.pdf

Federal Aviation Administration. (1977). Operational approval of airborne long-range navigation systems for flight within the North Atlantic MNPSA (AC 120 -33). Available online at http://rgl.faa.gov/Regulatory_and_Guidance_Library/rgAdvisoryCircular.nsf/0/ab20bddd342482b1862569ea00695ec7/$FILE/AC120 -33.pdf

_______. (2011). *Aeronautical Information Manual (AIM).* Available online at www .faa.gov/regulations_policies/faa_regulations/

_______. (2011). *Federal Air Regulations Part 61: Certification: Pilots and Instructors.* Available online at www.faa.gov/regulations_policies/faa_regulations/

_______. (2011). *Federal Air Regulations Part 91: General Operating and Flight Rules.* Available online at www.faa.gov/regulations_policies/faa_regulations/

______. (2011). *Federal Air Regulations Part 97: Standard Instrument Procedures.* Available online at www.faa.gov/regulations_policies/faa_regulations/

______. (2011). *Federal Air Regulations Part 135: Commuter and On-Demand Operations.* Available online at www.faa.gov/regulations_policies/faa_regulations/

______. (2011). Reduced vertical separation minimum (RVSM). Available online at www.faa.gov/about/office_org/headquarters_offices/ato/service_units/enroute/rvsm/

3

Operational Criteria

Learning Objectives: After reading this chapter you should be able to:

- Outline the career path of an aviation department manager
- Justify a corporate flight department
- Draw an organizational chart for a typical corporate flight department
- Recite the position descriptions for corporate flight department
- Prepare a standard operating procedure for a corporate flight department
- Explain the guidelines for flight and duty time as practiced in the corporate world
- Assess the need for a work-life balance in the corporate world
- Calculate the number of pilots needed based on both flight hours and number of days a pilot is needed

THE FLIGHT DEPARTMENT

A business aviation flight department is a functional blend of assets, personnel, and processes, combined to provide the ultimate in customer service: the definitive convenience and flexibility of a corporate aircraft. Business aviation can trace its foundation back to the early days of flight (Chapter 1). The roots of this viable industry realistically took seed when the National Business Aviation Association (NBAA) was founded in 1947 by a small group of dedicated chief pilots and executives who envisioned a future for this segment of aviation. What began as the company plane soon morphed into the corporate jet by 1960. Viewed as a private convenience for a select few, the business aircraft has become a staple of corporate culture and the expectation of many progressive executives.

Managing a corporate flight department can be a daunting task. The vast majority of aviation managers began their careers as pilots or mechanics. A few began the path to leadership through the operational discipline of administrative support or scheduling. Regardless of the pathway to a career in business aviation, managing a flight department was typically not one their initial career goals. Pilots simply wanted to fly. Maintenance technicians worked diligently to gain the requisite skills in order to maintain those beautiful machines. Management, leadership, and being responsible for the overall safety, security, and financial well being of an entire group, are not the typical dreams of the novice aviation professional.

Business aviation requires more from individuals than does the work-life expectations of a scheduled air carrier. The fact that a pilot is an excellent aviator is a given in business aviation. The expectation that a technician can troubleshoot a discrepancy and provide a timely solution goes without question in the corporate world of aviation support. Business aviation demands that the basic skill sets of associates are covered and completed in a professional manner. The challenge of working within the aviation support structure of a corporation is to ensure that all of the other aspects of the discipline are accomplished. Those aspects are defined and outlined in this chapter.

The business aviation industry is composed of operations that vary in complexity from NetJets to a Navajo flown by a professional pilot who works for a feed company based in Casper, Wyoming. Aircraft are collectively managed by aviation companies, who hold charter certificates under the guise of FAR Part 135. Major corporations own or lease a fleet of business jets based in multiple locations. High net worth individuals operate a dedicated business aircraft for the purposes of transportation of a select few in the course of the promotion and development of the owner's interests. Aircraft from Boeings to Bonanzas are utilized as transportation tools in this vibrant alternative to commercial lift.

Why Form an Individual Flight Department?

Time savings/flexibility: Use of a corporate flight department results in a reduction of non-productive time for executives and middle managers by providing point-to-point service. Time is also saved because corporate/business aircraft are able to use smaller airports closer to final destinations, as opposed to the use of a commercial airline service. A final, and most important, way that time is saved is that a corporate aircraft has the ability to serve as an airborne office. This allows greater productivity while flying to the destination than would be the case for commercial flight. Another important advantage of using a corporate flight department is that they are able to provide on-demand service. This allows the executive the flexibility and freedom to set his or her own travel schedules or change destinations en route, which would be impossible when traveling via the commercial airlines.

Cost of Operation: When you operate your own aircraft with a competent aviation manager employed by your organization, his or her responsibility is to control costs within the guidelines of a pre-approved budget (Chapter 10). Properly applied, budgetary controls coupled with solid Standard Operating Procedures (SOPs) may offer a lower cost alternative than a management company and certainly lower than a fractional provider, given roughly 400 hours of use a year.

Security: The owner is personally aware of each crew member in the flight department. They are in turn dedicated to the safety and security of the owner. They have an obvious vested interest in the safety and security of the principal and his family. Aviation department personnel become quickly aware of the special needs of the principal passengers (i.e., small children, elderly parents, media exposure, confidential information, etc.) as they relate to security.

Confidentiality: Who is on board and where they are going is information only for those whom the principal chooses to inform.

Customer Service: Owning and operating a personal aircraft should be the ultimate in customer service. You are never late; when you arrive the aircraft departs. Because your employees schedule, maintain, and operate your personal jet, your specific needs are in the forefront of every trip's planning and execution. The guidelines of your operation are tailored to meet your expectations, not dictated to you by the operational principles that direct a managed aircraft or fractional provider. With your own aviation department, your company will have greater flexibility.

Integrity of Operational Needs: With your own department, you control the aircraft maintenance program as well as the flight crew's training program. Your personnel control all the information concerning the travel needs, ground transportation, lodging, and business meeting plans. There is an expectation of direct and honest feedback when issues arise concerning the company aircraft.

Pride of Ownership: For your family and guests, your aircraft takes on a special meaning when they understand that the pilots, flight attendants, and support personnel all work for you. You have reached a personal and/or business plateau that enables you to own and operate a private form of transportation that only a limited number of members can claim to be theirs. You designed it, built it, and now you operate it. Your employees are a part of your team, instead of someone else's team.

The organizational structure of a business aviation department will vary with the diversity and relationship with its parent corporation. For the purposes of discussion and learning, Figures 3.1 and 3.2 are offered as typical

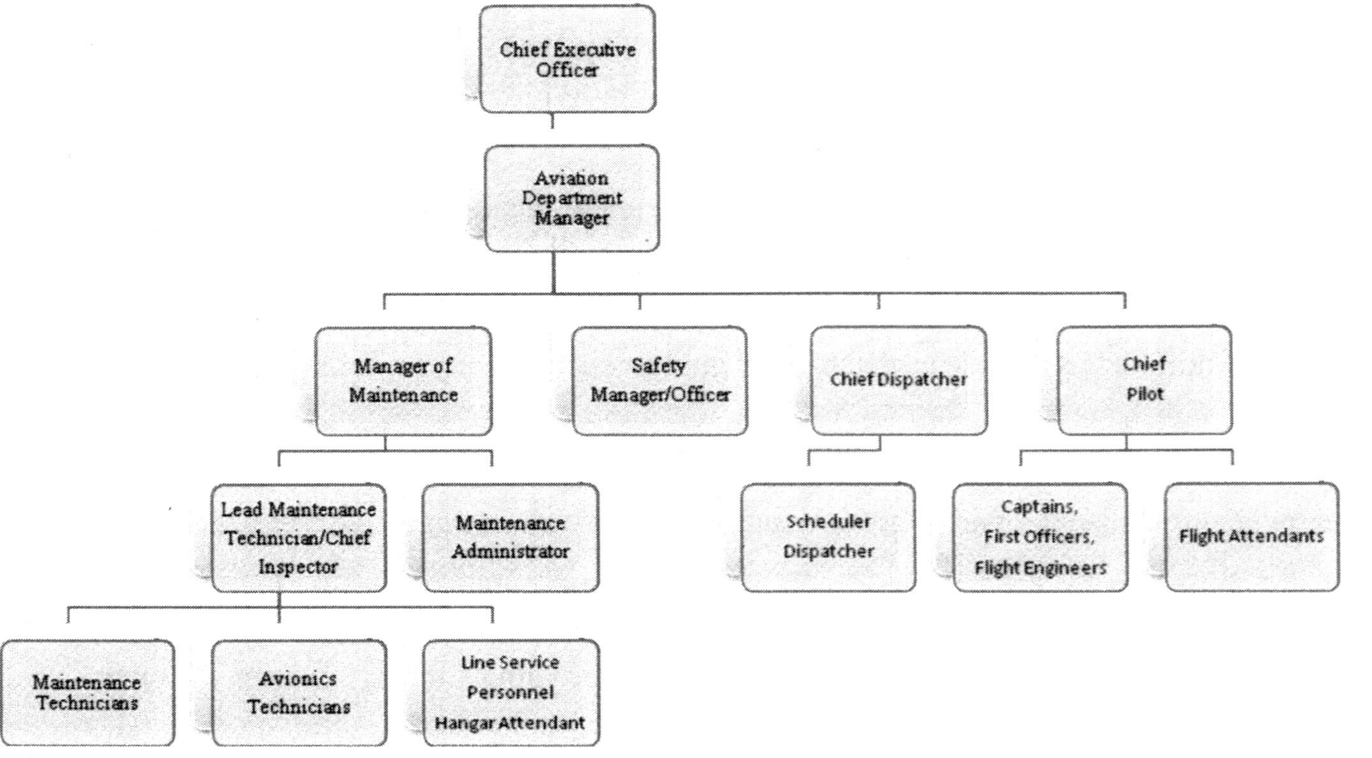

Figure 3.1 Sample corporate flight department reporting chart: large department. Developed by the authors.

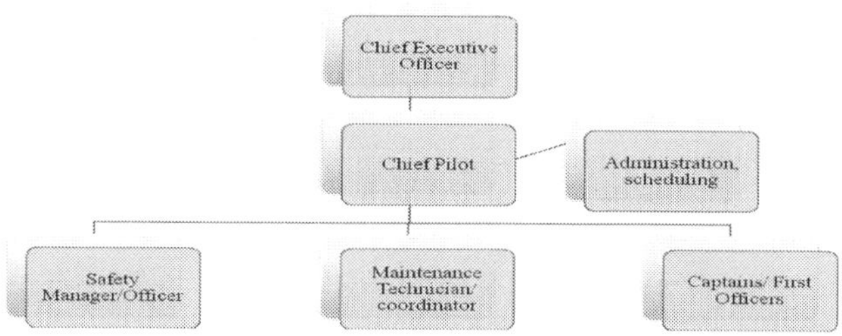

Figure 3.2 Sample corporate flight department reporting chart: small department. Developed by the authors.

organizational structures of a single-base, corporate-owned and -flown, business aviation department. Variations from this structure will be influenced by the number of associates and aircraft that are being managed. The aviation department under discussion has an aviation department manager (ADM), a chief pilot, a manager of maintenance, a safety officer/manager as well as the appropriate number of pilots, mechanics, and administrative support personnel.

During the course of a business aviation career that is highlighted with the opportunity to become an aviation manager, you may be offered the prospect of building a flight department from scratch. If that is the case, it would be wise to already have a sense of what tools are necessary to launch the new venture. As inclusive as the authors have attempted to make this text, there is no substitute for experience. As the reader's career grows, it is very important to learn from those professionals who work with you as well as those you work for. Once the chance is offered to provide leadership and guidance to a business aviation department, the learning curve only gets steeper. Hopefully your ascent to aviation management is elevated through a solid background of professional credentials and managerial development over time.

Whether the department you are managing is small or large, one of the most important factors to remember is that you cannot get the job done without the buy-in from the other members of your flight organization. That especially holds true for the senior executive who you will be reporting to. (How to work with senior management is discussed more thoroughly in Chapter 14.) It is critical to your success as an aviation manager to have a solid working relationship with your boss and those in the corporate structure above that position. These are your customers and you are in the customer relationship business. The professionals who work for you, or with you, are the ones who will deliver the customer delight or dissatisfaction. Your working relationship with your aviation team must be a positive and nurturing one. As an aviation manager you will have to dig in and work very hard to provide the essential tools and support for your department to function. Most senior officers within the corporation will view your operation as a cost center that doesn't produce value. It is the unique challenge of the business aviation manager to change that opinion shared by those above you in the organizational structure. They are all understandably competent in their jobs, but when the subject of the corporate aircraft arises, their knowledge is typically clouded by past perceptions. Senior executives have a clear understanding of the mission of the corporation and the contribution of their individual efforts to the company's success. They don't, however, understand how you and your department function: how you do what you do and why it costs so much to provide the services you offer.

Let's begin by looking at the complexity of several jobs within a typical business aviation department. It is important to note that the size and scope of a flight organization will allow more delegation of duties and responsibilities as it grows. That growth will, by the nature of the operation, create many new aspects that will have to be broken down into tasks and assigned to individual members of the team. Whereas a single aircraft flight department may only have two pilots, the manager holding the title of chief pilot, a multi-aircraft group may require additional layers of management to provide the proper level of necessary oversight. Regardless of the size of the department, the basic functions of each job must be accomplished. The following groups of position responsibilities are provided to offer insight as to how complex the task of business aviation can become.

Position Descriptions

Aviation Department Manager (ADM): The ADM reports to the senior corporate executive assigned overall responsibility for the flight department. The ADM position is responsible for formulating plans and policies, directing the execution of parent company policies, establishing personnel, operations, and equipment standards. The ADM works with appropriate corporate support functions to build and maintain the flight department budget; prepares monthly reports for senior management concerning monthly budgetary variances and operational performance; coordinates with the maintenance manager when scheduling aircraft into applicable inspections and maintenance, and manages the operational scheduling of all flights. The ADM manages the process of personnel interviews of flight department personnel and directs the training of all members of the organization. He or she coordinates with the operations department to obtain the necessary diplomatic clearances prior to departure for all flights into or over foreign countries. The ADM manages the revision, distribution, and accountability of the company manuals; supervises procurement, distribution, and posting of all information or memoranda relative to changes affecting company policy and procedures; ensures prompt reporting, filing, and follow-up action on any incident reports to the appropriate FAA agencies. The ADM may delegate functions to other personnel, but retains responsibility. The ADM must be highly knowledgeable of the entire contents of all company manuals, pertinent operations specifications, and all Federal Aviation Regulations pertaining to the flight department's operations; be responsible for maintaining all company records; and provide leadership and direction to ensure that high standards of performance are maintained in the areas of safety, compliance, costs, and quality. The ADM is responsible for communication and administration of corporate policies and goals to assigned personnel to ensure a continuing understanding of the company's commitment to safety and compliance; coordinates strategic growth plans with marketing/planning, finance, flight operations, and other departments; establishes operating procedures that, when followed, will ensure that all flight operations are continuously in compliance with applicable Federal Aviation Regulations, operations specifications, and all other applicable federal, state, and local regulations. The ADM ensures that safety policies and procedures are fully implemented in the respective areas; ensures that safety corrective action plans are implemented in response to findings resulting from external audits or from the Internal Evaluation Program activity; chairs the flight operations safety committee; performs or delegates the duties of the alcohol and drug prevention program manager. The ADM has the authority to ensure that safety is the first consideration in all operations. He or she hires flight operations personnel who meet established company standards; terminates flight operations personnel who fail to meet company standards; maintains operational control of all flight operations including the orderly and safe dispatch of company aircraft as outlined in 14 CFR part 135, if applicable (also maintains a copy of the load manifest required by FAR 135.63(c) for a period of at least 30 days); and terminates any or all flight operations due to safety, compliance, or security concerns.

Chief Pilot: The chief pilot (CP) is responsible for the coordination of all operational policies, standardization, and training matters for flight crew personnel. The CP maintains oversight of flight operations and the training of flight crew members. The CP prepares and maintains proficiency records, flight schedules, reports, and correspondence pertaining to operational activities; maintains the currency of any and all aircraft checklists, cockpit or cabin, ensures that each aircraft has the appropriate standard operating procedures, manuals, safety equipment, charts, database updates, documents and approvals necessary to conduct appropriate flights within the rules and regulations of local and national governing authorities. The CP is responsible for the dissemination of information to all crew members as it pertains to routes, airports, NOTAMS, navigational aids, and company policies; submits to FAA all reports required pertaining to flight crews; designates check pilots to ensure all flight crews conform to standard procedures outlined in applicable FAA regulations and company policies, and to ensure that all pilots maintain current qualifications and receive proficiency checks as required by FAA and the company; works with the operational/scheduling department to ascertain available flight crew members and establish personnel duty hours. The CP, as with the ADM, must be highly knowledgeable of the entire contents of all company manuals, pertinent operations specifications, and all Federal Aviation Regulations pertaining to the flight departments operations. Provide direct supervision to crew members to ensure the highest levels of safety and to ensure that they meet the highest standards of performance in accordance with all aspects of the company guidelines. Maintain oversight of contract training providers, training records for pilots, flight attendants, and check airmen. Perform any additional duties assigned by the director of operations.

Safety Manager/Officer: This position reports to senior management, directors, managers, and supervisors; the aviation department manager, VP of operations, or when appropriate, to the president of the aviation entity. Duties include the management and regulatory compliance of safety related matters. The safety manager/officer is responsible for developing, implementing, and maintaining a comprehensive safety program for the company as documented in the safety management system manual; administers the safety management system; is a member of the departmental safety action groups that meet quarterly to discuss findings and concerns within the operational departments; and oversees and guides the internal evaluation program as outlined in the company internal evaluation program manual. The safety manager/officer plays a primary role in the review and evaluation of the company's emergency response plan. Conducts periodic safety evaluations and training programs for flight and ground operations, maintenance programs, and if appropriate, other aviation-related operations. The safety manager/officer acts as a Continuing Airworthiness Surveillance (CAS) auditor in safety-related areas as requested by the chief inspector. He or she maintains records of audit activities and safety recommendations made to various company officials and monitors planned flight operating programs, procedures, and practices. He or she also monitors industry safety concerns that may have an impact on operations; reviews, monitors, and catalogues employee-generated safety hazard reports and recommends action to various departments and corporate officers; investigates (independent of investigative and review activities by other departments, the FAA, or the NTSB) selected significant events, incidents, and accidents; and makes timely safety recommendations to the safety review board, and the president. The director of safety position should be autonomous and work independently from all operating divisions. He or she is the liaison between the company, the FAA, the NTSB, other government agencies, and industry safety organizations and associations and ensures that findings and concerns are addressed by upper management from each functional area. He or she requests specific action from any company director on safety-related issues; brings safety-related issues where a satisfactory resolution was not achieved at the director level to the attention of the most senior position; requests assistance in conducting safety-related audits from the directors and, via them, other department heads and staff; participates in relevant company meetings; calls intra- or inter-department meetings to discuss and resolve safety-related issues; and initiate corrective action when safety-related events, activities, or trends are identified.

Manager of Maintenance: The manager of maintenance reports to the aviation department manager and is responsible for the airworthiness of all company aircraft. Duties include managing a continuous surveillance, analysis, and operational irregularity process; ensuring that all necessary work records are properly executed; and providing leadership and direction for the maintenance services function. The manager of maintenance is responsible for the management of all maintenance manuals, service bulletins, airworthiness directives, and any other technical data pertinent to the operation. This person ensures that high standards of performance are maintained in the areas of safety, compliance, costs, and quality; approves contract maintenance vendors; coordinates the training requirements of maintenance department personnel; acts as mentor and coach to subordinates within the department and maintains a process of evaluation and development of all personnel assigned; delegate to second tier maintenance technicians who have demonstrated the desire and ability to supervise functional areas of maintenance; and communicate corporate policies and goals to assigned personnel in order to ensure compliance with the organization's commitment to safety and integrity.

Pilot-in-Command: Reports to the chief pilot. The pilot-in-command (PIC) is responsible for the safe and efficient conduct of all assigned flights. The PIC may delegate functions to other personnel but retains responsibility for all aspects of the flight. The PIC must determine that his crew is legally and professionally qualified for the flight, adequately rested, and properly attired. He or she is responsible for checking the maintenance/flight logs to ascertain the aircraft's airworthiness. It is important for the PIC, working with the dispatch mechanic, to determine that the planned flight will not interfere in any scheduled maintenance plans. This position is responsible for planning each flight assignment and for briefing the crew regarding purpose of the flight, weather, range, weight, cruise control data, airport facilities, and navigational aids. The PIC supervises aircraft loading. The responsibility for proper weigh and balance calculations for each flight rests with the PIC. This person ensures that cargo is properly secured and that onboard equipment and provisions for passengers' comfort and safety are adequate for the assigned flight. Upon passenger arrival, the PIC verifies the identity of each passenger and ensures that all baggage is properly secured and none is left behind at the point of departure. Prior to departure, the PIC should communicate with scheduling/dispatch to validate that no passenger or passenger belongings were inadvertently neglected at the departure point. Approaching the destination airport, the PIC is responsible for having validated the passenger's transportation and other special needs. Following shutdown, the PIC should ensure that the passengers and their luggage are secured in the appointed mode of transport and that a cellular phone number contact has been passed to the lead passenger. Many view the role of PIC as a position that has command authority over passengers as well as fellow crew members from the time they report for duty until they go off duty. This position has responsibility for flights within a trip packet from the moment when the aircraft is released to the PIC until the trip is concluded.

Second in Command: Reports to the chief pilot. The second in command (SIC) is administratively responsible to the chief pilot but is functionally responsible to the PIC on each assigned flight. Most flight departments work to improve the professional skills of the SIC to enhance the opportunity to upgrade to PIC whenever the person holding flight status as a SIC gains sufficient experience through training and practical flight knowledge. It is the role of the SIC to back up the PIC and monitor the aircraft's performance during flight.

Command and Sequence of Command: The pilot-in-command is responsible for the integrity of the company aircraft from the instant that it is released to the PIC until the trip has been completed and the aircraft is returned to the custody of the maintenance department. The PIC is also no longer responsible for the aircraft if he or she has been relieved of that responsibility during a crew change during an en route stop or an extended stopover away from the company base hangar. The pilot-in-command must have authority over all crew members from the time they report for duty until the duty period has ended. In addition the PIC must also have command authority over the passengers, regardless of whether the operation is commercial in nature, during the course of an emergency, or whenever a decision of go/no-go must be made. The SIC provides backup and assistance to the PIC during the course of all flight operations where they are collectively working together as a cockpit crew. The PIC should make every opportunity available to the SIC for learning and enhancement of aviation expertise. Whenever conditions allow and under the approval of the PIC, the SIC should share in the execution of takeoffs and landings. This can be accomplished from the right seat in a fixed wing aircraft, the left seat in a rotary wing aircraft. If the SIC is rated in the aircraft and company policy allows, the PIC and SIC may switch cockpit seat positions prior to engine start. The SIC will in that instance make the takeoff and landing from the left seat while the PIC monitors and assists during the flight. Regardless of seat position, the SIC is responsible for assuming the PIC's responsibility and authority in the event that the PIC is incapacitated during flight. That responsibility should end upon landing and with the assignment of a relief PIC.

THE PROCESS

With all the people and capital assets put together, what, one may ask, does business aviation offer to their passengers that the airlines do not tender to their customers? The most important differential between these two vital and vibrant aspects of aviation is that business aviation operates on the passengers' schedule while the commercial air carriers mandate that their customers function on the airline's fixed schedule. The old adage in business aviation is that "the boss is never late." Others include, "We always have on-time departures." Business aviation obviously is subject to weather and traffic delays just as are the airlines, but with more than 5,000 airports from which to choose versus less than 500 served by commercial carriers, business aviation extends a greater degree of flexibility. "You go where you want to go whenever you wish to depart."

With an airline you look at options and book the trip accordingly. With business aviation, you generate a trip request. That request, when circulated through the approval process, generates the scheduling of an aircraft and crew. The request may be a simple out-and-back the same day to attend an important business function or as complicated as a multi-day trip with multiple destinations each day. The trip typically is initiated by a senior executive or authorized person who may request use of the corporate aircraft. The communication is usually managed by the administrative assistant of the "requestor" and is sent to the office of the person who is authorized to approve trips. Many companies use a computer-generated trip request form. Authorization is based on cost vs. benefit; the perceived business benefit weighed against the operating cost of the trip (see Chapter 10). Approval of the request brings the flight department into the picture. A trip approval may often require a review by the scheduling office within the flight operation to ascertain the feasibility of the requested transportation.

Once the trip becomes a scheduled event, the pre-departure workload begins. The scheduling office, one person in most business aviation departments, will then take the requested information and put the trip together in a trip sheet format. A flight crew is assigned, including both PIC and SIC. Hotels, ground transportation, catering, and airport facilities are selected including the fixed base operator (FBO), fuel is verified, driving times from the airport to business address are confirmed, and en route flight time corroboration, passenger manifest generation, and special circumstances notification are completed. The assigned fight crew will work with scheduling to ensure that their portions of the tasks are completed in a timely manner. Scheduling should know prior to filling the trip that the crew members are current and qualified in all aspects of their flight duties. Crew rest following a previous flight by either crew member should also be taken into account when scheduling a flight. Prior to departure on the day of the flight, one or both crew members should run a flight risk analysis tool (FRAT), (Chapter 12) to ascertain the dispatchability of the trip as it relates to predetermined risk factors.

An underlying fact of each business aviation operation is that the aircraft or one of the aircraft in a multi-plane group will be available for the proposed trip. Working day to day, the maintenance effort (Chapter 4) provides the ultimate availability of the company asset for use. Airworthiness is the cornerstone of the entire operation. Without the methodical application of the practice of sound maintenance principles, the opportunity to conduct flight operations would not exist. A skilled chief of maintenance is as integral to the modern business aviation department as is the chief pilot and therefore should share the same organizational reporting level. Whereas in the past, promotion to the aviation department manager (ADM) position always came through the office of the chief pilot, today, more and more ADM positions are being filled by former manager of maintenance personnel.

Preparation for the flight certainly requires effort on the part of the pilots and mechanics; however, the aircraft must be stocked with the requisite food and beverage items. It must also be clean. The image of a professionally managed and maintained flight department begins with the passengers' first impression of the aircraft as they prepare for boarding. When the department operates out of its own hangar and office space, every time a passenger enters that facility, they are validating the management process. This point cannot be overemphasized. If the executives who fly aboard the company aircraft feel like they could literally eat off the hangar floor, they will not have any worries about how well the department functions.

With the flight plan filed, maintenance logs reviewed, pre-flight complete, ice/coffee/catering aboard, aircraft fueled and in position for passenger boarding, preparations are complete. The final task is passenger boarding. Most medium to large corporate jets are equipped with an auxiliary power unit (APU). These small turbines provide electrical power and pneumatic air for environmental temperature control on the ground. The cabin should therefore be well lit and comfortable before boarding. Prior to passenger arrival, all cockpit checks up to engine start should be complete. Upon arrival, each passenger should be handled with the same level of customer service.

The transition from auto to aircraft should be seamless and understood by all flight department members. Passenger and baggage handling requires a process, just as any other important aspect of the management of the organization. Who greets the passenger, who handles the bags, where the passengers wait prior to boarding, which pilot remains aboard with the APU running, who loads the bags, who verifies that everyone on the manifest is accounted for, how and when the passengers are briefed prior to taxi, and who closes the main entrance door are all issues that are just as important as who sits in the left seat to make the takeoff. A well-managed business aviation department has standard operating procedures for every aspect of its process (see Chapter 5).

It is critical to the future success of the flight department's contribution to the parent corporation that all crew adhere to an agreed upon set of SOPs (Chapter 5). During a flight there are many occasions where members of the crew are called upon to use their decision-making and piloting skills to further enhance the quality of the trip. Individual pilot techniques should never be discouraged. The goal of SOP implementation is to provide a universally understood level of safety and process. The end result: Passengers will experience that regardless of who is piloting the aircraft, the same professional level of service is being rendered.

The SOPs should also cover all aspects of the arrival process. Again, business aviation differs from commercial aviation in the attention to customer needs and expectations. On a commercial flight, once you step off the aircraft, onto the Jetway, away from the arrival counter, and into the terminal gate corridor, you and your continued travel arrangements are not the responsibility of the airline. Passengers aboard a corporate aircraft are monitored on a continual basis to ascertain any changes in current plans. A business aviation flight crew will be in communication with the FBO at the destination airport, prior to descent from cruise altitude, in order to verify all handling requirements for their passengers. Ground transportation confirmation is a critical aspect of the business aviation flight. An acknowledgement of the ground transportation prior to pulling up on the ramp is a key factor in customer service. The transition from aircraft to surface transport of the passengers and their baggage should be as seamless as possible.

At this point in the trip, the lead passenger should be aware of how to contact the flight crew. If changes in the remainder of the trip arise, the ability of the flight crew to adapt to those changes is greatly enhanced by receiving notice as soon as is reasonably possible. Often, the administrative assistant of the lead passenger will contact the corporate aviation coordinator/scheduler and they in turn will notify the crew. The coordinator/scheduler plays a crucial role in the overall communication process (Chapter 9).

FLIGHT AND DUTY TIME

At the beginning of 2011, the FAA is scheduled to incorporate new regulations regarding the amount of time that a flight crew may fly during the course of a duty period and the length of that duty period. Specific language regarding flight and duty time under Part 135 of the Federal Aviation Regulations is covered in 135.263 through 135.273. Many operations in the business community operate under these regulatory guidelines. The majority, however, operate under FAR Part 91 and are not required by regulations to adhere to a strict set of duty and flight time rules. Most of these flight departments reference the FARs as well as the NBAA *Management Guide* and the many offerings from the Flight Safety Foundation (FSF) over the past twenty years. In the February 1990, John Pope, one of the founding fathers of business aviation, wrote an article for the FSF publication *Accident Prevention*, "The flight and duty time dilemma":

> Regardless of the size of the aviation department, the company operations manual is the best means to spell out flight and duty guidelines and specific limitations. Aviation department managers find it difficult to be completely restrictive because the priorities may lie with the company's travel requirements and not with the pilot's fatigue factors. Therefore, it is more practical to state limitations as guidelines, and allow for exceptions with the concurrence of the department manager and the air crew.

In February 1997, the Flight Safety Foundation published "Principles and Guidelines for Duty and Rest Scheduling in Corporate and Business Aviation" (see Figure 3.3). This nineteen-page report was the result of more than two years of effort on the part of a committee of thirty business aviation professionals, chaired by Pat Andrews, Manager, Global Flight Operations, Mobil Business Resources Corp. This is one of the finest documents published on the subject of flight and duty limitations. The following two tables outline the findings and recommendations of the committee and have been referenced and adopted by the vast majority of professionally managed business aviation departments.

To ensure the optimum efficiency and performance of flight crews and to enhance the safety of flight, it is highly recommended to closely adhere to the above limitations outlining the length of a flight duty period and the amount of rest required for crew members. The PIC should always retain the authority to temporarily suspend a trip anytime he determines crew fatigue may affect safety of flight. Duty time commences when the flight crew reports for a scheduled flight. Crew report is defined as the time when the crew arrives at the point of departure and commences their pre-flight duties. Normally, a crew reports one hour prior to scheduled takeoff for a domestic flight and two hours prior to scheduled takeoff for an international

	Off Duty			Duty Period		Flight Time			
	Per 24-hour Period	Per Week	Other	Per 24-hour Period	Weekly, Monthly, Annually	Per 24-hour Period	Per Week	Monthly, Annually	
Two Pilots	10 hours	Minimum 36 continuous hours, including two consecutive recovery nights, in a seven-day period (calculated on a seven-day or 168-hour rolling basis) … or … minimum 48 continuous hours in a 10-day period	48 continuous hours on return home following duty period across multiple time zones	14 hours	There are not sufficient scientific data to provide specific guidance in this area; nevertheless, maximum cumulative duty periods should be adjusted downward over increasing time frames.	10 hours	There are not sufficient scientific data to provide specific guidance in this area; nevertheless, maximum cumulative flight time should be adjusted downward over increasing time frames.		**Standard**
	12 hours (following extended flight time)			14 hours		Up to 12 hours (requires that landings, maximum cumulative hours be restricted, with compensatory off-duty time)	Maximum of four cumulative hours of extension		**Extended***
	Off Duty			Duty Period		Flight Time			
Three Pilots (Augmented)	12 hours 12 hours	*(same as above)*	*(same as above)*	*Reclining seat:* 18 hours *Supine bunk:* 20 hours	*(same as above)*	16 hours** 18 hours**		*(same as above)*	

Figure 3.3 Flight Safety Foundation recommendations. Source: Flight Safety Foundation and NASA (in the public domain).

trip. The PIC may request an earlier show time if conditions require additional time for flight planning or aircraft preparation. Flight duty time ends when all post-flight inspections and activities are completed, normally 30 minutes after landing at a domestic airport, or one hour after landing at an international location. However, if any crew member is required to remain with the aircraft for repair or servicing, the flight duty period shall be extended to include that time. If flight duty limits are exceeded due to en route delays or unscheduled operational requirements, an additional amount of crew rest should be required before the next duty period begins. If the urgency of the mission dictates flying the aircraft for more than the number of hours available to the crew, the aviation department manager should position an entire relief crew to take over the aircraft and continue the flight.

Crew Rest

Crew rest is defined as the required period of time between flight duty periods that allows a crew member to receive a sufficient amount of uninterrupted rest to safely resume his flying duties. Referring to Figure 3.3, the recommended minimum crew rest in a 24-hour period is 10 hours, 12 hours of rest with an extended flight day. What is referred to as rest in this instance is the ability to rest. Travel time to and from home or a hotel is included in this allotment of time. Crews typically will have a meal or perhaps two during the rest period. The 10-hour figure quickly becomes less than 8 hours available for rest. Adherence to this or a similar schedule of formal policy concerning rest will prove to enhance the overall safety of the flight operation.

Variations on the Flight Safety Foundation recommendations when dealing with rest include statements such as these:

- Crew members will be scheduled for a minimum of 12 hours between the last landing of the duty day and the first takeoff of the following flight duty period. This time can be reduced on a one-time basis with the approval of the director of operations, when there is an urgent reason to continue a trip. At no time will crew rest be reduced to less than 10 hours.
- If a crew is required to exceed a 14-hour flight duty period, crew members will be scheduled for 14 hours of crew rest following the flight.
- If an aircraft is to remain in one location for an extended period of time and the captain determines that the crew needs rest, he may authorize the use of a hotel or day-room. If the crew is given 5 hours of uninterrupted crew rest, their flight duty time may be extended to 18 hours.

- On those occasions when an augmented flight crew (three pilots and a flight attendant) extend the duty day between 14 and 20 hours, the entire crew must receive a minimum of 14 hours rest between the duty day in question and the following duty day which may not exceed 14 hours with a maximum of 10 hours flying.
- After returning to home station from a trip lasting 6 days or more, all members of the flight crew will be given a minimum of 2 days of uninterrupted time off. To compensate for trips of longer duration, the director of flight operations will determine the appropriate amount of time off to be granted.

Work Days in Business Aviation

Retention of personnel is one of the many challenges faced by the business aviation manager. Whenever a valued associate accepts a position with another company or airline, or simply makes the choice to leave his or her current employer, it is important to comprehend the reasons why. As the aviation manager you can recognize an offer of promotion that would not be readily available with your flight organization. It is vital to understand that the reason for the separation is not work-life related. Initially the intoxication that follows one's first big break in the industry is eventually overcome by the sobering realization that flying the line or working long and arduous hours attempting to correct a puzzling discrepancy is not all glamour and glitz. Employees of business aviation flight departments work much harder than the public perception gives credit for. When an associate resigns to take a position that will afford more planned time off, that departure may indicate a glitch in the current scheduling system. As with any decision dealing with people, work and family, the explanation is usually more complicated than simply a quick answer, "I wanted more time with my family."

Having a sense of control over one's personal time is a key factor in maintaining a successful work-life balance. If the employee's family begins to feel that he or she has no time for them; if planned social events are constantly cancelled due to being called out on a trip or into the hangar to dispatch a flight; if personal vacations are interrupted in order to meet a pop-up requirement at the airport, retention is going to become a problem for the flight operation.

Business aviation, whether you are working for a private individual, major corporation, fractional provider, charter operation, or single turboprop with only one pilot in the company, demands a great deal of your time. Pilots and flight attendants in our industry understand the need to be on call. As the business of corporate transport continues to mature and the budgets get tighter, all aspects of the job come under closer and more detailed inspection. Flight crews work odd hours, late nights, long days, short days, long flights, short hops and are subject to the varied demands of the flight schedule. That workload is driven by the personality of each industry, corporate initiatives, values, and the particular needs and social posturing of the principal passengers. Flight crews prepare for each trip, execute each trip, rest between trips, are scheduled for standby or readiness duty to fly a pop-up trip and train to maintain proficiency. This is essentially their work product. Often that product requires down time with family and friends to recharge the personal batteries and provide a balance between the work life and personal life. How each organization handles this balance varies across the board. There are, however, some similarities in the manner in which current flight departments go about solving the work life balance. "For the vast majority of working Americans, weekends and weekday evenings are considered personal time, to use as they see fit. But for many of us in business aviation, those times are not inviolate; our industry doesn't adhere to 9-to-5 conventions or schedules" (*B/CA*, April 2004, Practical Manager).

To gain some perspective of how various companies are handling this issue, eleven highly respected corporate operators based within the continental United States were surveyed in order to determine if there were any commonalities as to how they treated the work product of their flight crews. Results of the survey are shown in Table 3.1. They varied in size from a two-aircraft operation to several that operated 11 aircraft located in multiple bases. The discussion points were kept to a minimum and were focused on flight crew work days: how they measured them, tracked them, limited them, and used this mechanism to enhance the work life balance.

Every department in this small sample was very specific about the number of days their crews are expected to work per month. The average of the group is 15.63 work days per month. The average number of scheduled personal days off was 5.4. The average number of pilots per aircraft is 3.23. The aircraft in the survey population are flown an average of 545 hours per year.

Working Hours

Because of the nature of the business aviation mission, working hours are often difficult to establish for all flight department personnel. The aviation department manager (ADM) is responsible for ensuring that the scheduled aviation support requirements of the corporation are met and that all necessary work is accomplished to support that effort. This may require adjustment of working days and duty hours. The chief pilot (CP) and manager of maintenance (MOM) accordingly coordinate work schedules to support the flight schedule and avoid interfering with required crew rest periods. Flight crews typically report for flying duty in

Table 3.1. Work Life Survey Results

		Work-Life Survey			
Company	*Work Days/ Month*	*Personal Days Off*	*Flight Hours/Year*	*Aircraft*	*Pilots*
1	16 to18 max	4 per month	500	5	16
2	15 to 20 max	10 per month	550	2	8
3	18 max	30 days per year	550	8	22
4	15 to 18 max	Informal—in progress	700	8	22(a)
5	15 is target	5 to 6 per month	600	11	48
6	16 is target	Bid the month prior (b)	450	11	36
7	13 to 15 max	4 to 5 per month	600	2	7
8	12 to 17 max	4 + Weekend (c)	560	4	13(d)
9	16 days average	10 off days per month	360	4(e)	12(f)
10	12 to 16	6 days per month (g)	500	Missing info	Missing info
11	12 to 14	4 hard and 4 soft	550	3	11

Notes:

a. Staffed for five aircraft.

b. Paid for flight days beyond 16 days. Personal days off are bid by the 15th of the month prior and flight crew can switch out days off with other qualified crew when necessary.

c. Off days are assigned by the 15th of the month prior. Weekend standby assigned for one aircraft. Crews are on hard days off during weekend that they are not assigned standby.

d. Includes two management pilots but does not include a flying aviation director. Three additional pilot positions currently open and interviewing.

e. Extensive international flights. Two other satellite bases, maintain similar work rules.

f. Does not include chief pilot and manager, who both fly.

g. Every second or third weekend per month, driven by the schedule, each pilot is given a three-day weekend off. These can be attached to both ends of vacation.

accordance with guidelines established as industry best practices: as previously mentioned, one hour prior to takeoff with domestic departures and two hours prior for international flights. Although flight department associates cannot be guaranteed weekends off, most corporate flight departments attempt to schedule a flight crew member for eight days off during each month to provide equivalent time for personal activities. Flight crew members are not usually required to maintain regular office hours during non-flying periods, but are expected to assist the CP and the MOM with operations-related work in the flight department offices, perform additional duties, and complete special assignments, when requested. The manager of maintenance is responsible for accomplishing as much scheduled and unscheduled maintenance work as possible whenever the aircraft are at home station. During these periods, maintenance personnel may be required to work additional hours.

Standby Days

One common thread among the larger departments in business aviation is the use of crews on standby. If the company has more than one aircraft, the expectation is that an aircraft will always be available for use. If at least one aircraft is not flying during a particular day and it does not have maintenance scheduled to be performed, that aircraft will typically be placed in a standby status. The ADM for a five-aircraft department recently revealed that while he often had the requirement to put a crew on standby, it was his opinion that standby did not work for his operation. The main reason was centered on the fact that standby is so uncertain. "How do you keep a crew on standby from 8:00 AM until 6:00 PM and then at 7:30 PM the call comes in for an immediate flight?" Do you use the crew that has been on an alert status all day to initiate a trip late in the evening? Do you use two standby crews, tough to do in a single-aircraft operation, to provide 24-hour coverage?

This particular Fortune 50 operator has averaged 500 hours per aircraft each year for the past ten years. "We have sixteen pilots for five aircraft, down two pilots at present, and our crews average eleven flight days per month, including overnights." He shared, "We are able to provide four personal days off per month per pilot and eighteen work days per month is our maximum." Another very experienced manager said, "When an aircraft is in the hangar, we have a standby crew available until 9:00 PM. Standby is definitely counted as work in our operation. With nine pilots and two aircraft, we can provide weekends off to our crews." This operator has two aircraft and nine pilots, including two management pilots. They schedule their crews so that every second or third weekend each pilot will have a three-day weekend.

How do you treat the standby day in your allocation of crew workload? From the time of notification of the pop-up trip, how much time is allotted for the alert aircraft and the standby crew to be airborne? The answer from the survey group varied from four hours to two hours, with the former representing the majority of the flight departments. One large operation with eleven aircraft in two bases replied that his standby crew, one per base per day, has to be able to report to the airport within one hour of notification. It is important to note that every flight department that participated indicated that a standby day was considered to be a workday and measured on an equal basis with a flight day, training day or administrative day by the flight crew.

SCHEDULED DAYS OFF

Quoting from a *B/CA* Practical Manager column published in October of 2004, "To your boss, the on-ground time that pilots have between flights is, essentially, time off. The fact that crews often spend days on the ground while away on a trip adds to this misconception. It is difficult to discuss the issue of duty days versus scheduled time off with passengers and senior executives. They view productivity and efficiency as the definitive measures of good management." A 9-to-5 employee considers his or her weekends as a period to unwind and relax with family and friends, away from the work environment. Most of us realize that in order to succeed in the business world, the hours of 9 to 5 for executive-level jobs are stretched several hours on both ends of that mythical eight-hour work day. Fast trackers with an eye toward the ivory tower will spend time at home and on weekends completing projects and/or catching up on work-related reading.

When one considers the business aviation world, there is no routine time to come and go from work. Weekends are more likely spent flying executives to a Monday morning meeting by taking them there on Sunday afternoon. Workdays can be fourteen hours or longer in length. One of the constant issues facing an aviation manager is the ability to provide scheduled time off for everyone in the flight department, not just pilots. It is sometimes easy to forget that the scheduler works odd hours, many of them at home taking calls from passengers making changes in a current itinerary or future trip. If the airplane is on a trip, the scheduler is providing flight following and serves as the point of contact should plans change. The maintenance staff comes to work before the pilots to ensure that the aircraft is completely airworthy. Chances are that the same mechanic may meet the aircraft at home base following a very lengthy flight day. Suffice it to say that work hours in a corporate aviation environment are never routine. The dilemma facing the manager can be a delicate balancing act of meeting the travel demands of the corporation's executives while providing sufficient time off for the aviation department associates to recharge their individual batteries.

Most working class people put in an average of 22 days per month and enjoy their weekends off. The challenge facing a business aviation manager is how to provide a somewhat matching amount of time off for departmental associates. The answer will depend upon how predictable the travel schedule is for the parent corporation, modified by the changeable nature of the type of trips typically flown, and the current level of staff in key positions. A well-respected veteran aviation manger confessed, "The more rules you write concerning work-life balance for your people the more difficult it is to enforce.... Our goal is to manage this issue on the basis of fairness and equity." He continued, "Our crew's average is 15 workdays per month, which definitely includes standby. We provide five to six days off for each crew member depending on how full the schedule is." The aviation department manager for a very active northwestern flight department is currently testing a PDO (personal days off) policy. "We are trying four PDOs for each pilot and stretching to five when we can," He indicated, "Our schedule is pretty hard and fast, not many changes, therefore we don't have standby in our mix. Our pilots fly long-stage-length trips and average 15 days per month on the road with at least 10 overnights. The nature of our operation is that we have hardly any day trips. My goal is to make sure that going forward, our crews have more of a work-life balance."

Work-Life Balance

Every conscientious aviation manager is concerned about their department's work-life balance. This may be the number-one factor in personnel retention within the industry. Balancing the manpower requirements of a corporate department, which by its nature provides the ultimate in flexibility to the corporation it serves, and keeping the associates responsible for the safe conduct of the aircraft and its passengers in a work-life balance that is acceptable to all parties, is the ultimate challenge. The author has been flying for 41 years, the last 35 in corporate aviation. I've observed and personally experienced the challenge that all managers face in regard to work-life balance. Executives typically do not understand what we do or how we manage our responsibilities. When it comes to flight crews, most executives view them as privileged—all kinds of time off and when they work all they do is fly. Sure they know that the hours can be long and the travel requirements can be demanding, but because they do not see the pilots and flight attendants sitting at a desk from 9 to 5 during the week days, executives have a tough time understanding why a pilot would want to have scheduled time off. "They seem to have all kinds of time on their hands," is a typical quote. Don't give up the struggle to provide your charges with some quality time off during the month. It is important to you and them that they have sufficient time to take care of their personal demands so when they report to work, they are focused on the job. The fact that you are paying attention to this issue is the first and most important step. How you deal with the particular aspect of your operation and your ability to enhance the work-life balance for your subordinates is directly related to how you are viewed and evaluated as a manager.

COST OF REPLACEMENT

When a flight crew member decides to leave his or her present position for another opportunity, quite a few things are put in motion simultaneously.

First, how much notice is the employee providing to the current employer? Personnel directors will tell you that the expected amount of notice for any associate is usually equal to the number of weeks of vacation that they are eligible for. That can vary from two to up to four weeks in most cases. For any employee in a key position that level of notice is never sufficient enough for the corporation. It is important to note, however, it is not uncommon for corporate flight departments to immediately take the departing pilot off the schedule whenever notice of departure is first given. Somehow, the chairman may not be comfortable flying with someone who has recently resigned from the company. Regardless of whether the associate leaving the firm is an administrative assistant, corporate officer, or pilot, the void in experience that remains after their departure is more often than not impossible to fill immediately. The company may find someone to fill in until a replacement is found, but in business aviation, that becomes somewhat difficult. Certainly in the case of a pilot, a large, well-structured flight department can simply move a junior pilot up to a more senior position to fill the shoes of the recently separated member of the group. The new hire would, in an ideal world, come into the bottom of the seniority list.

This replacement scenario is not as easy for the majority of the business aviation community. More than two-thirds of the business aviation flight departments in the United States are single aircraft operations. Often in a single aircraft operation, there may be only two pilots. More and more single aircraft operators are choosing to employ three full-time pilots to provide some sense of work-life balance to their crew members. When one of a very few decides to seek greener pastures, the impact is felt not only by human resources, but more directly by the remaining pilots whose workload just increased from filling the time or vacancy just created. How long it takes to bring a new hire up to speed on company policies and procedures is dependent on the individual and the department. How long until that flight crew member blends into the operation depends to a great degree on how accepting the team is to a new member. In a small flight department that transition may take some getting used to. In a larger group it is much easier to bring in a new person on the bottom of a seniority list than it is to inject a seasoned veteran into the left seat from the beginning.

Costs associated with hiring a replacement include training, moving, materials, and time. Training costs can include company orientation training, professional training at FlightSafety or CAE if the new hire is not qualified in your particular aircraft and the time to train in the specifics of your flight operation. Moving costs will vary with the internal policies of the company, but it would be difficult today to hire an experienced pilot without offering to move his or her family to where your operation is based. Other costs are uniforms, human resources time to process the new employee into the company's employment, and benefits programs. The end result, it takes usually requires more time than is anticipated until the new hire is onboard and up to speed. During this period, the department may be required to use temporary assistance or schedule the remaining staff at a higher level of intensity until the new team member is fully qualified. The amount of time will depend on the level of training and the distance of the relocation. A rule of thumb that seems to work in most cases is that the cost of a new hire can certainly approach and in some instances exceed one half of the annual salary that is being offered for the position in question.

JUSTIFICATION

One of the most difficult tasks that a business aviation manager faces in a corporate world, where manpower requirements are based upon efficiency and effectiveness, is the justification of work product of the associates within the company flight department. This is especially true when it comes to pilots. Senior management within the corporate structure may be committed to the valuable contribution of business aircraft to their executive productivity, security, and safety, but often remain unconvinced that the flight crew members accomplish any productive work beyond flying the company aircraft from point A to point B. The accepted view that pilots have, by the nature of their work, large amounts of time off, high incomes, and fairly glamorous lives, becomes a barrier to requests for additional manpower in order to meet the needs of an increased demand for business aviation support and increased flight hours.

It is not the intent of this text to fully explain the long and often arduous road undertaken by the novice pilot on his or her way to gaining the necessary experience and certifications which lead to the left seat of a business jet. It is important, however, to provide information to current and potential business aviation managers about manpower justification and the requirements of effectively staffing a multi-crew aircraft in support of the transportation needs of the parent company. First, two pilots are required, via regulations and peak workload activity, to operate a modern business aircraft. There are exceptions to this statement, within the turboprop and very-light-jet community of aircraft that are operated single pilot, but the overwhelming majority of corporate cockpits are occupied by two pilots.

The number of pilots employed by a business aviation flight department is dictated by the number of aircraft and the travel requirements of the corporation. A general rule of thumb used in pilot staffing discussions that has been around a long time is the need for three pilots (1.5 crew) per aircraft (NBAA 2009, pp. 1–17). Prior to making any calculation of the appropriate number of crew members for a particular flight operation, the philosophy of the level of service required needs to be fully understood.

What level of availability does the corporation expect from the aviation? The ultimate would be 24 hours a day, 7 days a week, with a flight crew available at a moment's notice. That, of course, is not a realistic expectation. Most corporate operators understand the travel patterns of their customers, their company executives. The vast majority of trips are planned well in advance with a minority of trips popping up at the last minute. With that in mind, scheduling crews is a matter of matching the trip requirements with the pilot's qualifications and availability. Computing the number of pilots necessary for a flight department has to begin with the amount of time available during each year. In order to measure the availability of a pilot it is necessary to understand how much time that a pilot will not be available. Factors such as training, medical exams, vacation periods, sick time, holidays, and meetings must be taken into consideration, when measuring non-availability. Each pilot will have a slightly different result due to seniority and experience. Figures 3.4 and 3.5 (NBAA 2009, pp. 1–13) illustrate this principle.

Pilot Availability (An Exercise)

This is a single-aircraft operation requiring two pilots to operate the aircraft and be available whenever the aircraft is available. How many pilots

Calculation of the Number of Pilots Based on Number of Days a Pilot is Needed

Each company could vary this calculation according to its own requirements. This sample calculation presumes a seven-day-a-week operation (the aircraft is available seven days a week) with a particular pilot available five days a week. Five pilots would be required if a five-day-a-week operation is used

Description	**Calculation**	**Totals**
Work days/pilot	52 weeks/year x 5 days/week	260
Days not available	• Vacation 15 days • Holidays 11 days • Sick leave 5 days • Training and physical examination 10 days	
Subtotal of days not available		41
Total days available for duty	260 days-41 days	219
Number of crew seats (2 per aircraft)	(2 aircraft x 2 pilots/aircraft)	4
Number of operating days/year	7 days per week	365
Number of flightcrew days/year	4 pilots x 365 days	1,460
Number of pilots required (rounded up)	1,460 flightcrew days required/ (219 days available)	7

Note: Does not take into consideration augmented or prepositioned flightcrew

Figure 3.4 Number of pilots needed (based on days available). Developed by the authors.

Calculation of the Number of Pilots Based on Estimated Flight Hours per Year This example could be beneficial for a company that expects future flightcrew needs to be similar to past needs. Each company can vary the calculation according to their own needs.		
Description	**Calculation**	**Totals**
Number of aircraft in fleet		3
Estimated number of flight hours/year (per aircraft)		450
Total flight time (fleet)	3 aircraft x 450 hours each	1,350
Number of pilots per aircraft		2
Duty/flight ratio*	3 hours duty/1 hour flight	3
Total number of pilot hours	1,350 flight hours x 3 (duty flight ratio)	8,100
Total hours available for duty	219** days x 8 hours per day	1,752
Number of pilots required	8,100 duty hours per year/ 1,752 hours available for duty	4.6
Number of pilots required (rounded up)		5

* This ratio assumes that a pilot spends at least 3 hours on duty for each hour in the air. The duty time includes preflight, postflight and ground time. The ratio could vary for a company that often requires long periods of waiting between flights on the same day.

** See figure 3.4 for calculation of days available for work.

Figure 3.5 Number of pilots needed (based on estimated flight hours per year). Developed by the authors.

are needed on staff to properly fill two cockpit seats and provide for all the appropriate professional and personal expectations? How many pilot days do we have available in any given year? This exercise also assumes that the department is staffed with a department manager/chief pilot and two additional captain-rated pilots.

An analysis of how many days each pilot is *not* available for flight during a calendar year:

Days:	Reason:
2	Physical
9	Holidays
28	Vacation days
12	Training
7	Meetings
58	Total, **not available.**

The aircraft is available to fly 365 days per year less a minimum of 10 days for annual maintenance: **355** days. Those 355 days of aircraft availability represents **710** pilot days (two pilots per aircraft). This assumes that each flight day will not overlap with the next, i.e., consecutive 14-hour days.

If a pilot is **not** available for **58** days per year, then he/she **is** available **307** days. This does not account for any expectation of scheduled days off during each month. Most people in non-executive positions (a reasonable comparison to a line pilot) do not work on weekends. There are 52 weekends per year, 108 days, 8 of which (16 days) could be used in conjunction with vacation, if the person had four weeks of vacation per year. For the sake of this analysis, assume that three pilots are eligible for four weeks of vacation per year; 108 weekend days less 16 vacation weekend days yields an additional **92** days that each pilot is **not available** for flight due to scheduled time off. Reducing **307** pilot days available by **92** days yields **215** days per year that a pilot is available to fly; given the premise of reasonable time off plus time for vacation, holidays, physicals, training and administrative meetings.

The flight department manager/chief pilot has additional duties that prevent him/her from being eligible for flight:

Days:	Reason:
16	NBAA meetings and seminars
12	Flight department staff meetings
48	Office duties 4 days per month
5	Planning and quarterly staff meetings
81	Total administrative days:

The flight department manager/chief pilot is available to fly **215** days less **81** administrative days: **134** days.

For the company flight operation, manager plus two line pilots, the total comes to **564** pilot days during the year. The aircraft, in order to be available to fly **355** days per year requires **710** pilot days (two pilots per aircraft); that is **146** pilot days more than are available, given the above analysis: That represents 68% of 215 pilot days that an additional line pilot could provide.

When the subject of scheduled days off for flight crew is discussed with senior managers, the lack of understanding of the use of a pilot's time leads to the conclusion that if they are not engaged in a flight activity that they are for all intents and purposes off. It is important to delineate the need for proper crew rest between flying periods. There is a distinction between an off day and a standby day. Effective business aviation teams are best managed with a consideration of an appropriate work-life balance for flight crew members. As an aviation manager, your success will, in part, be defined by your ability to deal with the human resource dilemma of properly staffing your cadre of pilots. A similar, but more explainable quality of work-life management issue occurs in the maintenance department (see Chapter 4). Early morning launches, late evening arrivals, scheduled maintenance during non-flight hours at the home base of operations and the need to be at work during one or both weekend days each week to support flight operations, poses unique challenges to the process of scheduling maintenance personnel.

REFERENCES

Cannon, Jim. (2004, Apr 1). Practical manager: Road tripping—When is on-the-road time your time, what can you do with it, and what, if anything, is prohibited? *Business & Commercial Aviation*, 98.

_______. (2004, October 1). Practical manager: Off duty but on call—The quandry. *Business & Commercial Aviation*, 140.

Flight Safety Foundation. (1997, Feb). "Principles and Guidelines for Duty and Rest Scheduling in Corporate and Business Aviation." *Flight Safety Digest* 16(2): 1–11.

National Business Aviation Association. (2009). *NBAA Management Guide*. Washington, DC. Retrieved from http://www.nbaa.org/admin/management-guide.

Pope, John A. (1990, Feb). The flight and duty time dilemma. *Accident Prevention* 47(2): 1–4.

4

Business Aviation Maintenance

Learning Objectives: After reading this chapter you should be able to:

- Describe the mission of a business aviation maintenance department
- Interpret the federal air regulations as they apply to the maintenance function
- Describe the relationship of maintenance within an aviation organizational structure
- Discuss the different types of maintenance used to maintain business aircraft
- Choose an appropriate inspection program for maintaining business aircraft
- Outline the requirements for a Minimum Equipment List (MEL)
- Construct a system for recording aircraft discrepancies

INTRODUCTION TO BUSINESS AVIATION MAINTENANCE

Poised on countless ramps and sequestered in thousands of hangars around the world the business aviation fleet of aircraft is maintained by a dedicated group of professional maintenance managers and technicians. Without the knowledge base and inherent skill sets of these key members of individual business aviation teams, those shiny, beautiful business jets would be of little use to the corporations who own them. Careers in business aviation maintenance offer varied and robust opportunities for the aspiring maintenance technician. Business aviation is driven by technological advances in airframe design and avionics development. Maintaining the seemingly ever-increasing inventory of business aircraft is accomplished by a diverse set of rules and regulations. In keeping with the theme of this book, Chapter 4 is focused on the inner-workings and inherent complexities of managing the maintenance function of a business aviation department.

Business aviation consists of, as mentioned in Chapter 1, a wide variety of operating styles: charter departments, fractional ownership companies, aircraft management organizations, privately owned and flown aircraft, and professionally flown and maintained corporate flight departments. It is with the latter operating philosophy that this text is focused upon. This segment of the industry has for decades been essentially self-regulated and has striven to emulate industry best practices under the guise of the NBAA and other industry advocate associations. Maintenance within this heavily populated segment of business aviation, more often than not, is the responsibility of a sole practitioner, the manager of maintenance. By far, single aircraft flight departments make up the majority of business aviation operations. The challenges faced by the maintenance manager, although increased due to the complexity of the makeup of the flight department, remain fairly common, regardless of size. Many would argue that maintaining one aircraft is often more difficult than a fleet, due to the inherent level of support within a larger flight organization.

Some corporate operators as well as individual owners have chosen to outsource their maintenance to third party vendors. If the aircraft is flown under the guidelines of a charter certificate (FAR Part 135), the flight department's approved operations specifications will require that the organization have a director of maintenance (DM). The DM must supervise the approved maintenance program under the procedures specified with the flight department's general maintenance manual (GMM). A DM may choose to outsource the aircraft's maintenance or accomplish the maintenance himself. The most important factor in any business aviation maintenance oversight process is that the technicians doing the work must be certified A&P (airframe and powerplant) mechanics, in possession of a valid license, and have the requisite level of experience (FAR 65.83) working on the aircraft type; six of the previous 24 months.

For those business aviation flight departments that choose to conduct their maintenance in-house with a qualified maintenance technician, on staff, the program under which the maintenance is conducted may be structured in a variety of ways. Two aspects of maintaining an aircraft must be kept in mind at all times: the aircraft manufacturer's recommendations and the applicable guidance of FAA regulations. Whether maintenance is conducted in-house or outsourced, it is essential that the aircraft is placed under the auspices of a preventative maintenance program combined with a periodic inspection process. A multi-aircraft department will maintain all company aviation assets under a single system.

The purpose of business aircraft maintenance department is to support and maintain company aircraft in airworthy condition. Airworthy condition is defined as meeting established standards for safe flight, equipped, and maintained in condition to fly as determined by the FAA. The responsibility for aircraft maintenance is specified in the Federal Air Regulations. Specifically, Part 91.7 says that no person may operate a civil aircraft unless it is in airworthy condition and makes the pilot-in-command ultimately responsible for that determination. Part 91.403 further defines this responsibility by making the owner or operator responsible for maintaining the aircraft in an airworthy condition over time. Part 91.409 establishes required inspection programs and specifies who may conduct these inspections to return the aircraft to service. Other U.S. federal regulations and the International Civil Aviation Organization (ICAO) regulations require specific recordkeeping and a variety of other requirements for maintaining aircraft. These records must be kept for each aircraft, engine, and aircraft component to determine whether the aircraft has been maintained in an airworthy condition and in accordance with approved procedures. Further, the Federal Air Regulations hold the aircraft owner responsible for proper maintenance of their aircraft, regardless of how the aircraft is maintained or who performs the maintenance. The owner is further responsible for maintaining records that accurately reflect the state of airworthiness of the aircraft. It is important to note that it is the owner/operator that is held responsible and not the mechanic. Table 4.1 contains a brief summary of the Federal regulations that a corporate owner/operator must comply with in the areas of airworthiness directives, preventative maintenance, certification of mechanics, and general operating rules, to include maintenance inspections and record keeping.

Aircraft of U.S. registry must be maintained in accordance with these regulations. How they are maintained, or who actually does the maintenance, is up to the operator as long as it is under an approved program. There are a number of different ways that that an aircraft may be maintained, as will be discussed later in this chapter.

MAINTENANCE RESPONSIBILITIES: RESPONSIBILITY SPECIFIC TO THE MAINTENANCE FUNCTION

Aviation Department Manager (ADM): Responsible for ensuring that a viable maintenance program is in place. This program must be properly structured and approved by the governing authority relative to the type of flight operation. The ADM is responsible for approval of the maintenance budget prior to

Table 4.1. Maintenance Related Regulations

Federal Air Regulations Governing Corporate Flight Departments	
Airworthiness Directives	
FAR 39.1	Identifies unsafe condition that may exist in aircraft of the same type design
FAR 39.3	Prescribes inspections or limitations required for continued operation
Maintenance, preventative maintenance, rebuilding or alteration regulations	
FAR 43.5	Approval for return to service after maintenance
FAR 43.7	Identifies persons who are authorized to perform maintenance
FAR 43.9	Specifies content, form and disposition of preventative maintenance records
FAR 43.11	Specifies content, form and disposition of inspection maintenance records
Certification of airmen other than crew members	
FAR 65.81	General privileges and limitations for aircraft mechanics
FAR 65.83	Recent experience requirements for aircraft mechanics
FAR 65.85	Airframe rating: additional privileges
FAR 65.87	Powerplant rating: additional privileges
FAR 65.91	Inspection authorization requirements
General operating and flight rules	
FAR 91.7	Civil aircraft airworthiness
FAR 91.9	Civil aircraft flight manual, marking and placard requirements
FAR 91.203	Civil aircraft: certification required
FAR 91.213	Inoperative instruments and equipment
FAR 91.403	General maintenance continued airworthiness
FAR 91.405	Maintenance required
FAR 91.409	Inspections
FAR 91.411	Altimeter system and altitude reporting equipment and inspections
FAR 91.413	ATC transponder tests and inspections
FAR 91.415	Changes to aircraft inspection programs
FAR 91.417	Maintenance records
FAR 91.419	Transfer of maintenance records

submission of the overall budget each year. Within the flight department, the ADM will approve all maintenance plans for major work to be accomplished on the aircraft and the facility. As the workload within the maintenance function increases or decreases due to the addition or reduction in aircraft, the ADM is responsible for ensuring that the staffing levels are appropriately maintained. In regard to safety, the department manager is ultimately responsible to ensure that the hangar and ramp spaces provide a safe working environment for all company employees and that an effective safety management system is part of the overall safety culture of the flight department.

Manager of Maintenance (MOM): Responsible for the airworthiness of all aircraft within the flight department. This is a company mandate. This is the expectation of the corporation that hired someone with the experience to take on such a challenge. Airworthiness does not legally, however, under the guidelines of FAR Part 91, Subpart E, become the responsibility of the manager of maintenance. Under Part 135 or Part 121 operations, it's a different story. For the purposes of this chapter, we are dealing with the discipline of maintenance under Part 91. Managing the maintenance of a business aviation organization consists of planning all aspects of the daily workload and any upcoming major maintenance. The maintenance manager is responsible for an effective troubleshooting and analysis scheme for aircraft located at home base as well as on the road. The manager of maintenance deals with many vendors and outside contracts. The quality of the parts, repairs, and the associated qualifications of those individuals and companies who support the aviation maintenance effort fall under the scope of the maintenance manager's responsibility. The maintenance manager is tasked with the regulatory requirements under Occupational Safety and Health Administration (OSHA), Environmental Protection Agency (EPA), Department of Environmental Protection (DEP) and the National Fire Protection Association (NFPA). The manager of maintenance is also the liaison with the FAA for letters of authorization; reduced vertical separation minimum (RVSM), minimum equipment list (MEL), and required navigation performance (RNP), to name a few.

One of the most important responsibilities assigned to the maintenance manager is the proper documentation of the aircraft records. It is critical that a formal process be incorporated into the procedures of the flight department that provide guidance for this vital function. A well-organized administrative maintenance process enhances the professional status of the flight department as well as maintaining the market value of the aircraft. There is no excuse for incomplete or missing aircraft maintenance records.

The hangar and the various pieces of support equipment contained therein are all inherent aspects of the job. In a large flight department, the manager of maintenance will have an organizational structure consisting of a variety of technical specialists. Accompanying the responsibility of work assignments during a variety of schedule changes, the maintenance manager is tasked with controlling a large segment of the department's budget. Close coordination with the aviation department manager in all aspects of maintenance is vital to a professionally managed flight department.

Pilot-in-Command: The PIC must ensure that the aircraft is in an airworthy condition, prior to the initiation of any flight. In the world of FAR Part 91 operations, the PIC is legally responsible for the airworthiness of the aircraft. It is imperative therefore that the PIC fully comprehends the maintenance status of the aircraft. This is accomplished through the coordination of pre-flight and post-flight inspections, making certain that all maintenance documentation has been completed and is onboard the aircraft and a review is made of any discrepancies noted during previous trips. There may be carryover issues though the use of an approved MEL process. There may be issues with equipment that is not essential to flight (NEF), located in the cabin, that is not operating properly. All of these issues up to and including the aircraft's readiness for flight should be coordinated through a process that works for each individual flight department.

MAINTENANCE MANAGEMENT

The proper size and capability of the corporate aircraft maintenance organization depends on the number and type of aircraft, aircraft utilization, and proximity to contract maintenance support. In the case of one or two light twin-piston or turboprop aircraft, a single maintenance technician may be all that is needed to properly maintain the aircraft. Aviation quality-assurance standards call for an independent party to inspect all aircraft maintenance work in the interest of safety. Because of this, it is recommended that maintenance technicians work in pairs. The number of maintenance technicians increases with aircraft sophistication. For example, the ratio of technicians to aircraft is greater for large turbojet or turbofan powered aircraft, as opposed to light piston aircraft. There is also a greater need for specialized factory training to maintain these larger and more complex aircraft. An important factor to consider when staffing a maintenance organization is that more maintenance technicians are needed as the aircraft utilization increases, regardless of type aircraft. The NBAA has developed a formula for calculating the number of maintenance technicians needed based on hours flown, available work hours per year, and a standard ratio of four maintenance man-hours per flight hour. Under this formula, it is assumed that each maintenance technician will be available for productive work 1,577 hours per year, based on a 40-hour work week, and after non-productive time (vacation, holidays, sick leave, training, etc.) is removed. To determine the number of recommended maintenance technicians multiply the annual flight hours by four then divide by 1,577. As an example, assuming the estimated annual flight hours will be 850 per year, a total of (4 x 850) = 3,400 man-hours will be required to maintain each aircraft. Since each technician is available for 1,577 hours of productive work per year, to determine the total number of technicians needed to maintain the aircraft under these conditions, divide 3,400 by 1,577 to arrive at a total of two (rounded) maintenance technicians required to maintain the aircraft. This formula may be used for any number of aircraft or number of flight hours to yield a ballpark figure. The four man-hours per flight hour ratio may also be adjusted to a more representative value based on long-term usage for a specific aircraft.

Another important factor that will have an impact on the size of an in-house corporate aircraft maintenance organization is the proximity to contract maintenance support. Assuming the company wishes to contract a part of their aircraft maintenance out and a properly certified aircraft maintenance facility is available locally, the organizational structure of an in-house maintenance staff may be reduced by using this facility.

Inspection Programs: The most important aspect of a Part 91 aviation department maintenance inspection program is that it follows the original equipment manufacturer (OEM) recommendations and guidelines. This is also true for the maintenance inspection process for the engines. With few historic exceptions, the OEM and the engine manufacturer are completely separate companies. The recommended maintenance process for each manufacturer has been reviewed by the FAA during the aircraft certification process. Inspections are categorized in two distinct but interrelated forms: a continuous maintenance process and a periodic inspection system. Periodic inspections may be organized in several ways, but the most frequent manner is the annual inspection.

The continued airworthiness inspection program is certainly the key factor in a sound maintenance management process. Today, these programs are managed through a computerized list of daily, weekly, and monthly recommended practices. The OEM has a service responsibility to its customers to provide recommendations for and updated procedural checks to the specific aircraft type. The computerized continued airworthiness program within a business aviation department is designed around the scheduling of periodic maintenance, the forecasting of upcoming parts replacement that are time-driven versus on-condition, and the documentation of all maintenance performed through the use of work cards, system printouts and company reports.

An integral part of the continued airworthiness of the aircraft is a standardized pre-flight and post-flight inspection process. These procedures are found in the aircraft flight manual (AFM); a document that is produced by the OEM and, as with all publications of this type, periodically updated. Business aviation maintenance managers usually take the AFM procedures and enhance them into daily pre-flight and post-flight maintenance checks. With departures from home base or whenever a department maintenance technician is accompanying the company aircraft on the road, it is understood that a very important part of their duties and responsibilities is to conduct a proper pre and post flight of the aircraft. The PIC is, as emphasized many times, responsible for the airworthiness of the aircraft in the eyes of the FAA. Pilots, therefore, will conduct their own pre-flight and post-flight inspections, prior to and following the completion of each flight. This is critical to the overall maintenance effort. These daily conditional integrity reviews by the flight crew and maintenance technicians will often uncover the onset of an impending discrepancy. The fact that business aircraft spend countless days and nights away from home base highlights the importance of a standardized pre- and post-flight inspection process.

Airworthiness Directives: The *NBAA Management Guide* defines airworthiness directives as "FAA regulations that require inspection and/or modification to an aircraft after it has been certified...to ensure safe aircraft operation by identifying areas in an aircraft that need to be inspected or modified and/or have become unsafe during experience with the product." ADs arise occasionally due to a discovery, either in the field by a series of related events or from continued testing by the OEM, of an unforeseen design issue or a related use tendency that is determined to be material enough to cause the FAA to issue a maintenance alert. The FAA maintains a website that contains all ADs and Special Airworthiness Information Bulletins (SAIB), http://rgl.faa.gov. Until September of 2007, the FAA offered ADs in printed form. This is no longer the case. All ADs are offered electronically. When an AD is issued, the OEM will notify each operator of that particular aircraft type that the FAA has taken this action. It is mandatory that each operator comply with and appropriately document that compliance in the aircraft's maintenance records. The AD should be identified by:

- AD number
- Date of completion
- Description of work
- Airframe and engine time when the AD is completed
- Name of technician and his or her certificate number

Service Bulletins: These maintenance alerts are typically presented in three distinct types; (1) mandatory service bulletins, (2) recommended service bulletins, and (3) optional service bulletins. As an aircraft design matures, the OEM may uncover improvements to the original blueprint of the aircraft that will aid in more efficient operation of a part or increased life of a component. When this occurs, the manufacturer may issue an approved service bulletin (SB). A mandatory SB must be complied with in much the same manner as an AD and within a specified amount of time, usually with more time allowed prior to compliance than with an AD. Recommended SBs and optional SBs follow the logic of their descriptions. The judgment as to whether to accomplish these two forms of the SB process usually falls to the manager of maintenance. Whether SBs are completed as per the OEM's recommended procedures or, on occasion, the maintenance department decides to pass or forego the SB, a summary of all SBs should be recorded within the maintenance records of the affiliated aircraft.

Special Inspections: Business aircraft are very rugged transportation assets. They are subjected to extreme temperature fluctuations, pressure differentials, and a wide variety of weather phenomenon. Usually housed in hangars for protection, business aircraft spend long hours on transient ramps. Sometimes due to operational situations or inattention by the flight crew, aircraft may be subjected to an overweight landing, a hard landing, severe turbulence, lighting strikes, bird strikes, and foreign object damage (FOD). In these instances, a special inspection is necessary prior to returning the aircraft to service. OEMs have developed special inspection procedures and will upon request send technical representatives to assist the aircraft technician. The end result of a successful special inspection is the return to service of the business aircraft.

Airworthiness Release: Upon completion of designated maintenance procedures, ADs, SBs, or the various inspections criteria described above, an airworthiness release must be made by the licensed maintenance technician who performed the work. This release becomes a part of the permanent record of the maintenance of the aircraft. It may be completed by a designated technician at a certificated repair station and should in this instance not only contain the technician's certificate number and signature, but the repair station's certificate number as well.

Maintenance Test Flights: The *NBAA Management Guide* (Section 4.12.12) references FAR 91.407: "Good operating practice requires that an aircraft be flown before carrying passengers if it has been repaired or altered in a manner that may have changed its flight characteristics or substantially affected its operation in flight." When necessary, a maintenance test flight must be logged in the aircraft flight log and should concentrate on evaluating the specific component that had been the focus of the previous maintenance event. Flights such as this should be flown in good weather conditions and with a limited crew. Good management practices also mandate that the flight crew be highly experienced and proper briefings pre- and post-flight be formally held using a company maintenance flight check document, a standardized form.

Ferry Flights: If the need arises to transport an aircraft to a maintenance facility due to a component failure that has rendered the aircraft un-airworthy, a special airworthiness certificate (ferry permit) must be approved by the local flight standards district office (FSDO) responsible for the departure airport flights. As with the case of maintenance test flights, a ferry flight should not carry passengers and should be conducted with extreme care. Flights of this nature have a larger percentage of accidents and/or incidents than do other business aviation operations. Again, it is best to conduct flights of this nature in good weather conditions.

Service Centers: Whenever a significant maintenance event, planned or unplanned, occurs, in all likelihood, the need for outside assistance to complete the scope of the maintenance will involve working with a service center. Each service center should be OEM factory-authorized and be certified by the FAA as a repair station. Unplanned events will often limit the number of facility options due to the last-minute request for assistance. Planned major maintenance can be negotiated far in advance of the scheduled maintenance period and appropriately budgeted. Good maintenance management practice dictates that the manager of maintenance send out several requests for proposal (RFP) to various service centers in order to obtain quotes for planned events. Each RFP should be identical in proposed scope. Please refer to section 4.16.2 in the *NBAA Management Guide* and Figure 4.8 therein (Request for Proposal Template). It is also considered an industry best practice to have a company representative on-site during major maintenance periods. Their presence fosters communication and enhances the quality of the work by the service center.

Discrepancy Management: Aircraft discrepancy recording and control are important functions within a business aviation flight department. The principle source of maintenance actions, outside of scheduled maintenance, is generated by aircraft discrepancy reports. Discrepancies are maintenance requirements that may or may not affect the airworthiness of the aircraft. These "squawks" may originate with either a maintenance technician who discovered the fault while working on the aircraft, or in the process of dispatching it. Some squawks arise from items that are not essential for flight (NEF) and are generated in a section of the aircraft, often in the cabin, that does not affect the airworthiness of the aircraft. Discrepancies may also come from flight crews who discovered the fault during pre-flight, while in flight, or during a post-flight walk-around. The discrepancies should be recorded on a flight department generated form similar to the one shown in Figure 4.1.

These aircraft discrepancy reports serve as a written record of the recent maintenance history of the aircraft. The corrective action taken may be used as a portion of the official aircraft log to show that proper maintenance was performed on the aircraft to return it to service. Most flight departments have created an aircraft flight log that includes a section similar to Figure 4.2. The more detailed description of the discrepancy provided by the flight crew, the greater the assist to the maintenance department in troubleshooting. It is a good idea for a maintenance technician to meet the aircraft when it returns from flight so that a verbal debrief may occur. If a discrepancy affecting the airworthiness of the aircraft cannot be corrected before the next flight the MEL should be consulted to determine if the aircraft may be flown with this discrepancy. If maintenance is deferred (using the MEL process), it should be in accordance with the overall maintenance plan and the date for corrective action should be made a part of the official aircraft records at the time it is deferred. It is also important to maintain a deferred maintenance record. This listing can be in tabular form showing the date that maintenance was deferred, a description of the discrepancy,

Aircraft ____________ Time in Service ____________ Cycles ____________

Discrepancy		Corrective Action	
Pilot	.	Technician	Date
Part # taken off	Part # on	Part S/N off	Part S/N on

Figure 4.1 Aircraft discrepancy record. Developed by the authors.

corrective action taken, and the date work was completed and inspected. This maintenance record is not part of the official maintenance logbooks for the aircraft, merely a control document that follows maintenance practices and as an additional measure of efficiency of the maintenance process.

When an aircraft requires maintenance away from home base, the flight crew should consult with the maintenance manager by phone to discuss possible courses of action. Minor discrepancies may be corrected by a properly certified FAA technician with the proper log entries into the aircraft maintenance log. If heavy maintenance is required away from home base it is best to use a facility that possesses an FAA repair station certificate and has an established record of performance. In addition, the maintenance should be supervised by a properly qualified company maintenance technician, whenever possible.

SAFETY-RELATED MAINTENANCE PROGRAMS

In addition to strict adherence to the Federal Aviation Regulations, maintenance department managers should be very familiar with the oversight procedures mandated under the following governmental agencies and associations:

- Occupational Safety and Health Administration (OSHA)
- Environmental Protection Agency (EPA)
- Department of Environmental Protection (DEP)
- National Fire Protection Association (NFPA)

The Department of Labor enters the world of business aviation through the portal created by the maintenance function. Whether the maintenance spaces are rented, leased, or owned by the corporation, the fact that the hangar, offices, and ramp areas are places where scheduled work is completed brings them under the regulatory guidelines offered under Standard 1910, Occupational Safety and Health Administration. Table 4.2 highlights sections in the OSHA standard that appear to have the most concern to industry in general.

In business aviation, the areas of concentration within the maintenance department that require the most attention by the maintenance manager are:

- Scaffolding
- Fall Protection
- Ladder Safety
- Respiratory Safety
- PPE (Personal Protective Equipment)
- First Aid and Fire Safety
- Confined Spaces
- Recordkeeping
- Welding Safety
- Training

Many of these factors may not apply due to the size of the flight department. It is vital that the maintenance manager does not lose sight of the federal mandate within Standard 1910.6, Section 5(a)(1), which stipulates, "Each employer shall furnish to each employee, employment and a place of employment which are free from recognized hazards that are causing or are likely to cause death or serious physical harm to his employees."

AIRCRAFT DOCUMENTS AND DOCUMENTATION:

FAA Order 8900.1 is a vast document that contains the Flight Standards Information Management System. This mountain of a standard is 15 volumes

Table 4.2. OSHA Standards

Top 10—Most Accessed General Industry Standards
1. Bloodborne Pathogens—1910.1030
2. Hazard Communication—1910.1200
3. Respiratory Protection—1910.134
4. Occupational Noise Exposure—1910.95
5. Powered Industrial Trucks—1910.178
6. Permit-Required Confined Spaces—1910.146
7. Lockout/Tagout—1910.147
8. Hazardous Waste Operations and Emergency Response—1910.120
9. Guarding Floor and Wall Openings and Holes—1910.23
10. Personal Protective Equipment—1910.132

in length and contains guidelines for a variety of subjects: airman certification (Volume 5), aircraft, airport and security (Volume 8), compliance and enforcement (Volume 14), and aircraft equipment and authorization (Volume 4). Volume 4, Chapter 4 contains 11 sections providing guidance for minimum equipment lists (MEL) and configuration deviation lists (CDL). Section 2 of Chapter 4 contains the process on how to gain approval of a MEL for each aircraft that your particular company is operating. The MEL is very important to an aircraft owner/operator. This approved document identifies equipment that may be inoperative and still allow the aircraft to be dispatched for flight. The aircraft is identified by serial and registration number on the MEL that is issued by the FAA. It is very important to understand that all airworthiness items not included in the MEL must be operative in order to operate the aircraft. The final decision as to whether or not an aircraft is airworthy is made by the pilot-in-command. The PIC is responsible for making the determination as to whether or not a discrepancy that has been processed as an MEL item is material to the continued airworthiness of the aircraft.

All equipment on an aircraft must be operative for it to fly, except as provided under FAR Part 91.213. This part of the regulations identifies certain equipment that may not be on an MEL and specifies conditions and procedures that must be followed to allow an aircraft to legally fly without an MEL. This part also specifies when an aircraft must have an MEL and letter of authorization (LOA). Without an approved MEL, any discrepancy would cause the aircraft to be un-airworthy.

An integral part of the certification process for any aircraft manufacturer is the development of a master minimum equipment list (MMEL). This is the guide that will be used by individual flight departments when they take delivery of a newly manufactured or previously used aircraft. One of the first operational requirements whenever a new aircraft enters a business aviation fleet is the initial process of gaining an LOA for the operator to fly using a newly published MEL. Even if the previous owner had a MEL for the aircraft that they just sold to your company, your company must produce a new MEL for that aircraft. The local FSDO must approve this new MEL.

The MEL allows an operator to take advantage of the engineered redundancy within a modern aircraft; three hydraulic systems, each operated by dual pumps; twin alternators on each engine with a ram air turbine emergency electrical source; triple inertial reference systems; triple flight management systems; cockpit and cabin lighting systems; warning systems; etc. Redundancy allows a single unit within a system to fail and with the use of the MEL, a flight crew can still continue the trip. When an item in the MEL manual is identified as inoperative, the flight crew must make a log book entry and attach an inoperative sticker to the item in the cockpit.

Weight and Balance: Each aircraft must have an approved weight and balance (W&B) form onboard the aircraft at all times. This is another document that was produced when the aircraft was first put into service by the manufacturer and completion center. A weight and balance calculation should be made prior to each departure. It is common for FAR Part 91 operators to produce a binder with the various passenger seating options, including baggage, so that the remaining item to be added for the W&B to be complete is the fuel required for the leg being planned. The foundation for this document is the basic operating weight of the aircraft that is computed during the completion of the manufacturing process. It is a good practice to periodically, during a heavy maintenance period, have the aircraft re-weighed.

Flight Log: It is the responsibility of the PIC to ensure that all flight log book entries are accurate. Upon return to the home hangar, it is also the PIC's duty to hand in an accurate flight log for the entire trip. The items that should be included in a flight log are: aircraft time, landings, engine time as well as cycles, engine readings, fuel purchases, and fuel burn.

MAINTENANCE DOCUMENTS AND DOCUMENTATION

Referring once again to the *NBAA Management Guide,* an excellent flow chart of maintenance activity within a business aviation department is contained on pages 4–25 in the maintenance operations section. It details all of the normal actions involved in the management of the vast amount of paperwork required to run an effective business aviation maintenance program. With the advent of technological advances, this flow chart can be very easily converted to an electronic work documentation process. A very handy guide in the form of a checklist is found on pages 4–26 of the NBAA guide. It contains a listing of the necessary tasks to be performed in the event that logbook entries are required, painting was performed, interior work was performed, and/or major repairs or alterations were performed on the aircraft.

INVENTORY MANAGEMENT

An effective maintenance plan is centered on the time required for a technician to troubleshoot, identify, and repair a discrepancy. A key element of the plan is the availability of replacement parts whether they are *rotable* (repairable after use) or *expendable* (not reused). Another important aspect of the maintenance plan is a manageable inventory of parts most likely to be required. An Original Equipment Manufacturer (OEM) will periodically publish a list of high failure items for each aircraft type, based on historic repair data from the fleet. The maintenance manager should maintain an inventory of spare parts for each aircraft. The challenge of this inventory management scheme is fostered by the combination of inventory costs, probability of failure of a part, whether or not the anticipated repair can be delayed through use of the MEL, and the reliability of receiving parts from the OEM or other reliable sources via rapid shipment.

Parts inventory management of items on hand requires the development of a minimum-maximum ordering system; first, a determination of the minimum amount of a particular part that the flight operation could tolerate and secondly, a not to exceed on-hand total of that part when ordering additional numbers because the inventory level is approaching or has passed the minimum level. This strategy helps assure that a predetermined level of reliability can be applied from the maintenance department in regard to dispatch of the company aircraft.

All parts should have a code assigned and entered on a computerized inventory control form or program, depending upon the size of the flight operation (see Table 4.3). The code is assigned upon receipt and the part is then stored in an orderly manner for ease of retrieval. When selected from the storage area, a notation must be made in the parts inventory control form that the part is being used to accomplish a repair on the aircraft. Periodically, recommended every six months, a parts inventory audit, or reconciliation should be accomplished. This is straightforward for the expendable parts portion of the inventory, but is slightly more complicated when it comes to managing the rotable parts.

A rotable part is repairable and therefore will need to be sent out for repair while the replacement part is functioning in its place. These are typically more complex parts that also carry a much higher price for replacement. These costs can be reduced by using *loaner parts*. Loaner parts are replacement parts that are leased for the period of time that the original rotable part was out for repair. When the repair facility has corrected the fault in the original part and shipped it to the maintenance department, the loaner part is then removed from the aircraft and returned. Repair facilities will often offer loaner parts as an incentive to purchase services from their company.

If the maintenance manager has spare rotable parts, perhaps several of the same high-failure item part, when such a part is removed from inventory to correct a failure on the aircraft, the removed part can then, as previously mentioned, be sent out for repair. In this instance, however, a loaner part is not required. When a part is sent out for repair, a service order should be created. The service order process should ensure that the same part that was sent out is the part that is returned. This is an important aspect of proper inventory management. It is critical to the success of any business

Table 4.3. Aircraft Parts Inventory Form

Company Name
Aircraft Parts Inventory Form
Item ________

Date	*Order #*	*Part #*	*Serial #*	*Location*	*Condition*	*Value*	*Qty. Rec.*	*Qty. Used*	*Rmks.*

aviation department that quality parts are utilized in the maintenance of each aircraft.

Whenever an inspection is scheduled or any major maintenance is performed on a company aircraft, it is vitally important to document the removal and replacement of all parts. The *NBAA Management Guide* recommends the use of a "parts removal form" to "verify that all the components removed during the inspection have been reinstalled in the correct position."

MAINTENANCE TRAINING

Maintenance training is certainly a critical factor to the overall safety and integrity of any well-managed business aviation flight department. As with the case for pilots, a well-trained maintenance technician who is current with the procedures necessary to maintain the aircraft is one of the most significant aspects of the operation.

When a technician joins the flight department, if not current or experienced on company aircraft, time permitting, the technician should be sent to initial training with an outside vendor. Vendor training assures a standard level of excellence. Recurrent training for maintenance technicians is also of vital importance to maintain currency with new techniques and procedures that may not be available through other means. Periodic training sharpens not only the skills of the technician, but also increases that person's sense of professionalism and pride in the organization. When the opportunity is available and certainly on an annual basis, technicians as well as flight operations personnel should participate in training focused on supplemental topics, company policies and procedures, first aid, operation of emergency equipment, AED, emergency response plan (ERP) drills, support equipment operation, fall protection, confined spaces, and so on.

Detailed training records should be maintained for each technician and should parallel in scope the type of records maintained for the flight crew. Currency requirements can be calendared in the training records to include all FAA and OSHA stipulations.

TECHNICAL LIBRARY

A mandatory requirement for the effective management of a business aviation maintenance department is the inclusion of a technical library. Technology today allows electronic media to provide more portable and compact storage for operators. Regardless of whether the maintenance manager elects to continue with the storage of manuals on the bookshelves or within the company hard drive, the following are recommended as reference to manage the daily workload:

- FAA Regulations
- Manufacturer's Maintenance Manual
- Continued Airworthiness Maintenance Manual
- Online/Website Library
- Industry Publications
- Read and Initial Board

REFERENCES

Eatchel, T., and T. Woulf. (2008, Jul). 10 neglected construction safety concerns. *ISHN 42*(7): 32.

National Business Aviation Association. (2009, Spring). *NBAA Management Guide*, Washington, DC.

Occupational Health and Safety Administration. Standard number 1910. Viewed online at www.osha.gov/pls/oshaweb/owastand.display_standard_group?p_toc_level=1&p_part_number=1910

Saner, M. (2008, Jun). Voluntary standards requirements. *ISHN 42*(6): 42.

5

Standard Operating Procedures

Learning Objectives: After reading this chapter you should be able to:

- Explain and interpret the International Standards for Business Aircraft Operations as they pertain to various phases of a typical business aircraft flight
- Judge the importance of standard operating procedures on an aviation safety record
- Appreciate aircraft evacuation and survival procedures

Teamwork is critical to the enhancement of safety in the business aviation cockpit. Each phase of aircraft movement must be coordinated by a flight crew operating as a unified team. Every member of the team has a role to play. This chapter will outline in detail the steps necessary for two pilots to operate a business aircraft utilizing a set of standard operating procedures (SOPs) that are considered "best practices" throughout the industry. Each flight department's SOP will vary slightly, but most professionally managed business aviation organizations are very similar in operational conduct. The International Business Aviation Council (IBAC) introduced the IS-BAO program in 2002 to foster standardized, safe, and highly professional aircraft operations. This program is called the International Standard for Business Aircraft Operations and is a set of safety standard guidelines that are designed to serve as a code of best practice for aircrews. It is a well-known fact that standardization of aircrew flight procedures helps to prevent accidents. These safety standard guidelines are intended to build upon and improve the excellent safety record already established by business aviation.

Standard operating procedures (SOPs) are the foundation of effective crew coordination and a key component of crew resource management (CRM). Accordingly, operators of aircraft with two or more crew members shall establish and maintain a SOP for each type of aircraft operated that enable the crew members to operate the aircraft effectively and within the limitations specified in the aircraft flight manual (IS-BAO 2010, 6.1.1).

As discussed in Chapter 7 (Training), flight crews who either train together or train individually under identical structured standards will work together more effectively. It is very important to attend aircraft training courses on a regularly scheduled basis. This repetition raises the level of competency for every pilot. Between training sessions, it is the individual pilot's responsibility to review procedures and limitations. It is also extremely important for the application of effective cockpit resource management that flight crew members are as knowledgeable as possible of the functions and operational characteristics of onboard equipment. Flight crew must ensure they are using current reference materials and up-to-date procedures. A review of all reference materials used in the flight department should be conducted on a regularly scheduled basis. Typically, the director of flight operations or chief pilot will determine the frequency of these reviews. Before each trip, the crew pre-flight inspection will include a physical check of onboard reference materials to determine the expiration date of items such as aircraft credit cards, insurance policies, chart revisions, letters of authorization for the minimum equipment list, over-flight permits, MNPS airspace authorization, customs permits, etc. All pilots are expected to be knowledgeable of the provisions of the Federal Air Regulations (FARs) and the International Civil Aviation Organization (ICAO), as well as the procedures outlined in the Airman's Information Manual (AIM), and the International Flight Information Manual (IFIM). When there is any conflict in guidance with other procedural or regulatory directives, the more restrictive normally apply.

A copy of the standard operating procedures must be carried on board the aircraft and a copy issued to each aircraft crew member (IS-BAO 2010, 6.1.2).

Flight duties in a business aviation cockpit are generally shared equally, if both pilots are rated in the particular aircraft and have demonstrated competency sufficient for the mission at hand. Crews will typically swap seats, allowing the pilot manipulating the flight controls in the air and controlling ground operations to be in the left hand (captain) seat. Captain refers to the pilot performing duties from the left seat. First officer refers to the pilot performing duties from the right seat. The first officer position is normally one of support and back-up. The captain position is usually one of control of the physical aspects of the flight, including operating the flight controls, requesting configuration changes, and asking for particular checklists to be run at specified times during the flight.

The following terms and abbreviations are offered to standardize pilot responsibility and authority regardless of seat position:

The pilot-in-command (PIC) of the aircraft has full authority for the aircraft and the trip, and is responsible for the overall performance of the crew (Chapter 3). A PIC is designated by the flight schedule, which is published and/or posted prior to the day of the trip. The PIC will retain this authority for the duration of the trip, regardless of whether the aircraft is flying or on the ground, or which pilot seat position is occupied by the PIC. A second-in-command (SIC) is assigned to a pilot under the operational command of the PIC. The SIC will retain this responsibility for the duration of the trip, regardless of the seat position occupied by the SIC.

> *Before commencing a flight the pilot-in-command of an aircraft shall be familiar with the available flight information that is appropriate to the intended flight. The pilot-in-command shall not commence a flight unless it has been ascertained that the facilities available and directly required for such flight and for the safe operation of the aircraft are adequate, including communication facilities and navigation aids* (IS-BAO 2010, 6.2.1.1).

The pilot flying (PF) the aircraft, regardless of whether he or she is in the captain's (left) or first officer's (right) seat while manipulating the engine throttles and aircraft flight controls, is engaged in maneuvering the aircraft, whether utilizing the autopilot or manual control, requesting checklists and configuration changes, and generally managing the flight. The pilot monitoring (PM) the aircraft, regardless of whether he is in the captain's or first officer's seat, is actively engaged in the support role. The PM generally is responsible for running checklists, making radio calls, clearing for outside traffic, operating aircraft systems, assisting the PF with programming navigation equipment, and acting as safety observer.

> *Before commencing a flight the pilot-in-command shall be familiar with all available meteorological information appropriate to the intended flight. Preparation for every flight shall include: a review of available current weather reports and forecasts and the planning of an alternative course of action to provide for the eventuality that the flight cannot be completed as planned, because of weather conditions* (IS-BAO, 2010, 6.2.1.2).

Business aviation affords each member of the flight crew a more personal relationship with other crew members as well as the passengers. Regardless of the size of the flight department, small-group dynamics are commonly in place. Pilots are frequently scheduled to fly together and therefore spend a great deal of time with each other. Passengers very often become well acquainted with individual pilots. Even in the case of the largest business jets, the passengers will sit nearer the cockpit and be able to see and often hear conversations from the cockpit. It is imperative therefore that the flight crew makes every effort to operate as a coordinated team and provide the highest possible standards of safety and service for the passengers on the aircraft. Each individual is expected to contribute to the fullest extent and assist other crew members in performing at their optimum level of performance. No one should be criticized for correcting or questioning another crew member when, in the opinion of that individual, the action or inaction of the other person is contrary to the standards of the company or could affect safety of flight.

CREW AND PASSENGER BRIEFINGS

Flight crew and passenger briefings are essential to the safe conduct of a scheduled trip. The PIC will ensure that crew members are familiar with all aspects of each flight. When deemed appropriate and with the assistance of other crew members, passenger briefings should be made. These briefings, announcements, will be based upon information received from various available sources, before or during every flight. Passenger briefings may be given in person by one of the crew (preferred), in writing (cabin safety information card), or utilizing a cabin announcement system controlled from the cockpit.

The most important briefing offered to the passengers is the passenger safety briefing at the beginning of each flight. This can be awkward with frequent flyers or principal passengers, but quite often, some passengers will be unfamiliar with the use of emergency equipment or the location of and proper operation of emergency exits. It is recommended that a crew member gain the attention of the passengers prior to each departure to reinforce the importance of cabin safety and how serious the issue is to the aviation professionals aboard the aircraft. Cabin safety information cards should be easily accessible at each passenger seat. The passenger briefing may also include destination weather and cruise conditions report. Keeping in mind that a lengthy briefing will not produce the intended impact, each cabin pronouncement should be thorough but brief.

Prior to each departure, preferably before passenger arrival, all associated flight crew should meet to discuss weather conditions for point of departure, en route, and destination, Notice to Airmen (NOTAMS), the flight plan routing and estimated time enroute (ETA), the passenger manifest and any special needs, aircraft status from a maintenance perspective, passenger arrival coordination, and any pertinent layover arrangements for the aircraft and/or crew. Prior to engine start, the pilots should review and brief the departure airport terminal information (ATIS), the taxi diagram for the departure airport, the takeoff safety briefing, the departure procedures anticipated, and any takeoff and departure performance related data.

AIR TRAFFIC CONTROL (ATC) CLEARANCES

The first officer's position will typically copy clearances and acknowledge radio calls while the aircraft is on the ground. This enhances the division of labor and places the first officer position in full support of the captain, while on the ground. If the occasion arises that the PF will be operating the flight controls from the first officer seat, the PM in the captain seat will handle ATC communications in the air. When receiving an initial ATC Instrument Flight Rules (IFR) clearance prior to departure, it is desirable that both pilots listen to and write down the clearance. During international operations and all other lengthy departure procedures, it is recommended that both pilots be on the flight deck when the flight plan is inserted into the onboard computers. It is critical to the safe and professional conduct of any flight that the flight crew has a complete understanding of the assigned departure and initial en route segment of the IFR clearance. This can be especially difficult during international operations. International rules often will not allow the aircraft to receive an IFR clearance until it has been cleared for taxi. This will be discussed further and in greater detail in Chapter 6 (International Operations). Flight crews need to be especially cautious of receiving a departure clearance that was unplanned. If you read back a clearance just prior to taking the runway for departure, you will be expected to comply with the full clearance. This will be difficult to do if you were planning on a departure different in scope from the one you were just cleared for. It is suggested to become as familiar as possible with all possible standard instrument departures (SIDs) prior to engine start. The same caution holds in regard to arrival procedures at an international destination. Familiarization of all possible standard terminal arrival routes (STARs) during a cruise will be of great benefit if the aircraft is cleared to a waypoint off the plan for an arrival that was unanticipated. Briefing a complicated arrival during the descent phase of flight is not the safest course of action, but is sometimes necessary.

A word of caution is warranted here: Do not proceed along an unfamiliar route unless you are certain that you have the exact information for that route and have the ability to execute the specified procedures. If on the ground, request a delay until you are ready to go. If airborne, request vectors or a hold if unsure of how to proceed. You may gum up the works for a few minutes and experience the ire of a controller or fellow aviator, however, the safety-conscious professional aviator does not rush into a unknown situation. The best practice is to slow down until each pilot is comfortable with the clearance and the crew's ability to comply.

In-flight, when assigned a change of altitude or flight level by ATC, the PF will repeat aloud the new altitude, and the PM will acknowledge the clearance over the radio and set the new altitude in the flight guidance system. Once set, the PF will acknowledge the change of altitude. This procedure will greatly decrease the possibility of selecting an incorrect altitude. When assigned a change in heading or airspeed, the PF will verbally state the clearance, and the PM will acknowledge the clearance over the radio.

PILOT INCAPACITATION

Loss of consciousness or capacity to perform piloting skills in a normal and expected manner should alert the other crew member in the cockpit that the pilot is incapacitated. Incapacitate is defined as "to make legally ineligible." To incapacitate someone is to disqualify or disable them from performing their duties. Pilots share responsibility for monitoring one another's performance to ensure that the temporary or permanent incapacitation of one pilot does not result in loss of control or an unsafe operating condition. This is especially important when the aircraft is operating at low altitudes or anytime it is being flown without the aid of the autopilot. Business aviation pilots are keenly aware of the other pilots' flying techniques within the realm of standardized procedures. This intimate knowledge allows business pilots the luxury of understanding the other pilot's habits and norms. If the PF deviates from his or her expected norm, it is instantly recognizable by the other pilot (PM). Not all deviations from the norm are incapacitation issues, but when crews are very familiar with each other's operational patterns, it is very easy to spot an anomaly.

The PM will notify the PF whenever the aircraft deviates from an assigned course or altitude. If the PM suspects the PF has misunderstood a published procedure or an ATC instruction or if the PF does not respond and initiate a correction after the second call, the PM will determine that the PF is incapacitated to some degree and will assume control of the aircraft. Similarly, if the PM does not respond to an ATC radio call or a verbal request from the PF, the PF will call attention to the missed communication. If the PM still does not respond, the PF will determine that the PM is incapacitated to some degree and will take appropriate action. When a pilot determines that the other pilot is incapacitated to any degree, he will assume immediate control of the aircraft. Once the aircraft in under control, the degree of impairment can be discussed and/or evaluated. If additional action is deemed necessary, the impaired pilot may be removed from the cockpit with the assistance of other crew or passengers. A pilot should not hesitate in taking control of an aircraft if it is suspected that the other pilot is incapacitated to any degree, either temporarily or permanently. If it is determined that a pilot has suffered a partial or temporary incapacitation, the other pilot will fly the aircraft for the remainder of the flight. If a pilot has suffered a total incapacitation, he or she should be moved into the cabin. ATC should be notified that the aircraft is being operated by a single pilot and assistance will be requested, as the situation warrants. The most qualified or competent passenger or crew member remaining should occupy the PM position for the remainder of the flight. If the occupant of the captain position was the subject who became incapacitated, the first officer should move to the left hand seat and assume the captain position as well as the PIC responsibility if not already in that role. In this instance the most qualified passenger or crew member would assume the first officer responsibilities and the role of support and communications.

CHECKLISTS

When first assigned to fly a new aircraft, professional pilots rely heavily on the cockpit checklist to guide them through the complicated procedures of setting up the aircraft in a safe condition, running pre-start tests, starting the engines, performing functional checks prior to taxi, and initiating movement on the ground. Checklists continue to guide the crew through preparation for takeoff, after takeoff climb, cruise, decent, and before landing. Following the landing, the cockpit checklist directs the crew through the proper after-landing and shutdown procedures.

> *An operator shall establish a checklist for each type of aircraft that it operates and shall make the checklist available to the crew members. The checklist shall cover normal, abnormal and emergency operations and be consistent with the aircraft flight manual and related company SOPs and shall include an effective date or date of last revision* (IS-BAO 2010, 6.12.1).

Once a crew is more familiar with the aircraft, checklists are used as a constant reminder of the manner in which the flight department SOP specifies operational conduct of each flight. Business aviation crews take pride in their professionalism. Adherence to checklists, even though they have read them a thousand times, is a large portion of that professionalism.

> *Every crew member shall follow the checklist in the performance of their assigned duties* (IS-BAO 2010, 6.12.2).

The PF calls for a checklist at the appropriate segment of the flight and the PM will read and execute or challenge and wait for the PF to reply. If the PF does not ask for a particular checklist to be executed during a normal segment where the checklist is anticipated by the PM, the PM will announce that he is standing by for that particular checklist. Everyone can become distracted from time to time. Checklist discipline tends to abate distractions. Normally, the PM will run the checklist by verbally issuing a challenge for each action to be accomplished. The pilot who performs the action will then call out the appropriate response when the action has been completed. The PM, in many instances, may call out both challenge and response as the items are completed in the checklist. By verbally covering every item in the checklist, both pilots will remain aware of the progress of cockpit checks.

There may be times when checklist actions can be more efficiently performed before they are called for, such as items checked by the captain as he begins to taxi the aircraft (steering, brakes, anti-skid, etc.) or those that can be accomplished in a cockpit "flow pattern." It is sometimes preferable that some checklist actions be accomplished from memory, such as the initial after-takeoff items (gear, flaps, etc.), when full attention is required by both pilots to fly the aircraft and clear for other traffic. Critical emergency situations often require certain immediate actions to be accomplished without taking time to read from a checklist. Whenever actions are accomplished early or from memory, however, the checklist will verify compliance by verbally completing the entire challenge-response sequence. This procedure provides a double-check on all required actions and ensures that no item was missed.

Abnormal and emergency checklists, depending upon aircraft type, are typically called for as necessary by the PF. The consistent and standardized use of checklists will assist the crew in completing their tasks in a safe and efficient manner, and it will reduce the possibility of missing a required action. Checklists are normally performed using a flow pattern followed by either a challenge and response or a read-and-execute procedure.

The following list of checklist categories is typical of most flight operations in business aviation. It is not representative of an all-inclusive list of items.

1. Before Power-Up
2. Before Start
3. Starting Engines
4. After Start
5. Taxi
6. Line-Up
7. After Takeoff

8. Cruise
9. Decent
10. Before Landing
11. After Landing
12. Shutdown
13. Securing

Note: Pre-flight and post-flight checklists may be added to the above list, but it is the opinion of the author that inclusive but concise is the watchword when it comes to checklists. It is also the opinion of the author that you can functionally check items on a periodic basis. Unless the flight manual mandates particular functional checks on each flight leg, it is best to exercise functional systems on a scheduled basis.

Cockpit checklists can be on one sheet, typically double-sided. They should be laminated with clear plastic to ensure their integrity. Often, aircraft are equipped with electronic checklists. These are easy to use and should have a way to indicate that an item has been covered before moving on to the next item. Every operation is a little different in its checklist appearance and use in the cockpit. Regardless, standardized use of checklists during flight operations is a very important safety tool.

PRE-FLIGHT

When the aircraft is departing from the airport where it is domiciled, the maintenance technician assigned to the departure will complete a pre-flight inspection of the aircraft prior to movement to the starting position on the ramp. This pre-flight inspection should be conducted using a company standard pre-flight inspection checklist. At least one of the pilots will also perform a less detailed oriented pre-flight once the aircraft has been positioned on the ramp. Both pilots may choose to inspect the aircraft prior to boarding. Close attention must be paid to all exterior panels to ensure they are stowed and latched. Typically the refueling panel is one of the most neglected panels on a business jet. Pre-flight duties can be shared among the pilots, but typically the PIC will be completing flight planning and gathering weather data, while the SIC will be giving the aircraft a look-see. That inspection by the SIC will blend into the cockpit and cabin area when appropriate. Fueling should be accomplished with sufficient time remaining before departure for the crew to continue their pre-flight duties in an efficient but relaxed manner. One pilot will be present during refueling. Fuel balance is critical and should be managed during refueling to avoid balancing using the aircraft's fuel system during pre-flight.

An aircraft shall not be refueled when passengers are embarking, on board or disembarking unless it is properly attended by qualified personnel ready to initiate and direct an evacuation of the aircraft by the most practical and expeditious means available. When refueling with passengers embarking, on-board or disembarking, two-way communication shall be maintained by the aircraft's intercommunication system or other suitable means between the ground crew supervising the refueling and the qualified personnel on board the aircraft. Note: Additional precautions are required when refueling with fuels other than aviation kerosene or when refueling results in a mixture of aviation kerosene with other aviation turbine fuels, or when an open line is used. Note: There may be airport restrictions on the use of radio communications during refueling operations (IS-BAO 2010, 6.2.9).

The cockpit preflight checklist should be completed with sufficient lead time to allow the aircraft to be set up and ready for departure 30 minutes before the scheduled departure time. All en route charts should be accessible, all flight management system (FMS) data should be entered, all radios tuned and set for departure, clearance received and briefed, initial altitude and clearance transponder set. The ease of flow following engine start is enhanced with the proper setup of the communication radios. Departure frequency should be set in the # 1VHF standby slot, ATIS set in #1 VHF active slot, ground control frequency set in #2 VHF active slot and tower frequency set in #2 VHF standby position. Each pilot should conduct a flow-pattern check of their respective cockpit areas. This is followed by a challenge-and-response checklist review.

PASSENGER SAFETY BRIEFING

A crew member will conduct a complete passenger safety briefing for all passengers prior to the first flight of the day. On subsequent legs, new passengers who board the aircraft should be briefed. As a minimum, the briefing will cover the following items: when, where, why, and how carry-on baggage is required to be stowed; smoking; seatbelts and harness restraints; emergency exits; emergency equipment, fire extinguishers, and oxygen; seatbacks and tables in upright and stowed position. For flights that will traverse large bodies of water, the location of life rafts and life vests should be briefed, including a demonstration of donning and inflating.

The standard safety briefing may be modified for regular/recurring passengers who are familiar with the aircraft and route and have repeated exposure (e.g., company president) to that type of flight (IS-BAO 2010 6.11.2).

Where the foregoing safety briefing is insufficient for a passenger because of that passenger's physical, sensory, or comprehension limitations or because that passenger is responsible for the care of another person on board the aircraft, the pilot-in-command shall ensure that the passenger is given an individual safety briefing that meets their individual needs (IS-BAO 2010, 6.11.3).

An operator shall ensure that a passenger safety briefing card is readily available at each passenger's seat that contains, in printed or pictographic form, information on at least the following safety features of the aircraft: the location and operation of emergency exits, the location and use of the passenger oxygen system, the location of life jackets and life rafts, and the location of emergency equipment on board the aircraft (IS-BAO 2010, 6.11.5).

TAKEOFF PERFORMANCE

The PIC is responsible for ensuring that all aircraft performance parameters are satisfactory for safe operation. These include: maximum gross takeoff weight, runway limit, second-segment climb, obstacle clearance, and standard instrument departure climb requirements. If takeoff performance data, as listed in the checklist tabs, are not deemed satisfactory for determining aircraft performance, the data must be computed or checked using the aircraft flight manual. Prior to takeoff, both pilots will verify that pertinent V-speeds are "boxed" (Gulfstream Flight Guidance Panel indicating performance computations have been loaded in the FMS and the aircraft is in a takeoff configuration) and a verbal acknowledgement will be made.

In applying the Standards of this section, account shall be taken of all factors that significantly affect the performance of the airplane (such as: mass, operating procedures, the pressure altitude appropriate to the elevation of the aerodrome, temperature, wind, runway gradient, and condition of runway, i.e. presence of slush, water and/or ice, for landplanes, water surface condition for seaplanes). Such factors shall be taken into account directly as operational parameters or indirectly by means of allowances or margins, which may be provided in the scheduling of performance data or in the comprehensive and detailed code of performance in accordance with which the airplane is being operated (IS-BAO 2010, 6.2.8).

FLIGHT CLEARANCE

The pilot-not-flying will call for the flight clearance, copy the clearance, and make the read-back. The pilot-flying will monitor the call to note any discrepancies. The crew will review the clearance and ensure complete understanding. Whenever possible, the clearance should be received prior to passenger arrival. The navigation computer will be programmed with the departure and route of flight. In addition, initial course, heading, and altitude assignments will be entered. The SID and instrument approach plates for the departure airport and takeoff alternate airport will be kept immediately available to the pilots. The PIC normally will not proceed with ground operations until the flight clearance has been received, reviewed, and is understood. During international operations, it is common to taxi without a clearance. Departure instructions and en route clearance may often be withheld until approaching the departure holding point on the airport. Care must be given to this added distraction to normal procedures. The crew must be aware and understand the departure and route clearance prior to accepting takeoff clearance.

BEFORE START

The before-start checklist is normally initiated with both pilots sitting at their stations and wearing their seat belts and shoulder harnesses. The PIC may at his discretion complete the before-start checklist or ask the SIC to complete it prior to the main entrance door closing.

STARTING ENGINES

The right engine may be started with only one pilot in the cockpit, if an outside observer is in position to provide visual acknowledgment of clearance to initiate start. The left engine may not be started until the main entrance door is closed and confirmed secure.

AFTER-START

The after-start checklist should be run by the pilot-not-flying issuing the challenge and the pilot-flying responding. The checklist is to be completed prior to calling for taxi clearance.

TAXI

Runway incursions have become an area of large concern in the aviation community. The mix of aircraft utilizing the services of an airport also highlights the mix of experience on the part of flight crews. It is critical that a strict discipline of outside vigilance be maintained during aircraft movement on all airport surfaces. This is not just necessary during the taxi phase; ramp integrity is also extremely important. Regardless of the aircraft's position on the ramp, whether located at a fixed base operator (FBO) or in a designated parking space at a major airport, it is important to make a good visualization as you approach the aircraft prior to flight. Discuss with the line crew how they plan to direct your departure from the ramp area following engine start. Begin your airport situational awareness before you climb aboard the aircraft. Share your thoughts with the other pilot. Understand how you are positioned relative to the initial taxiway and also to the active runway. Once in the cockpit, the airport taxi diagram should be referenced to refresh your route to the active runway holding area.

The airport taxi diagram will contain the appropriate frequencies for ATIS, ground, ramp control (large airports), and tower. When operating at major airports like JFK, LAX, ATL or ORD, to name a few, read and understand when you may be required to switch to alternate ground control frequencies during taxi. Most international airports have a ramp control frequency. In such instances, be aware of the language barrier and it is always best to ask for clarification before proceeding. Many require an initial call-up for permission to start. Ensure that you are aware of the local ground procedures before initiating start. Radio integrity and discipline are critical. Frequencies at busy airports are clogged with instructions to other aircraft. Be prepared to copy and read back all taxi instructions.

Clearance left and right will be acknowledged prior to initiating taxi. After the aircraft has cleared the immediate ramp area, the crew will complete the taxi checklist using the standard challenge-and-response method. Items are to be completed as soon as practicable without interruption in flow. Note: Distractions and disruptions while executing checklists have historically been the first link in the classic accident chain. Checklists are to be adhered to and their importance not taken lightly. During taxi, checklists can themselves prove to be a distraction. A professional flight crew can balance checklist execution with taxi compliance. This is achieved by maintaining good cockpit discipline.

During taxi, outside integrity is critical. Most incursions on taxiways and runways are caused by miscommunication and lack of outside visual integrity by one or more members of the crew. When approaching taxi intersections that contain other aircraft or any runway, active or not, the crew should suspend checklist execution until the aircraft has taxied beyond the potential conflict zone. It is recommended to confirm verbally all runway crossings with ground control.

TAKEOFF BRIEFING

The PF will give a complete takeoff briefing prior to the first flight of the day. Subsequent briefings for the same crew may be abbreviated by making reference to the original "standard briefing" and clearly stating any necessary changes. For every takeoff, the PF will verbally review the power settings and V-speeds for that flight. A typical takeoff briefing is listed in the next paragraph. The briefing may include additional information, depending on weather conditions and the familiarity of the crew: takeoff procedures and V-speeds calls; departure runway; initial clearance headings and altitudes for a SID, if used; navigation equipment settings; abort procedures below 80 knots and below V1; approach procedure for immediate return; takeoff alternate airport; and questions and discussion. If the departure procedure is complicated in nature, it is recommended that the crew conduct the takeoff briefing prior to starting engines.

Briefing Example: *"This will be a performance takeoff. V-speeds are posted." "We will use runway 26. Our clearance is to maintain runway heading to 3,000 feet. My instruments are set for a heading of 260, and I have the 265 inbound course set to the (station) VOR." "We will use standard company procedures to abort the takeoff. If we have an emergency after V I will continue to fly the aircraft and climb to 2,000 feet. You handle the radios and checklists. We will both identify and agree on the movement of any critical switches. We'll plan to turn left to re-enter for a VFR downwind. Any questions?"*

CHECKLIST PROCEDURES

The before-takeoff checklist is to be completed when the aircraft is cleared onto the active runway. The first officer will complete the checklist using the challenge-and-response procedure. From this point on, the PM will be responsible for running the checklists, as they are called for by the PF. The tower will clear the aircraft from the holding point short of the active runway, onto the active runway with one of two standard procedural clearances: *"N1234 is cleared for takeoff,"* or *"N1234 is cleared to line-up-and-wait."* The previous standard for the latter clearance was *"N1234 is cleared into position-and-hold."* This was changed in September of 2010 (NBAA 2010).

"F.A.T.S." CHECK

A final check will be made prior to takeoff roll to ensure the aircraft is properly configured for takeoff: The pilot-flying will usually initiate this prior to starting the takeoff roll.

F. Flaps, set for takeoff
A. Airbrakes, retracted
T. Trim, set for takeoff
S. Speeds, reviewed and boxed.

TAKEOFF

The takeoff phase of flight is one of the most critical, and the crew must maximize aircraft performance in the event of an abort or a mechanical failure after V_1. Pilots will strictly adhere to approved flight manual procedures throughout the takeoff phase of flight.

All turbojet-powered airplanes or those with a maximum takeoff mass exceeding 5,700 kg, shall be able, in the event of a critical power-unit failing at any point in the takeoff, either to discontinue the takeoff and stop within either the accelerate-stop distance available or the runway available, or to continue the takeoff and clear all obstacles along the flight path by an adequate margin until the airplane is in a position to comply with 6.2.8.3.b. Note: "An adequate margin" referred to in this provision is illustrated by examples included in Attachment C to ICAO Annex 6, Part I (IS-BAO 2010,6.2.8.3.a).

Marginal Conditions

A captain-qualified pilot will perform the takeoff from the left seat whenever any of the following conditions exist:

- Published or observed weather is less than 100-foot ceilings or 3/4 of a mile visibility.
- A crosswind component is equal to or greater than 20 knots at 90 degrees.
- The balanced field length for takeoff equals the runway available.
- Braking action is reported as poor.

Takeoff Procedures

The PM will perform the following duties and call-outs:

- Ensure that the auto-throttles are engaged by the PF.
- Call "Power set," to confirm that the minimum EPR power setting has been attained.
- Call "Airspeed alive," to confirm that both airspeed indicators are functioning.
- Call "80 knots," as the aircraft accelerates through that speed on both airspeed indicators.
- Call out "Abort," if the takeoff should be discontinued for any reason. Assist the PF in completing the abort procedures described below.
- Call out each posted V-speed as it is attained.

The PF will perform the following duties and call-outs:

- Advance the throttles and engage the auto-throttles.
- Initiate abort procedures, when required, by bringing the throttles to idle and applying brakes; deploy the thrust reversers. Call "Abort," and follow the procedures described below.
- To preclude an unintentional abort attempt, the PF will remove his hand from the throttles when the PM calls "V," and he will keep both hands on the yoke for the remainder of the takeoff.
- Rotate to the command bars in the go-around position when the PM calls "VR." Hold the takeoff attitude until the aircraft is safely airborne, and then transition to the climb phase.

Abort Procedures

Sound cockpit operational policy maintains that the PF will not question the "Abort" call of another crew member, but will immediately reject the takeoff if he can safely do so. After the aircraft is stopped, the cause for the call-out can be discussed. A takeoff will be aborted for any suspected or actual discrepancy or any warning light noted by a crew member prior to the aircraft reaching 80 knots. After 80 knots and prior to V, an abort will be initiated only for indications of fire, bleed overheat or engine failure, loss of directional control, runway obstruction, or thrust reverser deployment. The PF is responsible for initiating action to abort a takeoff, but any member of the crew can call "Abort" if, in that person's opinion, the aircraft should not take off. When the decision is made to reject the takeoff, the PF will call "Abort" and make the initial throttle reduction. The pilots will follow the abort procedures as called for in the aircraft flight manual and as pre-briefed by the PF, and the aircraft will be brought to a stop as quickly as possible by using maximum braking action, use of ground and flight spoilers and thrust reverse. When the aircraft is safely under control, the PM will notify the tower and back up the PF with the appropriate checklist and communication procedures.

AFTER TAKEOFF

The PF must devote full attention to flying the aircraft immediately after takeoff. Unless required by a SID, or to comply with noise-abatement procedures, no turns will be made before reaching circling minimum altitude, and no power reductions will be made until reaching an altitude of 1,000 AGL. The PM will monitor performance instruments and perform the immediate after-takeoff checklist items, but full attention will be paid to clearing for outside traffic at low altitudes and during the initial portion of the climb.

Immediate Checklist Items

Immediate checklist items on the after-takeoff checklist are performed from memory. Additional checklist items will not be performed at low altitude to avoid the pilots' attention being drawn inside the cockpit. Immediate items include:

PF: Following rotation, and confirming the "positive rate" call from the PM, call "Gear up," "FLCH,", "Flaps up," "Set heading," and "VS" when normal departure sequence dictates.

PM: Call "Positive rate," confirm gear retraction, set FLCH, retract Flaps, reposition heading bug to conform to departure clearance, set VS, and manually set departure speed if ATC procedures require a departure speed different than the standard provided by the flight management system (FMS). In addition, change to departure frequency and disarm the ground spoilers.

Checklist Procedures

Landing Gear: The PM will monitor the flight performance instruments and call out "Positive rate," at which point the PF will confirm the climb and call "Gear up." The PM will raise the gear handle, confirm a safe indication, and repeat "Gear up."

Flap Retraction: Upon reaching VFS and at a minimum of 400 feet AGL, the PF will call for "flaps up." When this call is made, the PM will double check the airspeed to ensure that flap-retraction speed has been reached. He will then raise the flaps, confirm they are positioned properly, and call, "Flaps Up."

Performance Take Off: Unless the runway available is greater than 1,000 feet of the balanced takeoff runway requirement from the FMS performance computer, a performance takeoff will always be used. Flex takeoff power will be utilized on all other occasions. This practice provides cooler top-end temperature for the engines and promotes engine life. If visible moisture and +8 degrees are present, anti-icing will be used and posted on the performance computer of the FMS. The PF will call for the completion of the after takeoff checklist after passing 10,000 feet MSL.

CLIMB

Climb power settings and speeds recommended by the aircraft operating manual will be used, whenever possible. If engine performance is automatically controlled, the crew will monitor power settings to ensure they are in accordance with expected performance parameters. During the climb portion of the flight, both pilots will remain at their stations until reaching cruise altitude. When passing 10,000 feet, or sooner at the discretion of the PIC, if seated on the jump seat, the flight attendant may be released from cockpit duties to begin cabin service. The use of auto-pilot is recommended during the climb, so crew members can maintain a close watch for outside traffic. For the same purpose, computer navigation equipment should not be reprogrammed until the aircraft is above 10,000 feet MSL, unless it is necessary to comply with a change to the ATC clearance. During hours of darkness, cockpit lighting should be kept at low levels to afford maximum outside visibility. When altitude clearances are received from ATC, the PM will respond to the radio call, and the PF will acknowledge hearing the call by verbally stating the assigned altitude.

Altitude Call-outs

During the climb, the PM will make the following call-outs:

- "One thousand feet to go," when approaching 1,000 feet below an assigned altitude.
- "Level at (altitude)," if it appears that the PF may overshoot an assigned altitude.
- "Reset to flight level 180," when passing 18,000 feet or another transition altitude, as a reminder to reset the altimeters to indicate flight levels and to turn off taxi/recognition lights.
- The PF will verbally acknowledge all altitude calls and make the following specific responses to PM call-outs: "Out of (passing altitude) for (assigned altitude)" when alerted by the aural tone or the "One thousand feet to go" call from the PM.
- "Correcting to (assigned altitude)" when warned of an overshoot.
- "Altimeter set to 29.92," when advised of passing the transition altitude.

CLIMB TRANSITION CHECKLIST

The climb transition checklist will be performed approaching 18,000 feet MSL or at 10,000 feet MSL if cruise altitude is below flight level 180.

CRUISE

The PF will call for the cruise checklist to be completed after leveling off at initial cruise altitude. The aircraft will be operated at a favorable cruise altitude, taking into account an appropriate balance between performance considerations (fuel requirements, winds, etc.) and passenger comfort (cloud clearance, turbulence, etc.). Safety will never be compromised for the sake of passenger comfort or convenience. Both pilots will remain at their stations with seatbelts fastened except when one pilot is required to perform duties related to the operation of the aircraft or to attend to physiological needs. The operation and condition of all navigation and communications equipment, aircraft systems, and performance instruments will be continually monitored by the flight crew. Once comfortably airborne and established en route, a message should be sent to the dispatch/operations assistant. En route, pilots will update and destination weather on a periodic basis. A minimum of two time–en route checks will be completed on each flight. Under normal circumstances, pilots will fly a constant Mach or airspeed, following flight plan fuel flows, to minimize fuel use. In addition, pilots will monitor fuel consumption to ensure that they can reach the destination with sufficient reserves. At least two fuel-remaining checks will be completed on each flight. During oceanic crossings, position and fuel logs are very important. As a rule of thumb, the crew should monitor and plot the current position every 15 minutes.

> *The airplane shall be able, in the event of the critical engine becoming inoperative at any point along the route or planned diversions from, to continue the flight to an aerodrome at which the Standard of 6.2.8.3.c. can be met, without flying below the minimum obstacle clearance altitude at any point* (IS-BAO 2010, 6.2.8.3.b).

Crew Oxygen Requirements

If one pilot leaves the cockpit when the aircraft is at an altitude above FL 350, the other pilot will wear his oxygen mask. The PIC will also ensure that all other oxygen requirements are met, as outlined in FAR 91.211.

> *A flight to be operated at altitudes at which the atmospheric pressure in personnel compartments will be above 10,000 ft (less than 700 hPa) shall not be commenced unless sufficient stored breathing oxygen is carried to supply: all crew members and at least 10% of the passengers for any period in excess of 30 minutes that the pressure in compartments occupied by them will be between 10,000 ft. (700 hPa) and 13,000 ft. (620 hPa); and all crew members and passengers for any period that the atmospheric pressure in compartments occupied by them will be above 13,000 ft. (less than 620 hPa). A flight to be operated with a pressurized aircraft shall not be commenced unless a sufficient quantity of stored breathing oxygen is carried to supply all crew members and passengers, as is appropriate to the circumstances of the flight being undertaken, in the event of loss of pressurization, for any period that the cabin altitude would be above 10,000 ft. (less than 700 hPa). In addition, when an aircraft is operated at flight altitudes above 25,000 ft. or an altitude from which the aircraft cannot descend safely within four minutes to 13,000 ft., there shall be no less than a 10-minute supply of oxygen for all occupants* (IS-BAO 2010, 6.2.6).

DESCENT

When descent clearances are received from ATC, the PM will respond to the radio call, and the PF will acknowledge hearing the call by verbally stating the assigned altitude. The flight crew will attempt to receive ATIS information early enough to allow time for thorough preparation for the approach and landing. Approach plates will be reviewed and discussed, if necessary, and kept ready for use. All checklists to be completed during the descent phase of the flight should be completed before reaching 10,000 feet MSL or getting into high-density traffic areas when full attention is required outside the cockpit. The PF will call for the descent checklist when the aircraft begins its let-down. The transition checklist will be performed approaching FL 180. If the cruise altitude was below FL 180, this checklist will be completed immediately after the descent checklist. The in-range checklist should be completed upon reaching 10,000 feet MSL.

Altitude Call-outs

During the descent, the PM will make the following call-outs:

- "One thousand feet to go," when approaching 1,000 feet above an assigned altitude
- "Level at (altitude)," if it appears that the PF may overshoot the assigned altitude
- "Reset to eighteen thousand," when passing FL 180 or another transition altitude, as a reminder to reset the altimeters to indicate MSL readings and to turn on taxi/recognition lights
- "Ten thousand," when passing 10,000 feet MSL, as a reminder to reduce airspeed to 250 knots
- The PF will verbally acknowledge all altitude calls and make the following specific responses to PM call-outs
- "Out of (passing altitude) for (assigned altitude)" when alerted by the aural tone or the "One thousand feet to go" call from the PM
- "Correcting to (assigned altitude)" when warned of an overshoot
- "Altimeter set to (current altimeter setting)," when advised of passing the transition altitude

Approach Briefing

The approach briefing is a vital element in the safe completion of a flight. The information shared between crew members will significantly enhance their performance as an integrated team. The briefing should be completed before the aircraft enters the high-density traffic area or begins maneuvering for the approach. A full IFR approach briefing will be conducted whenever the reported or forecast weather conditions are below Visual Flight Rules (VFR) minimums or if an instrument approach is expected or requested. The instrument approach plate will be used for reference during the approach briefing.

The PM will brief the following items: landing data for the approach runway, destination weather, and altimeter setting. The PF will brief the following items: STAR procedures or arrival route and altitude restrictions; review approach plate profile and note obstacles, altitudes, entry procedures, timing, printed notes, etc.; runway in use—length (vs. distance required), lighting, nav-aids, airport layout, and obstacles; minimums—check and set minimum descent height (MDH) or minimum descent altitude (MDA); missed approach point and procedures; alternate airport.

Approach Briefing Example

"We will expect radar vectors for the ILS to runway 07 at UBE. The transition altitude is 14,000 feet. Our sector altitude is 3,400 feet, with the UBE VOR as a reference point. The UBE VOR is nearly co-located, and its frequency is 110.8. The highest obstacle is 1,066 feet MSL, located northeast of the airport. The airport elevation is 15 feet. The TCH is 55 feet, with the TDZE at 23 feet."

"The localizer and DME frequency is 110.1. The inbound course is 068 degrees, with glide slope intercept near 6.1 DME. We will expect to cross the VOR at 5,000 feet and descend to be at 2,000 feet prior to the 6.1 DME inbound. A middle marker will help us determine the missed approach point. Time to missed approach is 2 minutes and 32 seconds from the 6.1 DME. For the missed approach, we can initially expect a climb straight ahead to 500 feet, and then make a right turn to the east, climbing to 3,000 feet. The decision altitude is 223 feet for the full ILS approach. Decision height is 200 feet. The minimum runway visual range (RVR) is 600 meters. Do you have any questions?"

Circling Approach Briefing

In addition to the items included in the IFR approach briefing described above, the following subjects should be briefed and discussed for circling approaches: approach category (D) minimums; entry; direction and pattern of the circling maneuver; aircraft configuration during the circling approach; speeds to be flown; missed approach procedure. Special attention must be given to terrain and obstruction clearance altitudes, as shown on approach charts.

VFR Approach Briefing

The VFR approach briefing should include pertinent aspects of the IFR briefing. If the runway of intended landing is identified with sufficient time for the crew to tune and identify approach aids, this should be accomplished prior to entry into the airport control environment. During visual approaches, especially at airports without a control tower, special vigilance outside the cockpit must be maintained. Uncontrolled airports can become quickly congested with a variety of aircraft. Speed differentials and intervals in the pattern may vary widely. Caution must be maintained during all phases of a VFR approach and landing. Radio calls as to the position of your aircraft and other aircraft is essential to the conduct of safe VFR pattern integrity.

Visual Descent Point

A VDP should be calculated before flying any non-precision approach. The VDP is that point along the final approach course from which a 3 degree glide slope from the MDA allows a touchdown within the first 1,000 feet of the landing runway. If an approach does not have a published VDP, use the following guidelines:

LOC/VOR/DME Approach

To calculate the distance of the VDP from the runway, multiply the height of the MDA above the airport by 0.3. Use the answer (expressed in miles) and adjust the final approach DME by that amount.

Example:	Field elevation	= 2,000′ MSL
	MDA	= 1,500′ MSL
	Height of MDA above airport	= 500′ AGL
Calculation:	500 × 0.3	= 1.5 miles from the runway to VDP.

Timed Approach

To calculate the time from the FAF to the VDP on a timed approach, multiply the height of the MDA above the airport by 0.1 and subtract the answer (expressed in seconds) from time-to-miss.

Example:	Field elevation	= 2,000′ MSL
	MDA	= 1,500′ MSL
	Height of MDA above airport	= 500′ AGL

Calculation:	500 × 0.1	= 50 seconds
	Time to miss	= 2:55
	Time to VDP	= 2:55 - :50 = 2:05

APPROACHES

The instrument approach is a demanding phase of flight that requires both vigilance and accuracy. Pilots must adhere to published approach procedures. Deviations from published procedures or assigned clearances are not authorized unless a crew member notifies ATC and/or declares an emergency. The PM will tune in all available navigation aids and set them up to provide the air crew with additional reference information for the approach. This applies to either instrument or visual approaches. The PM will monitor the performance of the instrument approach, make all normal callouts, communicate via the VHF radio as necessary, and identify approach frequencies, and in a paper environment retain the approach plate during the approach. Extraneous conversation and activities are to be completed prior to decent below 10,000 feet AGL and should not take place after passing the final approach fix (FAF).

Weather Restrictions

The PF will normally couple approaches to the autopilot anytime the ceiling is less than 400 feet AGL and/or the reported visibility is less than one mile or 5000 RVR. Note: This is a recommended procedure at the end of a long duty day or a particularly fatiguing flight. If the autopilot fails or other instrumentation is lost or degraded, the approach may proceed at the PIC's discretion. An approach to an airfield should not be attempted if any of the following weather conditions are determined to exist by ATC, by an authorized observer, or by a pilot report within the preceding 15 minutes:

- The ceiling is 100 feet below published minimums
- The visibility is below published minimums
- The approach-end RVR is below the published minimums

It is important to note that once the aircraft has passed the FAF, the approach may be flown to minimums, even if a weather update reports conditions falling below those listed above.

Stabilized Approach Configuration

Whenever possible, the PF should establish a stabilized final landing configuration at or before reaching the FAF. For visual approaches, a stabilized final configuration should be established no lower than 1,000 AGL. The airspeed is to be maintained within Vref + 20 knots. Flight below Vref is not authorized. The target airspeed under stable conditions is Vref + 10 knots. On non-precision approaches and during circling maneuvers, it may not be possible to establish final landing configuration until later in the approach. In such instances, the pilot will stabilize the approach as soon as possible before landing. When operating the aircraft with an engine out or in other emergency conditions, the PIC will determine the optimum time to establish final landing configuration. That configuration will be applicable to the nature of the emergency and in compliance with the aircraft flight manual.

Pilot-Monitored Approach (PMA)

Pilot-monitored approach (PMA) procedures were developed to help a flight crew transition from instrument to visual flight conditions and land the aircraft during low-visibility conditions. Experience has shown this to be one of the most hazardous segments of a low-visibility instrument approach. It is always important to brief a procedure such as the PMA prior to descent below 10,000 feet AGL. PMA procedures call for the first officer to fly the instrument approach from the right seat making all standard configuration changes and position calls, until the aircraft reaches the MDA/MDH. The captain monitors the approach and maintains the outside visual scan. Approaching minimums, the captain determines if sufficient visual cues exist to continue the approach and land the aircraft. At that point, the captain will take over the controls, simultaneously confirming verbally and fly the aircraft from the left seat to complete the approach and landing. If a landing cannot be made, the first officer will continue to fly the aircraft and execute the missed approach.

There are several advantages to using a pilot-monitored approach. The captain is in a visual position to be able to evaluate if the approach should be continued at the MDH/MDA. This procedure reduces the tendency of the pilot flying the aircraft to go below the glide slope when approaching the runway during a low visibility approach. If a missed approach is required, the first officer, as the PF, is able to make a more responsive go-around. Properly executed, the PMA is a demonstratively better method of performing a low-visibility instrument approach.

To be effective in using PMA procedures, the crew must be properly trained. A crew is authorized to perform pilot-monitored approaches only when both crew members have completed training on PMA procedures and successfully practiced the required number of pilot-monitored approaches (typically during simulator training). If either member of the crew has not completed PMA training, the captain will fly approaches from the left seat, using standard instrument approach procedures.

Weather Criteria

A PMA-qualified crew may elect to use PMA procedures whenever the destination airport is reported to be below VFR conditions (1,000-foot ceiling or three miles visibility).

The autopilot will be coupled to the right side for the PMA whenever the destination weather is reported to be below 400-foot ceiling or one mile visibility/5000 RVR. When engaged, the autopilot should be left engaged until the aircraft reaches the lowest authorized engagement altitude. If any navigation or flight guidance equipment has failed, the PIC will determine if a coupled approach is acceptable. PMA procedures stipulate that control of the aircraft be transferred from the first officer, who flies the instrument portion of the approach from the right seat, to the captain, who flies the visual portion of the approach to landing from the left seat. It is imperative that the transfer of control be positive.

Control should be transferred to the first officer prior to the aircraft descending below 10,000 feet or reaching a point 30 nautical miles from the airport, whichever occurs first. When the first officer takes over the controls, the autopilot will be coupled to the right side. The crew will confirm that all checklists up to the "before-landing checklist" are complete. The captain will assume responsibility for running the remainder of the checklists and will take over ATC communications.

The left seat pilot must not take control of the aircraft until he has positively identified the runway environment and has determined that he can visually complete the approach to landing. To assume control of the aircraft, the captain will use both a verbal command and a physical action. The captain will call, "I have the runway and the aircraft," and will simultaneously bring his hand up from below and behind the throttles, lifting the first officer's hand off the throttles. After control is transferred, the first officer will assume responsibility for monitoring the instruments, sink rate and airspeed, through the landing phase and will take over radio communications.

APPROACH SEQUENCE CALL-OUTS

The call-out procedures outlined in this chapter should be used on all approaches, regardless of whether the aircraft is being flown by the captain from the left seat or the first officer from the right seat. If the PM notes and calls out any deviation from approach procedures or performance standards, the PF is expected to acknowledge the call or immediately correct for the deviation. If, after two calls, the PF does not respond, the PM will call "Go around," and take appropriate action, as described in "Pilot Incapacitation."

The pilot flying (PF) will make the following standard call-outs during an instrument approach:

- "Localizer alive," as the CDI leaves the fully deflected position when intercepting the ILS approach course.
- "Course alive," as the CDI leaves the fully deflected position when intercepting the non-precision approach course.
- "Glide slope alive," as the GSI leaves a fully deflected position when intercepting the glide slope.
- "Descent altitude is (state altitude), missed-approach instructions are (state initial actions), comparator warning light is extinguished," at the final approach fix inbound. (The call, "No flags" will be substituted for "Comparator warning light is extinguished," if a comparator warning system is not installed in the aircraft.)
- "1000 above," when 1000 feet above minimums. (The PM will confirm the call.)
- "500 above," when 500 feet above minimums.
- "100 above. Approaching minimums," when 100 feet above minimums. (The PM will confirm the call and begin a heads-up scan to view the runway environment.)
- "Minimums. Going around," at the MDH/MAP, if the PM *has not* called, "Lights" or "Runway." (Upon making the "Minimums. Going around" call, the PF will initiate the published missed-approach procedure.)
- "Minimums," at the MDH/MAP, if the PM has called, "Lights" or "Runway." (The PF should continue flying the approach and expect a transfer of control at any time, but no later than published minimums. It is critical that the PF monitor the instruments, with particular emphasis on airspeed and vertical speed after the "minimums" call.)
- "You have the aircraft," after the pilot in the captain's position has called, "I have the aircraft," and has taken physical control of the aircraft. (After transferring control, the first officer will resume normal right-seat duties, including the monitoring of instruments and ATC communications.)
- "Going around," at published minimums, if the pilot in the captain's position has not called, "I have the runway and the aircraft," and taken physical control of the aircraft. (Upon making the "going around" call, the PF will immediately execute the published missed-approach procedure.)

The pilot monitoring (PM) may make the following call-outs during the approach:

- "Rate of descent," for any excessive rate of descent. (Below 5000 feet AGL, except on final approach, the rate of descent will not exceed one-half the absolute altitude remaining. On final approach, the rate of descent will not exceed 1000 feet per minute.)
- "Check altitude," whenever the PF deviates 100 feet above or below an assigned altitude.
- "Check airspeed," whenever the airspeed falls below V_{ref} or, if inside the FAF, below V_{ref} +10.
- "Check course," whenever the CDI is displaced one-half dot or more during a precision approach; the CDI is displaced one-half dot or more when the aircraft is inside the FAF on a non-precision approach; the bearing needle is displaced 5 degrees or more from the desired course during an ADF approach.
- "Check glide slope," whenever the GSI is displaced one-half dot or more.
- "Lights," when visually acquiring one of the following: strobes, approach lights, or other markings identifiable with the approach end of the runway.
- "Runway," when visually acquiring the threshold or runway surface or one of the following: VASI, REIL, threshold lights, runway lights, touchdown zone lights, edge or centerline lights.
- "I have the aircraft," when certain that a safe landing can be made from the current position. (After making this call, the PM will physically take control of the aircraft and complete the visual approach to landing.) The pilot in the first officer's position will respond, "You have the aircraft."

The aircraft will not continue the approach below the published MDH/MDA unless: the aircraft is in a position from which a landing can be made on the intended runway using normal maneuvers and a normal rate of descent; the flight visibility is equal to or greater than those prescribed for the approach procedure being used; the PM has called "Lights" or "Runway," satisfying the visibility criteria to complete the approach. If the PM loses sight of the runway environment any time after calling "Lights," he will immediately call, "Go around," and the PF will execute the published missed approach. The aircraft will not descend below the published decision height until the pilot in the captain's position has the runway environment clearly in sight and has physically taken control of the aircraft.

MISSED APPROACH

Either pilot may command a go-around for any reason at any time. The PF needs only to call, "Going around" and execute the maneuver. When the PM calls "Go around," the PF must immediately execute the published missed approach procedure. Control of the aircraft should not be transferred to initiate the go around, except for pilot incapacitation or a mechanical malfunction that requires the aircraft to be flown from the opposite side. Either pilot may be required to fly a missed approach, depending on when or for what reason the missed approach is initiated.

The missed approach will be reviewed during the approach briefing. Both pilots must understand the published procedures and be familiar with initial missed-approach headings and altitudes. Once the missed approach is initiated, the PF may fly the complete published approach from whichever position he is in. The PM assumes all duties normally assigned to the first officer position, including ATC communication, programming flight management systems, and executing checklists. The PM will monitor the missed approach procedures as described in the published approach plated. Normal checklist call-outs concerning aircraft-configuration changes will be made by the PF and confirmed by the PM.

The PF will confirm the position of the flight director prior to engaging the autopilot. If a transfer of control is required for a subsequent approach, or diverted to an alternate airport, the transfer will be made only under the following conditions:

- The aircraft is established at the final missed approach altitude
- All configuration changes have been completed
- The check list is completed to the before-landing check

CIRCLING APPROACH

The circling approach is the most difficult and one of the most hazardous operations performed, because the crew is required to maneuver the aircraft in close proximity to the ground after making the transition from instruments to visual conditions. The success of the maneuver depends on careful planning, a thorough briefing, good crew coordination, and precise flying. Circling approaches must be flown using a conservative philosophy. A circling approach should not be attempted in marginal conditions or if the crew has any reservations about the appropriateness or safety of the maneuver.

Category D circling minimums should be used for all turbojet aircraft. One pilot must have continual visual reference with the airport. The pilot who can best maintain visual reference with the active runway should fly the initial portion of the circling approach. Full attention of the PF is required outside the aircraft to keep the runway in view and position the aircraft for landing. The PM must closely monitor instruments and call out any deviations in airspeed of ±5 knots and altitude of ±50 feet. The PM should also advise the PF of excessive bank angles or rates of descent.

Because the aircraft will be maneuvering, the crew may elect to delay configuring the aircraft for landing until established in the airport traffic pattern. It is important to note that the aircraft should be in at least an approach flap configuration and the airspeed in a range for ease of maneuverability. If the circling maneuver is being flown from the right seat, and the pilot in the captain's position determines that the aircraft is in a position from which he can comfortably complete the visual approach to landing, he will call "I have the aircraft," and use prescribed procedures to take the controls. Following the transfer, the first officer will monitor the approach, paying close attention to altitude, airspeed, angle of bank, and rate of descent.

If instrument conditions are encountered during the circling maneuver, or if the PF loses visual contact with the airport environment, a missed approach must be executed immediately. The PF will initiate a climb while turning the aircraft toward the landing runway. When established on the missed approach course for the instrument approach flown, the PF will complete the published missed approach procedure. Control will not be transferred during the missed approach, except for pilot incapacitation or a mechanical malfunction that requires the aircraft to be flown from the opposite side.

BEFORE LANDING

When the destination airport does not have a tower in operation at the time of intended arrival, the following procedures are recommended:

- No straight-in approaches to landing are authorized without verbal confirmation from a ground observer of all traffic.
- Published VFR pattern procedures must be briefed and complied with.
- Configure to approach flaps early and conform to normal airport traffic speeds.
- Make all appropriate call-outs on the published monitored frequency or local unicom.

It is advisable to contact the local FBO via telephone prior to departure in order to gain any additional information concerning local conditions.

BEFORE-LANDING CHECKLIST

The before-landing checklist should begin when the PF calls for the landing gear to be lowered. Items on the checklist may be deferred to later in the approach, but should be completed before the aircraft reaches 500 feet AGL. Upon receipt of landing clearance or announced decision to land at an uncontrolled airport, both landing lights should be turned on during daylight as well as night operations.

LANDING

Both pilots will devote full attention to outside references and traffic throughout the landing phase and until the aircraft is safely clear of the landing runway. The after-landing checklist shall not be initiated until after the aircraft has cleared the active runway and the tower or ground.

> *The airplane shall, at the aerodrome of intended landing and at any alternate aerodrome, after clearing all obstacles in the approach path by a safe margin, be able to land, with assurance that it can come to a stop or, for a seaplane, to a satisfactorily low speed, within the landing distance available. Allowance shall be made for expected variations in the approach and landing techniques, if such allowance has not been made in the scheduling of performance data* (IS-BAO 2010, 6.2.8.3.c).

ABNORMAL PROCEDURES

An abnormal situation will be dealt with on a priority basis and integrated into the flight-related duties being performed. Each action should be based on the effect of the action on the operation of the aircraft and the ability to continue the mission. At all times, the PF will devote his/her attention to flying the aircraft. The PM will assist the PF by examining the cause of the abnormality and discussing alternative actions recommended by the manufacturer's quick reference handbook (QRH). The abnormality is thus addressed using an effective cockpit resource management (CRM) process. If immediate action is not required, the crew should complete any checklist in progress before dealing with the abnormality. Because a malfunction can affect multiple systems or produce multiple caution indicators the crew should deal with abnormalities using the system hierarchy: engines, electrics, and hydraulics.

EMERGENCY PROCEDURES

Emergency procedures have been developed by the original equipment manufacturers (OEM) to assist the crew in responding to foreseeable, but potentially dangerous situations or systems malfunctions. While it is desirable that pilots have a thorough knowledge of emergency procedures, OEMs are trending away from the need to commit certain emergency checklist items to memory. A QRH should be readily available to each pilot's seat position for instant reference to any emergency that may arise during the course of flight operations. During annual or bi-annual recurrent simulator training, experienced flight crews have ample opportunity to practice their skills in handling aircraft emergencies. In between training sessions it is extremely important that business aviation crews continue to refer to and familiarize themselves with the contents of the OEM's QRH.

Hurried actions can lead to an even more serious situation. Therefore, the PF should maintain the integrity of critical operating systems to ensure they are not inadvertently shut down or disabled during the execution of QRH procedures. These systems include: operating engine controls, generator, and engine fuel supply. Both pilots should identify and agree upon the movement of any switches or controls of critical systems. The PM will read the challenge item in the checklist, place his/her hand on the appropriate switch or control, and state the response action to be taken. He/she will not move the switch or control until the PF has visually confirmed the selection and verbally agreed with the action to be taken. At all times during an emergency, the main priority of the PF is flying and maintaining control of the aircraft. Good CRM dictates that the PM run all checklists called for by the PF, and continues to assist the PF by monitoring aircraft performance and navigation.

IN-FLIGHT EMERGENCIES

Declaring an Emergency

The safety of passengers and crew rests on how rapidly emergency assistance is requested and rescue forces are alerted. It is critical that notice of an emergency situation is communicated to ground support services. Any circumstance that requires priority handling or could possibly result in a crash landing or ditching must be transmitted for effective coordination. When declaring an emergency, set transponder to code 7700. Transmit the following message on the assigned air-ground frequency, emergency frequencies 121.5 or 243.0, and/or the maritime distress frequencies 2182 or 4125 kHz. "Mayday, Mayday, Mayday, this is (aircraft identification), (position), (altitude), (ground speed), (true course), (fuel remaining in hours), (description of emergency), (intentions), (assistance required)." Comply with information and clearances received. Accept the communications control offered by the ground radio station, and do not shift frequency or shift to another ground station unless absolutely necessary or instructed to do so. Keep the controller informed of the current status of the situation.

Cabin Preparation for Planned Forced Landing or Ditching

In the event of a forced landing on an unimproved surface, preparations in the cabin must be as complete as possible, given the time available:

- One crew member will brief the passengers about the situation and review landing and evacuation procedures.
- Instruct the passengers to review the airplane briefing card, including the general evacuation plan. Also review the operation of seat belts, doors, emergency exits, life vests, lifelines, life rafts, and anything else pertinent to the situation.
- Complete the bracing position announcement.
- Assign primary and secondary exits to passengers.
- Assign competent passengers to aid less able passengers. The use of a buddy system is recommended to ensure that everyone is accounted for.
- Place hand luggage, loose items that cannot be stowed securely, and potentially dangerous articles in the lavatory and secure the door.
- Turn off the galley power and secure the galley.
- Open all doors between the cabin and cockpit.

Ditching

The possibility of a series of events culminating in an open-water landing of a modern business jet is extremely remote. This has occurred in the past, but only in a few instances where poor planning due to lack of international experience led to fuel starvation over the water. That said, aviation history has proven, time and time again, that the unplanned event, the never-before-imagined situation, has and will continue to occur. "Hope for the best, but plan for the worst," is attributed to an English proverb, "Good is I graunt of all to hope the best, But not to liue still dreadles of the worst" (1565 Norton and Sackville *Gorboduc* I).

When considering the subject and the aforementioned proverb, the author can think of no better example than US Airways Flight 1549, January 15, 2009 (Sullenberger 2009). The professionalism of the entire crew and the coolness of the pilots during an extremely stressful situation is an example for all of us to emulate. Flight 1549 involved a denigration of thrust, due to the ingestion of birds in both engines. A river ditching became the best of relatively few options. Open-water ditching on a large lake or in the ocean would ordinarily offer more time for planning and preparation by the crew and passengers.

In the unlikely event that an ocean ditching was the last option available, the crew should be aware of a report known as the Automated Merchant

Vessel Report System (AMVER). Every merchant vessel on the North Atlantic has filed a sail plan with a computer in New York giving the intended route, speed, and so on. If an aircraft is in trouble with a ditching possible, the crew may contact the Coast Guard or air traffic control and ask for AMVER information. In approximately 10 minutes, the crew should have the name and location of every merchant vessel within 100 miles of the aircraft's reported position. Oceanic control will report the emergency situation to the Coast Guard. The Coast Guard then initiates the AMVER system. This expedites a seagoing vessel to the area.

Once the decision has been made to ditch, the Captain should take advantage of ditching assistance provided by a seagoing vessel. If available, any nearby ship will provide the surface wind, the recommended ditching heading, and the sea condition. The ship can also give radar vectors to a ditching near the ship when weather is a factor. Set up a pattern for the ditching in close proximity to the vessel that will standby to pick up passengers and assist in any way. The crew should determine the best ditching heading, using information based on weather reports and reading sea conditions. Normally, there is a primary swell and one or more secondary swells, often moving in different directions. During daylight, the primary swells can be best observed from an altitude of 10,000 to 12,000 feet. Secondary swells become visible at lower altitudes. During nighttime, the landing lights should be used to illuminate the surface of the sea. If the surface wind is more than 35 knots, the ditching should be made into the wind, regardless of the direction of the swells. However, a ditching into the upslope of a swell should be avoided. If the surface wind is less than 35 knots, ditch parallel to a major swell.

If possible, the landing should be accomplished while engine power is available to permit maneuvering to a favorable touchdown area. Water contact should be made at minimum speed and at the lowest descent rate possible. The pitch attitude should be limited to not more than +6 degrees.

Passenger Communications

It is extremely important that passengers and other crew members be kept advised of the emergency and directed to take appropriate actions. If a crash landing or ditching is about to occur with little or no warning, the captain or designated crew member must announce, "Attention! Fasten your seatbelts immediately! Prepare for an emergency landing."

With a planned ditching, a designated crew member must instruct the passengers on use of the life vest:

> Remove the life vest from under your seat. Open the bag containing the vest. Remove the vest from the bag. Hold the vest so the word TOP is up. Place the

vest over your head. Take the strap at the bottom of the vest, place it around your waist and buckle the strap. Tighten the strap around your waist. Do not inflate the vest inside the cabin. As soon as you leave the aircraft, inflate the vest by pulling down sharply on one of the two red handles. Pulling the second red handle will give more inflation if needed later. The vest also has a manual inflation tube in case more air is needed. Look at the passenger safety information card to see how the vest is used.

A designated crew member must instruct the passengers on the proper bracing position:

> Adjust all seat backs to the vertical position and put the tray tables up. Remove dentures, glasses, and shoes. Take all sharp objects from your pockets. Remove your necktie and loosen your collar. Fasten your seat belt as tightly as possible. When you hear the "Brace for landing" command, fold your arms and rest them on your knees. Bend your body forward as far as possible, and place your head firmly on your arms. If available, hold a pillow, blanket, or clothing in front of your head to cushion the impact. Stay in this position until the aircraft has come to a complete stop. Then, follow the instructions of the crew and assist others in evacuating the aircraft.

The PIC will inform the passengers when to take appropriate actions to prepare for a forced landing or ditching:

- 1000-foot alert: "Passengers, be seated."
- 500-foot alert: "Standby for landing/ditching."
- 50-foot warning: "Brace for landing."

Evacuation from the Aircraft

The PIC will give the order to evacuate the airplane when the airplane has come to a complete stop. When the command to evacuate is given, the evacuation must be executed in a prompt, but orderly, fashion. If possible, the SIC will leave the cockpit first and move to the designated exit point, if it is aft of the main entrance door, to assist in passenger evacuation. Upon securing the aircraft, the PIC will assist at the forward exit door. The suitability of an exit must be considered before it is opened. Some considerations are its height above the ground or waterline, and its proximity to any fire. Passengers should be directed to the nearest suitable exit, and urged to move rapidly through it.

Land Evacuation

After landing, passengers must be instructed to clear the exit area and move without delay to a safe distance from the aircraft to reduce the risks or injury from a fire or explosion. Passengers exiting ahead of the wing should move to a point well forward of the aircraft nose. Those exiting behind the wing should move a safe distance behind the aircraft, but off to the side of the path of the landing and away from any spilled fuel.

Water Evacuation

After ditching, each crew member must quickly move to the assigned exit to position life rafts and assist in evacuating passengers from the aircraft. Life rafts will not be removed from their stowage areas nor should an exit be opened until the aircraft has come to a complete stop. The over-wing emergency exit can then be opened and the lifeline attached, one end to the inside and the other end to the wing attach point. This should be accomplished by the crew member who has opened the emergency exit. The life raft should be removed from its stowage area, the retaining lanyard secured to the lifeline, the raft lifted through the exit and inflated. The raft should be boarded initially by two able passengers to assist the others during boarding. The first person aboard the raft should assure raft inflation and, to the extent possible, hold the raft away from damaged aircraft structures. The second on board will assist other passengers in boarding. Depending on the seas and extent of injuries, people may be transferred directly from the aircraft into the life raft. If unable to board directly, passengers should be instructed to inflate their life vests after they exit the aircraft. Persons on the wing should hold on to the wing lifeline. Those in the water should hold on to a life raft heaving line to avoid drifting or being washed away.

Persons entering the raft will be instructed to sit with their backs against the rail and their feet toward the center. No one should be allowed to stand. Sharp objects, including shoes that can damage the raft, should be removed. Persons should move on hands and knees, and unnecessary movement should be restricted. When everyone is aboard the raft, the lanyard may be cut and the sea anchor deployed immediately. It is recommended to keep the rafts as close as possible to the floating aircraft, because the size of the aircraft would be easy to spot by search and rescue teams. Life rafts should not be tied together, unless the seas are very calm. All loose equipment should be secured when not in use so that it is not washed overboard.

Survival

When all passengers have been evacuated and are safely away from the aircraft, a member of the flight crew may be assigned to remove any emergency equipment or personal items that would be of use in a survival situation. Such items include, but are not limited to, fire extinguishers, flashlights, crash ax, portable oxygen bottles, first aid kits, blankets, clothing, food, and water. Mental attitude cannot be overemphasized when discussing survival. The crew must demonstrate confidence that rescue is simply a matter of time. Crew members should mix with the passengers and demonstrate an interest in them. Crew members should not group together or disassociate themselves from the passengers. The proper mental attitude will help sustain a strong will to live, even when one's physical condition is at its lowest point. The primary responsibility of the PIC and members of the crew is the welfare of the passengers and one another.

REFERENCES

International Standard for Business Aviation Operations (IS-BAO). (Jan 1, 2010). The International Business Aviation Council, Montreal.

National Business Aviation Association. (2010, Sep 27). Don't forget: "Line-up-and-wait" starts this week. *NBAA Update #10-39.*

Sullenberger, C. B. (2009). *Highest Duty.* New York: Harper Collins.

6

International Operations

Learning Objectives: After reading this chapter you should be able to:

- List all of the considerations needed for planning an international flight
- Describe the contents of a trip folder for a typical international flight
- Summarize the ICAO oceanic procedures used for aircraft separation and entry when crossing the North Atlantic and Pacific regions
- File an international flight plan and decode all weather reports needed to support international flight

Daily business aviation flight operations within the confines of North America have become so familiar and therefore routine in nature that a seasoned crew might liken the experience to taking a trip in the family car. Obviously having made such a comparison, the intent is not to lessen the amount of professional planning and meticulous effort that is undertaken with each and every flight. The point being, the air traffic control system, although currently antiquated, is very well managed; flight crews are extremely well trained; aircraft are reliable and quite sophisticated; and the attention to customer service within the business aviation community is just plain outstanding. Thousands of business aviation flights take place every day. The industry has grown exponentially since its inception (see Chapter 1). However, even today, the percentage of business aviation departments that fly internationally, beyond Canada, Mexico, and the Caribbean, remains relatively low. Conducting flight operations outside of the confines of the United States is not overly complex; it does, on the other hand, require specialized skills and considerable experience.

Normal aircraft and crew operational procedures remain essentially the same. Added to this familiar base of knowledge are a set of process-based guidelines that provide for flight over large bodies of water, in non-radar environments, to non-English-speaking nations, utilizing procedures adopted by the international aviation community, but differing slightly from FAA and Air Route Traffic Control (ARTC) mandates. Scripted and well-briefed preparation for international flights is mandatory. Planning for each trip by in-house staff must be supplemented by outside agency participation. In today's international flight environment, computerized flight planning, over-flight permission, landing rights, fuel uplifts, ground handling, and payment of airspace and airway fees must be coordinated through the assistance of a licensed and qualified international support agency.

Annex 2, "Rules of the Air," of the International Civil Aviation Organization (ICAO) regulations, is the primary guide when conducting international flights. Flight crew members shall also comply with the provisions of Parts 61 and 91 of the Federal Air Regulations, even when flying outside United States–controlled airspace, when the FARs are more restrictive than the provisions of ICAO or foreign government regulations, and when the FARs do not violate or conflict with them. Extended range operations are defined as those conducted on planned routes that exceed 180 minutes flying time at the one-engine-inoperative cruise speed under standard conditions in still air from an adequate airport. Note: See Advisory Circular AC 120-42B for information published by the FAA on extended range operations (IS-BAO, 2010, 6.2.7).

When operating outside the contiguous United States or Canada most business aviation flight departments typically utilize the services of an international handling company. The handling agent acts on behalf of the flight department, its client, to obtain landing permits, fuel uplifts, over-flight authorization, ground transportation and hotel reservations for passengers and crew, international weather, computerized flight planning, and flight following. The handling company will also assist the flight department in the payment of trip expenses associated with landing and airspace usage fees. There is of course a cost associated with this service, but the coordination required for such an undertaking is very time-consuming for most business aviation operations and therefore the added expense is easily justifiable. Having a local representative meet the aircraft at the international destination and shepherd the passengers and their baggage through customs, immigration, and into prearranged ground transportation is an enhancement to the overall customer service mission of a professionally managed business aviation flight department.

International operations necessitate that the flight crew maintain a currency level not to exceed initial or recurrent training in operational procedures within a 24-month period preceding an international flight. This can be accomplished at most professional training centers as an added enrichment course, or by attending an international seminar. Some countries, Brazil for example, require that both pilots are rated on the aircraft, prior to entering their airspace. Others have variations in their entry requirements for passengers and crew. The former Soviet-bloc countries use the metric system for their altimetry levels and approach altitude heights. Parking at a major international airport can be a daunting task, due to differences in communication procedure and the use of English, the common language of international aviation. Couple this with weather and night operations into an airport where the crew has never before ventured and the experience of the crew weighs even more heavily in its ability to function professionally.

The opportunity to make errors in procedure and judgment is increased when conducting international flight operations. When international trips are scheduled, it is very important to use that occasion to increase the knowledge base of the pilots within your organization. Pairing two highly experienced international pilots on the same trip is certainly desirable. If the flight department has a number of pilots who lack commensurate expertise, you would be advised to allow a mix of experience in order to allow for professional development. Of note to the aviation manager, international crew experience is, with the above limitations, at the discretion of the flight department. The aircraft configuration, in order to operate within the confines of international airspace, especially over water operations, is covered under the following:

FAR Part 91, Subpart F (Large and Turbine Powered Multiengine Airplanes and Fractional Ownership Program Aircraft); Sec. 91.511; Radio equipment for overwater operations.

(a) Except as provided in paragraphs (c), (d), and (f) of this section, no person may take off an airplane for a flight over water more than 30 minutes flying time or 100 nautical miles from the nearest shore unless it has at least the following operable equipment:

(1) Radio communication equipment appropriate to the facilities to be used and able to transmit to, and receive from, at least one communication facility from any place along the route:

(i) Two transmitters.

(ii) Two microphones.

(iii) Two headsets or one headset and one speaker.

(iv) Two independent receivers.

(2) Appropriate electronic navigational equipment consisting of at least two independent electronic navigation units capable of providing the pilot with

the information necessary to navigate the airplane within the airspace assigned by air traffic control. However, a receiver that can receive both communications and required navigational signals may be used in place of a separate communications receiver and a separate navigational signal receiver or unit.

(b) For the purposes of paragraphs (a)(1)(iv) and (a)(2) of this section, a receiver or electronic navigation unit is independent if the function of any part of it does not depend on the functioning of any part of another receiver or electronic navigation unit.

(c) Notwithstanding the provisions of paragraph (a) of this section, a person may operate an airplane on which no passengers are carried from a place where repairs or replacement cannot be made to a place where they can be made, if not more than one of each of the dual items of radio communication and navigational equipment specified in paragraphs (a)(1) (i) through (iv) and (a)(2) of this section malfunctions or becomes inoperative.

(d) Notwithstanding the provisions of paragraph (a) of this section, when both VHF and HF communications equipment are required for the route and the airplane has two VHF transmitters and two VHF receivers for communications, only one HF transmitter and one HF receiver is required for communications.

(e) As used in this section, the term "shore" means that area of the land adjacent to the water which is above the high-water mark and excludes land areas which are intermittently under water.

(f) Notwithstanding the requirements in paragraph (a)(2) of this section, a person may operate in the Gulf of Mexico, the Caribbean Sea, and the Atlantic Ocean west of a line which extends from 44°47′00″ N / 67°00′00″ W to 39°00′00″ N / 67°00′00″ W to 38°30′00″ N / 60°00′00″ W south along the 60°00′00″ W longitude line to the point where the line intersects with the northern coast of South America, when:

(1) A single long-range navigation system is installed, operational, and appropriate for the route; and

(2) Flight conditions and the aircraft's capabilities are such that no more than a 30-minute gap in two-way radio very high frequency communications is expected to exist. (FAR Part 91.177,Amdt. 91-296, Eff.8/6/07)

AIRCRAFT DOCUMENTS

Prior to departure from home base on a trip that includes an international destination, it is important to verify that the aircraft has the proper documentation aboard and that it is current. Some of this requirement should be attended to weeks prior to departure. Some can be left until the day before or the day of, but attention to those items which may require substantial lead time in order to maintain currency will understandably need immediate attention. It is professionally embarrassing to the crew and potentially costly to the flight department if a required document is either missing or out of date. These items should be checked aboard the aircraft before the start of an international trip.

- Letter of flight authorization
- Aircraft registration certificate
- Airworthiness certificate
- Radio license
- MNPS/RVSM/RNP 10/RNP 5/B-RNAV/P-RNAV certification
- U.S. customs over-flight permit
- Customs bond
- *Guide for Private Flyers*
- Fuel cards
- *Jeppesen Airway Manuals*—international manuals or trip kit
- ICAO flight plans
- Navigation logs
- General Declarations
- Customs Declarations—United States
- Tourist/immigration cards—United States and foreign destinations if available
- TSA waiver—appropriate to the operation
- Insurance certificate—including Mexican waiver and war risk rider
- Aircraft flight manual
- Company international operations manual
- Aeronautical Information Publication (AIP)—available online; International Flight Information Manual (IFIM)
- MEL (minimum equipment list)
- Company flight operations manual
- Maintenance log books
- Import documents if required
- Weight and balance manual and forms—appropriate to the operation
- U.S. customs decal, current date and properly displayed

Passengers are expected to have all personal documents current and available at the time of departure. These include passports, visas, tourist cards (usually supplied by the crew en route), immunization records, letters of invitation, diplomatic clearances, and so on. The passengers are also expected to comply with all customs requirements for those countries to be visited. A reminder of pertinent documents required for destinations on the itinerary should be provided to each passenger as soon as is feasable. This is usually handled by the flight department's scheduling office. The flight department should council the passengers of their personal responsibilities during international travel, but should not be held accountable for their actions or lack of preparation. As passengers arrive at the departure airport, prior to boarding the aircraft for an international trip, a final reminder to ensure that passports are in a conveniently accessible location serves as a final document check for the flight. If a passenger has forgotten to bring his or her passport to the departure airport, contingency plans are much easier to implement than realizing that fact en route or upon landing at a foreign destination.

The potential hazards to passengers and crew from security or health related issues in many destinations around the world should be taken into consideration when planning an international flight. Many business aviation departments, taking the lead from their parent corporations, restrict flights into high-risk areas. In other words, the corporate jet is not going there. Several excellent websites provide sufficient information to make an informed decision concerning security and health related risks:

CDC Website—www.cdc.gov/travel
The World Health Organization website—www.who.int/en
U.S. Department of State website—www.state.gov/travel

INTERNATIONAL TRIP PLANNING

While preparing for an international trip, crew members must allow sufficient time for flight planning to avoid delays and reduce the frustrations that typically occur due to the different laws and regulations governing travel in foreign countries. Thorough knowledge and careful planning practices are essential to comply with the many requirements for diplomatic clearances or invitations, landing and over-flight rights, aircraft and personnel documentation, customs declarations, and so on. The pilot-in-command (PIC) for the trip should be responsible for contacting the international handling agency and providing all available information regarding the trip, to include the planned itinerary, names of crew members and passengers, and any special requests. The PIC should coordinate all communications and planning with the flight department's scheduling office. Once underway an international trip should be followed very closely by the scheduling office. Establishing a central point of communications with the scheduling office is the most efficient means of reacting to changes, reaffirming and confirming scheduled services during the trip, and communicating progress and availability of the passengers to the appropriate corporate staff at company headquarters.

Prior to contacting the handling agency, the PIC should run preliminary flight plans to ensure that no flight during the trip will have inadequate fuel reserves or a "wet footprint." This can be accomplished in-house using available planning software, or by asking the agency to run some estimates of time en route and fuel burns for any flight legs that are in question. This exercise will also validate the proposed itinerary as to the sequence of flight legs within the overall trip schedule. In order to gain valuable experience, the PIC may delegate this duty to the first officer, but should stay on top of all planning data. Close attention must be paid to any over-water sequence and should include equal-time-points for twin engine, single engine with drift down, and loss of pressurization. The first officer should work closely with and assist the PIC throughout the planning process to stay abreast of all requests for, confirmations of, and changes to the itinerary and flight plans. Both pilots should ensure that the aircraft is ready for the trip, including such things as required documents, manuals, life vests, rafts, and other survival equipment. Both pilots should utilize an international operations checklist when planning any aspect of the trip.

INTERNATIONAL OPERATIONS CHECKLIST

- Passport/visa/tourist card requirements
- Airman certificates and medicals
- Crew ID—international
- Immunization/inoculation requirements
- Customs/immigration requirements—entry information
- Local holidays at destinations
- Airport curfews
- Airport layout
- Landing/SLOTs/over-flight permits
- Military permits
- Fuel arrangements
- Ground handling/parking permits
- Communication devices/cell phones/laptop computer
- Security in and around the airport
- Fees/charges and the form of payment
- Flight times and the fuel requirements
- Flight duty times and crew rest requirements
- Crew accommodations and transportation

TRIP FOLDER

A trip folder containing all reference materials and documentation for the trip should be assembled by the flight crew prior to departure on an international trip. Items normally included are:

- Itinerary (including Greenwich mean time (GMT) and local times)
- Crew/passenger names

- Crew/passenger passport numbers
- Crew/passenger hotels and numbers
- Handling agent information; names of contacts and representatives (telephone numbers and e-mails)
- VHF/HF frequencies
- The ICAO-administered Aeronautical Fixed Telecommunication Network (AFTN) address (for flight plan filing)
- Airport information (facilities, curfew, services)
- Requests and acknowledgments for permits and handling
- American embassy information (locations, contact names and numbers)
- List of English-speaking doctors and hospitals
- List of technical-support representatives for aircraft manufacturer and equipment vendors
- Customs/immigrations forms
- ICAO flight plan forms
- Weather folder
- NAT Track information, if needed
- Copy of the current flight plan
- Security Risk report
- Notice to Airmen (NOTAM) information
- Oceanic plotting charts
- Flight plans for alternative routes
- Landing cards

One of the most demanding aspects of international flying is oceanic operations. Going east to Europe or west to Asia from North America, a business aviation flight crew is required to navigate over large bodies of water. This navigation is in a non-radar environment incorporating specialized procedures and skill sets. Defined tracks, or routes, are utilized for example from the western coast of the United States to Hawaii. Variable tracks, such as the North Atlantic Track (NAT), define the designated routes over the North Atlantic, published daily as "Track Messages," and vary as to the time of day and the prevailing wind patterns. Plotting charts are used by international crews to back-up Global Positioning System (GPS)–based flight management systems that provide primary navigational guidance from waypoint to waypoint. Position reports along oceanic routes are made in a precise format and are dependent upon the accuracy of a synchronized Coordinated Universal Time (UTC) or GPS clock. This is the area of the world aviation airways that spawned Reduced Vertical Separation Minimum (RVSM), due to the increasing demand for airspace over the North Atlantic.

In 1978, the International Civil Aviation Organization (ICAO) initiated studies to investigate the feasibility of reducing the vertical spacing between aircraft to increase the number of aircraft that could utilize a given airspace while maintaining an acceptable measure of safety. The detailed plan called for the reduction of the vertical space between aircraft from 2,000 feet to 1,000 feet at flight levels above 29,000 feet (MSL), adding six more flight levels. Completed in 1988, these studies proved the goal of RVSM was attainable and RVSM was capable of offering increased traffic density, preferred routing and fuel economy. Above all, it offered all these advantages with the highest levels of safety. Implementation of RVSM was initiated with an evaluation phase in the North Atlantic in 1997. This evaluation phase was followed with full implementation in this region in October 1998. Since then, many other regions around the world have incorporated RVSM as well. The FAA, Eurocontrol, Nav Canada and other regional agencies supported ICAO in its efforts and have since initiated their own vertical separation programs. The FAA has published its final ruling on the RVSM mandate. It states that the FAA will require all aircraft and flight crews operating in Domestic Reduced Vertical Separation Minimum (DRVSM) airspace to be RVSM compliant as of January 20, 2005 (Duncan Aviation, 2004).

High frequency (HF) radio communications date back to before World War I and are still in use in areas out of range of Very High Frequency (VHF) communications capabilities. Invented by Marconi, HF radio communications are supplemented by the selective-calling radio system (SELCAL).

On December 17, 1902, a transmission from the Marconi station in Glace Bay, Nova Scotia, Canada, became the first radio message to cross the Atlantic from North America. On January 18, 1903, a Marconi station built near South Wellfleet, Massachusetts in 1901 sent a message of greetings from Theodore Roosevelt, the president of the United States, to King Edward VII of the United Kingdom, marking the first transatlantic radio transmission originating in the United States (http://en.wikipedia.org/wiki/Guglielmo_Marconi)

OCEANIC OPERATIONS

Transitioning from an IFR flight plan to an oceanic route is a relatively simple procedure if the crew has planned for this transition. The oceanic clearance should be received, verified, and accepted long before the aircraft approaches the oceanic boundary. En route charts contain the appropriate frequency to request the oceanic clearance, but experienced international crews already have the frequency noted on their flight plan along with the appropriate position when the controlling agency may be first contacted. Prior preparation is critical when operating in international airspace. A professional flight crew should be able to copy and read back an oceanic clearance without a misstep. Oceanic clearances contain an entry point, en route waypoints consisting of latitude and longitude positions, the exit point, a clearance altitude, and a Mach speed to be flown while within the airspace. Even if the aircraft is cleared to fly a specified track by its alphamnemonic designation, the controlling agency requires a read back to include each waypoint on that track. When requesting an oceanic clearance, the crew must compute an estimated time of arrival (ETA) at the oceanic entry point by factoring in the estimated time en route (ETEs) from the master flight plan and convey that ETA to the clearing authority.

Clearance is usually received from air traffic control (ATC) approximately 200 miles before reaching the gateway fix when flying eastbound from North America. If a clearance has not been received when the flight is within 20 minutes of the fix, the crew must call the appropriate agency (Gander, New York, Shanwick, or Santa Maria Oceanic Control) on either VHF or HF and request the oceanic clearance. During westbound flights from Europe:

- North of 50N—Contact Shanwick before 02W
- South of 50N—Contact Shanwick before 01W
- South of 45N—Contact Santa Maria OAC at least 20 minutes before crossing the OAC boundary. Contact Santa Maria radio on HF

Pertinent information on clearances can be found on the Atlantic (H/L) 1 en route chart. In 1997 more than 300,000 flights crossed the North Atlantic and annual traffic growth rates have been projected to increase by at least 10%. The North Atlantic airspace is one of the busiest in the world. As mentioned earlier in this chapter, normal land-based communications and radar surveillance are not available over the North Atlantic. Horizontal and vertical separation of aircraft is ensured through a strict set of parameters and procedural disciplines.

Clearances for Pacific crossings are usually received on the ground prior to takeoff. If the clearance is delayed until after the aircraft is airborne, as is the case in the Atlantic, the clearance must be received before the aircraft crosses the oceanic entry point. A good pre-departure technique when conducting oceanic operations is to test the HF radios long before takeoff. At minimum, before entering oceanic airspace, the crew must perform a functional test of HF radios, and will ensure that all navigation equipment used for the trip is in working order.

Mach number technique must be used for all oceanic operations. The controlling agency can only plot the approximate position of aircraft, based on position reports; this method is used to ensure proper spacing between aircraft along oceanic routes. Pilots must maintain their Mach number within a tolerance of +.01, unless a change is granted by ATC. After leaving oceanic airspace, the pilot is expected to continue to fly the flight plan Mach number until ATC authorizes a change in airspeed. Pilots must notify oceanic control if their ETA at the next reporting point changes by +3 minutes when operating on a designated track, or by +5 minutes when operating off the designated track system.

ORGANIZED TRACK STRUCTURE

To handle the heavy air traffic between the United States and Europe, an organized track structure (OTS) is built every 12 hours (due to constant weather changes). The entire Atlantic Control Area:

- Reykjavik (to the North Pole)
- Shanwick and Gander Oceanic
- Santa Maria Oceanic—North of 27°N
- New York Oceanic—North of 27°N but excluding the area west of 60°W and south of 38°30′N

The North Atlantic Track Structure (NATS) is a region of controlled airspace where IFR rules apply. Pilots flying a North Atlantic Tracks (NAT Tracks) are expected to use the Mach number technique to smooth the flow of traffic and enable en route step-climbing.

COMPOSITE ROUTES

There are fixed airways (composite routes) in the Pacific which are operational 24 hours a day. These composite routes are located in U.S.-controlled oceanic/arctic airspaces called control areas (CTAs) or flight information regions (FIRs). Pursuant to the Chicago Convention, the United States accepted responsibility for providing ATC services over the domestic United States and within certain areas of the western half of the North Atlantic, the Gulf of Mexico, the Caribbean, and the North Pacific. Within these CTAs/FIRs the United States applies oceanic separation procedures consistent with ICAO regional procedures.

Standard ICAO oceanic procedures apply to Pacific routes, with minor differences (in spacing and separation) from those on Atlantic routes. In the Pacific, Oakland Oceanic CTA extends out to 165E (to the Tokyo CTA) and to 130E (Manila FIR). As a result, the FAA controls most of the Pacific airspace. There are five routes that make up the North Pacific (NOPAC) routes between Alaska and Japan. The two northern routes are for westbound traffic, and the three southern routes are for eastbound flights. An organized route system, made up of six composite routes (ATS routes), is used for aircraft operating between Hawaii and the Los Angeles/San Francisco area. The routes are between FL290 and FL410 and use the same rules as the NOPAC routes.

OCEANIC COMMUNICATIONS

As mentioned earlier in this chapter, beyond approximately 200 nautical miles from a land-based VHF communication station, HF radio is used as the main communication source for oceanic operations. A recent advancement in communications technology allows satellite reporting and communication over water via the aircraft's flight management system. This is accomplished using automatic dependant surveillance-contract (ADS-C) and controller pilot data link communications (CPDLC). ADS-C and CPDLC have been in use in oceanic regions since 1995 (Rockwell Collins, 2007, p. 1). This is the future of oceanic flight communications. Today only a few business aviation departments have this capability. As has been the case with other technological advancements, ADS-C and CPDLC will become more commonplace during the next decade. "Air travel requirements mandate airlines to maintain two-way radio contact with their aircraft, but the abundance of voice communication over the designated frequency can be so great that it presents operational problems" (Business Editors, Business Wire, New York, Dec 1, 2000, p. 1.

Most operators continue to use HF as their primary means of oceanic communication. The HF frequencies used en route are determined not only by the particular route flown, but also by atmospheric conditions and the time of day. Generally, lower frequencies are used during the night and higher ones during the day. Each oceanic center has groups of HF frequencies assigned. These frequencies can be found in numerous resource locations, but most crews utilize the en route chart for the particular part of the world to pick up area frequencies. When receiving the oceanic clearance, the crew may request the "primary" and "secondary" HF frequencies. It is mandatory, while en route, that the primary HF must be monitored. There is a great deal of background/static noise on most HF radios. In the early days of oceanic flight, radio operators were used to maintaining HF listening watches. That duty later on fell, with two-pilot cockpits, to the pilot not flying the leg. During the on-first contact with the controller, the crew should perform a SELCAL (Selective Calling Radio System) check so the HF frequency does not have to be continually monitored by the crew. If the controlling authority needs to communicate with the crew, they will send a transmission through a ground-based encoder that is specific to that aircraft. An onboard alert tone and light will be initiated in the cockpit by the encoded signal thereby notifying the crew to reply.

POSITION REPORTS

As is the case when operating in any non-radar environment the aircraft crew is required to make position reports at all designated reporting points or at certain designated lines of latitude and longitude. When crossing the boundaries between oceanic control areas, a position report is made to the airspace controlling authority responsible for the airspace being entered. Over the Atlantic, on east and west tracks, position reports are required at each 10-degree line of longitude if the aircraft can cover that distance in one hour or less. Similarly, if the aircraft cannot reach the next 10-degree line of longitude in one hour, an intermediate position report is required at each 5-degree line of longitude. Similar timing rules apply for aircraft flying on north and south tracks. Position reports are required at each 5 degrees of latitude, with intermediate reports required for slower aircraft.

In the Pacific, position reports are required at mandatory reporting points indicated along fixed routes on the en route charts. If the aircraft cannot fly between mandatory reporting points in one hour and twenty minutes or less, mid-point reports are required at intermediate points, also printed on the charts. Position reports for flights along non-published routes will be made at significant points listed in the flight plan, or as instructed otherwise by ATC.

POSITION REPORT FORMAT

A position report to ATC should include the following in the order specified:

- Aircraft identification
- Position—over a mandatory reporting point
- Time (UTC) over the position
- Flight level
- Next fix and time (UTC)
- Name of the following fix
- Optional temperature and wind readings

An example of a position report and the controlling agency's response: (Aircraft) "Gander, N123JC, Position." (Gander Center) "N123JC go ahead." (Aircraft) "N123JC position 51N 40W at 0310; Flight Level 410; estimate 52N 30W at 0358; 52N 20W next. Temperature minus 54, wind

260 diagonal 60, over." (Center) "Roger N123JC, position 51N 40W at 0310, 410, 52N 30W at 0358." In this example, 51N 40W represents the position of north 51.00.0 and west 040.00.0. Proper position reporting requires brevity, due to the high volume of communications on HF. This format should be used for all HF position reports, substituting waypoint names for latitude and longitude when so indicated on the en route charts.

A position report is required at all Atlantic, Pacific, and European FIR boundaries. When departing from United States or Canadian cities, reports should be made at all compulsory reporting points on the FIR boundary. On the North Atlantic plotting chart, there are blue triangles printed on the FIR boundaries that represent the transition from local to oceanic control. For those flights departing gateways in Newfoundland (Gander, St. John's, and Stephenville), there are no triangles along the FIR from St. Anthony south to Gander. East of Gander the first mandatory reporting boundary is at longitude 50W. No named reporting points are designated on the European FIR boundary, so position reports must be made using latitude and longitude coordinates. The same is true of Guam and Tokyo CTA/FIR. The flight crew should expect ATC to require confirmation approaching and reaching all FIR boundaries.

HF COMMUNICATIONS FAILURE

In the unlikely event that HF radio communications are lost, the flight is expected to continue by the last assigned oceanic clearance. Every effort should be made to relay position reports on the VHF guarded frequency, 121.5, or in the Atlantic, air-to-air frequency, 131.8. Traditionally, oceanic aircraft have always monitored 123.45, in order to render communication assistance to other aircraft within VHF range. Over the Pacific the same procedures exist with the addition of VHF frequency, 128.95.

NAVIGATION PROCEDURES

Industry best practices mandate that flight crews not only file flight plans for each proposed flight leg, but maintain a copy of the flight plan in the cockpit as reference during the flight. Today, technology has advanced the art of navigation from a desktop exercise using a chart, a ruler, map, protractor, Jeppesen CR-3, and a #2 pencil. Now crews are equipped with laptops, iPads, smart phones, and GPS-driven flight management systems with moving map displays. Both weather and winds at altitude are available in a current format. These advancements have caused many crews to become complacent in the navigation phase of flight operations, especially during domestic flying. When it comes to international flight operations, any complacency, especially pertaining to navigation, cannot be justified. Flight planning and navigation require skill and diligence during international operations. Reviewing approach charts, standard arrivals, departures, and en route charts, well ahead of arrival, provides the crew with a familiarity of navigational procedures and waypoints that will come in handy when it's time to use them. Not being familiar with the name of or where to find an important intersection on a local chart, following a six- or eight-hour ocean crossing, is unprofessional and inexcusable.

To avoid human entry errors, loading an international flight plan into the aircraft's FMS should incorporate a two-person process of insertion and verification. Computerized flight planning and modern communication techniques allow for the plan on file to be received and downloaded electronically. Despite this convenience, it is critically important that this process be overseen by one pilot and verified by the other. During the previous decades of organized oceanic operations, hundreds of navigation errors have been recorded. The vast majority of those errors have been flight crew–induced during initialization or in the course of updating while en route. A time-proven manner of avoidance of crew induced navigational error is to double-check all FMS initial and updated position entries by either pilot. When an oceanic clearance is received, the flight crew should plot the waypoints on an oceanic plotting chart to ensure the coordinates received in the clearance match the coordinates that were programmed into the FMS. If there are any revisions to the flight plan, they will be entered in the correct position on the master flight plan and the old waypoints crossed out. An initial plot may take place, prior to departure, that represents the requested oceanic clearance. Once the clearance is received, as is often the case when traveling eastbound from the United States, a second plot should be made.

PROPER EN ROUTE PROTOCOLS

As soon as it becomes practical after departure, one crew member, typically the pilot monitoring (PM), should record the actual departure time on the master flight plan. This allows an accurate estimate to a gateway that may be fast approaching (examples: westbound out of London or Glasgow) and to have an accurate ETA to the destination. The estimate provided by the FMS may not initially be as accurate as the crew may wish. It also will not necessarily provide an accurate ETA to an FIR boundary or initial track entry point during climb-out when the controling agency may be requesting an estimated time of arrival at a particular fix along the flight routing. In addition to the time to each fix along the flight plan, the crew should have an estimate of how much fuel will be remaining at each fix. Before takeoff the PM should record the total fuel load on the master flight plan and in parallel with listing each waypoint's ETA, the PM should note the estimate of the total fuel remaining at each fix.

Passing the oceanic gateway outbound, the crew should perform a gross-error check to ensure the long-range navigation equipment is performing properly. This is accomplished by flying directly over the gateway, if practicable, and verifying that the aircraft is on the proper outbound course. Short-range navigation facilities may be monitored and compared to detect any deviations. This will help to detect any errors in the position updates since departure.

Approaching each waypoint, the crew should review the master flight plan and record all pertinent information, such as the fuel remaining and elapsed time. At this time it is important to check that the present and following waypoint are in accordance with clearance that was received by ATC. Overhead each waypoint, the crew should ensure that the aircraft turns in the proper direction and that the heading and mileage conform to the master flight plan estimates. Once passing an en route waypoint in any non-radar environment it is important that the crew make a position report as soon as possible. Each cardinal clock position, on the hour, quarter past, half past and three-quarters past the hour, diligent navigational discipline dictates that the crew plots the actual position of the aircraft using the FMS/GPS coordinates to determine if they are on course and within the tolerances of the oceanic procedures. Each mark should fall directly on the plotting charts route directory that was drawn by the crew, prior to entering the oceanic airspace. At the inbound gateway, the crew should cross-check VOR/DME positioning if available, but continue to navigate using the FMS/GPS. In the event of a contingency, the crew will immediately notify ATC to inform them of the situation and, if required, request a revised clearance. A clearance should be received before any action is taken to change altitude or the route of flight. If ATC cannot be notified, the crew should broadcast their request on 121.5 until a clearance is received.

LONG-RANGE NAV FAILURE

If one long-range navigation system fails before takeoff, the crew should consider the following options:

- Delay the departure until the system is repaired.
- File a revised flight plan using special routes which have been issued for aircraft with partial loss of navigation capability.

NOTE: These routes are available only if the remaining navigation equipment meets the MNPS, and the requirements in ICAO Annex 6, Part 1, (see Chapter 7) are met using short-range navigation aids. Request a clearance above or below MNPS airspace.

If one long-range navigation system fails after takeoff, but before the aircraft reaches the oceanic boundary, the crew should consider the following options:

- Land at an en route airport that has suitable repair capabilities, or return to the departure airport.
- File a revised flight plan using the special routes described above.
- Request a clearance above or below MNPS airspace.

If one long-range navigation system fails after the aircraft crosses the Oceanic Control Area (OCA) boundary, the crew may continue to operate the aircraft in accordance with the oceanic clearance received, recognizing that the reliability of the total navigation system is significantly reduced. If, after entering oceanic airspace and losing one navigation system, the remaining system fails or gives an indication of degraded performance, the flight crew must immediately advise ATC of the loss of navigation equipment. After assessing the circumstances, consult with ATC to select one of the following optional courses of action:

- Continue to destination
- Divert to a suitable alternate
- Turn back
- Obtain an appropriate clearance from ATC prior to any deviation from the current oceanic clearance
- Keep a special lookout for possible conflicting traffic, and use all available outside lights
- Using VHF radio, attempt to establish voice contact with adjacent aircraft to assist in maintaining separation
- Monitoring the Honeywell ring laser gyro (Laseref), plot the aircraft position on the plotting chart every 5 minutes

If no instructions are received from ATC within a reasonable period (approximately 10 minutes) after notifying them of the loss of navigation systems, the pilot should clear the oceanic track and use dead-reckoning procedures to continue the flight.

- Immediately climb or descend 500 feet, if at or below FL290; or 1,000 feet, if above FL290

- Initiate a turn 90 degrees right/left of course, preferably in a direction away from any organized track in the area.
- Continue on the 90-degree offset heading until 30 nautical miles from the original assigned track. Use timing procedures to estimate the distance flown. (If ground speed is 360 knots, or 6 nautical miles per minute, fly the offset heading for 5 minutes.)
- When offset by 30 nautical miles, turn back to the original heading to parallel the original track and continue the flight.
- Plot new waypoints (now offset by 30 nautical miles from the originals), using the heading and ETE between points on the master flight plan to define them. Note: The ETA to the next waypoint will be later than planned because of the time spent flying to the offset course (5 minutes in the example above). Adjust all subsequent ETAs by that amount.
- Over each waypoint, turn to maintain a new course, if required, using the magnetic compass. Make note of the course, time of waypoint passage, time to the next point, fuel remaining, and fuel burn between points on the master flight plan.
- Continue to monitor both the assigned HF frequency and the appropriate VHF frequency (121.5, 131.80 Atlantic; or 128.95 Pacific) for any position reports in the vicinity. Use the information on winds and temperature aloft to update flight plan estimates.
- Monitor all Volmet reports en route to select a suitable alternate landing site if the weather is below VFR at the intended destination.
- If radio contact can be re-established, advise ATC of the situation and actions taken. Request an amended clearance, if necessary.

EQUI-TIME POINT

The equi-time point (ETP) is that position along the route of flight where the time to return to a suitable airport with all systems operating normally, or in the case of a loss of an engine or loss of pressurization, is equal to the time to proceed on to a suitable airport. The ETP for the loss of pressurization will not be the same as that for an engine failure, because of the differences in airspeed with one or both engines operating. In addition, each ETP will be based on aircraft performance at a lower, but different flight altitude (loss of pressurization necessitating a much lower cruise altitude than loss of engine), the TAS and winds at the lower level must be used in computing the flight times.

Distance from the last suitable airport to the ETP can be computed by using the following formula:

ETP = (T × GSr)/(GSr + GSc)
T = Total distance from the departure of the last suitable airport.
GSr = The ground speed to return from the equi-time point back to the last suitable airport, based on the winds and TAS at the lower altitude.
GSc = The ground speed to continue from the equi-time point to the next suitable destination airport, based on the winds and TAS at the lower altitude.

EN ROUTE PROCEDURES

Radar control is not as prevalent outside the continental United States. An international flight crew must focus their attention on flying the published airways and approaches. They must be familiar with the different airspace requirements, ICAO symbols, and preferred routes. When making the transition from oceanic routes to the en route and terminal portions of the U.S. domestic portion of the flight, the crew must also be mindful of the differences in clearance procedures and terminology to be encountered.

Transition Altitude/Transition Level

Transition Altitude: Climbing out of an airport, the aircraft passes through a series of altitudes (not flight levels) until reaching an altitude at which the altimeter setting changes from QNH (station setting) to QNE (standard setting). Transition altitudes are normally printed on standard instrument departures (SIDs), standard terminal arrivals (STARs), as shown on the instrument approach plates.

Transition Level: Descending to a destination airport, the aircraft passes through a series of flight levels (not altitudes) until reaching a flight level at which the altimeter setting changes from QNE (standard setting) to QNH (station setting). Transition levels are *not* normally printed on approach plates because they vary from day to day, depending on the local barometric pressure. ATC normally tells the pilot to change to QNH when reaching a certain flight level.

Airways will be printed with one or two altitudes, one of them followed by the letter "a." The altitude *without* the "a" is the minimum en route altitude (MEA), which will assure terrain clearance and/or minimum reception altitude for navigation. Published minimum altitudes must be observed closely because it is not unusual, in some countries, to be cleared for an approach when the aircraft is a hundred miles or more away from the airport. The flight crew must ensure that they do not descend below the MEA or minimum sector altitude (MSA) until the aircraft is established on a published segment of the approach or, during daylight hours, they have the airport in sight. This is especially important during radar vectors, or whenever a crew member is not sure of an altitude clearance by reference to an approach plane. There are no airspeed restrictions below 10,000 feet, as in the United States. However, there are speed limit procedures (SLP), which are designated at points on an arrival that require a reduction in speed.

METEOROLOGY

When conducting international operations, pilots will be issued weather forecasts and observations using formats and codes different from those in the United States. Weather forecasters will use terms such as terminal aerodrome forecast (TAF), routine weather report (METAR), and special weather report (SPECI) and will assume they are understood. This task has become more real-time oriented today than in years past due to advancements in cockpit capabilities and the overall communication process. It is important, however, to have some working knowledge of how to read and interpret international weather reports.

VOLMET REPORTS

Volmet reports are meteorological (Met) reports, significant weather (Sigmets), and forecasts for selected airports that are broadcast at specified times on HF frequencies. The HF frequencies and times of broadcast can be found on the Atlantic Orientation Chart or in the meteorology section of the Atlantic Jeppesen binder. Because Volmet reports give the most current weather available, the flight crew should make every effort to regularly monitor and copy these weather forecasts while en route.

TERMINAL AERODROME FORECAST (TAF)

A TAF is a printed weather forecast consisting of groups of number and letter codes which indicate forecast weather conditions. The following is an example of a typical TAF:

EGGW 1212 33025/35 0800 71SN 9//005 INTER 1215 0000 39BLSN 9//000 GRADU 1516 33020 4800 38BLSN 7SC030 TEMPO 1620 85SNSH GRADU 2122 33015 9999 WX NIL 3SC030 RAPID 00 VRB05 9999 SKC 680304 590359 02102.

METAR (ROUTINE METEOROLOGICAL AVIATION WEATHER REPORT)

A METAR is a printed weather observation reported at one-hour or half-hour intervals. The following is an example of a typical METAR.

METAR 0100 EGGW 30006 CAVOK 06/M02 992 06452293

SPECI (SPECIAL WEATHER REPORT)

A SPECI is a special report used to supplement METARs at intermediate times when significant weather changes are observed. The SPECI report is printed in the same format as a METAR. The following is an example of a typical SPECI.

SPECI 1215 EGGW 33025/33 0700 R0600/30 38BLSN 9//005 04/01 1013

HOW TO READ A TAF, METAR, OR SPECI REPORT

TAF Codes are found in various planning documents and instructional publications. Weather codes are universal. The same codes that are used in the TAFs are used in the METARs and SPECIs. Some of the unique features of international weather reports and forecasts are explained below.

- Station Identifier: Uses the ICAO four-letter identifiers.
- Valid Time: All times are reported in UTC. Weather reports show the time of the observation, in hours and minutes. Forecasts show the range of the forecast time period. The first two digits are the beginning time, and the last two digits are the ending time. Forecasts will cover as much as 24 hours and may be subdivided into several time periods. NOTE: In some forecasts, the four-letter ICAO identifier is replaced with a different code. The first two digits indicate the length of the forecast. "BB" indicates a 9 hour forecast, and "00" indicates an 18-24 hour forecasts. The second pair of digits are the first two letters of the ICAO identifier, which indicate the country location. For example, if a TAF begins with "00LS," it means an 18- or 24-hour forecast for LS (Switzerland).
- Surface Wind: Speed is reported in knots for the last 10 minutes. Peak gust is reported when it exceeds the average wind by 10 knots.
- Visibility: Reported in meters. Prevailing visibility is the minimum in any direction.
- RVR: Reported in meters.
- Cloud Amount: Reported in oktas (eighths of sky coverage). When the sky is obscured, vertical visibility into the obscuration is reported. The

term "partial obscuration" is not used overseas. NOTE: Either one of the following conditions constitutes a ceiling: The lowest layer covering 5 oktas or more, or an obscuration.

- Cloud Height: Reported in feet or meters, depending on local practices.
- Temperature: Reported in degrees Celsius.
- Altimeter Setting: Reported as QNH (station setting) in hectopascals.
- CAVOK: A term meaning "Ceiling and Visibility OK," used in place of visibility, weather, and cloud code groups, when visibility is 10 km or more, there are no thunderstorms, cumulonimbus, or precipitation, and no clouds below 5,000 feet.

INTERNATIONAL OPERATIONS: TERMS AND DEFINITIONS

ACC: Area control center
ADCUS: Advise customs
ADIZ: Air defense identification zone
ATS: Air traffic services
ATS Route: A specified route designed for channeling the flow of traffic as necessary for the provisions of air traffic services
Cabotage: Transportation of goods and/or personnel from point to point within a foreign country
Cruising Level: A level maintained during a significant portion of a flight
ETP: Equal time point
FIR: Flight information region
GCA: Ground control approach
ICAO: International Civil Aviation Organization
IFIM: *International Flight Information Manual*
METAR: Routine meteorological aviation weather reports
MNPS: Minimum navigation performance specifications: The standard deviation of lateral track errors shall be less than 6.3 nautical miles. The proportion of the total flight time spent by aircraft 30 nautical miles off the cleared track shall be less than 1 hour in about 2,000 flight hours. The proportion of the total flight time spent by aircraft between 50 and 70 nautical miles off the cleared track shall be less than 1 hour in about 8,000 flight hours. Aircraft are normally certified if they are equipped with two independent and operational GPS/IRS based long-range navigation systems.
Okta: A measure of cloud cover (equal to one-eighth of sky coverage). Five oktas constitute a ceiling.
PSR: Point of safe return
QFE: An altimeter setting used in some nations that causes the altimeter to read zero feet when on the ground

QNE: An altimeter setting used at, or above, the transition altitude (normally FL 180 in the United States)

QNH: An altimeter setting that causes the altimeter to read field elevation when on the ground

SPECI: Special weather report for aviation

TAF: Terminal aerodrome forecast

UDA: Upper advisory area

UTA: Upper control area

UIR: Upper information region

UTC: Coordinated Universal Time; Expressed as "Zulu"

Wet footprint: That portion of an over-water flight that, in the event of an in-flight engine failure or other mechanical problem, the aircraft will not have enough fuel to reach a suitable airport.

INTERNATIONAL OPERATIONS CHECKLIST

Trip Departure Date ______________________

Initial flight planning actions:

_____ Required stops
_____ Refueling stops
_____ Routes
_____ Over-flight permits required
_____ Destination airport
_____ Destination permits/slots
_____ Prepare flight itinerary

Clearances:

_____ Prepare trip folder
_____ Over-flight permits requested
_____ Over-flight permits received
_____ Landing permits/slots requested
_____ Landing permits/slots received

Crew/Passengers:

_____ Passports
_____ Visas
_____ Airman certificates
_____ Flight medical certificates
_____ Crew ID badges
_____ Immunization if needed:
_____ Cholera
_____ Smallpox
_____ Tetanus
_____ Typhoid
_____ Yellow fever
_____ Plague

Aircraft:

_____ Registration
_____ Airworthiness certificate
_____ Radio license
_____ Insurance certificate
_____ Aircraft flight manual
_____ MNPS certificate
_____ Letter of flight authorization

Publications:

_____ Company operations manual
_____ *International Flight Information Manual*
_____ Maintenance log book

_____ FlightSafety International. procedures manual
_____ OAG International

Communications:

_____ VHF operational check
_____ HF operational check
_____ Spare earphones
_____ Spare microphone

Navigation:

_____ Plotting chart
_____ High and Low en route charts
_____ Approach charts
_____ MNPS certified equipment

Inspection Services:

_____ Passenger list
_____ Crew list
_____ Customs forms
_____ General Declarations
_____ Personal Declarations

Survival Equipment:

_____ Survival kit
_____ Medical kit
_____ Raft
_____ Life jackets

Security:

_____ Aircraft locks
_____ Security tape
_____ Risk assessment
_____ Company security briefing

Miscellaneous:

_____ Extra commissary
_____ Money
_____ Credit cards
_____ Letters of credit, if needed

INTERNATIONAL SERVICES COORDINATION SHEET

Trip Departure Date:____________________

FBO/Handling Agent

_____ Fuel reservations

_____ Type of fuel payment

_____ Parking arrangements

_____ Security details

Hotel Reservations

_____ Crew hotel

Location ______________________

Confirmation numbers ___________

_____ Passenger hotel

Location ______________________

Confirmation numbers ___________

Catering ordered

_____ Number of meals

_____ Type of food

_____ Special orders

_____ Delivery instructions

_____ Time

_____ Location

Ground transportation

_____ Vehicles suitable for passenger needs

_____ English speaking driver for passengers

_____ Crew transportation

_____ Flight plans (ATC and navigation)/Weather

_____ One copy to hotel four hours before takeoff

_____ One copy to FBO/handling agent

Instructions for Completing the International Flight Plan

Figure 6.1 contains FAA form 7233-4, the form used to file an international flight plan. Detailed instructions for completion of the form follow the illustrated form.

General

1. Use BLOCK CAPITALS when completing each item.
2. Adhere closely to the prescribed formats and manner of specifying data.
3. Commence inserting data in the first space provided. Where excess space is available leave unused spaces blank.
4. Insert all clock times in four figures UTC.

Form Approved OMB No. 2120-0026
09/30/2006

U.S. Department of Transportation
Federal Aviation Administration

International Flight Plan

PRIORITY

<=FF

ADDRESSEE(S)

<=

FILING TIME

ORIGINATOR

<=

SPECIFIC IDENTIFICATION OF ADDRESSEE(S) AND / OR ORIGINATOR

3 MESSAGE TYPE

<=(FPL

7 AIRCRAFT IDENTIFICATION

—

8 FLIGHT RULES

—

TYPE OF FLIGHT

—

<=

9 NUMBER

—

TYPE OF AIRCRAFT

WAKE TURBULENCE CAT.

/

10 EQUIPMENT

— /

<=

13 DEPARTURE AERODROME

—

TIME

<=

15 CRUISING SPEED

—

LEVEL

ROUTE

<=

TOTAL EET

16 DESTINATION AERODROME

HR MIN

ALTN AERODROME

2ND ALTN AERODROME

<=

18 OTHER INFORMATION

—

<=

SUPPLEMENTARY INFORMATION (NOT TO BE TRANSMITTED IN FPL MESSAGES)

19 ENDURANCE

HR MIN

— E/

PERSONS ON BOARD

P/

EMERGENCY RADIO

UHF VHF ELBA

R/

SURVIVAL EQUIPMENT

POLAR DESERT MARITIME JUNGLE

/

JACKETS

LIGHT FLUORES UH VHF

/

DINGHIES

NUMBER CAPACITY COVER

COLOR

D /

<=

AIRCRAFT COLOR AND MARKINGS

A/

REMARKS

N /

<=

PILOT-IN-COMMAND

C/

)<=

FILED BY

ACCEPTED BY

ADDITIONAL INFORMATION

FAA Form 7233-4 (7-93)

Figure 6.1 International flight planning form. Source: FAA (in the public domain).

5. Insert all estimated elapsed times in four figures (hours and minutes).

6. Shaded area preceding Item 3—to be completed by ATS and COM services, unless the responsibility for originating flight plan messages has been delegated.

7. Complete Items 7 to 18 as indicated hereunder.

8. Complete also Item 19 as indicated hereunder, when so required by the appropriate ATS authority or when otherwise deemed necessary.

Note:

The term "aerodrome" where used in the flight plan is intended to cover also sites other than aerodromes which may be used by certain types of aircraft, e.g. helicopters or balloons.

Note:

Item numbers on the form are not consecutive, as they correspond to Field Type numbers in ATS messages.

Item 7: Aircraft Identification

(Maximum 7 Characters) The registration marking of the aircraft (e.g. N1234HS)

Item 8: Flight Rules and Type of Flight

One of the following letters to denote the category of flight rules with which the pilot intends to comply:

I if IFR; V if VFR; Y if IFR first; Z if VFR first

(Note: If indicating either Y or Z, specify in Item 15 the point or points where a change of flight rules is planned. For Type of Flight, insert one of the following letters to denote the type of flight when so required by the appropriate ATS authority: S if scheduled air transport; N if non-scheduled air transport operation; G if general aviation; M if military; X if other than any of the defined categories above.)

Item 9: Number and Type of Aircraft and Wake Turbulence Data

Insert

(1) The number of aircraft, if more than one.

(2) Type of aircraft (two to four characters)

Insert

(A) The appropriate designator as specified in ICAO Doc 8643, Aircraft Type Designators,

Or

(B) if no such designator has been assigned, or in case of formation flights comprising more than one type, insert ZZZZ, and SPECIFY in Item 18 the number(s) and type(s) of aircraft preceded by TYP/.

(3) Wake turbulence category (one character)

Insert an oblique stroke followed by one of the following letters to indicate the wake turbulence category of the aircraft:

(A) H—HEAVY, to indicate an aircraft type with a maximum certificated takeoff mass of 136,000 kg or more;

(B) M—MEDIUM, to indicate an aircraft type with a maximum certificated takeoff mass of less than 136,000 kg but more than 7,000 kg;

(C) L— LIGHT, to indicate an aircraft type with a maximum certificated take off mass of 7,000 kg or less.

Item 10: Equipment

(1) Radio Communication, Navigation, and Approach Aid Equipment

Insert one letter as follows:

(A) N—if no COM/NAV/ approach aid equipment for the route to be flown is carried, or the equipment is unserviceable,

OR

(B) S—if standard COM/NAV/ approach aid equipment for the route to be flown is carried (see Note 1 below),

AND/OR

(C) Insert one or more of the following letters to indicate the COM/ NAV/approach aid equipment available and serviceable:

A (Not allocated); I Inertial Navigation; R RNP type certification (see Note 5)

B (Not allocated); J (Data Link) (See Note 3); T TACAN

C Loran C; K MLS; U UHF RTF

D DME; L ILS; V VHF RTF

E (Not allocated); M Omega; W RVSM

F ADF; 0 VOR; X NAT MNPS

G (GNSS); P Precision RNAV in Europe; Y 8.33 Frequency Split in Europe

H HF RTF Q; (Not allocated); Z Other equipment carried (See note 2)

(Note 1: Standard equipment is considered to be VHF RTF, ADF, VOR, ILS, and B-RNAV in Europe, unless another combination is prescribed by the appropriate ATS authority.)

(Note 2: If the letter Z is used, specify in Item 18 the other equipment carried, preceded by COM/ and/or NAV/, as appropriate.)

(Note 3: If the letter J is used, specify in Item 18 the equipment carried, preceded by DAT/ followed by one or more letters, as appropriate.)

(Note 4: Information on navigation capability is provided to ATC for clearance and routing purposes.)

(Note 5: Inclusion of letter R indicates that an aircraft meets the RNAV or RNP type prescribed for the route segment(s) and/or route(s) concerned.)

(2) Surveillance Equipment

Insert one or two of the following letters to describe the serviceable surveillance equipment carried:

(A) SSR equipment:

(a) N—Nil

(b) A—Transponder—Mode A (4 digits—4,096 codes)

(c) C—Transponder—Mode A (4 digits—4,096 codes) and Mode C

(d) X—Transponder—Mode S without both aircraft identification and pressure-altitude transmission

(e) P—Transponder—Mode S, including pressure-altitude transmission, but no aircraft identification transmission

(f) I—Transponder—Mode S, including aircraft identification transmission, but no pressure altitude transmission

(g) S—Transponder—Mode S, including both pressure-altitude and aircraft identification transmission

(B) ADS equipment:

DADS capability

Item 13: Departure Aerodrome and Time (8 Characters)

(1) Departure Airport

Insert

(A) The ICAO four-letter Location Indicator of the departure aerodrome,

OR

(B) If no Location Indicator has been assigned, INSERT ZZZZ, and SPECIFY, in Item 18, the name of the aerodrome, preceded by DEP/,

OR

(C) If the flight plan is received from an aircraft in flight, insert AFIL, and SPECIFY, in Item 18, the ICAO four-letter Location Indicator of the location of the ATS unit from which supplementary flight plan data can be obtained, preceded by DEP/,

(2) Time

Insert

(A) For a flight plan submitted before departure, the estimated off-block time (HHMM)

OR

(B) For a flight plan received from an aircraft in flight, the actual or estimated time over the first point of the route to which the flight plan applies.

Item 15: Route[AU under (1), (2), and (3), please clarify, especially the points under (3) Route.]

(1) Cruising Speed (Maximum 5 Characters)

Insert the first cruising speed; insert the True Air Speed for the first or the whole cruising portion of the flight, in terms of:

(A) Kilometers per hour, expressed as K followed by 4 figures (e.g. K0830), or

(B) Knots, expressed as N followed by 4 figures (e.g. N0485), Or

(C) Mach Number, when so prescribed by the appropriate ATS, to the nearest hundredth of unit Mach, expressed as M followed by 3 figures (e.g. M082).

(2) Cruising Level (Maximum 5 Characters)

Insert the planned cruising level for the first or the whole portion of the route to be flown, in terms of:

(A) Flight level, expressed as F followed by 3 figures (e.g. F085; F330); or

(B) Altitude in hundreds of feet, expressed as A followed by 3 figures (e.g. A045; A100); or

(C) Standard metric level in tens of meters, expressed as S followed by 4 figures (e.g. S1130); or

(D) Altitude in tens of meters, expressed as M followed by four figures (e.g. M0840); or

(E) For uncontrolled VFR flights, the letters VFR.

(3) Route (including changes of speed, level and/or flight rules)

(A) Flights along designated ATS routes

Insert

(a) If the departure aerodrome is located on or connected to the ATS route, the designator of the first ATS route,

Or,

(b) If the departure aerodrome is not on or connected to the ATS route, the letters DCT followed by the point of joining the first ATS route, followed by the designator of the ATS route.

Then,

(c) Insert each point at which either a change of speed or level, a change of the ATS route, and/or a change of flight rules is planned

(Note: When a transition is planned between a lower and upper ATS route and the routes are oriented in the same direction, the point of transition need not be inserted.)

followed in each case by

(d) the designator of the next ATS route segment, even if the same as the previous one,

OR,

(e) DCT, if the flight to the next point will be outside a designated route, unless both points are defined by geographical coordinates.

(B) Flights outside designated ATS routes

Insert

(a) Points normally not more than 30 minutes flying time or 370 km (200 NM) apart, including each point at which a change of speed or level, a change of track, or a change of flight rules is planned.

Or

(b) When required by appropriate ATS authority(ies), define the track of flights operating predominantly in an east-west direction between 70°N and 70°S by reference to significant points formed by the intersections of half or whole degrees of latitude with meridians spaced at intervals of 10 degrees of longitude. For flights operating in areas outside those latitudes the tracks shall be defined by significant points formed by the intersection of parallels of latitude with meridians normally spaced at 20 degrees of longitude. The distance between significant points shall, as far as possible, not exceed one hour's flight time. Additional significant points shall be established as deemed necessary. For flights operating predominantly in a north-south direction, define tracks by reference to significant points formed by the intersection of whole degrees of longitude with specified parallels of latitude that are spaced at 5 degrees.

Insert

(c) DCT between successive points unless both points are defined by geographical coordinates or by bearing and distance.

Use only

(d) The conventions described below and SEPARATE each sub-item by a space.

(1) ATS route (2 to 7 characters)

The coded designator assigned to the route or route segment including, where appropriate, the coded designator assigned to the standard departure or arrival route (e.g. BCN1, B1, R14, UB10, KODAP2A).

(Note: Provisions for the application of route designators are contained in Annex 11, Appendix 1).

(2) Significant Point (2 to 11 characters)

(a) The coded designator (2 to 5 characters) assigned to the point (e.g. LN, MAY, HADDY), or, if no coded designator has been assigned, one of the following ways:

- Degrees only (7 characters): two figures describing latitude in degrees, followed by "N" (north) or "S" (south), followed by three figures describing longitude in degrees, followed by "E" (east) or "W" (west). Make up the correct number of figures, where necessary, by insertion of zeroes, e.g. 46N078W.
- Degrees and minutes (11 characters): Four figures describing latitude in degrees and tens and units of minutes followed by "N" (north) or "S" (south), followed by five figures describing longitude in degrees and tens and units of minutes, followed by "E" (east) or "W" (west).

Make up the correct number of figures, where necessary, by insertion of zeroes, e.g. 4620N07805W.

- Bearing and distance from a navigation aid: Identify the navigation aid (normally a VOR), in the form of two or three characters, then the bearing from the aid in the form of three figures giving degrees magnetic, THEN the distance from the aid in the form of three figures expressing nautical miles. Make up the correct number of figures, where necessary, by insertion of zeros, e.g. a point 180° magnetic at a distance of 40 nautical miles from VOR "DUB" should be expressed as DUB180040.

(3) Change of Speed or Level (maximum 21 characters)

The point at which a change of speed (5% TAS or 0.01 Mach or more) or a change of level is planned, expressed exactly as in 2) on the previous page, followed by an oblique stroke and both the cruising speed and the cruising level, expressed exactly as in paragraph A of this Item 15 and paragraph B of this Item 15 without a space between them, even when only one of these quantities will be changed.

Examples: LN/NO284A045

MAY/NO305F180

HADDY/N0420F330

4602N07805W/N0500F350

46N078W/M082F330

DUB180040/NO350M0840

(4) Change of Flight Rules (maximum three characters)

The point at which the change of flight rules is planned, expressed exactly as in 2) or 3) above as appropriate, followed by a space and one of the following:

(a) VFR if from IFR to VFR

(b) IFR if from VFR to IFR

Examples: LN VFR

LN/NO284A050 IFR

(5) Cruise Climb (maximum 28 characters)

(a) The letter C followed by an oblique stroke;

Then

(b) The point at which cruise climb is planned to start, expressed exactly as in 2) above, followed

by an oblique stroke;

Then

(c) The speed to be maintained during cruise climb, expressed exactly as in (a) above, followed by the two levels defining the layer to be occupied during cruise climb, each level expressed exactly as in (b) above or the level above which cruise is planned followed by the letters

PLUS, without a space between them.

Examples: C/48N050W/M082F290F350

C/48N050W/M082F290PLUS

C/52N050W/M220F580F620

and Oceanics Procedures

Item 16: Destination Aerodrome and Total Estimated Elapsed Time, Alternate Aerodrome(s)

(1) Destination Aerodrome And Total Estimated Elapsed Time (8 Characters)

Insert

(A) The ICAO four-letter location indicator of the destination aerodrome followed, without a space, by the total estimated elapsed time,

OR,

(B) If no location indicator has been assigned, insert)ZZZZ followed, without a space, by the total estimated elapsed time, and SPECIFY in Item 18 the name of the aerodrome, preceded by DEST/.

(Note: For a flight plan received from an aircraft in flight, the total estimated elapsed time is the estimated time from the first point of the route to which the flight plan applies.)

(2) Alternate Aerodrome(s) (4 Characters)

Insert

(A) the ICAO four-letter location indicator(s) of not more than two alternate aerodromes, separated by a space,

OR,

(B) if no location indicator has been assigned to the alternate aerodrome, insert ZZZZ and SPECIFY in Item 18 the name of the aerodrome, preceded by ALTN/.

Item 18: Other Information

(1) No Other Information Insert:0 (zero) if no other information

OR

Any other necessary information in the preferred sequence shown hereunder, in the form of the appropriate indicator followed by an oblique stroke and the information to be recorded:

(2) Estimated Elapsed Time Insert: EET/

Followed by: Significant points or FIR boundary designators and accumulated estimated elapsed times to such points or FIR boundaries, when so prescribed on the basis of regional air navigation agreements, or by the appropriate ATS authority.

Examples: EET/CAP 0745 XYZ0830

EET/EINNO204

(3) Revised Destination Airport Insert: RIF/
Followed by: The route details to the revised destination aerodrome, followed by the ICAO four-letter location indicator of the aerodrome. The revised route is subject to re-clearance in flight.
Examples: RIF/DTA HEC KLAX
RIF/ESP G94 CLA APPH RIF/LEMD

(4) Aircraft Registration Insert: REG/
Followed by: The registration markings of the aircraft, if different from the aircraft identification in Item 7.

(5) Selcal Insert: SEL/
Followed by: SELCAL Code, if so prescribed by the appropriate ATS authority.

(6) Operator Insert: OPR/
Followed by: Name of the operator, if not obvious from the aircraft identification in Item 7.

(7) Status Insert: STS/
Followed by: Reason for special handling by ATS, e.g. hospital aircraft, one engine inoperative, e.g.
STS/HOSP, STS/ONE ENG INOP.

(8) Type Of Aircraft Insert: TYP/
Followed by: Type(s) of aircraft, preceded if necessary by number(s) of aircraft, if ZZZZ is inserted in Item 9.

(9) Aircraft Performance Data Insert: PER/
Followed by: Aircraft performance data, if so prescribed by the appropriate ATS authority.

(10) Communications Insert: COM/
Followed by: Significant data related to communication equipment as required by the appropriate ATS authority, e.g. COM/UHF only.

(11) Data Link Capabilities Insert: DAT/
Followed by: Significant data related to data link capability, using one or more of the letters, S, H, V, and M, e.g. DAT/S for satellite data link, DAT/H for HF data link, DATN for VHF data link, DAT/M for SSR Mode S data link.

(12) Navigation Equipment Insert: NAV/
Followed by: Significant data related to navigation equipment as required by the appropriate ATS authority.

(13) Departure Airport Insert: DEP/
Followed by: Name of aerodrome, if ZZZZ is inserted in Item 13, or the ICAO four-letter location indicator of the location of the ATS unit from which supplementary flight plan data can be obtained, if AFIL is inserted in Item 13.

(14) Destination Airport Insert: DEST/
Followed by: Name of destination aerodrome, if ZZZZ is inserted in Item 16.

(15) Alternate Airport Insert: ALTN/
Followed by: Name of destination alternate aerodrome(s), if ZZZZ is inserted in Item 16.

(16) En-Route Alternate Insert: RALT/
Followed by: Name of en route alternate aerodrome(s).

(17) Remarks Insert: RMK/
Followed by: Any other plain language remarks when required by the appropriate ATS authority or deemed necessary.

(18) Aircraft Address Insert: CODE/
Followed By: Aircraft address (expressed in the form of an alphanumerical code of six hexadecimal characters) when required by the appropriate ATS authority. Example: "F00001" is the lowest aircraft address contained in the specific block administered by ICAO.

Item 19: Supplementary Information

(1) Endurance
After E/
INSERT: A four-figure group giving the fuel endurance in hours and minutes.

(2) Persons on Board
After P/
INSERT: The total number of persons (passengers and crew) on board, when required by the appropriate ATS authority. INSERT TBN (to be notified) if the total number of persons is not known at the time of filing.

(3) Emergency and Survival Equipment
(A) R/ (Radio)
(a) Cross out U if UHF on frequency 243.0 MHz is not available.
(b) Cross out E if emergency location beacon-aircraft (ELBA) is not available.
(B) S/ (Survival Equipment)
(a) Cross out all indicators if survival equipment is not carried.
(b) Cross out P if polar survival equipment is not carried.
(c) Cross out D if desert survival equipment is not carried.
(d) Cross out M if maritime survival equipment is not carried.
(e) Cross out J if jungle survival equipment is not carried.
(C) J/ (Jackets)
(a) Cross out all indicators if life jackets are not carried.
(b) Cross out L if life jackets are not equipped with lights.
(c) Cross out F if life jackets are not equipped with fluorescent.
(d) Cross out U or V or both as in R/ above to indicate radio capability of jackets, if any.

(D) D/(Dinghies) (Number)
(a) Cross out indicators D and C if no dinghies are carried, or
(b) Insert number of dinghies carried; and
(E) (Capacity)
Insert total capacity, in persons, of all dinghies carried; and
(F) (Cover)
Cross out indicator C if dinghies are not covered; and
(G) (Color)
Insert color of dinghies, if carried.
(H) A/(Aircraft Color and Markings)
Insert color of aircraft and significant markings.
(4) N/(Remarks)
Cross out indicator N if no remarks, or INDICATE any other survival equipment carried and any
other remarks regarding survival equipment.
(5) C/ (Pilot)
Insert name of pilot-in-command.

The following is a list of informational documents and websites that may be used for further reference:

1. FAR/AIM
2. Advisory Circular 91-70—Oceanic Operations
3. Advisory Circular 20-138A—Airworthiness Approval of GNSS Equipment
4. Advisory Circular 90-96A—Approval of U.S. Operators and Aircraft to Operate under FIR in European airspace Designated for B-RNAV and P-RNAV
5. International Flight Information Manual (IFIM)
6. North Atlantic MNPS Airspace Operations Manual
   www.paris.icao.int/documents_open/files.php?subcategory_id=108
   www.nat-pco.org/nat/CurrentNAT%20IGA.pdf
7. ICAO Annex 1—Personnel Licensing
8. ICAO Annex 2—Rules of the Air
9. ICAO Document 4444—Air Traffic Services (PANS-ATM)
10. ICAO Document 7030—Regional Supplementary Procedures (NAT and Pacific Supplementary procedures and Contingency Procedures)
11. ICAO Document 8168—Aircraft Operations (PANS-OPS)
12. ICAO Document 9574—Manual on Implementation of a Vertical Separation Minimum
13. ICAO Document 9613—Manual on Required Navigation Performance (Performance-Based Navigation Manual)

14. Oceanic Errors Safety Bulletin
    www.paris.icao.int/documents_open/show_file.php?id=290
15. International NOTAMS
16. Local Country Aeronautical Information Publications (AIPs)
17. Advisory Circular 91-85—Authorization of Aircraft and Operators for Flight in RVSM Airspace
18. FAA Website—Oceanic and Offshore Operations (WATRS Plus Structure)
    www.faa.gov/about/office_org/headquarters_offices/ato/service_units/enroute/oceanic/
19. FAA Website—Pacific CNS Requirements
    www.faa.gov/about/office_org/headquarters_offices/ato/service_units/enroute/oceanic/pacific_cns/
20. FlightSafety International Operations Manual
21. U.S. Coast Guard Navigation Center (GPS Info)
    www.navcen.uscg.gov
22. U.S. Department of State—Travel Information including Warnings and Alerts
    travel.state.gov/travel/cis_pa_tw/tw/tw_1764.html
23. CDC Website—Travelers' Health wwwn.cdc.gov/travel/
24. Eurocontrol—The European Organization for the Safety of Air Navigation
    www.eurocontrol.int/

REFERENCES

Duncan Aviation download blog; www.duncanaviation.aero/news/artciles/2004.

Business Editors, *Business Wire.* (2003 Dec 1). New York, p. 1.

Federal Aviation Administration. (2003). *Code of Federal Regulations,* Part 91, Subpart F—Large and Turbine-Powered Multiengine Airplanes and Fractional Ownership Program Aircraft (Part 91.501).

_______. (2007). *Code of Federal Regulations,* Part 91, Subpart B—Flight Rules (91.177, Amdt. 91-296, Eff. 8/6/07).

_______. (2008). *Extended Range Operations with Two Engine Airplanes* (AC-42B).

_______. (2010). *International Flight Information Manual* (IFIM).

International Business Aviation Council. (2010). *An International Standard For Business Aircraft Operations* (IS-BAO).

Rockwell Collins; www.rockwellcollins.com/~/media/files/unsecure.

7

Training

Learning Objectives: After reading this chapter you should be able to:

- Outline an overview of the training needed to support a corporate flight department
- List the different types of management training needed
- Debate the reasons for management training
- Distinguish between proficiency and recurrent training
- Explain the rationale for crew resource management (CRM) training
- Outline the regulatory requirements for FAR Part 135 training

OVERVIEW OF TRAINING

This chapter will outline the requirement for training and discuss methods used to develop training programs. Training is very important in maintaining the safe and efficient operation of a business aviation flight department. Many flight departments operate a fleet of aircraft with dozens of pilots and mechanics. Others, approximately 70% of the business aviation industry, operate one aircraft and employ less than half a dozen people to manage and maintain that company asset. Due to the complexity of the aircraft and the regulatory environment in which it functions, the employees who work on and fly this expensive corporate asset must be experienced and very well trained. Not only are these assets expensive, the implied exposure on the part of the operating company in the event that an accident or incident occurs could also be very costly. Due to the high level of financial risk exposure, insurance companies will not insure the aircraft and the operation unless the pilots receive appropriate initial and recurrent training. A formal training process should include appropriately certified maintenance technicians who work on the aircraft. The FAA outlines many of the regulatory training requirements for pilots, mechanics, and other crew members in the *Federal Aviation Regulations Aeronautical Information Manual.* Finally, the International Civil Aviation Organization (ICAO) has training requirements for aircraft that operate over the oceans and from one country to another. These regulatory training requirements were created in the interest of safety when conducting international operations and are mandatory for crew members flying within these environments.

In its role of regulating civil aviation to promote safety, the FAA has established training requirements for pilots, maintenance technicians, and other support personnel within a business aviation flight department. These requirements are expressed in the form of regulations that are binding on all certificated personnel. Due to the self-regulated nature of business aviation, many industry best practices related to training have been developed by the National Business Aviation Association (NBAA) and adopted by member companies. This chapter will also touch on the need for management training and other non-aviation related training for support personnel. This chapter will also cover annual pilot proficiency training, assuming the flight department is operating under a FAR Part 135 certificate. Maintenance technician training requirements for attaining the Airframe and Powerplant (A&P) certificate will be included, as well as aircraft specific training requirements for maintenance technicians needed to be able to work on complex aircraft. Standard operating practices explaining how the typical business aviation flight department goes about meeting FAA training requirements will be discussed in detail.

TYPES OF TRAINING

Training to support a business aviation flight department can be separated into three broad categories. These categories are: (1) management training, (2) flight and maintenance training, and (3) operations-related training. The personnel who receive these various types of training are shown in Table 7.1.

One of the major responsibilities of the flight department manager is to maintain a properly trained staff. Operating a modern corporate flight department requires many specialized skills in many different disciplines. Managing the aircraft equipment and physical plant requires experience and specialized training. Managing the human resource function can be just as challenging to the business aviation manager. This requires management

Table 7.1. Types of Business Aviation Training

Management Training	*Operational Training*	*Operations-Related Training*
Aviation department manager	Pilots (chief pilot, captains and first officers)	Scheduler
Manager of maintenance	Flight attendants	Dispatcher
Chief pilot	Maintenance technicians	Administrative Assistants
Manager of safety	Maintenance foreman/chief inspector	
	Line service personnel	

training to be able to motivate and direct personnel toward overall organizational goals. Technical and managerial skills tend to degrade with time and should be refreshed on a periodic basis. Due to technological changes, new aircraft and equipment are constantly being introduced into the business aviation community. The modern day flight department manger must keep current with innovation. Whenever the opportunity arises to promote or upgrade aviation department personnel, consideration should be given towards additional training required to allow them to function in their new roles. Specialized pilot training is required by federal aviation regulations in the interest of safety. Specialized organizational specific training is also required for new hires to make sure they comprehend in the flight department's role in the overall corporate structure. It is understandable that a business aviation flight department needs a comprehensive training plan. Development of such a plan rests with the corporate flight department manager. A training plan should be outlined regardless of the size or number of aircraft operated. The training plan should include training in the areas of pilot and mechanic proficiency, communications and leadership skills, decision-making, motivational theory, conflict resolution, group dynamics, organizational behavior, financial management, flight operations and safety program management. Each training plan should be structured to meet the needs of the organization. The NBAA has developed training programs to assist the flight department manager, as will be described in the next section.

MANAGEMENT TRAINING

Aviation personnel work very hard to develop their individual professional skills. Pilots and maintenance technicians are incentivized to constantly learn new methods of doing a better job as they mature in their professions. This ethic is not unique to aviation, but it is definitely part of the culture of business aviation. Several of the skills that have been historically missing from the line pilot and technician tool kit are the ability to manage the financial aspects of company assets as well as motivating and leading flight department personnel. Business aviation was being led, in the early days, by individuals who were promoted into managerial positions by seniority and almost always without the benefit of any management training. This apparent lack of developmental foresight within the industry led to the creation of the Professional Development Program (PDP) by the NBAA. The champion of the PDP who fought political and budgetary constraints to make it a reality was Rod Kauber, then manager/chief pilot of Mutual of Omaha. Rod and Gary Kiteley, then executive director of the University Aviation Association (UAA) presented a paper at the Flight Safety Foundation Corporate Aviation Safety Seminar in 1996, calling for the development of management training in the business aviation community. A joint task force was established later that year by the NBAA and UAA. This working group was composed of eight academic professors with management degrees who were teamed with eight experienced corporate flight department managers. It took this task force over 18 months to construct the initial PDP management curriculum consisting of 27 modules. The curriculum was written in such a way as to make it available via distance delivery online or by conventional class room instruction. These programs have been expanded and are now made available through a variety of venues, including in print and online resources. They are delivered via distance learning through educational institutions and in presentations given at the NBAA's industry events.

The program was launched in 1998 and has been a rousing success. In 2011 the NBAA website, www.nbaa.org, listed 51 PDP courses, 20 of which are offered online through Embry-Riddle Aeronautical University. Course titles range from human resource management, emergency planning, community relationships, safety management systems, maintenance reliability certification, flight operations manuals, to corporate aviation management. Numerous seminars are held that are specifically designed to provide PDP credits for the attendees. At the 2011 NBAA annual meeting and convention six PDP courses were scheduled for participants during several days prior to and following the yearly event.

The initial success of the PDP process led to the development of a certification program for business aviation managers. First proposed in 2001, NBAA's certified aviation manager (CAM) examination evaluates professional development knowledge though a written test designed to measure proficiency in the five subject areas of: leadership, personnel management, operations, technical and facilities services, and business management. This certification program validates knowledge in these areas and is a very important qualification milestone to assuming a position of leadership within a corporate flight department. Information concerning the CAM test can be found on the NBAA Website at URL: www.nbaa.org/prodev/cam/application/. The qualification process incorporates a point system accumulating in seven areas combining the applicant's professional experience, educational history, and industry involvement. When the point level meets the criteria in each area, an applicant is eligible to take the test. Once the test is successfully completed, the applicant receives an official document confirming that he or she is an NBAA certified aviation manager. This certification is recognized throughout the corporate aviation community and is an important milestone in the career development of a corporate aviation department manager.

In addition to the CAM initiative in 2001, the Schedulers and Dispatchers Committee of the NBAA initiated a subset of the PDP process tailored to the professional development of business aviation schedulers. This innovative effort created the Schedulers Professional Development Program (SPDP). This program provides course offerings designed to meet the professional development needs of schedulers and dispatchers. The SPDP curriculum contains 30 learning modules that have been specifically incorporated to enhance the expertise of those schedulers who are not employed as professional dispatchers. The NBAA formally recognizes individuals who have completed at least six of the modules.

The NBAA Maintenance Committee has proposed an aviation maintenance technician certification program. The certification process is currently under development by the committee working with the National Center for Aerospace & Transportation Technologies (NCATT) and a host of other strategic partners. This initiative has been named Project Bootstrap. The goal of this initiative is to raise the educational and professional bar for aviation technicians though the development of a certification process. Once fully implemented, this program will **oversee** the awarding of an aviation maintenance technical engineer (AMTE) certificate. The AMTE credential will be awarded to those individuals who will be able to combine the A&P, IA and avionics skill sets with a required 10-year contiguous experience history. The goal of this program is to improve safety and quality while providing educational growth opportunities for maintenance technicians.

FLIGHT CREW TRAINING

Pilot training standards in business aviation were first set using established guidelines from World War II. Ground-based classes were followed by "dual" instruction in the air. As the business aviation industry expanded, it became necessary to document individual company standards into recurrent training programs. The FAA had, at the time, an abundance of inspectors who provided check rides and type rating rides aboard company aircraft. Flying expensive company aircraft for training quickly gave way to the use of simulators for the majority of instructional purposes. The first cockpit simulations had been incorporated into "Link" trainers during the late 1920s. Simulation technology would evolve in parallel with new aircraft development.

In 1951 a pilot by the name of Al Ueltschi "took a $15,000 mortgage on my house and opened the doors to FlightSafety" (Ueltschi 1997, p. 44). He began his commercial aviation career with Pan Am in 1926. Juan Trippe, the founder of Pan Am, purchased a business aircraft to move within the United States; his airline was restricted to international operations. Al was assigned as Mr. Trippe's personal pilot (Ueltschi p. 37). Mr. Ueltschi instinctively understood that business aviation would need a training provider in the near future. He installed the first of many cockpit simulators in his headquarters at LaGuardia Airport. "While those simulators were a vast improvement over what preceded them, they were imperfect to say the least. They had no visual systems, their instrumentation was nonstandard, and they relied on racks of vacuum tubes, which were always failing" (Ueltschi p. 54). The jet age within business aviation was rapidly approaching. Crews needed standardized training in systems and emergency procedures. Standard procedures training began to catch on within the business aviation community.

Today, FlightSafety, www.flightsafety.com, and CAE SimuFlite, www.cae.com, dominate the business aviation external training market. Both of these vendors provide a wide variety of training modules for flight crews and maintenance technicians under FAR Part 142. Their core offerings are focused on the ground and simulator instruction programs for literally every business aviation aircraft that has an airworthiness certificate. Crews today during the course of a flight manage the cockpit. External training vendors provide standardized crew training, not just pilot training. Digital instrumentation has replaced the "steam gauges" of the 1960s and before. Everything is now displayed electronically. Technology has transformed the training environment as well. Today a pilot sits inside a classroom in front of two or more computer screens. An entire training curriculum can be downloaded onto a memory stick. Home-based ground school is a reality. Level D, six-axis, full motion simulators have become standard in the pilot training industry. The venerable FAA began allowing type rating pilot certification rides to be taken in simulators, decades ago. Simulators, as far back as the mid 1980s, were sophisticated enough that a pilot could earn a rating as pilot-in-command on an aircraft that he or she had never actually flown.

FAA TRAINING REGULATIONS

Mandatory training requirements for pilots and other crew members are contained in the federal air regulations. Table 7.2 contains a list of the applicable Part 61 federal air regulations that apply to business aviation pilot training while conducting non-commercial operations under FAR Part 91.

FAR section 61.56 contains a regulatory requirement that a pilot must undergo a flight review each 24 months by an authorized instructor before acting as pilot in command (PIC) of the aircraft. This is a basic minimal requirement for all non-commercial operations of any aircraft operating in the U.S. airways system. The flight review is tailored to the aircraft, but as a minimum, the pilot must demonstrate an understanding of the flight rules spelled out in part 91 and be able to properly execute all maneuvers and procedures for safe operation of the aircraft in all phases of flight. This part also sets the minimum ground and flight training time requirements as well as basic content of the training. The training and flight review may be in an aircraft for which the pilot is rated, or it may be in an approved simulator or flight training device. That device must be representative of the aircraft, provided it is available in accordance with an approved course given at a flight training center operating under a Part 142 certificate. Once the flight review is complete, a pilot may continue to act as pilot-in-command until it is time for the next review, as long as the recent flight experience requirements, as specified in FAR section 61.57, are maintained. There is a more stringent requirement under FAR section 61.58 for operation of an aircraft requiring more than one pilot. For aircraft certified in this manner, a PIC proficiency check is required to be taken by a pilot-in-command every 12 months. The *NBAA Management Guide* recommends that recurrent training be accomplished every 6 to 12 months at a reputable training center. It is important to note that many business aviation departments operate more than one type of aircraft. Pilots are often required in the case of multiple

Table 7.2. Pilot Training Regulations

FAR Part 61 Regulations Impacting Pilot Training	
Part 61 –	Certification: Pilots and Instructors
FAR 61.3	Requirements for certificates, ratings, and authorizations
FAR 61.31	Type rating requirements
FAR 61.56	Basic training and flight review requirements
FAR 61.57	Recent flight experience to include landings, night, and instrument requirements
FAR 61.58	PIC proficiency check requirements for aircraft requiring more than one crew

aircraft models to maintain currency on two different aircraft types. In this instance, FAR 61.58 proficiency checks can be completed in one aircraft type every 12 months, rotating aircraft on an annual basis. This meets the requirements of subsection (a)(1) and (a)(2) of section 61.58. Sound aviation management practices would dictate that in this instance, the interval between training cycles is too long. The recommended practice in the case of operating multiple aircraft is to send each pilot to refresher training at professional training center every 6 months, rotating aircraft types.

The standards for a proficiency check are much higher than for a flight review. The standards for this check are the same as that required to obtain a type rating, to meet subpart K of Part 91 requirements, or that required by the commercial air carriers (Parts 121, 125, or 135). This proficiency check may be in an aircraft for which the pilot is rated, or it may be in an approved simulator or flight training device that is representative of the aircraft, provided it is given in accordance with an approved course given at a flight training center operating under a Part 142 certificate. Safety experts agree that it is more prudent to train in an approved simulator than it is in the company aircraft. Although the cost of flying a business jet for the purposes of training may be justified when comparing the expense of training with a professional center, it is not considered to be an industry best practice and is universally discouraged.

To maintain landing currency, FAR section 61.57 requires three takeoffs and three landings (for both day and night) in the last 90 days. This is a continual requirement that rolls over every 90 days. The landing requirements may also be accomplished in a flight simulator or flight training device (FTD), provided it is a part of an approved Part 142 training program. In order to maintain instrument currency, FAR section 61.57 requires that six instrument approaches be made in the past six months with three hours of logged instrument time. Once a successful check ride is complete, and the pilot makes the required number of instrument approaches in the required time period, the pilot may continue flying under instrument conditions until it is time to have another instrument proficiency check ride. This part also requires experience at entering a holding pattern and intercepting and tracking courses to maintain currency. In the event this currency is not maintained, a pilot must undergo an instrument proficiency check given by an examiner or other person who is authorized by the FAA. Once the instrument proficiency check is successfully completed, the pilot is again considered fully qualified to act as the pilot-in-command using the same currency criteria as before. The instrument proficiency check may be performed in a representative aircraft, or a flight simulator/flight training device operating under an approved Part 142 certificate.

In order to function as a PIC on an aircraft with a gross takeoff weight in excess of 12,500 pounds, the pilot must pass an oral and flight check (FAR

61.31) that results in the awarding of a type rating on that aircraft. This requirement also applies to aircraft that are turbine powered, but do not meet the gross weight limitation. During a pilot's career, this process will be completed quite a few times as aircraft are sold and replaced with a different type of aircraft or a new aircraft is added to the aviation department. This training may be obtained in the aircraft, or a flight simulator/flight training device operating under an approved Part 142 certificate.

Initial training is provided for crew members who have not previously qualified as a crew member on a particular aircraft. Recurrent training is required for crew members to remain current in the aircraft in which they normally function as a crew member; one where they have previously received initial training. Recurrent training is therefore given at periodic intervals to assure that crew members remain familiar with aircraft systems, limitations, abnormalities, and emergency procedures. Modern business aviation aircraft are very reliable and will operate for long periods of time before an abnormality occurs. The infrequency of systems failures and rarity of emergency situations arising tends to, over time, lull very experienced pilots into a false sense of security. Recurrent training sharpens systems knowledge. It tends to reassure pilots of proper procedural flows. It reacquaints each pilot with the location and interpretation of abnormal and emergency checklists. As will be noted throughout this text, the job of flying the aircraft expertly and safely should be a given in the business aviation community. Without question, that is the number one priority of the business aviation pilot. Unfortunately the primary responsibility that the flight crew undertakes when they place passengers aboard a business jet, in lock step with safety, is the level of personal service available to the customer. These customer service issues become the challenge, before, during, and following the conclusion of a business aviation flight. The fact that the aircraft performed flawlessly and the crew was excellent in manipulating the controls can be overshadowed if the catering is stale or the ground transportation is not on time when the flight arrives. Recurrent training is a must in the business aviation community. Pilots are called upon to display more than just excellent operational skills.

Transition training is required to qualify a crew member to serve in a position for which he or she has previously been qualified on another aircraft. This training is necessary for a lateral transfer to a different type of aircraft. It is generally not as intensive as initial training because the crew member has been qualified in this position and only needs to gain the knowledge needed to do the same job on a different aircraft. Differences training is the training required by the FAA for a crew member who has previously been qualified for a position on a given type of aircraft needed to serve in the same position on a variation of that aircraft. In this case the aircraft is very similar, but a small amount of training is needed to account for the differences in the aircraft. Upgrade training is more comprehensive in nature because this is the training needed to move from second-in-command to pilot-in-command on the same type aircraft. The training needed in this case that needed to function as the PIC and is not so much aircraft specific, but more in the areas of leadership, division of responsibility, human factors and teamwork. The final type of pilot training needed is requalification training. This type of training is the training needed to requalification after one has failed to maintain currency in the aircraft due to lapsed instrument proficiency, or a lack of testing within the specified time periods. In this case, time is the enemy and retraining is required to regain proficiency before a check ride is administered. These definitions are regulation-based and should be included in pilot training programs developed by the corporate flight department.

CREW RESOURCE MANAGEMENT

Decades past, especially following World War II, flight crews were made up of very experienced pilots who adhered to the philosophy that the captain was always right and that the captain's decisions were never to be challenged. Clearly that culture arose from the military backgrounds of the majority of those veterans; however, much of the "god-slob" rigidity was in place due to the fact that most captains of that era grew up in aviation flying by themselves. Prior to World War II multi-crew cockpits were not the standard of the day. Following the war, U.S. airlines flourished as converted military transports became civilian transportation vehicles. In the ensuing 35 years a number of accidents occurred that were the result of poor cockpit decision-making. Errors in judgment on the part of the captain in many instances were not challenged or discussed by other flight deck crew members. Clearly something had to be done. In 1979 NASA conducted a workshop to validate communications, leadership, and decision-making in multi-crew cockpits. The resultant finding was the beginning of crew resource management.

Crew resource management (CRM) training is required to be given to all crew members by fractional ownership programs operating under Part 91, Subpart K. The regulatory requirement for this training is contained in FAR section 91.10739(f). CRM training is also required by the scheduled airline operating under Parts 121 and 135. This training is required to be given to all pilots and flight attendants and focuses on situational awareness, communication skills, teamwork, task allocation, and decision-making. Dispatch resource management (DRM) training is also required to be given by the scheduled airlines to all of their aircraft dispatchers. There is no mandatory regulatory requirement to provide CRM training for a business aviation flight department operating purely under FAR Part 91; however, the NBAA strongly encourages it and recommends that this type training be provided every two years. This CRM training provides business aviation crews with the skills they need to operate more effectively as a team. It is designed to improve communication, situational awareness and task management skills to help the crew make better decisions.

The NTSB, NASA, and the FAA also strongly support CRM training in the interest of safety. Recommendations for CRM training can be found in Advisory Circular 120-51B, titled "Crew Resource Management Training." The majority of business aviation flight departments find it more efficient to send their pilots to an approved Part 142 training center to receive their aircraft-specific initial and recurrent training each year. Vendors, FlightSafety and CAE SimuFlite, for example, offer a number of supplemental training modules including CRM training, as a part of their aircraft-specific training programs. Most business aviation operators elect to include this type training as part of a package obtained while the pilots are receiving their initial or recurrent training. The NBAA strongly urges that flight attendants be included in CRM training when they are employed as part of the flight crew. Whenever possible, schedulers, maintenance personnel and all others connected with flying operations should be encouraged to be familiar with and/or attend CRM training.

TRAINING MANUALS

The *NBAA Management Guide* recommends that business aircraft operators initiate training programs for flight crew in order to standardize procedures and to ensure competency. In section 2.2.2, the *NBAA Management Guide* lists the minimum regulatory standards under which a Part 91 operator can ensure the proficiency and currency of pilot certificates and ratings.

The list below contains those items that each flight crew member should have or be able to obtain to be considered "legal" to fly airplanes or rotorcraft under Part 91 of the Federal Aviation Regulations.

- Pilot Licensing
  - Commercial (Airline transport pilot preferred)
  - Instrument
  - Multi-engine (if applicable)
  - Land, sea (as applicable)
  - Airplane, rotorcraft (as applicable)
  - Aircraft specific type rating (FAR Part 61.31, 61.63)
  - Biennial flight review, or pilot-in-command check (FAR Part 61.58, Part 125.281, Part 135.297)

- Medical certificate
  - Class (1st, 2nd, or 3rd)
  - Frequency (as applicable)
- Recency of flight experience
  - Day—takeoffs and landings
  - Night—takeoffs and landings
  - Instrument currency and instrument competency check
- Second-in-command training requirements
  - High-altitude endorsement
  - Jet transition course (if transitioning from turboprop or rotary-wing aircraft)
  - FCC radio license (international operations)
  - Part 91 requirements (if applicable)
  - Part 91 Subpart K requirements (if applicable)
  - Part 125 requirements (if applicable)
  - Part 135 requirements (if applicable)
  - International operations training (if applicable); RVSM, MNPS, RNP
  - Domestic reduced vertical separation minimum (DRVSM) training (if applicable)
  - FAA and company training requirements for use of supplemental help
  - FAA and company training requirements for cross training (various category or type aircraft); if applicable, trainee must meet the requirements of the company for pilot experience and proficiency for use on two or more different pieces of equipment. The company should be aware that pilot proficiency decreases if the pilot is assigned to more than two aircraft and that this practice should be discouraged.
- Rotorcraft-specific training
  - Helicopter IFR procedures, to include: helicopter ILS procedures, helicopter point-in-space approaches, GPS approaches to heliports
  - Chart and flight orientation of specific heliports and airports
  - Helicopter route charts and operations in high-density airspace (Class B)

Individual flight departments develop training programs with variations in standard operating procedures (see Chapter 5) based upon the performance characteristics for each type of aircraft. The training program, however, should conform to the rules contained within the regulatory requirements. Table 7.3 contains a list of the federal air regulations contained in Part 91 Subpart K that are required to develop a pilot training program for a fractional ownership flight operation. Due to the complexity of these regulations and the cost of conducting the training and check rides in the company aircraft, as mentioned previously, most business flight departments elect to train their pilots by sending them to an approved training center. These vendors have high-tech full-motion simulators that are certified by the FAA to conduct training and check rides. Regardless of how the training is accomplished, individual training records should be maintained on each crew member to show that they are being trained in accordance with the FAA regulations. This is not mandatory under Part 91, but is required by FAR Parts 91 K, 135, and 121. Formalizing a training manual, designating a person responsible for training, monitoring the training performance of company pilots, and maintaining accurate records of flight crew training and qualifications, again, is not mandatory under FAR Part 91. These actions are, however, examples of good management practices and are in place within well-run business aviation departments.

Initial training for pilots who are assigned to a new aircraft is typically two to three weeks in length, depending upon the size and complexity of the business aircraft. The first week of training is an immersion of classroom instruction, where aircraft systems, hydraulic, electrical, pneumatic, flight controls, power plant, pressurization, air conditioning, fuel systems, and aircraft performance are covered in detail. Modern training centers are marvels of technology. Long removed from the overhead projectors and schematics with multicolored grease pencil additions, instruction is given utilizing digital projections, multi-screen work stations for each student and memory stick renditions of

Table 7.3. Training Related Regulations

FAR Part 91 Regulations Impacting Pilot Training	
Part 91 Subpart K—Training-Related Rules for Fractional Ownership Operations	
FAR 91.1073	Training program: General
FAR 91.1063	Testing and training: applicability and terms used
FAR 91.1065	Initial and recurrent pilot testing requirements
FAR 91.1067	Initial and recurrent flight attendant crew member testing requirements
FAR 91.1069	Flight crew: instrument proficiency check requirements
FAR 91.1071	Crew member: tests and checks, grace, training to accepted standards
FAR 91.1075	Training program: special rules
FAR 91.1077	Training program and revision: initial and final approval
FAR 91.1079	Training program: curriculum
FAR 91.1081	Crew member training requirements
FAR 91.1083	Crew member emergency training
FAR 91.1087	Approval of aircraft simulators and other training devices
FAR 91.1097	Pilot and flight attendant crew member training programs
FAR 91.1099	Crew member initial and recurrent training requirements
FAR 91.1103	Pilots: initial, transition, upgrade, requalification, and differences flight training
FAR 91.1105	Flight attendants: initial and transition ground training
FAR 91.1107	Recurrent training

full-blown training manuals. The second and, if necessary, third weeks are consumed with ancillary training subjects and simulator training. Most initial training curricula include a minimum of six to seven simulator periods of three to four hours each, with the final session culminating in a check ride.

Recurrent training sessions normally last two to three days, again, depending upon the aircraft type. Sessions include a variety of training such as a classroom review of aircraft systems, a variety of equipment failures, and new regulations or procedures as well as several simulator sessions designed to review emergency procedures. Topics such as wake turbulence, wind shear encounters, and escape maneuver training can also be included in recurrent training sessions. CRM training is usually emphasized during both initial and recurrent training. Supplemental subjects, for example MNPS currency certification, are also available at professional training centers.

TRAINING RECORDS

It is recommended that training records be maintained for all flight department personnel. Many subjects pertinent to company policies, such as facility safety, CPR, AED, and first aid, may be provided on a periodic basis to all associates. It is important to ensure that proper records are maintained on these and other subjects; for example, recurrent review of support equipment and company vehicle associated with the aviation department. Maintenance technicians and flight crew personnel receive more training than operations personnel and that training should be appropriately documented and maintained in an orderly fashion. The following list is offered as an example of the contents of a pilot training record:

1. Data sheet listing the full name, current local address, and home phone number of the flight crew member
2. Copies of FAA certificates, radio telephone operator permit, and other required documents
3. Copy of most recent medical certificate
4. Certificates of completion or other documents showing completion of all initial and recurrent training courses conducted at contract training facilities or any training performed in-house
5. Proof of last pilot proficiency check for each aircraft in which a pilot is maintaining currency
6. Copies of correspondence that reflects on the training performance of the associate, and any resulting letters of commendations or letters of counseling

Note: this is a minimum recommended list.

FAR PART 135 PILOT TRAINING REQUIREMENTS

Federal regulations require that an organization wishing to operate a business aircraft for commercial purposes must obtain an FAR Part 135 certificate. Today, a number of business aviation flight departments that were originally conducting operations under FAR 91 have elected to obtain a Part 135 certificate or to be certified under the auspices of an established certificate holder. Offering unused aircraft availability for charter returns revenue to the aircraft owner and can significantly offset the cost of operation. It is however, more expensive to maintain and often equip a Part 135 aircraft due to the imposed regulatory requirements.

Record keeping requirements are much greater under FAR Part 135 than under FAR Part 91. A charter operation is required to have a training manual that is approved by the local flight standards district office (FSDO). Any revisions must also be approved by the FAA FSDO principal operations inspector (POI) prior to updating each employee manual. A Part 135 flight department must also have a series of operations specifications approved by the FSDO. These OpsSpecs dictate in detail what the operator can and cannot do in the normal course of flight operations and maintenance. The operator must have an approved General Operations Manual (GOM) and a General Maintenance Manual (GMM). All of these manuals must be written and approved by the local FSDO before the charter certificate is issued. These manuals contain the procedures and policies to be used by the certificate holder's flight, operations, and maintenance personnel. The manuals also contain the operations specifications covering the geographic area where operations may be conducted and conditions authorized (IFR, VFR, etc.). The operations specifications also specify the type of approaches authorized. Because the manuals are approved under regulatory control of the FAA, they must be complied with at all times. There will be occasions where a Part 135 flight department may operate under Part 91, but the requirement to maintain the aircraft, train the crews, and administratively manage the flight department under Part 135 is still in effect. Individual training records must be kept on each pilot as specified in FAR, Subpart B—Flight Operations, 135.63.

Table 7.4 contains the training related regulations needed to develop an FAR 135 training program. These requirements are very similar to those required for the fractional owners. Anyone desiring to apply for a FAR 135 certificate should review these regulations for compliance.

MAINTENANCE TECHNICIAN TRAINING

The NBAA recommends that corporate flight departments require that their maintenance technicians hold an FAA Airframe and Powerplant (A&P)

Table 7.4. FAR Part 135 Training Requirements

FAR Part 135 Commuter and On-Demand Operations Rules	
Part 135 Subpart H—Training	
FAR 135.323	Training program: General
FAR 135.327	Training program: Curriculum
FAR 135.329	Crew member training requirements
FAR 135.335	Crew member emergency training
FAR 135.339	Initial and transition training and checking
FAR 135.341	Pilot and flight attendant crew member training programs
FAR 135.343	Crew member initial and recurrent training requirements
FAR 135.345	Pilots: Initial, transition, and upgrade ground training
FAR 135.347	Pilots: initial, transition, upgrade and differences flight training
FAR 135.349	Flight attendants: initial and transition ground training
FAR 135.351	Recurrent training

certificate. As an individual, one must have this certificate in order to perform maintenance work on an aircraft. Criteria for obtaining this certificate is found in Subpart D of FAR Part 65. Completion of the program of study normally requires between 18 and 24 months with a total of at least 1,900 hours of instruction given in three areas. Required areas of study in the powerplant portion of the curriculum include inspection, reciprocating and turbine engine theory and repair, instrument systems, fire protection systems, electrical systems, lubrication systems, ignition and starting systems, fuel metering systems, fuel systems, induction and airflow systems, cooling systems, exhaust and reverser systems, propellers, unducted fans, and auxiliary power units. The airframe part of the A&P curriculum includes inspection, wood, sheet metal composite, covering, finishes, welding, assembly and rigging, hydraulics, pneumatics, cabin atmosphere control systems, instrument systems, communication and navigation systems, fuel systems, electrical systems, position and warning systems, ice/rain control systems, and fire protection systems. The third or "general" part of the curriculum includes electricity, technical drawings, weight and balance, hydraulics and pneumatics, ground operation of aircraft, cleaning and corrosion control, basic mathematical calculations, forms and record-keeping, basic physics, maintenance manuals and publications, and applicable federal regulations. Once the program of instruction is complete, the applicant must take a comprehensive set of tests. These written tests are followed by a practical test, including an oral examination administered by a designated mechanic examiner (DME). Maintenance technicians may choose to acquire an inspection authorization (IA) added to their certificate. An IA is allowed to perform annual inspections on aircraft and sign off for return to service after an aircraft is in for major repairs or alterations. The certification requirements and limitations, including renewal requirements, are contained in 14

CFR Part 65. In order to obtain an IA the maintenance technician must be licensed for a minimum of three years and actively exercising the rights of an A&P for the two years prior to the date that the IA examination is to be taken. Once the technician completes the exam with a passing grade, he or she will qualify to have the IA added to their A&P certificate.

Obtaining the A&P certificate provides the maintenance technician with the basic knowledge needed for an entry-level position with a business aviation flight department. The ever-increasing sophistication of today's modern aircraft requires that maintenance technicians receive additional aircraft specific training once on the job. An important qualification of the maintenance technician in today's environment is the individual's ability to grasp the operation of an aircraft's systems and solve related complex problems. The experience needed to do the job is acquired over time by on-the-job training and specialized factory training on the type of aircraft operated by the company. Aircraft maintenance expenditures represent a significant portion of the annual costs of an aircraft's operational budget (see Chapter 10). As the annual budget is in the process of development, the technician in charge of aircraft maintenance should be prepared to provide predictive cost parameters based upon upcoming inspections and expected operational maintenance costs. Improper corrective action by the maintenance technician can compound these costs exponentially. Development of a comprehensive maintenance training program can be one of the most effective ways by which an aviation department can promote cost effectiveness and maintain the expected high levels of safety. The NBAA recommends that each operator develop a written training program for its maintenance personnel to ensure that the technician is familiar with and competent in the assigned duties of the position. Maintenance technician training should go beyond the basic technical training to include both oral and written communication skills.

The training program should consist of initial and recurrent training courses in each type of aircraft operated and maintained by the company. These aircraft specific courses should focus on aircraft and systems familiarization. They should also emphasize diagnostic testing and line troubleshooting techniques that are designed to promote efficient and cost-effective operations. Maintenance technician training can be divided into four types as shown on Table 7.5.

The NBAA recommends that training should not be treated as a one-time event in which all knowledge is expected to be imparted over a period of days or weeks. Rather, training should be structured to support the ongoing daily operations of the aviation department. In addition to training for technical competency, aviation department managers should work to foster a team environment in which all personnel understand their role in the organization and their impact on the economic and operational efficiency of the department.

Table 7.5. Types of Maintenance Technician Training

1. *Initial training*: by aircraft type covering airframe and powerplant maintenance procedures. This training is provided by the aircraft manufacturer, with training sessions scheduled once a year. They should include training aids to acquaint the maintenance technician with proper operation of the aircraft.
2. *Recurrent training*: by aircraft type, or if qualified on two aircraft types with alternate training every six months.
3. *In house training*: on-the-job training (OJT) for apprentice technicians and technicians who have not had initial training on a particular type aircraft.
4. *Management training*: for maintenance managers; attendance at seminars or short courses designed to enhance maintenance management skills.

SURVIVAL AND FIRST AID TRAINING

Holding with the operational philosophy that flight operations personnel should train for all possible contingencies, it has been a standard practice since the inception of business aviation to conduct periodic survival training. The lives of passengers and aircrew could possibly depend upon survival training. Both could be exposed to a situation where the aircraft is forced to make a landing in a remote part of the world. Much of the world is covered with water, so there is also a need for ditching and cold water survival training. Realizing this, the NBAA Safety Committee recommends that first aid and emergency situation training be conducted each year and that ditching and water survival be conducted every two years. Cardiopulmonary resuscitation (CPR) training should also be included as a part of first aid training. The value of first aid has applications both on and off the aircraft and can be also used to self-treat in an emergency. There are numerous vendors available to assist in developing survival and first aid training courses. The NBAA has a "Products and Services" section on their website that lists vendor capabilities. The FAA also has training videos available from their website. CPR and first aid training packages are available from the American Heart Association or the local fire department. Many business aircraft today carry automated external defibrillators (AED) as part of the emergency equipment inventory. It is very common to see AEDs at airports, shopping malls, and corporate headquarters. Recurrent training in the use of an AED is recommended for all operators.

REFERENCES

The Link Trainer, http://autospeed.com/cms/title_the-link-trainer

Ueltschi, A. L. (1997). *The History and Future of FlightSafety International.* New York: FlightSafety International.

8

Human Resource Management

Learning Objectives: After reading this chapter you should be able to:

- Assess the importance of human resources in running a business aviation department
- Outline the initial skills needed for each job required to run a business aviation department
- Relate the operational duties of each position within a business aviation department to an overall organizational structure
- Interpret the personnel policies used to manage a business aviation department

HUMAN RESOURCES

Perhaps the most underrated factor in building and managing any organization, especially a business aviation flight department, is human resources. People affect every decision you will make as an aviation manager. People maintain and control the aviation assets you have acquired on behalf of the company. Policies and procedures are built as guidelines for the expected conduct of personnel within your organization. People interact with outside vendors, internal associates, senior officers of the company, and their co-workers at the airport. The men and women working with and for you each have a life outside of the job. The various personalities, skills, educational backgrounds, experience levels, and abilities to adapt to change heavily influence the character and professional reputation of your flight department.

The best lessons of how to manage people are not taught in school. It is an acquired talent, developed over the length of your career, on the job. Many people learn from the mistakes of others. Observing how not to manage, what doesn't work, is often gleaned through negative experiences. The counter is just as true. What does, in fact, motivate and inspire others is observed by paying attention to good managers that you have been exposed to early on. Emulating the attributes, or people skills, of successful managers is very valuable later on in your management development. Over the course of the past several decades, seminars and developmental courses have been constructed to enhance human resource management. Aviation, however, has lagged behind in the advancement of factors relating to the positive management of personnel.

It is critical to infuse an atmosphere of professional respect within your organization. Respect flows both ways. Disagreements will always occur, but respect for others above and below you on the managerial ladder will in the long run bolster your ability to effectively manage and work with people. Aviation can be a very unforgiving discipline when it comes to certain pilot-related errors. Often the mistakes that are made by individuals can become causal in an incident or accident. There is a natural tendency to discipline those who err. In the post–WWII birth of business aviation, the "God-Slob" cockpit environment produced a generation of captains and copilots who learned how not to work as a crew. Cockpit resource management (CRM) principles developed in the 1970s have proven to be effective in handling crew coordination and communication when faced with operational abnormalities.

"Business aviation, whether you are working for a private individual, major corporation, fractional provider, charter operation or single turboprop with only one pilot in the company, demands a great deal of time. Pilots and flight attendants in our industry understand the need to be on call. As the business of corporate transport continues to mature and the budgets get tighter, all aspects of the job come under closer and more detailed inspection. Flight crews work odd hours, late nights, long days, short days, long flights, short hops and are subject to the varied demands of the flight schedule. That workload is driven by the personality of each industry, corporate initiatives, values, and the particular needs and social posturing of the principal passengers. What flight crews do to prepare for each trip, execute the trip, rest between trips, put themselves in a standby or readiness mode to fly a 'pop-up' trip, and train to maintain proficiency, makes up their work product. Often that product requires down time with family and friends to recharge the personal batteries and provide a balance between the work life and personal life. How each organization handles this balance varies across the board. There are however some similarities in the manner which current flight departments go about solving the work life balance" (Cannon 2008, p.70).

ORGANIZATIONAL STRUCTURE

Within the organizational structure of a midsize or larger business aviation department (two or more aircraft), the aviation department manager (ADM) is responsible for all aspects of flight operations and maintenance. The maintenance function falls under the direction of a manager of maintenance (MOM) and the flight operations function reports to the chief pilot (CP). All maintenance personnel typically report to the MOM and all flight personnel report to the CP. It is important to note that this theoretical business aviation department represents a minority of the total U.S. business aviation community, approximately 30%. The majority of business aviation flight operations are single aircraft departments with less than six company associates. In this instance, the ADM may also be the CP. In many cases, one person will wear all three management hats. For the sake of discussion we will first review the organizational structure of a more complex flight department. Figure 8.1 represents a typical organization chart for a business aviation department.

The aviation department manager is the organizational point of contact for all aviation-related matters. The areas of responsibility would include, but not be limited to, employees, facilities, equipment, flight scheduling, aircraft operations, and maintenance. The ADM is responsible for the overall administration of the flight department in accordance with general business practices of the parent corporation. The chief pilot is responsible for the day-to-day flight operations of company aircraft in accordance with the policies of the parent corporation, the procedures outlined in the general operations manual of the aviation department, and procedural guidelines established by the aircraft manufacturer, the Federal Aviation

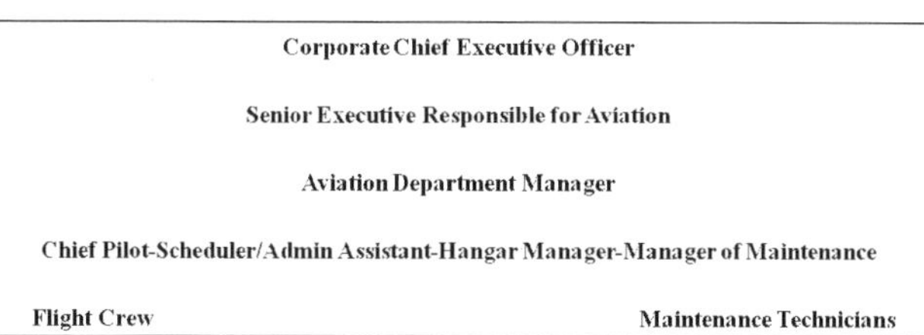

Figure 8.1 Organizational chart: large multi-aircraft business aviation department. Developed by the authors.

Administration, and other governing and regulatory organizations. The manager of maintenance is responsible for the overall maintenance and repair of company aircraft. All personnel assigned to the maintenance and appearance of the aircraft report to the MOM. The MOM also supervises maintenance performed at contract maintenance facilities.

For those operations that have the capacity to occupy an individual hangar owned or leased by the corporation, where the size of the flight department is sufficient in scope, the job of hangar manager may be added to the duties and responsibilities of the MOM, or may be a stand-alone position. The hangar manger is responsible for aviation office spaces, hangar spaces, fueling equipment, as well as all associated support equipment within the hangar facility.

Within the confines of the hangar or administrative office space available, the scheduler or operations assistant is responsible for the scheduling of passengers aboard company aircraft, arranging for travel-related needs of the flight crew members and when necessary, the travel-related needs of the passengers. This position is typically responsible for maintaining an array of flight-documentation records as well as assisting the ADM in special projects (see Figure 8.1).

The more typical organizational structure associated with a single aircraft operation in business aviation is represented in Figure 8.2. One aircraft does not require the level of additional support personnel or facilities to effectively manage its contribution to the parent corporation. It is more the exception than the rule that a single-aircraft flight department would have a dedicated hangar and support equipment in place. More often, a fixed-based operation (FBO) or some form of shared facilities will provide the office and hangar storage that is necessary for a single-aircraft operation. Personnel within a smaller department will of necessity wear several hats when it comes to duties and responsibility. It is more common for the chief pilot to be responsible for management of the flight department in a single-aircraft operation. The MOM will typically be the only full-time licensed mechanic on staff and the flight crew may only consist of the CP and one

Corporate Chief Executive Officer

Senior Executive Responsible for Aviation (Optional)

Aviation Department Manager/Chief Pilot

Scheduler/Admin Assistant -Manager of Maintenance-Flight Crew

Figure 8.2 Organizational chart: single aircraft business aviation department. Developed by the authors.

additional pilot. In a small flight organization, the scheduling duties may fall to an administrative assistant of a senior corporate executive. It is all a matter of scale and budgeting.

HIRING

In general, it is important to develop a policy and philosophy to hire the best-qualified person for any open position. Internal candidates should be considered before outside sources are pursued. A formal policy should be developed as to how all potential candidates for employment are initially screened, interviewed, and offered the position that has become available. Candidates under consideration for employment will be expected to meet the minimum standards as set forth for each position. As will be discussed later in this chapter, each job in the department should have a full description of duties and responsibilities. Each job should have a set of minimum standards for consideration. In some instances, each applicant for a flight crew, maintenance, or administrative/operations position may be subject to screening by an external personnel consulting agency. The use of such firms often becomes necessary when the current applicant pool does not meet the minimum standards developed for employment. The external agency should test and interview the most highly qualified candidates and submit their findings and recommendations to the aviation department manager. Special attention must be given to the candidates' licenses, logbooks, and any other records to determine overall experience. In addition, a background investigation must be conducted and all references checked. Within a specified amount of time following the employment offer to a candidate, it is advisable that the candidate successfully pass a specified drug screening process. A formal drug screening program for the aviation department should be in place and should mirror the current process in use by the parent corporation.

Most corporations prohibit or discourage the hiring of members of the same family if the positions filled by family members places them in close proximity to each other in the workplace. There have been several instances where husband and wife work as pilots together. Other situations have arisen where one spouse was a pilot and the other was a cabin attendant. These situations are not common and few have been successful long term. Guidance from the parent corporation should heavily influence policies at the aviation department level.

A formal interview process should be in place that allows the final group of candidates to be interviewed by a predetermined cross-section of the managers associated with the aviation department. Human resources at the corporate level should be consulted when instituting any policy dealing with company personnel. Policies in place within the aviation department must mirror the parent corporation's employee practices. People work very efficiently in a system where the rules are clear and understandable. When confusion exists as to work expectations, hours, duties, pay, and benefits, the work product will not have the same level of quality and throughput. The same holds true when recruiting personnel to fill new or replacement positions. During the interview, offer, and acceptance phases of the hiring process, the new employee should clearly understand the level of work expectation as well as the level and means of compensation. The opposite side of that human equation should also be clear; the employer has every right to fully understand the capabilities of the potential employee. Hiring someone that will be intimately involved with the safe operation of a corporate aircraft, with all of the inherent responsibility attached, should be as thorough a process as possible.

"For the vast majority of working Americans, weekends and weekday evenings are considered personal time, to use as they see fit. But for many of us in business aviation, those times are not inviolate; our industry doesn't adhere to 9-to-5 conventions or schedules" (Cannon 2004).

INITIAL QUALIFICATIONS/SKILLS

Pilots: Pilot qualification criteria can and will vary from company to company. Of particular note is the reliance on the number of flight hours that are used for recruiting and advancement. Experience and skill are not necessarily measured in the number of flight hours a pilot has accumulated. The environment in which a pilot has flown and the experience gained in a multiple-crew cockpit is often used as a more meaningful measure of competency and eligibility for promotion. Although an FAA type rating in the aircraft that the company is currently operating is desirable, strong consideration should be given to the candidate who will best fit into the culture of the department. The following list of job qualifications is offered for discussion purposes:

- Level I—(Copilot)—High school graduate. Four-year degree or equivalent is preferred. Holds a valid FAA airline transport rating (ATP) and first-class medical certificate. Minimum of 2000 flight hours. Meets 61.55 second-in-command qualifications. Restricted to right seat only. Authorized to fly from left seat at discretion of captain.
- Level II—(Type-Rated Copilot)—Meets or exceeds entry-level copilot requirements. Minimum of 2500 flight hours. Three years experience as a professional pilot. Type-rated in assigned aircraft and recent experience includes 61.58 check in-aircraft or level C (or greater) simulator. Authorized to fly left seat at discretion of captain.

- Level III—(Co-Captain)—Meets or exceeds type-rated copilot requirements. Minimum of 3000 flight hours. 1000 hours as pilot-in-command (PIC). Minimum of five years experience as a professional pilot. Meets 61.57 recent flight experience: pilot-in-command requirements. Captain qualification is limited to one type of aircraft. Other restrictions may apply as directed by the chief pilot.
- Level IV—(Captain)—Meets or exceeds co-captain requirements. Minimum of 3500 flight hours. 1500 hours as PIC. Minimum of eight years experience as a professional pilot. May hold captain qualification on two types of aircraft.
- Level V—(Senior Captain)—Meets or exceeds captain requirements. Minimum of 5000 flight hours. 2000 hours as PIC. Minimum of ten years experience as a professional pilot. May hold captain qualification on two types of aircraft. Qualified as PIC for international flight destinations. Functions as an assistant to the chief pilot in the management of flight safety, standardization, and training programs and may serve as chief pilot in his absence, assigned by and under the supervision of the aviation department manager.
- Level VI—(Chief Pilot)—Meets or exceeds senior captain requirements. Bachelors degree or equivalent is required. Minimum of 7000 flight hours. 3000 hours as PIC. Extensive international experience in heavy jet aircraft. Fifteen years experience as a professional pilot. Experience in the management and development of operational procedures, flight safety, standards, and training programs. Functions as an assistant to the aviation department manager and may serve as the manager, when appointed, in his or her absence.

Maintenance: Of equal importance to the safe and efficient operation of any business aviation flight department, the maintenance department must be staffed with skilled technicians. This vital function not only ensures a mechanically sound aircraft, it provides critical support in consideration of the dispatch reliability of the aircraft. Without the ability to manage planned and unplanned maintenance, the corporation will not always have a ready-to-operate asset.

- Maintenance Apprentice—High school graduate, technical school preferred. Currently attending technical school or recent graduate looking for first employment opportunity as a maintenance technician.
- Maintenance Technician—High school graduate, technical school preferred. Current A&P, three to five years of previous experience as an aircraft mechanic. Experience working on company aircraft type is desired.
- Maintenance Lead Technician—High school graduate, technical school preferred. Current A&P, six to ten years. Supervisory training within

current corporate structure. Maintenance technician experience with company two years preferred.

- Manager of Maintenance—High school graduate, college degree preferred. Current A&P, with IA preferred. Ten to twelve years, including two years as a supervisor. Previous training on type aircraft and engines operated by the company is preferred.

Ancillary Support Positions—Depending upon the complexity of the organization, as previously discussed, the business aviation flight department by necessity must have a central point of contact for all scheduling and communications pertaining to the operation of the aircraft. This position is critical to the ability of the department to provide timely and cost-effective transportation. The scheduler becomes the liaison between the executives and the flight crew. If the department is of sufficient size that the corporation owns or leases a private hangar facility, it is advisable to have a person within the organizational structure who is responsible for the physical plant and the appearance of the aircraft. If the aircraft is of sufficient size to warrant the use of an onboard cabin service and safety professional, it is recommended that the department be staffed to provide that level of customer service.

- Scheduling/Dispatch/Operations Assistant—High school graduate, college degree preferred. Proficiency in typing and office administration, computer proficiency, with knowledge of business aviation software programs. Demonstrated abilities in aircraft scheduling, recordkeeping, finance, accounting and budgeting. Excellent interpersonal and communication skills.
- Hangar Manager—High school graduate. Proficiency in towing, maintaining support equipment, overall maintenance of facility, and appearance of aircraft knowledge.
- Flight Attendant—High school graduate, college degree preferred. Five years minimum experience with a corporate flight department or airline. Passenger safety training and flight crew coordination training preferred. Excellent interpersonal and communication skills.

PILOT CURRENCY REQUIREMENTS

Within a well-organized business aviation department, the scheduling function will maintain the currency records of each crew member and provide reminders as to any impending lapse in currency. It is, however, each flight crew member's responsibility to maintain all applicable currency requirements, in accordance with the appropriate guidance of the governing

Federal Aviation Regulations. If a pilot is having difficulty completing a currency requirement, the chief pilot or, if absent, the aviation department manager should be informed well before the due date, so measures may be taken to avoid any loss of currency. It is each pilot's responsibility to maintain a pilot log in accordance with Federal Aviation Regulations. This log will include all information necessary to document currency requirements, including:

- Day and night takeoffs and landings
- Actual instrument time
- Night hours flown
- Actual or simulated instrument approaches, including holding currency
- Simulator/Flight training and documentation of proficiency examinations

Most flight departments track aircraft and crew hours using a computerized logbook program. This is typically maintained by the operations scheduler or assistant utilizing the flight department scheduling computer. Each pilot should receive a monthly update as to flight time in aircraft specific type and their currency requirement status. When a pilot first joins a business aviation department, the opportunity to enter past flight experience in the scheduling software should be offered, but is not mandatory.

MEDICAL QUALIFICATION

The FAA medical directive concerning medical requirements for business aviation pilots, under Part 91, does not mandate that the PIC hold a first-class medical certificate; a current second-class is sufficient. "A second-class medical is required for those intending to exercise the privileges of the commercial pilot certificate. It is possible to obtain a commercial pilot certificate while holding a third-class medical, but the licensee cannot exercise privileges beyond that of a private pilot" (FAR Part 61.23). It is however, the excepted standard practice for the vast majority of flight departments that their pilots all hold, with sufficient flight hours, an airline transport pilot license and a first-class FAA medical certificate. "First class certificates are required for those intending to be pilot-in-command in an air carrier operation requiring an airline transport pilot (ATP) certificate. Other operations, including those under Part 91, may require a first-class medical for insurance purposes, although it is not a federal requirement in such cases" (FAR Part 61.23). Many operators require a first-class examination once a year, six-month expiration, and allow the pilot to lapse to a second-class for the last six months of the twelve-month period. Pilots have the right to choose their medical examiners.

DUTIES AND RESPONSIBILITIES

Within the organizational structure of each business aviation department, the management and performance of critical functions can be outlined by a set of duties and responsibilities for each position. The following list of tasks for the position of aviation department manager, chief pilot, manager of maintenance, dispatch/operations assistant, captain and flight attendant are offered for illustration purposes. The relative complexity of an individual business aviation department will be dictated by the size and scope of the company operating business aircraft.

AVIATION DEPARTMENT MANAGER

The aviation department manager (ADM) is responsible for the safety, efficiency, and measurable performance of the flight department. The ADM is the immediate supervisor for the chief pilot (CP), manager of maintenance (MOM), and the dispatch/operations assistant (OA). The duties of the aviation department manager include, but are not limited to, the following:

- Formulate, coordinate, and implement policies and procedures for the safe and efficient operation of the flight department.
- Plan, manage, and control the scheduling, dispatch, operation, and maintenance of assigned aircraft and crews, within the bounds of company policy, to satisfy the travel needs and requests of authorized passengers.
- Ensure all associates' compliance with international, federal, state, and local regulations that apply to corporate aircraft operations, maintenance, and reporting.
- (Optional if qualified) Fly as pilot-in-command on company aircraft on a regularly scheduled basis, maintaining full currency and proficiency as a captain. Note: Many business aviation ADMs have a maintenance background and are not pilots.
- As the flight department's senior member, represent the flight department in all operational and administrative matters. Prepare, review, and/or approve all reports required by the FAA or other governing organizations.
- Establish and maintain an internal safety program such as safety management systems (SMS) to ensure compliance with approved operational, maintenance, and industrial safety practices.

- Provide for the selection, indoctrination, training, and upgrade of flight department personnel. Maintain the organizational development of the department.
- Establish and maintain a program for annual performance evaluations for all associates.
- Prepare and submit an annual operating budget to provide for continued operations of the aircraft and all support requirements. Monitor the budget on a monthly basis and make required reports to management.
- Review invoices approved by department heads for payment. Resolve any questions about the appropriateness of any invoice and ensure its accuracy.
- Review and approve expense reports for all direct-reporting associates and ensure all expenses are fully documented and explained before payment.
- Remain informed on aviation equipment, products, and services. Forecast and recommend to management any required capital purchase of new equipment. Approve and/or recommend the selection and design or modification of aircraft and associated equipment.
- Ensure the timely dissemination of all pertinent corporate and industry information to associates.
- Delegate authority and assign collateral responsibilities, additional duties, and special projects to other flight department associates, as required, to accomplish the administrative support requirements and to maximize department efficiency.
- Establish and maintain records of all completed flight activity and other supporting data. Keep historical records in sufficient detail and for appropriate periods of time to respond to internal and external audits, investigations, reports, etc.

CHIEF PILOT

The chief pilot (CP) is directly responsible for the implementation of the operations section of the general operations manual (GOM). All flight crew members report directly to the CP. It is the CP's responsibility to ensure the professional quality of each cockpit crew. The duties of the CP include, but are not limited to, the following:

- Fly as pilot-in-command on company aircraft on a regularly scheduled basis, maintaining full currency and proficiency as a captain.
- Provide for the selection, indoctrination, training, and upgrade of cockpit flight department personnel. Provide ongoing supervision for assigned associates.

- Establish and maintain a program for annual performance evaluations for all assigned associates. Recommend all upgrades when appropriate.
- Conduct flight checks on a periodic basis to ensure compliance with company SOPs.
- Establish a training program for all flight crew associates that ensures currency requirements and fosters professional development and growth. Maintain all training records for flight crew associates.
- Gather statistical data on a monthly basis that will validate the scheduling criteria for currency, compliance, fairness and workload balance. These data will be submitted to the director of flight operations.
- Constantly review standard operating procedures (SOPs) as they apply to individual aircraft and the overall operation. Issue all appropriate operations notices to the director of flight operations for approval.
- Work closely with the dispatch/operations assistant in the scheduling of all flights. Approve operations into nonstandard airports in conjunction with or in the absence of the director of flight operations.
- Construct and distribute an annual calendar which details training and vacations for all flight department associates.

MANAGER OF MAINTENANCE

The manager of maintenance is directly responsible to the aviation department manager for the airworthiness of all company aircraft and the integrity of the hangar and associated support equipment. He or she will ensure that inspections, maintenance, and repair of the aircraft are conducted in accordance with Federal Air Regulations (FAR) and the aircraft manufacturer's directives and bulletins. The duties of the manager of maintenance include, but are not limited to, the following:

- Direct the overall maintenance program for the flight department to ensure assigned aircraft are kept in the highest possible state of airworthiness and cleanliness.
- Support the internal safety program to ensure compliance with approved maintenance and industrial safety practices. Ensure that all maintenance safety regulations, as required by federal, state, and local authorities, are observed. Periodically inspect safety and emergency medical equipment and supplies.
- Provide for the selection, indoctrination, training, and upgrade of maintenance technicians. Provide ongoing supervision for assigned associates.
- Establish and maintain a program for annual performance evaluations for all assigned associates.

- Establish and carry out approved preventive maintenance inspection programs approved by the FAA and aircraft manufacturers.
- Implement policies and procedures for the safe and efficient operation of the maintenance department. Coordinate and recommend changes to policies and procedures, when required.
- Maintain valid licenses and certificates required to perform maintenance and inspection duties.
- Procure and maintain a personal set of tools sufficient to accomplish assigned aircraft maintenance tasks. Specialized tools specific to aircraft type will be supplied by the company. Note: Many business aviation departments supply a complete set of tools to maintenance personnel, the ownership of which is earned out over time.
- Supervise, monitor, and inspect the work of assigned, temporary, or contract maintenance personnel.
- Coordinate on a regular and frequent basis with flight crew members to obtain additional information when evaluating write-ups, to report back on findings and corrective actions, or to request in-flight operational checks.
- In conjunction with or in the absence of the DO, represent the aviation department on aircraft maintenance matters.
- When aircraft reside at the company hangar or maintenance facility, ensure the completion of all pre-flight and post-flight servicing and maintenance requirements, troubleshooting and repairs, inspections, preventive maintenance, and general upkeep of the aircraft.
- When aircraft are away from home station, coordinate with flight crews to monitor the maintenance status of the aircraft and ensure that necessary maintenance items are repaired or deferred in accordance with minimum equipment list (MEL) procedures, provide assistance in troubleshooting discrepancies, schedule maintenance work, and expedite parts deliveries.
- Be prepared to travel to the location of the aircraft to perform or supervise maintenance activities. Obtain and maintain passports and visas or tourist cards, current international certificates of vaccination, and other documents required to travel to foreign destinations.
- Determine if on-site staff supervision of work is required when an aircraft is taken to an outside maintenance facility for inspections, overhauls, modifications, or other major or extended maintenance procedures.
- Establish and maintain aircraft records in accordance with applicable FAA directives and manufacturer-approved aircraft maintenance programs. Ensure that all work performed away from home station is properly documented.

- Ensure that computerized maintenance records are completed and submitted in a timely manner. Review all reports and requirements to ensure accuracy and currency of the system.
- Keep a current library of maintenance regulations, manufacturer's inspection program documents, aircraft and engine manuals, and references for accessories, equipment, and components.
- Make necessary arrangements with outside vendors for invoicing and payment preparation.
- Maintain an appropriate inventory of spare parts and supplies and ensure that full accountability is maintained for all items.
- Monitor and control expenses in the maintenance area. Review and endorse invoices for payment. Resolve any questions about the appropriateness of any invoice and ensure its accuracy before forwarding it to the ADM for payment.
- Assist the ADM in the preparation of annual budget estimates by forecasting scheduled maintenance and estimating the costs of repairs, support equipment, inventory purchases, etc.
- Provide the ADM, the CP, and the OA with maintenance forecasts to aid in scheduling aircraft, especially when extended international flights are anticipated.
- Assume responsibility for cleanliness and general upkeep of the hangar, maintenance offices, and shop facilities, and associated equipment. Coordinate necessary service and repairs. Maintain relationships with vendors who provide appropriate preventative maintenance procedures on the facility, grounds, and safety and security support equipment.

DISPATCH/OPERATIONS ASSISTANT

The Dispatch/Operations Assistant (OA) reports directly to the ADM, in the administration of scheduling, service coordination and flight following of each planned trip for the aviation department. In addition, the OA is the primary point of contact for company associates on all matters pertaining to flights aboard aircraft operated by the company or chartered through outside vendors, and for other travel arrangements directly associated with these flights. The duties of the OA include, but are not limited to, the following:

- Plan and control the scheduling, dispatch, and operation of the aircraft within company policy to satisfy the travel needs and requests of authorized passengers.
- Maintain computer-based programs for flight scheduling.

- Maintain ongoing communication and liaison with corporate representatives and aviation department associates at home station to inform them of the location and status of the aircraft and crew. Coordinate additions to and deletions from passenger lists, and make necessary changes in planned itineraries.
- Coordinate the arrangements for ground transportation and hotel accommodations for the flight crews to ensure quality and cost efficiency is maintained.
- Prepare and print the flight schedules of all passengers aboard the aircraft, utilizing the current computer scheduling program and other automated systems, as required.
- Coordinate scheduling requirements and changes with operations and maintenance staffs.
- Maintain data for all flights of company aircraft into the recordkeeping program. Maintain charter flight activity.
- Maintain accurate records of flight activity for reporting and budgeting purposes. Compile, produce, and distribute reports, as required.

CAPTAIN

When assigned as pilot-in-command (PIC) for a trip, a captain assumes command responsibility for the aircraft and crew, and is operationally responsible to the chief pilot. When assigned as first officer, a captain is operationally responsible to the designated PIC for that trip. These relationships remain in effect, regardless of which pilot is flying the aircraft or which pilot seat is occupied. A captain's primary responsibility is to provide for the safe, comfortable, and economical operation of the assigned aircraft. While the captain may delegate flight-related duties to other members of the flight crew, the captain retains full responsibility for the aircraft and the overall performance of the crew. The duties of a captain include, but are not limited to, the following:

- Remain current and qualified in the assigned aircraft and be familiar with all regulations and procedures pertaining to its operation.
- Review all maintenance documentation to ensure the assigned aircraft is airworthy, with all required maintenance actions completed and signed off.
- Ensure that a complete pre-flight inspection of the aircraft is performed before each trip, and perform a walk-around inspection between flights.
- Ensure that the assigned aircraft is clean, properly serviced, and stocked with all provisions needed for a flight.

- Ensure that all members of the assigned crew are fully qualified, properly rested, and prepared for flight, have all required licenses and certificates in their possession, and are briefed on all specific requirements of the trip.
- Plan and review all aspects of an assigned trip, arrange for en route support requirements, and file flight plans. Use the services of international handling agents, when required, to complete necessary arrangements.
- Ensure that all crew members and passengers have, in their possession, valid passports and visas or tourist cards for the countries to be visited, current international certificates of vaccination, and other documents required for any specific destination.
- Ensure that all crew members and passengers comply with customs, immigration, and agricultural regulations of all countries of entry.
- Compute aircraft performance data and brief crew members.
- Fly the aircraft and supervise the performance of the crew to complete all pre-flight, in-flight, and post-flight assignments.
- Provide for the safety and comfort of passengers, and satisfy their needs and requests, within the limits of sound operational procedures.
- Provide for the servicing, maintenance, and protection of the aircraft at all times while away from home station. Coordinate closely with the COM for advice and assistance with maintenance requirements.
- Train and indoctrinate first officers to assist them in preparing for upgrade to captain status. Assist in training other crew members in the performance of their duties, when required. Provide individual appraisals to the CP, when requested, for preparation of associates' annual performance evaluations.
- Complete all required aircraft forms, logs, records, and reports. Perform additional administrative duties and special projects, as assigned by the CP.

FLIGHT ATTENDANT

When specifically requested or whenever the director of operations deems it necessary to provide the assistance of a flight attendant on passenger flights, a highly qualified flight attendant may be assigned to a trip. This will ensure the safety and integrity of the passenger compartment. The flight attendant is operationally responsible to the pilot-in-command for that flight. A flight attendant is primarily responsible for servicing of the aircraft cabin when it travels to locations where such care may not be adequately provided. The flight attendant will assist the cockpit crew in the operation of the aircraft and attend to the safety and service needs of the passengers. The duties of a flight attendant include, but are not limited to, the following:

- Before and after each flight, perform a thorough interior inspection of the aircraft cabin to confirm that it is prepared for the next mission. Ensure that all servicing needs are completed.
- Before and after each flight, perform a thorough inspection of the cabin and ensure it is cleaned, serviced, and stocked for the next mission. Particular attention will be paid to the availability, condition, and inspection dates of emergency equipment, the replenishment of cabin stores, and the receipt and storage of catering orders.
- Assist in the loading and unloading of passengers and their baggage and perform other services, as required, to expedite passenger arrivals and departures.
- Conduct safety briefings and ensure passengers know where safety and survival equipment is located and how to use it.
- Assist the cockpit crew, when the jump seat is occupied by the flight attendant, by acting as safety observer during takeoff and initial climb and during descent and landing. Scan for outside traffic, monitor instruments, or perform other duties, as requested.
- During en route phases of flight, perform assigned cabin duties. Monitor all activities in the aircraft and inform the captain of any situation or irregularity that could affect safety of flight.
- Serve food and beverages in accordance with company standards and applicable health regulations.
- In the event of an emergency, direct the actions of the passengers and assist them, when required, in the use of oxygen masks, emergency equipment, exits, etc. Check on the condition of the cockpit crew and perform other duties, as required by the situation.

PERSONNEL POLICIES

Human resources guidelines presented in this section are meant to augment those established by the parent corporation. In the event of conflicts, the ADM should seek guidance and clarification from the corporate human resources department. A copy of the flight department GOM should be issued to each associate at the time of hiring. Each GOM should be appropriately labeled with a tracking number to ensure the integrity of company publications and a means of updating periodically. A reference copy of the GOM should be maintained in the flight department's administrative files.

PERSONNEL RECORDS

Personnel records are an important aspect of human resource management. Previous experience, including education and past employment, should be included via a resumé upon initial employment. The contents of each employee's record will be dictated by corporate human resource policy. Any associate may review his or her own personnel records upon request to the human resources department. Copies of additional materials during the tenure of the employment of each associate should include at least the following:

- Data sheet listing the full name, current local address, and home phone number of the associate.
- Emergency actions data card, including names, addresses, and phone numbers of family members or other persons to contact in the event of an accident, incident, or serious illness.
- Hiring documents, including date of hire.
- Current position description, including documentation showing selection for or promotion to the current position.
- Copies of annual performance evaluations.
- Copies of correspondence that reflect on the performance of the associate, and any resulting letters of commendations or letters of counseling.

Pilot Records

An individual record of each pilot used in operations under FAR Part 135 must be kept for at least twelve (12) months after it is made and will include the following:

- Full name of the pilot.
- The pilot certificate (by type and number) and ratings that the pilot holds.
- The pilot's aeronautical experience in sufficient detail to determine the pilot's qualifications to pilot the aircraft in operation under FAR Part 135.
- The pilot's current duties and the date of the pilot's assignment to those duties.
- The effective date and class of the medical certificate that the pilot holds.
- The date and result of each of the initial and recurrent competency tests and proficiency and route checks required by FAR Part 135 and the aircraft flown during that test or check.

- The pilot's flight time in sufficient detail to determine compliance with the flight time limitations of FAR Part 135.
- The pilot's check pilot authorization, if any.
- Any action taken concerning the pilot's release from employment for physical or professional disqualification.
- The date of the completion of the initial phase and each recurrent phase of the training required by FAR Part 135.

JOB CLASSIFICATIONS

Associates who perform managerial, supervisory, or professional responsibilities are classified as exempt associates. This includes pilots, flight attendants, and maintenance personnel. Exempt associates are salaried and do not receive overtime pay. Note that some states classify maintenance personnel as nonexempt.

Outside employment on a temporary basis is discouraged by most business aviation departments. Although an employee's spare time is certainly his or her own, days off and vacation periods are provided to obtain critical rest and relaxation in order for them to be well rested and available for flight duties. Insurance coverage and questions of liability further complicate the issue when an aviation employee performs part-time work for other flight operations. Serious liability considerations may exist if one of your employees who has trained with you and is insured under your corporate umbrella is involved in an incident or accident while acting as a pilot for another corporation.

VACATION

Vacation policy is defined by corporate human resources policy. However, due to the special circumstances involved in the varied schedule workload, pilots and maintenance personnel usually accrue vacation days at a rate of two weeks during the first year, anniversary date to anniversary date, and similarly, two weeks during the second year. Vacations normally are approved on a first-come, first-served basis, but often it is necessary to ask flight crews to plan their vacations around maintenance down periods. However, depending on the size of the organization, no more than one flight crew member and one maintenance person may be scheduled for vacation and/or training at any given time. Department heads have to ensure that flying schedules and training periods are covered. A vacation request is typically not approved if it conflicts with an existing training schedule. If there are competing requests for vacation, the affected individuals may be able to resolve the conflict and request new dates. Vacation normally should be completed within the credited year. The DO may authorize the carryover of additional days only if the work schedule prevents an individual from using his vacation entitlement. Vacation time not used during the year, under normal circumstances, may be lost.

PERFORMANCE EVALUATIONS

A formal performance evaluation of all aviation department personnel should be conducted on an annual basis. A more informal, mid-year evaluation may be conducted in order to briefly meet with each employee/associate and ascertain how things are progressing. Although most employees tend to want to meet less than more, any opportunity, formal or informal, to provide praise or constructive feedback tends to be viewed far more as a positive than a negative. The ADM may specify a shorter period for an evaluation, if an associate's performance requires more frequent attention. The evaluation process is intended to be a two-way exchange of information. The annual review is typically used for goal setting and provides an excellent opportunity to discuss not only the professional attributes of each associate, but the opportunities for advancement that are in the future. However, an associate may request a verbal evaluation from a supervisor at any time to obtain feedback on job performance or to revise goals. Appraisals become a permanent part of the associates' personnel records. The evaluation form should be specifically designed for flight department associates, but must conform to the company's human resource standards.

PERSONAL APPEARANCE

Professional conduct and performance on the job are critical to an employee's success. In the business aviation community, a professional appearance on the part of company associates is very important to the enhancement of maintaining the professional image of the aviation department. Standards of dress and appearance should be defined in the general operations manual. Whether the company requires that a business suit and tie, an airline-style uniform, or casual business dress be worn, the entire department should maintain the same standard of appearance while in the workplace. As noted throughout this text, business aviation is all about customer service. If the aviation department is not constantly striving for the ultimate in customer service, the executives (customers) within the corporation will seek transportation support through alternate means. Sustaining the professional image of the department is a key factor in the overall reflection of the value added by the aviation staff.

The style of dress should be outlined for associates in order to cover instances where aviation employees are actively involved with work, visiting other company facilities, traveling on company business, and attending training courses at remote locations. Each individual should understand that in each of these instances, they are not only representing themselves, but they are representing the aviation department and the corporation that it serves. At all times, whether on duty or off-duty at intermediate destinations, associates should maintain a neat, clean, and well-groomed appearance.

WORKPLACE APPEARANCE

Of equal importance, the appearance of the hangar, aircraft, and work spaces is critical to the professional image that is projected by the aviation department. If the hangar is clean and the support equipment is stored properly when not in use, the projected image is that the aircraft and crews are equally, to use an old Navy term, "squared away." Structure and appearance project management skills. The executives who support the flight department's mission to provide transportation services to the corporation will certainly feel more comfortable flying aboard the aircraft that you are operating if they have a sense that the aircraft are well maintained. Coupled with personal appearance, the image that the workplace projects sets the stage upon which the overall representation of a safe and well managed flight department is viewed.

PERSONAL CONDUCT

Associates should be counseled and discouraged from participating in any activity that would create a poor impression of the flight department or the parent corporation or reflect unfavorably on themselves as company employees. Because of the unique relationship between flight crew members and their passengers, aviation department associates must be able to comfortably switch between a purely professional role, when providing air transportation and associated services, and a more relaxed and personal role, when invited to participate in social or recreational events. They must not allow informal friendships that may develop during social events to interfere with their professional service as a crew member. And they must not disclose or misuse any confidential information discussed or overheard during meetings with executives and business associates of the company.

Aviation personnel must be careful about discussing anything about the company, its business practices or plans, or its associates in the presence of persons who could misunderstand or misuse the information. Close attention should be paid and prior approval should be requested from the ADM before participating in any of the following activities:

- Making a speech or public statement that includes information about company operations or company personnel or business interests
- Writing for a publication, responding to a survey, or answering an author's or reporter's questions about the company or the aviation department
- Joining an organization or participating in a group activity as a representative of the company

To illustrate the impact extracurricular activities can have on the flight department mission, the following excerpt from an article in *B/CA* magazine is included (Cannon 2003):

> The cell phone goes off late in the day. You had just completed the first draft of next year's budget and sent it on to your boss for review. One of your senior captains is on the line informing you of an incident that has just occurred. It's not the aircraft that was involved, it's the other pilot. This was the afternoon of the second day of a three-day trip which included two nights at Vail. With an entire day to themselves, both pilots and the flight attendant decided to go skiing. This had been planned well in advance on their part, and arranged by scheduling because all three crew were experienced skiers: Interesting to note that you were not aware of this particular crewing arrangement that coincided with their common interest in winter sports.
>
> Yours is a large flight department with multiple aircraft and flight crew. The unwritten policy and usual practice has always been to, whenever possible, schedule crewmembers on trips to a destination that is meaningful to them personally. If someone's parents are near a common stopover, or the college they attended is in close proximity to an overnight on a football weekend, or both pilots are golfers and Scottsdale is on the schedule, your dispatch/scheduling associates usually try their best to pair up those who wish to be involved. You've probably endorsed this in the past because you understand full well the nature of business aviation. Pop-up trips, and changes in time and destination are common occurrences in our industry. Whatever you have been able to do to ease the personal pain of the impact of the schedule on your flight crew's lives has been important to the overall well-being of your department. More often than not, you've tried to accommodate requests for off-time, vacation, and personal preferences. That effort on your part, you've just realized, has been adopted by the majority of your personnel, to include activities during the hours of down time on the road.

So here you are with one of your young aviators in a hospital near Vail, with a compound fracture of the left femur. Outcome: emergency surgical intervention and prognosis of three to six months of convalescence. Result: you are down one crew member for quite a while. Impact: increased expenses due to hiring of a temporary pilot, and increased workload on the remaining flight crew. Since you are in the office and you're certain that your boss is also in, you pick up the phone, instead of e-mail, and deliver the news that you will be down one aviator for quite a while. His response catches you off-guard and has you scrambling for an appropriate response. "Why were the pilots out skiing when they are on a company trip?" are the words coming into the earpiece. It is a great question, but one which you hadn't really, up until this point, contemplated before.

It's certainly worth discussing the next opportunity you have to gather your aviators together. The subject for discussion shouldn't necessarily be what someone can or cannot do, but the overall responsibility that we have as employees to the company that is signing our paychecks every two weeks.

DRUG AND ALCOHOL USE

The nature of business aviation does not allow for any compromise of the safety and security of individuals who travel on the company aircraft. Therefore, each flight department is tasked with preventing any illegal drug use or any substance abuse (including prescription and nonprescription drugs, alcoholic beverages, or other intoxicants) by flight department members. Employees must be aware that they cannot report for work or attempt to perform any portion of their job responsibilities while under the influence of drugs, alcohol, or other intoxicants. Many corporations have incorporated policies which prohibit employees from using any drugs (for other than medical purposes) or consuming alcohol at any time while on the company aircraft, on company premises, or at any other location during duty hours. For flight crew members, the industry-wide accepted prohibition of alcohol consumption extends to 12 hours before the performance of flight duties. The prohibition of medical drug use typically extends to 24 hours before flight, unless a physician certifies, in writing, that flight duties can be performed while on medication.

Aviation employees will be expected to participate in a voluntary drug and alcohol screening program that incorporates a random selection process. Any associate who refuses to submit to testing may be subject to personnel action, up to and including dismissal from the company. A pre-employment screening will most likely be required. Any evidence of illegal drug use or substance abuse will be grounds for immediate removal from all duties directly associated with the aircraft. Dismissal from the company upon proof of substance abuse would be expected to follow in short order.

PILOT RETIREMENT

The retirement of any aviation associate is hopefully an occasion to celebrate. Following a long career in the industry, one of your employees has chosen to voluntarily separate from the company and take a break from full-time employment. If your company has a defined retirement program, there may be incentives in place to encourage senior associates to make the decision to retire at a predetermined point in time. Absent a defined plan, most corporations today do not offer this benefit, thus the decision to retire rests entirely with the individual. When the subject of pilot retirement is weighed, the discussion often centers on the appropriate age for a senior aviator to step down from the cockpit.

The following, "Pilot Retirement: When and How?" is taken from *Business & Commercial Aviation*, April 2006:

> At what point do you believe that it is appropriate for business aviation pilots to retire? The simple answer is that it doesn't matter what you think about how old someone should be before they retire, you cannot, by federal law, force someone to retire. There are great examples of senior pilots who are flying today past the age of 70. They are exceptional to say the least. Your dilemma as an aviation manager is to find a way to meet both the needs of the company and your aging pilot population.
>
> As the aviation manager, regardless of the size of the company or your staff, you may find it interesting to approach your senior passengers and inquire as to what their feelings are concerning senior citizens working in the cockpit of the company aircraft. Some will naturally find it comforting to see all that gray hair or lack of hair in general, up front. Probing a little deeper with the question of how long a senior pilot should be allowed to manipulate the controls of their multi-million dollar asset with its strategic cargo, you will receive answers all over the board. Some will say they don't have a problem with a 60-year-old as captain of the company jet. Others may stretch that age up to 65. Most will, to be honest, have concerns about what the appropriate age should be.
>
> Most of us work under state labor law regulations that are classified as, "employment at will." Certainly as business aviation pilots, we do not have union representation or are not paid by the hour. With few if any exceptions, we are salaried employees who can be terminated for cause at any time. What we cannot be terminated for in any state in the United States, is being too old. While our airline brethren are forced by the FARs to retire at age 65, under the current

regulatory atmosphere, business aviation pilots who operate under Part 91 are free to continue to ply their chosen craft indefinitely. When to retire? The answer will vary with each individual. Financial stability, health, family situation, working environment, and where you live will possibly all have an influence on the decision. Often, the needs of the company to move on with staffing and developmental issues may come into conflict with a senior pilot who is hesitant to announce his or her retirement.

What happens when you have a program similar to those offered above and a pilot, who is approaching eligibility to participate, declines the offer? One option would be to reassign that pilot to a non-flying job within the corporation. If you do so, be aware that if you fill that pilot's slot with a much younger pilot, the specter of age discrimination may raise its ugly head. If the aging pilot is placed into another position within the company, pay and benefits should remain the same. The question would be whether the pilot who had elected not to take an incentive package and retire from the cockpit can put up with a 9-to-5 job five days a week. While this may seem petty or nothing to worry about, you do need to contemplate all aspects of this tricky issue when proposing a specialized retirement program for your company's pilots.

PILOT DISABILITY

"Disability is defined as 'a disabled condition, incapacity, handicap, legal incapacity or disqualification.' According to a recent disability rate study, 90% of disabilities in the US are due to illness. The remaining 10%, due to injury" (Cannon 2008a). Statistically, three in ten Americans will become disabled for three months or longer before they reach the age of 65. During their working lives, one in five will suffer a disability that lasts more than one year. One in seven will be disabled for five years or more. As a pilot, what can cause you to become disabled? What restricts you from receiving a first class medical certificate?

FAR Part 67—Medical Standards and Certification; Subpart B—First Class Medical:

67.103 Eye: Distant—Near—Color.

67.105 Ear, nose, throat, and equilibrium: Hearing is demonstrated by the applicant through normal conversation during the physical. Few, if any, FAA medical examiners use a tone audiometric test.

67.107 Mental: Personality disorder, psychosis, manifest delusions, hallucinations, disorganized behavior. Bipolar disorder. Substance dependence, alcohol, sedatives, hypnotics, opiates, or central nervous stimulants such as cocaine, amphetamines and similarly acting psychoactive drugs. No substance abuse within the preceding two years. No other personality disorder, neurosis, or other mental condition.

67.109 Neurologic: Epilepsy, a loss of consciousness without medical explanation, transient loss of control of nervous system function without medical explanation. No seizure disorder, disturbance of consciousness, or neurologic condition.

67.111 Cardiovascular: Myocardial infarction, angina, coronary heart disease, cardiac valve replacement, permanent cardiac pacemaker implantation, or heart replacement.

67.113 General medical: Clinical diagnosis of diabetes. No other organic, functional, or structural disease, defect, or limitation that the federal air surgeon, based on the case history and appropriate, qualified medical judgment relating to the condition involved, finds.

If one of your staff becomes disabled and cannot return to work, he or she may be required, following the use of available sick time, to go on short-term disability. This is an insurance-driven process, purchased by the employer for each employee, and is designed to provide a portion of the disabled employee's salary for a period up to 90 days in duration. Many employers offer an optional long-term disability benefit which may be purchased by the individual employee or the cost is more often shared by the employee and the employer. Long-term disability insurance is designed to extend the benefit for up to two additional years, if the disability continues past the initial 90-day period. During both short and long term disability, the employee can expect to earn approximately 60% of the salary that they were earning prior to the disability. "Approximately 50% of large and mid-size companies offer Long Term Disability to their employees" (Cannon, 2008a).

The test for short-term is an either or situation: Has the disabled employee lost the ability to perform his or her normal job (occupation test)? Has the disabled employee lost the ability to earn more than 80% of his or her pre-disability pay (earnings test)? During the short-term period of disability benefit, the employee must qualify under one or the other, not necessarily both. The test for long-term is slightly more complex; typically, you must qualify under both tests. Long-term disability payments are taxable to the employee, if the coverage is provided by the employer. Just because the employee qualified for short-term disability does not mean that he or she will automatically qualify for long-term disability.

Disability programs are in place to protect the employee in case of a disability, but designed to incentivize the disabled employee to return to the workplace. The odds of not qualifying for an FAA medical sometime during a pilot's career are higher than you might think. Harvey Watt &

Table 8.1. U.S. Census Bureau 2006 American Community Survey

Category	Employed Population	Employment Disability	Percentage
Male: 16–20 years	10,939,399	292,648	2.6%
Female: 16–20 years	10,552,739	219,121	2.1%
Male: 21–64 years	84,582,607	6,313,321	7.5%
Female: 21–64 years	87,493,471	6,842,158	7.8%

Company stipulates, "As a pilot, you are more likely to lose your medical certificate during your career than you are to die." Table 8.1, from the 2006 U.S. Census Bureau, outlines the overall disability claimant figures for that year.

Employer-Sponsored Plans—This is packaged with a myriad of insurance offerings in most employees' company benefit programs. The employee does not pay for this insurance. All benefits received under an employer-sponsored plan, paid for by the employer, is taxable income to the recipient. Many states require employer paid disability programs.

Individual Disability Insurance Plans—This option is available to you at any time, but if your employer offers long-term disability insurance as part of your benefit package, you might want to balance the cost of an additional plan that you pay for. If you are paying for the policy, and you are disabled, the plan benefits to you are tax-free. The catch is that your supplemental insurance will be secondary to your employer's primary disability benefit. The result: you will, long-term, collect, say, 60% of your pre-disability pay from your employer's plan and then 15 to 20% of your pre-disability pay from your personal plan. Disability insurers will not, even in conjunction with another carrier, make you whole on your pre-disability pay.

Workers' Compensation—Every state in the United States requires employers to provide workers' compensation insurance. If you are injured on the job, workers' compensation insurance will pay a portion of your pre-disability income, typically two-thirds. It also will act as a form of medical insurance by paying medical bills related to the injury on the job. Workers' compensation insurance, depending on the state, may also provide coverage for economic loss created by the injury, past and future, general damages for pain and suffering, and benefits payable to the dependents of the employee if the injury on the job results in death. Most long-term disabilities are not covered by workers' compensation. The National Safety Council, *Injury Facts, 2004,* found that only 10% of long-term disabilities occurred at work. Most disabilities are not work-related.

State Disability Insurance—A few states, California, Hawaii, New Jersey, New York, and Rhode Island, as well as Puerto Rico, provide short-term disability for their residents. This coverage can run for up to six months.

Social Security—This is available to all citizens and acts as a floor beneath all the other disability programs. It was constructed and is available to prevent "abject" poverty. This is most often coupled with medical coverage for the disabled party. Social Security Disability is designed for those persons whose disability is so severe that they are unable to find gainful employment. Social Security Disability begins to pay benefits on the six-month anniversary date of the disability.

Veteran's Administration—If you are a veteran, you can qualify for long-term disability that will supplement the long-term coverage from your employer's policy. The difficulty for most disabled vets is that the VA will only pay disability to the most severely disabled. You would have to be in such a disabled condition that you could not work in any capacity before the VA would provide disability benefits.

LOSS OF LICENSE

National Business Aviation Association (NBAA) members may note that Harvey Watt & Company offers special packages to NBAA-member-company pilots. Harvey Watt has been serving the corporate aviation community since 1951. If you are not able to fly as a result of sickness that is insured through Harvey Watt, their payment schedule to you may be as long as 48 months and may be as much as $5,000 per month. There is a waiting period of six months before you can receive benefits. That six-month period allows most pilots an opportunity to regain their medical certificate and resume their careers. This particular insurer has three distinct monthly benefit plans as well as a lump sum plan that pays up to $250,000, if you qualify. It is important to remember that this is a supplemental plan that you can purchase with tax-free benefits or your company can purchase with the benefit paid to you in pretax dollars.

Pilots don't fit neatly into an employer's insurance portfolio. Most of the time, you are "out of network." The nature of what you do for a living is the exception rather than the normal 9-to-5 corporate office environment. When it comes to disability coverage and how well you might qualify should you lose your medical benefits, you might want to start asking the questions now, rather than after the fact. If your company's insurance carrier balks at the thought of disability for a pilot who cannot fly for a period of time, supplemental loss-of-license may be the best option.

MORE INFORMATION ON DISABILITY INSURANCE

Life and Health Foundation for Education
www.life-line.org
America's Health Insurance Plans
www.ahip.org
Department of Veterans Affairs
www.va.gov/
Social Security Administration
www.ssa.gov/
A.M. Best Company, Inc.
www.ambest.com
Fitch Ratings
www.fitchibca.com
Moody's Investor Services
www.moodys.com
Standard & Poor's Insurance Ratings Services
www.standardandpoor.com
Weiss Research
www.weissratings.com

The following is taken from the author's article, "Finding Balance," *Business & Commercial Aviation*, October 2008:

> When a flight crew member decides to leave his or her present position for another opportunity that has just been offered, quite a few things are put in motion simultaneously. First, how much notice is the—for discussion let's limit this to a pilot—employee providing to the current employer? Personnel directors will tell you that the expected amount of notice for any associate is usually equal to the number of weeks vacation that they are eligible for. That can vary from two to up to four weeks in most cases. For any employee in a key position that level of notice is never sufficient enough for the corporation. Regardless of whether the associate leaving the firm is an administrative assistant, corporate officer, or pilot, the void that remains after their departure in experience with the company is more often than not impossible to fill immediately. Perhaps you can find someone to fill in until they are up to speed, or even have the person leaving the company mentor the replacement during the notice period.
>
> Certainly in the case of a pilot, a large well-structured flight department can simply move a junior pilot up to a more senior position to fill the shoes of an experienced captain who has just given notice of imminent departure. The new hire would, in an ideal world, come into the bottom of the seniority list. Important to note, however, it is not uncommon for corporate departments

to immediately take the departing pilot off the schedule whenever notice of departure is first given. Somehow, the chairman may not be comfortable flying with someone who has given notice to his company.

The replacement scenario is not as easy for the majority of the business aviation community. Often in a single aircraft operation, there may be only two pilots. More and more single aircraft operations are choosing to employ three full time pilots to provide some sense of work-life balance to their crew members. When one of a very few decides to seek greener pastures, the impact is felt not only by human resources, but more directly by the remaining pilots whose workload just increased from filling the time or vacancy just created.

How long it takes to bring a new hire up to speed on company policies and procedures is dependent on the individual and the department. How long until that flight crew member blends into the operation depends to a great degree on how accepting the team is to a new member. In a small department, that may take some getting used to. In a larger group it is much easier to bring in a new person on the bottom of a seniority list than it is to inject a seasoned veteran into the left seat from the beginning.

Costs associated with hiring a replacement include: training, moving, materials and time. Training costs can include company orientation training, professional training at FlightSafety or CAE if the new hire is not qualified in your particular aircraft, and the time to train in the specifics of your flight operation. Moving costs will vary with the internal policies of the company, but it would be difficult today to hire an experienced pilot without offering to move his or her family to where your operation is based. Materials cost include uniforms and human resources' time to process the new employee into the company's employment and benefits programs. Time includes the fact that until this person is onboard and up to speed, you may be required to use temporary assistance or if fortunate to have a larger staff, work the staff at a higher level of intensity until the new team member is fully qualified. The amount of time will depend on the level of training and the distance of the relocation. A rule of thumb that seems to work in most cases is that the cost of a new hire can certainly approach and in some instances exceed one half of the annual salary that is being offered for the position in question.

REFERENCES

Cannon, Jim. (2004). Road tripping. *Business & Commercial Aviation* (B/CA), April 2004, 98.

_______. (2006). Pilot retirement: When and how. *Business & Commercial Aviation* (B/CA), April 2006, 95.

_______. (2008). Disability and the corporate pilot. *Business & Commercial Aviation* (B/CA), November 2008, 34.

_______. (2008). Finding balance. *Business & Commercial Aviation* (B/CA), (October), p. 73.

Federal Aviation Administration. (1996). *Code of Federal Regulations, Medical Standards and Certification, Subpart B- First Class Medical Certificate* (Part 67.101-113). Retrieved from http://rgl.faa.gov/Regulatory_and_Guidance_Library/rgFAR.nsf/0/062014b7986e11cb86257157006a6c8d!OpenDocument

_______. (2009). *Code of Federal Regulations, Medical Certificates: Requirement and duration* (Part 61.23). Retrieved from http://rgl.faa.gov/regulatory_and_guidance_library/rgfar.nsf/b4a0cab3e513bb58852566c70067018f/0e9c9d6aa9b4c6738625768f005c2e1a!OpenDocument

National Safety Council. 2004. *Injury Facts.*

9

Teambuilding and Communications

Learning Objectives: After reading this chapter you should be able to:

- Assess the importance of teambuilding to the business aviation department
- Demonstrate an insight into the importance of good communications to small group dynamics
- Outline the performance appraisal system as used in the business aviation department
- Tell how scheduling works in a business aviation department

The profession of aviation, regardless of the discipline, is very demanding. Developing your professional skills as an aviator or maintenance technician requires a commitment of not only money, but years of diligent effort. It doesn't happen overnight. This is a vocation where a pilot or mechanic must, as the saying goes, earn his or her stripes. That phrase implies an investment of time and on-the-job training. As a young professional, the initial steps on your developmental ladder are achieved in a relatively short period. Pilots accumulate flight hours and pass credentialing milestones for the private, instrument, commercial, and airline transport pilot certificates. Mechanics spend several years in training, apprentice themselves, pass oral and practical tests, and attend formal schools.

Remember when you were very young and you couldn't wait to get older? That same internal drive to achieve affects young professionals as well. Patience is a certainly a virtue in business aviation. Early in one's business aviation career, the desire to acquire another type rating, to qualify as captain, to fly the next interesting trip to an exotic destination, and to be compensated at a higher rate, creates a level of impatience that is often difficult to manage. There is much to learn and as the aviation manager of a group of young professionals you have the perfect opportunity to work on their development. Forming a core of aviation personnel that will deliver safe and efficient executive transportation is a challenging endeavor.

LEADERSHIP

Putting together high-performance teams in a small-group environment is indeed demanding. Assuming the mantle of leadership of a business aviation flight department first and foremost removes the pilot or maintenance technician from the floor of the hangar or the cockpit of the aircraft and refocuses his or her duties and responsibilities. Where you were once "one of the guys," you now are the boss. Where you were a team member, you are now a team leader. This is an important transition and is not to be taken lightly or without a clear understanding of the consequences and personal sacrifice involved. During the course of building a career, developing professional skills, acquiring additional attributes on the job and perhaps through educational pursuits, the aspiring manager dreams of the day when he or she will be promoted to chief pilot or manager of maintenance. When that day arrives, one of the important personal conversions that must occur is that the newly appointed manager is then also the leader of the team.

John Sheehan, author of *Business and Corporate Aviation Management* and longtime consultant to the industry, shared his thoughts on leadership:

> Without this critical element all the rules in the world won't make an organization perform well. There must be a means of transmitting a vision of what the organization is all about to get people to achieve excellence. If policies and procedures are merely enforced the operation will lack spirit and a sense of direction that mark great organizations. Note that *leadership* is required, not merely *management skill*. Inspiration, a sense of direction, counseling, and a role model are the elements that separate the leader from the manager. Management is obviously needed, but leadership wins in the end; good leaders can hire good managers, not the other way around. Leaders may already be good managers or they can get by with minimal management skills; managers often have a harder time becoming leaders. Yet, it has been proved many times that leaders can be and are made on a regular basis. The best part about becoming a leader is that if the leader-in-training truly believes in the organization's mission, and feels passionate about delivering safety, service and value, the battle is half-won. Passion seems to be the key; without it you may just be play-acting.

TEAMBUILDING

As with any construction process, building an effective team begins with a foundation. Without a solid base of support from the parent corporation, a business aviation flight operation will always be subject to the destabilizing effect of external factors. Most, if not all, of those factors will be beyond the influence of the aviation manager. In 2008, owning and operating a business jet was politically embarrassing to many organizations. Corporations whose leadership swayed in the direction of media opinions and quarterly financial results placed the company aircraft on the auction block, dismissed aviation staff, and simply rejected any notion that they were involved in the "wasteful practice" of operating a business jet. This certainly did not occur to the majority of flight operations, but it did to a sufficient enough number so that the value of the average operational aircraft decreased in value by more than 40%.

This phenomenon served as an important lesson to aviation mangers throughout the industry. The departments that survived the recession of 2008–2010 had established the validity of their services to the corporation long before the heads of the Big Three automakers asked Congress for forgiveness for using their company jets to transport them to the hearings. It is critical that a solid base of support exists from the parent corporation for the business aviation function. With that support, a team is much easier to build and develop—development that relies upon the relationship of the personnel within the team as the dynamic that is enhanced through effective leadership by the aviation manager.

Behavioral scientists in the United States were recognizing the value of teamwork by the 1940s. "The emergence and growth of the quality movement in the 1980s created a proliferation of teams and teambuilding in organizations" (Wesner 2010, p. 44). Forming teams where employees were empowered to participate in how their work product was standardized began to catch on. Although the dictatorial boss still existed, that form of incentive toward quality and process improvement was slowly disappearing. The famous Russian writer Leo Tolstoy is given credit for the phrase, "All happy families are alike; every unhappy family is unhappy in its own way" (Kipp 2000, p. 138). In addition to the synergetic effect of teamwork at achieving organizational goals, an important reason to build a team in a business aviation department is the fact that each of the functional job areas is highly dependent on the others. This is true not only in the cockpit, but also in other functional areas of the organization. This interwoven nature of the workplace jobs makes it essential that a high-performance team be built early on in the management process.

Working with people is one of the most challenging and yet rewarding experiences of a manager's life. In the cockpit, there are clearly drawn lines of authority and responsibility, based upon traditional values, the mission at hand, company standard procedures, resource management principles, and the working relationship of a professional flight crew. On the hangar floor, regulatory guidelines dictate many maintenance procedures; however, the ability of an individual maintenance technician to creatively troubleshoot, repair, and place the aircraft in an airworthy status by correcting discrepancies brings a unique aspect to the workplace. Regardless of the discipline, working with your subordinates rather than having them work for you is the recommended path. When people feel empowered and appreciated they tend to take ownership of whatever process they are working under. Teamwork is the path and leadership is the key.

Some additional thoughts from John Sheehan on teamwork:

> This is an often maligned and misunderstood term that is the capstone of successful flight departments. This means everyone rowing in the same direction, helping where they can, pitching in when the tough work falls on just a few—these are all examples of people working under a sense of mission toward a common goal. Team members don't really care who gets the credit or glory—they all benefit from it. What is the secret to good teamwork? Teams are formed and fostered by leaders and coaches who care. They are nurtured through a shared sense of mission, mutual respect, and enjoyment of a job well done. And, having a little fun along the way serves to reinforce the concept. While flight and maintenance crews are natural teams due to their daily tasks, real teamwork occurs when members of the flight department work together on non–job specific projects such as operations manual rewrites, hangar restoration plans, and aircraft suitability analyses. When people work together outside of their comfort zone, teamwork can happen.

One of the many challenges facing the aviation manager is how to allocate personnel resources. Within every operation there exists a laundry list of functions that must be periodically organized, developed, allocated, and controlled. Aviation entities run most effectively when they function through a set of guidelines. These rules inform all members of the aviation team how the corporation wishes that safe and effective flight operations be conducted. The seasoned aviation manager will ensure that these guidelines or manuals adhere to industry best practices. There are many examples to follow when constructing operational manuals. The National Business Aviation Association (NBAA) has created a *Management Guide,* for use by its members as a template for guideline creation. The International Business Aviation Council (IBAC) has created and promoted the concept of safety management systems (SMS) through its International Standard for Business Aviation Operations (IS-BAO) standard. The FAA has a laundry list of operations specifications for business aviation departments offering charter services under the approval of FAA Part 135 charter certificates.

These specifications are very useful when considering implementation of Part 91 criteria.

How detailed an operator, Part 91, wishes to be is often dictated by the resources that are available to create, implement, and manage operational guidelines for the flight department. Most operations adhering to this discipline have incorporated a general operations manual (GOM), a general maintenance manual (GMM), a safety management system (SMS) manual, an emergency response manual (ERP), standard operating procedures (SOP) for each aircraft type, and a training manual (TM) covering all aspects of training. For those flight departments that consist of one aircraft and four or five total personnel, these functions cannot be fully covered by the limited resources within the department, but can be condensed and combined to mirror the intent of a set of guidelines to follow. As noted in Chapter 2, Part 91 flight departments are not scrutinized to the level of a Part 135 charter organization. The flexibility to incorporate changes within the company's aviation guidelines without FAA approval provides the Part 91 operation more autonomy. This self-sufficiency allows a small flight department to integrate many of the manuals and guidelines into a single document, tailored to their particular operation.

A much larger business aviation entity may also choose to delegate many of the daily administrative duties and responsibilities to nonmanagement staff in order to foster a more participatory workplace. Delegation also provides individuals to demonstrate their motivation to advance within the management structure of the group. A proven way of allowing participation by most if not all of the departmental members is to form specialized teams. With the understanding at the outset of putting together functional teams so that the additional workload does not place an undue burden on the flight department, it merely offers developmental opportunities for those participants who wish to partake. Each flight department should already have a safety committee (team) consisting of members from each discipline—flight, maintenance, and administration—typically chaired by the safety officer or safety manager. Other team opportunities are communications, facility, customer service, standardization, policy, and training. Staffing teams with members from each functional area of the department also fosters relationships between maintenance technicians and pilots, line service and scheduling, senior managers and relative newcomers. Teams should meet at least once per quarter and should have agendas, minutes, and a chairperson. Participation will serve to educate and empower all aviation associates in the functioning of the department. Empowerment leads to a sense of ownership, which in turn has proven to be a powerful tool in creating effective work environments.

Setting aside time for team meetings within the scope of an active business aviation department is a difficult undertaking. A larger flight organization is more likely to be able to offer a participatory team environment than a smaller one-aircraft department. Being small doesn't mean that many of the team functions just described cannot be implemented; they simply have to be refocused and condensed. Communications within a small-group environment that consists of three to six individuals can be very effective if the atmosphere of empowerment has been established by an effective team leader.

> Dysfunctional teams . . . often unwittingly bar the door to change, whether pursued in the guise of strategic planning, reengineering, work redesign, or cultural transformation. They handle the inevitable conflicts badly, conduct themselves according to unwritten rules that limit their effectiveness, and waste time in "violent agreement." Members bludgeon one another over differences in mindset and style. They tacitly consent not to learn from their collective experience for the sake of keeping peace in the family or "staying safe." Alternately, everyone speaks his/her mind but no one ever changes it (Kipp 2000, p. 138).

SMALL-GROUP DYNAMICS

Managing a single-aircraft flight department involves some unique skill sets that may not be as prevalent in a larger, more complex business aviation operation. These requisite set of people skills focus upon personality fit and professional continuity among a finite number of personnel working in very close quarters. Flying with the same person day after day, working in the hangar with the same person either under your supervision or looming over you week after week, can lead to some interesting behavioral dynamics. Running a small flight operation is akin to being involved with a second family. The job, by its nature, dictates that members of the aviation team spend more time with each other than they do with their families. At home you influence your children for the sake of their development and well-being. With your significant other the challenge is to mutually work toward achievable goals. Working with other professional adults in a close environment requires that the manager develop unity and teamwork on a far more personal level than is required in a larger, more complex, organization.

Leadership in a small group is enhanced less by insistence or intimidation and more by coaching and cheerleading. Politically, be less of a bureaucrat and more of a diplomat. When you are having a bad day, everyone in your department will know it. You cannot hide behind the office door or somewhere within the hangar complex. Chances are, you don't have an office or the company does not own the hangar your aircraft is sheltered in. The office, to most single-aircraft managers, is the cockpit they work in. That office more often than not has another occupant, resulting in close quarters and not much in the way of private, quiet, reflective workspace.

The very nature of a small group mandates that everyone is pulling together in the same direction. As the manager you must gain the confidence of everyone you work with. If they feel that they can be themselves and have honest communication and feedback, you are on the path that will provide you with the necessary ingredients to effectively lead the organization. Prior to you being able to count upon the team's dedication to your leadership, you must win their trust. Your reputation as a professional practitioner and a reliable manager follows you very closely in the business aviation industry. If your ego gets in the way of your desire to have a cohesive team or if your management style is leadership through intimidation, you will not be able to keep your team members in place. People want to be part of something positive. They also want to feel like they are making a contribution that is appreciated by their employer and fellow associates. As the leader of a small group, you have direct control over these factors.

If your goal is to manage, work on your personal managerial development with a focus on certain aspects of small-group management. Learn the basics: how to get along with people and encourage them to use their gifts and talents instead of simply working for you. Work with your parent corporation to assess and provide needed services. Your company is your customer. The quality of the services that you and your team provide requires constant attention. Focus on developing your people and in turn, you will grow.

COMMUNICATION

The portable communication device that we all take for granted today, still called a cell phone, has virtually eliminated the possibility that you cannot get in touch with a member of your organization. One thing for sure, at the creation of this text, if the authors were to sing the praises of an application offered though AT&T, Verizon, Sprint, or countless other carriers, by the time the reader were to arrive at this spot in the book, technology would have advanced far beyond the point of reference. The cell phone via either voice or data has revolutionized communication in the world. The author can still recall standing tall before his then chief pilot in the summer of 1980, being admonished for purchasing a "beeper" in order to be more readily available to the flight department's scheduler. Our standby policy at the time dictated that you had to be within five rings of answering your home telephone or you were in violation of the operations manual. The chief pilot was not happy with my acquisition and felt that I had overstepped the bounds of company policy. "Those are mechanical devices and are prone to failure," my boss ranted. "You are not allowed to use that as a substitute for your home phone." While many would criticize my then-leader for his short-sightedness, remember that the first desktop computers were then just being produced. He had learned to fly when cockpits were a maze full of round dial instruments and the primary long-range navigation systems were subject to various amounts of drift. I relate the personal memory to impress upon you the ongoing need to keep abreast of technology, especially in communications. Hopefully we have all learned that in this marvelous technological age almost everything imagined can be created. What was somehow beyond the grasp of my old chief pilot back then pales in comparison with new applications on smart phones that allow crews to submit expense reports, file flight plans, obtain current weather, run pre-flight risk analysis, get directions to any address, and, oh yeah, receive a phone or text from dispatch alerting them to a pop-up trip. The iPad was just approved by the FAA for airline crews to carry aboard during flight. All of the en route charts, company manuals, quick-reference materials, performance, and more are contained on these seemingly magic tablets. Communications, how we send and receive information and data will continue to evolve and provide capabilities we haven't even thought of yet.

PERFORMANCE APPRAISAL

As mentioned in Chapter 8, "Human Resource Management," the performance appraisal represents the annual opportunity for the aviation manager and his or her direct reports to sit down and discuss how well they worked together during the year. Some organizations require mid-year personnel appraisals that are designed to reinforce goals and expectations. The style and timing of the performance appraisal will depend upon the parent corporation's personnel review process. The following "Employee Performance Appraisal" is included as a compilation of ratings and values. It is far more comprehensive than the typical appraisal, but is offered for the purpose of discussion and development. Writing and delivering an effective performance appraisal is a managerial skill that takes time to master. This can be an intense exercise for both the manager and the employee and should be approached in a planned and purposeful manner. This can be the most effective communication tool at the aviation manager's disposal.

Business Aviation Department
EMPLOYEE PERFORMANCE APPRAISAL

______________________ Employee Name	______________ Hire Date
______________________ Position Description	__________ Years in Position
______________________ Supervisor Name	

Notes for the Appraiser:

Please complete this form with care. Base your evaluation on the employee's performance during the current rating period only. Whenever possible, use objective, quantifiable measures to evaluate performance. Some categories will not apply to the employee being reviewed. In that case, use the "Not Applicable" rating. Specific examples of behavior that illustrate performance should be noted in the remarks. An employee whose work does not meet the standards for the position should be rated accordingly, informed of the problem areas, and advised of the actions necessary to bring his or her performance to an acceptable level within an appropriate time frame. Written comments should be structured to motivate, rather than criticize, the employee. Ask the employee to submit the "Employee Goals" sheet before your meeting.

The Weighted Concept

Because of the normal career progression steps within a flight department, an aviation staff member will become more responsible for higher-level duties as he or she gains experience and earns additional professional ratings and certificates. For example, a qualified captain or maintenance shop lead technician will be more involved in administrative matters than an entry-level person, and less accountable for management responsibilities than the chief pilot or manager of maintenance. For that reason, this performance appraisal form is weighted to properly evaluate an employee on his or her assigned aviation responsibilities. A matrix worksheet will assist the evaluator in converting the ratings to a properly weighted score, based on the employee's job and experience level.

Ratings:

1. **Outstanding:** Exceeds company standards: Performance meets and often exceeds business aviation standards. Employee consistently performs above aviation industry levels. Actively promotes safety. Employee has made significant contributions

to the ability of the organization to carry out its mission responsibilities.

2. **Superior:** Meets company standards: Performance meets and often exceeds FAA and aviation industry standards. Consistently high service standards are provided and significant end results are being achieved. Performance at this level is expected from a fully trained and highly experienced aviation professional.

3. **Acceptable:** Meets industry standards: Performance meets accepted FAA and aviation industry standards on a consistent basis. Employee has met and maintains certification requirements in all technical areas. An employee operating at this level of performance is considered competent and safe to operate and/or maintain the aircraft.

4. **Needs Improvement:** Below industry standards: Performance is at times below the level required for unsupervised operation and/or maintenance of the aircraft, but satisfactory progress is being made to becoming fully qualified. Trainees who have not mastered all technical aspects of the job may fall in this rating category.

5. **Unacceptable:** Compromises safety: Performance is below the minimum acceptable level required to work in the aviation industry. Work associated with the operation and or maintenance of the aircraft must be monitored to ensure safety.

6. **Not Applicable:** Work not rated: Category of work does not apply to this employee or was not performed or observed during this rating period.

Note: Use Part A (pages 3–4) for pilots, or Part B (pages 5–6) for maintenance personnel.

SECTION ONE: TECHNICAL AND OPERATIONAL PERFORMANCE

Part A. Flight Operations

1. **Safety**: Consider the pilot's overall commitment to safety of flight while operating the aircraft. Does the individual analyze situations and take the safest alternative? How does the pilot balance the needs

of the passengers and the requirement to make conservative go/no-go decisions?

CIRCLE RATING:	X (Not Rated)	5	4	3	2	1
Remarks						

2. **General Piloting Skills:** Consider a pilot's overall flying technique and decision-making ability. How is the pilot's basic flying technique (smoothness and accuracy)? Are the pilot's decision-making and appropriateness of actions based on aircraft situational awareness?

CIRCLE RATING:	X (Not Rated)	5	4	3	2	1
Remarks						

3. **Cockpit Procedures:** Consider the pilot's performance of cockpit duties as specified by the aircraft flight manual guidelines and supplemented by the business aviation flight operations manual. Emphasis should be placed on pilot teamwork (compliance with checklist procedures, standard call-outs, monitored approach procedures, etc.).

CIRCLE RATING:	X (Not Rated)	5	4	3	2	1
Remarks						

4. **ATC Procedures:** Consider the pilot's ability to understand and comply with FAA air traffic control procedures as well as ICAO procedures while engaged in international flight operations. Emphasis should be placed on pre-flight planning, familiarity and compliance with air traffic control procedures, oceanic procedures, ground handling at foreign destinations, etc. How well does he or she complete and file flight plans, copy and read back clearances, understand and follow ATC directions and clearance changes?

CIRCLE RATING:	X (Not Rated)	5	4	3	2	1
Remarks						

5. **Performance Planning and Management:** Consider the pilot's familiarity and use of performance charts and his or her in-flight management of performance. Also rate the pilot on his or her ability to work out reduced-performance figures, knowledge of weight-and-balance forms, and ability to determine most effective aircraft configuration for the situation at hand.

CIRCLE RATING:	X (Not Rated)	5	4	3	2	1
Remarks						

6. **Familiarity with Aircraft Systems and Equipment:** Consider the overall knowledge about the aircraft this pilot is assigned to fly. How well does he or she know the aircraft systems, engines, operating limitations, flight characteristics, and emergency procedures?

CIRCLE RATING:	X (Not Rated)	5	4	3	2	1
Remarks						

7. **Aircraft Systems Management:** Consider the ability of this pilot to understand and manage aircraft systems using safe and proper procedures. Emphasis should be placed on navigational and flight management systems.

CIRCLE RATING:	X (Not Rated)	5	4	3	2	1
Remarks						

8. **Crew and Passenger Communications:** Consider the employee's ability to communicate in a flight environment. How well does the pilot communicate with other crew members on operational matters? How effectively does he or she communicate essential information to passengers? Emphasis should be placed on conducting required briefings, dealing with passenger requests, and providing assistance with customs and other regulatory agencies.

CIRCLE RATING:	X (Not Rated)	5	4	3	2	1
Remarks						

9. **Maintenance Liaison:** Consider how the employee complied with maintenance procedures and directives that involve the flight crew. Does the pilot understand MEL procedures and fill out maintenance forms clearly and correctly? Does he or she perform pre- and post-flight inspections and look after the maintenance needs of the aircraft when away from home station? Is there a cooperative working relationship with maintenance personnel?

CIRCLE RATING:	X (Not Rated)	5	4	3	2	1
Remarks						

10. **Goals:** Rate and describe the employee's progress and/or completion of stated goals in the flight operations area.

CIRCLE RATING:	X (Not Rated)	5	4	3	2	1
Remarks						

Section Score:
Ratings: ___ + ___ + ___ + ___ + ___ + ___ + ___ + ___ + ___ + ___ = _____ Total
Item # 1 2 3 4 5 6 7 8 9 10 _____ # Items
Section Total divided by the # of Items rated in this section = ________
Average Sec. 1-A

Part B. Maintenance Operations

1. **Safety:** Consider the maintenance technician's use of safe work practices and overall commitment to safety while servicing and maintaining the aircraft. Emphasis should be on the individual's consistent use of shop safety practices, proper use of equipment, and his or her ability to analyze situations and take the safest alternative. How does the technician balance the priorities of meeting operational requirements and his or her completion of open maintenance discrepancies?

CIRCLE RATING:	X (Not Rated)	5	4	3	2	1
Remarks						

2. **General Maintenance Skills:** Consider the technician's overall maintenance skills and ability to complete assigned tasks. Emphasis

in rating this area should be placed on basic mechanical knowledge and aptitude, the appropriate use of tools, equipment, manuals, and references.

CIRCLE RATING:	X (Not Rated)	5	4	3	2	1
Remarks						

3. **Familiarity with Aircraft Systems and Equipment:** Rate the technician's overall knowledge of aircraft systems. Comment on those specific areas (i.e. electrical, avionics, and hydraulics) in which the employee excels or needs additional study and familiarization. Consider recommending schools to either improve performance or allow specialization.

CIRCLE RATING:	X (Not Rated)	5	4	3	2	1
Remarks						

4. **Performance of Specialized Skills:** Consider the technician's knowledge and use of training and specialized skills in highly technical areas. Has the employee used acquired skills and taken the initiative in repair work calling on his or her special talents? Does the employee share the technical knowledge with others?

CIRCLE RATING:	X (Not Rated)	5	4	3	2	1
Remarks						

5. **Inspection Program Procedures:** Rate employee's familiarity of and compliance with the manufacturer's approved aircraft preventive maintenance inspection program. Is the employee familiar with the requirements of the program, completing them in a timely manner? Are the documentation requirements completed and submitted in a timely manner?

CIRCLE RATING:	X (Not Rated)	5	4	3	2	1
Remarks						

6. **Knowledge and Compliance with Technical Manuals:** Rate the technician on his or her effectiveness in using technical-library references for systems familiarization, troubleshooting, maintenance work procedures, etc. Evaluate how well manuals and publications are posted and maintained.

CIRCLE RATING:	X (Not Rated)	5	4	3	2	1
Remarks						

7. **Parts Ordering and Inventory Procedures:** Rate the employee's performance in ordering, tracking, and receiving aircraft parts and supplies, logging them into inventory, and keeping track of on-hand inventories, exchange items and/or repairable items.

CIRCLE RATING:	X (Not Rated)	5	4	3	2	1
Remarks						

8. **Flight Engineer and Cabin Attendant Duties:** Rate how well the technician performs when assigned crew duties as a flight engineer. Consider his or her performance of servicing and maintenance duties when away from home station, crew coordination, and passenger service skills.

CIRCLE RATING:	X (Not Rated)	5	4	3	2	1
Remarks						

9. **Operations Liaison:** Consider how this technician understands and supports operations requirements and directives that affect the maintenance function. Does the employee understand scheduling priorities, crew duty considerations, and operational reporting requirements? Is there a cooperative working relationship with the pilots and scheduler?

CIRCLE RATING:	X (Not Rated)	5	4	3	2	1
Remarks						

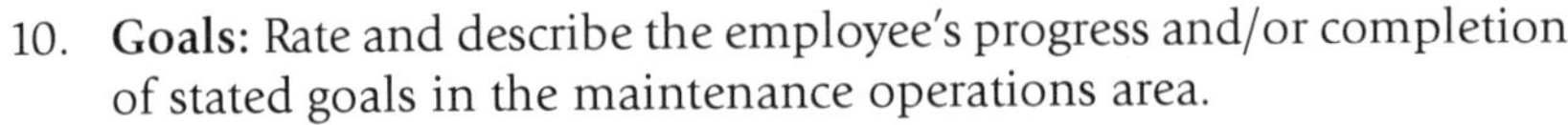

10. **Goals:** Rate and describe the employee's progress and/or completion of stated goals in the maintenance operations area.

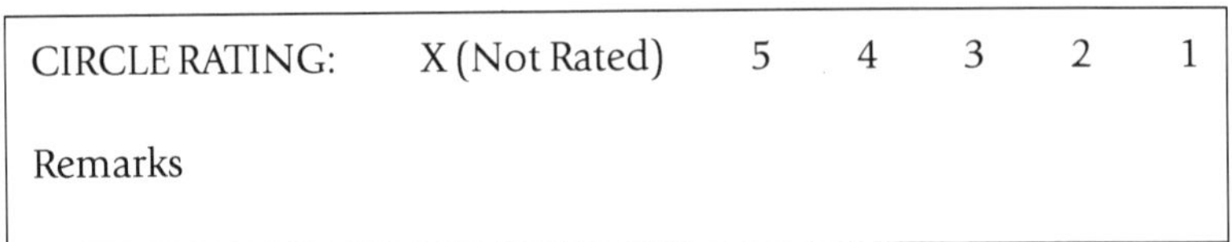

CIRCLE RATING: X (Not Rated) 5 4 3 2 1

Remarks

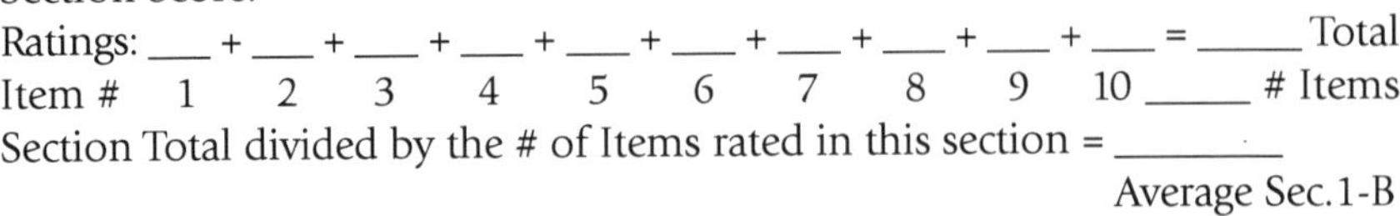

Section Score:

Ratings: ___ + ___ + ___ + ___ + ___ + ___ + ___ + ___ + ___ + ___ = _____ Total

Item # 1 2 3 4 5 6 7 8 9 10 _____ # Items

Section Total divided by the # of Items rated in this section = _______

Average Sec. 1-B

SECTION TWO: PROFESSIONAL PERFORMANCE

1. **Quality of Work:** Consider the accuracy, thoroughness, neatness, clarity, and technical competence of work performed. Additional factors to consider are the effectiveness of the volume of work produced as well as the speed and consistency of output.

CIRCLE RATING: X (Not Rated) 5 4 3 2 1

Remarks

2. **Time Management:** Consider how the employee plans, prioritizes, and budgets the use of time. Does he or she have a good record of attendance and meeting deadlines? How are organizational skills used to make the best use of time?

CIRCLE RATING: X (Not Rated) 5 4 3 2 1

Remarks

3. **Initiative and Acceptance of Responsibility:** Consider the independent initiation of action by the employee within the scope of his or her job duties. Rate the ability to accept responsibility for given tasks and follow-through on assignments. Does the employee find ways to do the job better and offer useable suggestions to others? Does the employee volunteer for or participate in group tasks?

CIRCLE RATING:	X (Not Rated)	5	4	3	2	1
Remarks						

4. **Interpersonal Skills:** Consider the employee's cooperation and ability to avoid conflict or resolve differences with coworkers, supervisors, and subordinates. How effectively does he or she deal with external contacts, such as headquarters staff members, executives and other passengers, flight-line personnel, FBO representatives, etc.?

CIRCLE RATING:	X (Not Rated)	5	4	3	2	1
Remarks						

5. **Communication Abilities:** Rate the employee's ability to express ideas clearly and concisely. How carefully and accurately does the individual listen to others when communicating with them?

CIRCLE RATING:	X (Not Rated)	5	4	3	2	1
Remarks						

6. **Professionalism:** Rate the employee's conformance with corporate and organization standards of appearance and behavior. To what extent do the employee's demeanor and work habits contribute to the flight department's reputation for quality and service?

CIRCLE RATING:	X (Not Rated)	5	4	3	2	1
Remarks						

7. **Confidentiality:** Consider the employee's concern for revealing or releasing information to those not authorized to receive it. How does the employee deal with information overheard while traveling with executives and business associates?

CIRCLE RATING:	X (Not Rated)	5	4	3	2	1
Remarks						

8. **Self Development Efforts:** Rate the employee's interest and efforts to improve knowledge and performance through formal education, technical training courses, self-study or professional reading programs, health activities, etc.

CIRCLE RATING:	X (Not Rated)	5	4	3	2	1
Remarks						

9. **Safety Awareness and Participation:** Rate the employee's support of the flight department safety program. To what extent does he or she participate in or enhance safety initiatives taken to reduce risks and eliminate accidents?

CIRCLE RATING:	X (Not Rated)	5	4	3	2	1
Remarks						

10. **Goals:** Rate and describe the employee's progress and/or completion of stated goals in the professional performance area.

CIRCLE RATING:	X (Not Rated)	5	4	3	2	1
Remarks						

Section Score:
Ratings: ___ + ___ + ___ + ___ + ___ + ___ + ___ + ___ + ___ + ___ = _____ Total
Item # 1 2 3 4 5 6 7 8 9 10 _____ # Items
Section Total divided by the # of Items rated in this section = ________
Average Sec.2

SECTION THREE: ADMINISTRATIVE SKILLS

1. **Work Habits:** Consider the employee's ability to organize his or her office and work area, keep track of work in progress and produce completed work products in a neat and legible form.

CIRCLE RATING:	X (Not Rated)	5	4	3	2	1
Remarks						

2. **Accuracy and Completion of Forms:** Rate the employee on the accuracy of work-related forms, such as flight plans, flight logs, MEL records, work cards, and other maintenance forms. Are the forms filled out with complete, accurate, and legible information? Are they of consistent quality, kept in accordance with established business aviation and company procedures, and submitted in a timely manner?

CIRCLE RATING:	X (Not Rated)	5	4	3	2	1
Remarks						

3. **Recordkeeping Skills:** Consider how the employee compiles and maintains required records. Are they complete, well-organized and easy to find? Can he or she produce back-up copies or reports from the records in a timely manner?

CIRCLE RATING:	X (Not Rated)	5	4	3	2	1
Remarks						

4. **Effectiveness of Written Communications:** Consider the extent to which the employee expresses ideas clearly and concisely in letters, memos, reports, and other written communications. Are the style, format, and content of the documents appropriate for the purpose of the communication?

CIRCLE RATING:	X (Not Rated)	5	4	3	2	1
Remarks						

5. **Performance of Assigned Additional Duties:** Rate the employee's acceptance and performance of additional department duties. Did he or she assume full responsibility for accomplishing the ongoing objectives of the additional duty? Was an appropriate amount of time and initiative spent to achieve desired results?

CIRCLE RATING:	X (Not Rated)	5	4	3	2	1
Remarks						

6. **Performance of Special Projects:** Rate the employee's abilities to accept and complete special projects. Were the results satisfactory? Was the work accomplished on time without close supervision required?

CIRCLE RATING:	X (Not Rated)	5	4	3	2	1
Remarks						

7. **Cost Control/Conservation of Resources:** Consider the employee's understanding and concern for controlling expenditures and making efficient use of available resources. Does the employee avoid wasteful work practices? Are parts and supplies ordered, approved, and used in a conscientious manner?

CIRCLE RATING:	X (Not Rated)	5	4	3	2	1
Remarks						

8. **Liaison with Corporate/Department Administrative Staff:** Consider how the employee works with corporate staff members, the department secretary, and the scheduling department. Is the employee cooperative and supportive when asking for information or administrative support? Does he or she keep administrators informed of work, training and vacation planning, work-related requirements, etc.?

CIRCLE RATING:	X (Not Rated)	5	4	3	2	1
Remarks						

9. **Knowledge and Use of Computers and Office Equipment:** Rate the employee's ability to effectively use personal computers and software programs, to include use of scheduling, recordkeeping, word-processing, spreadsheet and/or maintenance inspection programs. Is the person able to operate other standard office equipment, when required?

CIRCLE RATING:	X (Not Rated)	5	4	3	2	1
Remarks						

10. **Goals:** Rate and describe the employee's progress and/or completion of stated goals in the administrative skills area.

CIRCLE RATING:	X (Not Rated)	5	4	3	2	1
Remarks						

Section Score:
Ratings: ___ + ___ + ___ + ___ + ___ + ___ + ___ + ___ + ___ + ___ = _____ Total
Item # 1 2 3 4 5 6 7 8 9 10 _____ # Items
Section Total divided by the # of Items rated in this section = ________
Average Sec.3

SECTION FOUR: MANAGEMENT SKILLS

Note: The terms "supervisor" and "manager" do not limit the evaluation to only those duties requiring the supervision of direct reporting subordinates. This section should be used to evaluate any supervisory or management responsibilities associated with any leadership role taken by or assigned to the employee. This may be in the performance of additional duties or special group projects, shift work supervision, work done in the absence of a supervisor or manager, in-flight management of an aircraft crew or the supervision of temporary workers.

1. **Promotion and Support of Safety Programs:** Consider how the employee influences others to perform their duties in a safety-conscious manner. How does he or she enhance the effectiveness of the department safety program?

CIRCLE RATING:	X (Not Rated)	5	4	3	2	1
Remarks						

2. **Personnel Supervision:** Rate the employee on the effectiveness of motivating subordinates and structuring their work performance. How well did the employee assign and distribute work, encourage goal setting, monitor performance, and conduct appraisals to enhance productivity?

CIRCLE RATING:	X (Not Rated)	5	4	3	2	1
Remarks						

3. **Development of Subordinates:** Consider the employee's ability to coach, cross-train and develop individuals, using personal meetings and in-house or external training sources. How does he or she delegate responsibilities to further the development of others?

CIRCLE RATING:	X (Not Rated)	5	4	3	2	1
Remarks						

4. **Setting and Enforcing Professional Standards:** Rate the employee's effectiveness in promoting good work standards and professional behavior. How does he or she maintain standards for attendance, punctuality, conformity to established work rules, accepted behavior, and orderly work areas? Is the supervisor an appropriate role model?

CIRCLE RATING:	X (Not Rated)	5	4	3	2	1
Remarks						

5. **Departmental Organization and Development:** Consider the employee's efforts to enhance the overall development of the flight department, by setting goals, establishing priorities, encouraging team-building and organizing for maximum efficiency.

CIRCLE RATING:	X (Not Rated)	5	4	3	2	1
Remarks						

6. **Budget Planning and Control:** Rate the employee's ability to accurately plan and effectively manage those budget items under his or her control. How does fiscal performance compare to plan? What factors have influenced his or her ability to control expenses?

CIRCLE RATING:	X (Not Rated)	5	4	3	2	1
Remarks						

7. **Problem Solving:** Rate how effectively the employee anticipates or identifies problems, evaluates information, recommends sound and financially responsible alternative solutions, coordinates actions

and reaches desirable outcomes. How do his or her solutions fit with corporate policies and established procedure?

CIRCLE RATING:	X (Not Rated)	5	4	3	2	1
Remarks						

8. **Communication/Liaison with Corporate Executives and Managers:** Consider how the employee works with executives, managers, and coworkers in the corporation and its subsidiaries. How well does he or she communicate with them on essential subjects and anticipate their needs for information? How does he or she balance the demands for service with the capabilities of flight department resources?

CIRCLE RATING:	X (Not Rated)	5	4	3	2	1
Remarks						

9. **Management Development Efforts:** Rate the employee's interest and efforts to improve knowledge and management performance through formal education, management or supervisory training courses, and self-study or professional reading programs.

CIRCLE RATING:	X (Not Rated)	5	4	3	2	1
Remarks						

10. **Goals:** Rate and describe the employee's progress and/or completion of stated goals in the management skills area.

CIRCLE RATING:	X (Not Rated)	5	4	3	2	1
Remarks						

Section Score:
Ratings: ___ + ___ + ___ + ___ + ___ + ___ + ___ + ___ + ___ + ___ = _____ Total
Item # 1 2 3 4 5 6 7 8 9 10 _____ # Items
Section Total divided by the # of Items rated in this section = ________
Average Sec.4

PERFORMANCE APPRAISAL WORKSHEET

Instructions: After computing the average scores for each of the four sections in this performance appraisal form, bring the section scores forward to this worksheet to complete the rating process. Each score will be multiplied by an appropriately weighted percentage factor, based on the job level of the individual being rated. The total of the weighted scores will be used as the overall evaluation rating.

1. In the grid below, circle the four weighted percentages in the column directly under the job description of the employee being evaluated. Copy them to the % column in the box (step 3).

WEIGHTED PERFORMANCE DISTRIBUTION GRID

	Entry Technician	Specialist	MOM	Dept. Mgr.
	First Officer	**Captain**	**Chief Pilot**	**Director**
Technical and Operational	70%	60%	50%	40%
Professional Performance	15%	15%	15%	15%
Administrative Skills	15%	20%	20%	10%
Management Skills	0%	5%	15%	35%
	100%	100%	100%	100%

2. Copy the average score from each section to the designated blank in the box in step 3.
   Section One, A or B: Technical Performance — Insert in Block (1)
   Section Two: Professional Performance — Insert in Block (2)
   Section Three: Administrative Skills — Insert in Block (3)
   Section Four: Management Skills — Insert in Block (4)

3. Multiply the Section Scores in Blocks 1, 2, 3, and 4 by the grid percentage figures from above.

Section Scores × Grid % = Weighted Scores

________ × ____% = ____________

________ × ____% = ____________

________ × ____% = ____________

________ × ____% = ____________

Total Score = ____________

OVERALL EVALUATION

Based on the Total Score of the employee, as computed using this appraisal package, check the overall evaluation rating in the line scale below to describe the employee's overall performance for this rating period.

5 . . . . : . . . . 4 . . . . : . . . . 3 . . . . : . . . . 2 . . . . : 1

Unacceptable Needs Improvement Acceptable Superior Outstanding

Note: A computed total score of 2.49 or less will result in an overall rating of Superior. A computed Total score of 2.50 to 3.49 will result in a rating of Acceptable, etc.

Review Period: ____________ **Overall Rating:** ________________

What recommendations are made for training or an improvement plan? If so, when should it be completed? __________________

Overall Comments or Summary: ________________________________

____

____

____

____

____

____

____

____

____

____

______________________ ____________

Supervisor Signature Title –

I have read and discussed the ratings and the evaluator's comments in this performance appraisal form with my supervisor, and I have ____ have not ____ attached comments.

__________________________ ______________

Employee Signature Title -

EMPLOYEE GOALS

The following goals have been set for accomplishment during the next evaluation period. They have been agreed upon by the supervisor and the employee during the appraisal interview. At least one goal is suggested for each of the major rating areas. Additional sheets should be attached, if required to describe goals.

Technical Performance Goal:
Professional Performance Goal:
Administrative Skills Goal:
Management Skills Goal:

__________________________ __________________________

Employee Signature Supervisor Signature

Supervisor Comments:

SCHEDULING

Each operational division of a business aviation department is essential to the process of delivering effective transportation services to the parent corporation or organization. The paramount communication factor within the department is the scheduling function. Whether the operation consists of a single aircraft or is made up of a multi-airplane fleet, a position should be created, or an additional duty should be assigned, that provides oversight to and maintains a scheduling/dispatch/recordkeeping function. This position documents the scheduling and service needs of passengers, coordinates the availability of assigned aircraft and crew members, assists in accomplishing pre-departure arrangements for air crews and passengers, monitors the progress of missions, and verifies the flight logs. There is a clear differentiation between scheduling and dispatch. In order to dispatch a trip, the person holding the operational position of dispatcher, must have a current FAA Dispatcher Certificate. Dispatch entails placing professional value judgments upon the trip, generating flight plans, looking at runway performance issues, and evaluating the anticipated weather conditions. These tasks are typically completed by the PIC, but when a licensed dispatcher is involved with the scheduling process, they are able to discern issues regarding a proposed trip, prior to flight crew assignment. Within the ranks of many FAR Part 135 charter departments a licensed dispatcher plays a very important role in charter management and crew scheduling. Most FAR Part 91 scheduling positions in business aviation are filled with very qualified and experienced individuals who, although not licensed, understand the subtleties of putting a flight together and perform most if not all of the expected duties of a dispatcher.

Preliminary information about the trip will be gathered and an informal request for approval is then generated. A standardized form, scheduling sheet, should be used to relay, electronically, information about the passengers, itinerary, and flight-related services, including in-flight catering and ground transportation, to the scheduler at the flight department. The scheduler should initially train and periodically brief the executive assistants of authorized users of company aircraft on flight request procedures to ensure that information provided is sufficient to effectively process the requests. The scheduler should review the passenger lists submitted by requesting office and ensure that travelers are authorized or approved in accordance with company policy. It is important that a complete and accurate passenger list be assembled and filed for each leg of a trip. To conform to federal tax laws governing the use of United States–registered corporate aircraft, full names and affiliations must be recorded for each passenger, along with a brief description of the business purpose of their travel. If the trip is conducted under FAR Part 135 regulations, the passenger list will have to be compared to the Department of Homeland Security "No Fly List" to ensure compliance with current federal policy. The scheduler should coordinate with the appropriate individuals to obtain additional information about passengers, when required. Part 91 operations are not required to fulfill this requirement for domestic flights, but if the trip is international, the passenger manifest must be fixed by a minimum of one hour prior to departure and must be submitted for review. That applies when returning to the United States as well.

Typically business aviation flight departments will not transport passengers other than those requested and/or approved by executives authorized to request the use of a company aircraft. Exceptions may be considered for the following:

- Maintenance test flights: Maintenance technicians who are directly involved in the conduct of in-flight maintenance or evaluation of aircraft systems or equipment.

- Training flights: Authorized FAA check airmen and/or certified flight instructors who are actively training or evaluating department crew members.
- Emergency flights: Flights authorized by the company for humanitarian reasons; Corporate Angel Network and Angel Flight, for example.

The scheduler should inform the director of flight operations of all approved flight requests. The director of flight operations and/or chief pilot should review the mission parameters and other operational factors, validate the availability of aircraft and crew members, and accept or reject the trip. In the absence of the aviation department manager, the chief pilot would exercise operational control. Today, many flight departments are using pre-departure risk analysis tools such as Flight Risk Analysis Tool (FRAT) to ensure that scheduling and flight crews are reviewing all substantive factors prior to departure (Chapter 12, FRAT).

As changes occur, the scheduler will circulate a computer-generated aircraft scheduling report to inform the staff of planned aircraft use and open travel dates for the year. It is very important that the scheduler become the single point of contact for all information that may impact the flow of the original trip plan. Without the scheduler receiving and sending accurate change information, a communication disconnect will inevitably occur. Crews should consistently notify the scheduler with updates on the progress of each flight leg. The scheduler will in turn notify executive staff of arrival and departure times, either estimated or actual. The executive staff will communicate any requests that vary from the trip sheet that may impact the original plan. These changes would then be relayed to the crew and aviation management staff in the event that the change requests impact the overall risk factors and or viability of the proposed flight profile. In the event a trip request changes during the non-business hours preceding a trip, the scheduler is responsible for contacting all concerned parties, including passengers, other crew members, and maintenance personnel.

REFERENCES

International Business *Aviation* Council. (2011). *International Standard for Business Aircraft Operations* (IS-BAO). Retrieved from www.ibac.org/is_bao.

Kipp, Michael F. and Mary Ann Kipp. (2000). Of teams and teambuilding. *Team Performance Management*. 6(7/8): 138

National Business Aviation Association. (2010). *NBAA Management Guide*. Retrieved from www.nbaa.org/admin/management-guide/

Sheehan, John J. (2003). *Business and Corporate Aviation Management: On-Demand Air Travel*. New York: McGraw Hill.

Wesner, Marilyn S. (2010). Organizational learning: The enduring influence of organization development. *Organization Development Journal* 28(3): 41–46.

10

Budget and Capital Management

Learning Objectives: After reading this chapter you should be able to:

- Recite the four phases in the annual financial planning process
- Formulate a corporate flight department budget
- Construct a corporate flight department capital budget
- Discuss variable costs and fixed costs
- Explain how projected flight hours may be used to plan a budget
- Spread an expense budget
- Distinguish the difference between timesharing, interchange, and joint ownership
- Discuss how personal use of the company aircraft is viewed by the IRS

When you first begin the journey focused on becoming a professional maintenance technician, pilot, flight attendant, or operations specialist, financial forecasting is not one of the skills that you expect to acquire along the way. Surprisingly, for many who first move into a management position within business aviation, it is very important to possess a basic understanding of how capital is allocated and how costs are measured. Management of the day-to-day issues, department personnel, the company aircraft, support equipment, regulatory requirements, and the daily flight schedule take up a lot of an aviation manager's time. A close second in the overall consumption of the manager's time is financial matters.

It is important to understand one very critical truth concerning the business of business aviation, it costs a lot of money to purchase, outfit, house, crew, maintain, and operate a corporation's aircraft. As the aviation manager, you are responsible for a cost center that does not deliver an offsetting revenue stream. Your department is a financial burden to the company. The product that the men and women on your team produce is often difficult to measure. Time savings is a product that has worth; however, opinions vary greatly on how to quantify this service in dollars and cents. Due to this inherent conflict of how a company justifies owning and operating a business aircraft, many executives within the corporation will be skeptical of how much value your flight department adds to the bottom line. This is your political sparring match. It never goes away. When company profits are soaring, justification of the company jet is placed on a back burner. During difficult economic times, the aviation department will be looked at under a microscope.

It varies from one organization to another, but the annual financial planning process for a company can be broken down into four distinct phases: (1) planning, (2) budgeting, (3) recording, and (4) controlling or tracking. As the aviation manager, you will be intimately involved with the first two of these phases. To assure that company objectives are met, the planning phase is normally interwoven with and tied to the company strategic plan. This phase also usually involves company senior executives who set sales projections or production goals for the next year. These sales and production goals are then used to develop the revenue side of the annual budget. In order to properly plan for the upcoming year's activity, the aviation manager is required to comprehend the amount of expected flying during the budget period. Setting expectations for the upcoming year requires a full understanding of the previous year's flight history. The company may have been engaged in a developmental process during the past several years that is now complete. That process would have called out the company aircraft more often than normal. Working with the senior executive to whom you report in order to gain insight into the amount of transportation support the corporation will need during the upcoming budget year is a key element in your planning process. Meeting with other senior executives that have the authority to request the company aircraft is also very important. During these brief meetings, ascertain the amount of business and personal usage each executive is planning for in the upcoming budget cycle. Combined with these forecasts and full knowledge of the nature of previous year's flight activity, the aviation financial planning phase begins with a solid forecast of the upcoming year's flight hours. A critical step in this forecast is to coordinate with the maintenance manager to ascertain any planned maintenance that will take the aircraft out of service during the upcoming year. The next step in the process is forecasting the flight hours for each month during the next year. Understanding the frequency of flight operations is essential in order to properly distribute the variable cost portion of expected expenses throughout the budget period; more on variable costs later in the chapter.

The second phase in the financial and accounting process is called the budgeting phase. Before proceeding with an explanation of this phase, it is important to understand what is meant by the term "budget." The budget is a company's set of formal (written) statements of management's expectations regarding sales, expenses, production volume, and various financial transactions for the upcoming fiscal year. The aviation manager is typically only involved with two types of budgets: (1) annual operational budget and (2) capital budget. Both of these aviation-related budgets involve expenses based upon forecast need.

Capital budget items consist of major purchases that do not occur on a predictable basis. Capital goods also have an indentified useful life and may be amortized (to write off the cost over a period of time). Capital budget items require more justification before being approved. Justification for capital items could be shown by using certain financial tools; a detailed cost/benefit analysis, or a return on investment (ROI) study. Examples of capital budget items for a business aviation department would be the purchase of a new hangar, a new aircraft, or development of a fuel farm. Overhauling an engine, repainting the aircraft, and/or completely renewing the interior of an aircraft are also good examples of capital expense items.

The operational budget for a corporation is usually subdivided into smaller budgets for separate divisions that are functioning as individual business units. The business aviation department is an example of such a unit. The aviation manager's duties and responsibilities include preparation and submission of the annual departmental operational budget. The overall company budget is also the company's tool for both planning and control. At the beginning of the period, the budget is a plan or standard; and at the end of the period, it serves as a control device to help management measure the firm's performance against the financial plan so that future performance may be improved.

FIXED COSTS

The annual operational budget is concerned with the fixed and variable costs of operating all facets of the aviation department during the upcoming fiscal year (a corporations accounting year). Fixed costs are those items that are incurred by the flight department and must be paid on a periodic basis regardless of whether or not the aircraft is actually flown. These fixed or often referred to as "sunk" costs of operating a company owned aircraft are the expenses that commit the corporation to the aviation process. The largest of these is of course the aircraft itself. The cost of purchasing the aircraft is spread, in an accounting sense, over the designated "book" life of the aircraft. Company policy, referencing the guidelines of the Financial Standards Accounting Board (FASB) will designate a period of time over which the capital asset (aircraft) may be depreciated. The yearly amount of that depreciation schedule is calculated by subtracting the estimated salvage value, sales price at the end of the useful life of the aircraft, say 10 years, from the purchase price. The resultant figure is then divided by the number of years, 10, to yield the annual depreciation expense. When budgeting, the monthly depreciation expense for the aircraft will be one twelfth of the annual figure. If the corporation elects to lease the aircraft through a third-party financial institution, the monthly lease expense will replace the depreciation expense figure in the fixed portion of the budget. In order to depreciate an asset, you must own it. In this instance the financial institution owns the aircraft and leases it to your company; they receive the benefit, therefore, of the depreciation. This is typically the largest single monthly expense line item in the aviation manager's budget.

Large capital assets, a hanger that is wholly owned by the corporation, for example, may be treated in a similar manner. Other fixed costs associated with the operation of a business aviation flight department are: employee salaries and benefits; insurance; hangar support equipment that is not capitalized; annual training contracts; publications; software, and various miscellaneous administrative supplies. Fixed costs can be spread over the annual budget to coincide with the month when they are scheduled to be paid. Salaries and benefits are paid equally over the course of the year, with the exception of the month following annual reviews. In this instance, any anticipated average pay increase percentage should be applied to adjust this monthly line item. Again, the important distinction between fixed and variable costs is that variable costs are not generally incurred unless the aircraft is placed in operation.

VARIABLE COSTS

The costs of operating the aircraft expressed on a per hour basis are defined as variable costs. These may include fuel, oil, preventative maintenance, landing fees, flight planning services, crew expenses, catering, and designated reserve accounts for major maintenance projects. Fuel is the one variable cost that is difficult to estimate due to the volatility of pricing. Fuel is typically the largest variable cost in an aviation manager's budget. The maintenance manager is a key provider of current and viable estimates for hourly maintenance costs that can be projected forward. Although annual maintenance costs for major inspections may be closely estimated and hourly maintenance costs are often predicted within 5% of actual outlays, unanticipated costs of maintenance due to unplanned component failures can push the best of budget estimates beyond established variance limits. It is therefore recommended that an allowance for unplanned component failures, based on manufacturers high failure list analysis, be part of the variable budget process. Variable costs should be allocated throughout the annual budget on a basis of predicted flight hours per month. The best predictor of monthly usage rate is the historic departmental variations in average flight times from month to month in years past. Coupled with a good forecast provided by the executive management group concerning the upcoming years demand for the aircraft, the aviation manager is armed with a predictive tool that should bode well in the construction of a sound budget.

If understood and properly implemented, the annual financial planning/budgeting process can be used to the advantage of the corporate aviation department. To be an active participant in this process, the aviation department manager must have a basic knowledge of accounting procedures, financial terms and budgeting practices as used by the company. Without this knowledge of accounting terms and practices, the corporate aviation department manager may be at a disadvantage during the annual budgeting process. An understanding of the corporate strategic and short-term plans is also important in order to understand the direction that the company is going. Due to the size and complexity of the annual aviation budget, the aviation manager will most likely have assistance from a company associate within the finance department. This person will typically be the financial liaison to the aviation manager during the day-to-day coding and processing of invoices and the preparation of not only the budget, but additional financial forecasts as required during the year.

BUILDING THE BUDGET

Building a successful business aviation department budget starts with the right attitude. It can be thought of as a tedious and painful process that starts by setting short- and long-term budget goals that flow from strategic plans, with numerous submittals and re-submittals. A better way to think of it is to realize that the budget is the process that takes the abstract concept of providing on-demand company air transportation and gives it the resources necessary to bring the concept to reality. When thought of in this manner, one begins to realize how important the budgeting process is to completing the overall mission of the corporate aviation department. This gives motivation to complete the process. In addition to being properly motivated, the aviation department manager should study and understand the budgeting process as used by the corporation. Getting to personally know individuals in the accounting department that are responsible for preparing the budget can also be a great benefit because they can answer questions and provide assistance to help with the process.

Each year the budgeting process begins with the issuance of budgeting goals for each business unit within the corporation for the upcoming fiscal year. In years when the national economy is expanding and the company is doing well economically, the budget goals will be more liberal than in bad economic times. Budget managers should be aware of this and stay in tune with economic conditions. It is not a good idea to go against the tide and fight overly hard for a big budget increase in bad economic times. Budget goals are usually expressed by a desire to increase sales or profits by a certain percentage. This is usually a signal that conditions are favorable for an increase in individual business unit budgets. In the case of budget cuts, the options may be to cut out entire programs, or to eliminate individual line items in the overall company budget. Another approach is to have everyone take a percentage cut in their individual department budgets. If this happens, it is an indication that growth forecasts are not favorable and that budgets will have to be tightened. After the budget goals are set, budget worksheets are typically distributed that show the previous year's budget with actual expenditures. Spaces will be provided on these worksheets to fill in the amount requested for the next fiscal year. A column will be provided to indicate the percentage increase or decrease in the particular budget item from the previous year. Justification should be included for large increase requests. Once the worksheets are distributed, it is appropriate for the corporate aviation department manager to build the aircraft operation portion of the budget based on the number of planned flight hours for the next year. Table 10.1 shows a sample aircraft annual operating budget based on the NBAA template. This sample budget shows how the variable and fixed expenditures change for different hours of operation of the aircraft. In this case, the sample budget is calculated in such a way as to be specific to the aircraft and shows what the costs would be for a varying number of flight hours.

It should be noted that the cost per hour decreases as the hourly utilization increases because the fixed costs remain constant as the variable costs increase. Table 10.1 is an example of the differentiation of fixed and variable costs. Although the aircraft operational costs constitute the largest dollar value in a corporate aviation department budget, they are not the only items to consider when developing the annual budget. Salaries of all administrative personnel must be included. Non-aircraft-related cost items and fixed aircraft cost related items should also be included. Since fixed costs items remain approximately the same from year to year, the normal procedure is to use the previous year's budget as a basis for these type fixed cost items for the upcoming year's budget. It is appropriate to include a cost-of-living increase to personnel salaries, but most of the

Table 10.1. Sample Aircraft Annual Operating Budget

		Flight Hours Per Year		
	Cost Item	300	500	600
Variable/Direct Costs				
Fuel (price x GPH)	$650	$195,000	$325,000	$390,000
Maintenance				
Labor (hrs/flt hr x rate)	$90	$27,000	$45,000	$54,000
Parts	$80	$24,000	$40,000	$48,000
Engine reserves	$219	$65,700	$105,000	$131,400
Landing/Handling Fees	$12	$3,600	$6,000	$7,200
Crew Expenses	$120	$36,000	$60,000	$72,000
Catering/Supplies	$30	$9,000	$15,000	$18,000
Total Variable Costs	$1,201	$360,300	$600,500	$720,600
Fixed/indirect costs				
Crew Salaries	$180,000	$180,000	$180,000	$180,000
Employee Benefits	$10,500	$10,500	$10,500	$10,500
Hangar or Tiedown Costs	$5,000	$5,000	$5,000	$5,000
Flight Crew Training	$28,000	$28,000	$28,000	$28,000
Aircraft Insurance	$45,000	$45,000	$45,000	$45,000
Flight Publications	$2,500	$2,500	$2,500	$2,500
Miscellaneous	$4,500	$4,500	$4,500	$4,500
Total Fixed Costs	$275,500	$275,500	$275,500	$275,500
Total Costs		$635,800	$876,000	$996,100
Total Costs per hour		$2,110	$1,752	$1,660

other fixed costs normally remain the same from year to year. It is always good management practice to enter into contracts for multi-year periods for fixed-cost items such as insurance, training, and annual fee-based support products.

Each company has a different process of approving its budget and it would be impossible to include all the variations here. Table 10.2 is an example of how a typical budget worksheet may look. It contains the previous year's dollar values for each line item and the request for the next year's budget in a column format with variances and percent variances from the previous year. The reason is to allow senior management to see if there are any large changes in the budget from the previous year. The budget worksheet will conform to each company's standards, but will usually contain a description for each item to be contained in the next year's budget. The expense items for a corporate aviation department are also usually grouped as shown with personnel costs in a separate group. In the event a hangar is owned, these expenses are normally grouped together. If an aircraft lease is involved, all costs associated with the lease are usually grouped together.

Table 10.2 Budget Worksheet

Expense Description	*2010 Annual Budget*	*2011 Budget Request*	*$$ Variance*	*% Variance*
Personnel Costs				
Salaries	$ 616,603	$ 513,500	$ (103,103)	-20.08%
Insurance - Group Medical	22,376	27,560	5,184	18.81%
Payroll Taxes	41,919	38,512	(3,407)	-8.85%
Employer Contribution (401K)	8,659	9,715	1,056	10.87%
Administrative Fees	-	4,992	4,992	100.00%
Travel		16,600	16,600	100.00%
Training/Conferences	56,512	75,000	18,488	24.65%
Uniforms	4,772	4,000	(772)	-19.30%
Insurance – Disability	1,033	2,586	1,553	60.04%
Insurance – Worker's Comp	333	2,592	2,259	87.14%
Insurance – Life	373	594	221	37.15%
Physicals	5,492	2,500	(2,992)	-119.68%
Total Personnel Costs	758,072	698,151	(59,921)	-8.58%
Hangar Expenses				
Ac Spare Parts & Supplies	32,719	150,000	117,281	78.19%
Rent	114,000	114,000	-	0.00%
Security	-	4,840	4,840	100.00%
Office Expense	21,428	4,000	(17,428)	-435.70%
Insurance – Property	-	27,500	27,500	100.00%
Dues & Subscriptions	2,233	3,250	1,017	31.28%
Postage & Delivery	4,537	2,400	(2,137)	-89.06%
Equipment Rental	6,469	2,400	(4,069)	-169.56%
Plant Maintenance	-	1,200	1,200	100.00%
Cable Tv	859	650	(209)	-32.10%
Taxes & Licenses	7,167	-	(7,167)	-
Hangar Utilities	21,871	18,000	(3,871)	-21.50%
Commissary Supplies	3,371	10,000	6,629	66.29%
Hangar Maintenance	31,593	20,000	(11,593)	-57.97%
Other Hangar Expenses	77	-	(77)	-
Other Aviation Expenses	879	-	(879)	-
Fuel Farm Maintenance	6,475	3,000	(3,475)	-115.82%
Landscaping	6,963	4,284	(2,679)	-62.53%
Total Hangar Expenses	260,640	365,524	104,884	28.69%
Aircraft Lease	3,103,309	3,101,193	(2,116)	-0.07%
Aircraft Insurance	121,305	120,000	(1,305)	-1.09%
Aircraft Detailing	6,600	16,000	9,400	58.75%
Operational Dues & Subscriptions	4,493	36,000	31,507	87.52%
Aircraft Supplies	3,144	-	(3,144)	-
Other Aircraft Expenses	4,003	-	(4,003)	-
Total Aircraft Lease	3,242,855	3,273,193	30,338	0.93%

Flight Operation Expense				
Fuel	297,795	355,544	57,749	16.24%
Crew Expenses	172,353	130,144	(42,209)	-32.43%
Maintenance Parts	37,071	82,712	45,641	55.18%
Landing/Parking/Service Fees	12,452	58,800	46,348	78.82%
Catering	19,997	39,200	19,203	48.99%
Internation Handling Charges	23,437	25,000	1,563	6.25%
Total Flight Operation Expenses	563,105	691,400	128,295	18.56%
System Expenses				
Network	18,467	29,120	10,653	36.58%
Software	3,404	8,000	4,596	57.45%
Telephone	24,212	15,120	(9,092)	-60.13%
Total System Expenses	46,083	52,240	6,157	11.79%
Professional Services				
It Services	-	5,000	5,000	100.00%
Vendor A	109	-	(109)	-
Vendor B	7,679	-	(7,679)	-
Recruiting Services	667	-	(667)	-
Other Advisors	19,903	-	(19,903)	-
Total Professional Services	28,357	5,000	(23,357)	-467.15%
Depreciation And Amortization	56,715	13,888	(42,827)	-308.37%
Total Expenses	$ 4,955,827	$ 5,099,396	**$ 143,569**	**2.82%**

The flight operational expense items are transferred from the NBAA annual costs of operation template and included in the budget request. Other small items such as systems expenses and professional services are also usually grouped together.

Once the expense budget for the new fiscal year is approved, the next step is for the budget manager to spread the approved expense budget out over the fiscal year with planned expenditures for each month. Table 10.3 contains an example of how the personnel costs expense portion of the budget may look, once it is spread. This example is for a fiscal year starting on May 1 and only shows the first six months because of space constraints. Note that the planned expenditures may not be uniform for each month. Most accounting systems will also include a cost center and object code for each line item in the budget as shown on the example. Once the budget is spread and approved, the budget manager is responsible for monitoring the expenditures to see that they occur as planned each month.

Table 10.3. Example of Spread Expense Budget (over six months)

Fy 2011 Budget Submission Form
Xyz Group, Llc
Budget Manager: Joe Pilot
Department: Aviation/Cost Center 12345

Ln	*Object Code*	*Description*	*Annual Expense Budget*	*Spread Of Monthly Expense Budgets* May	June	July	Aug.	Sept.	Oct .
Budget Category: Personnel Costs (7001-7012)									
1	7001	Salaries	$513,500	42,792	42,792	42,792	42,792	42,792	42,792
2	7002	Insurance - Group Med.	$27,560	4240	2,120	2,120	2,120	2,120	2,120
3	7003	Payroll Taxes	$38,512	3209	3209	3209	3209	3209	3209
4	7004	Employer Contribution (401K)	$9,715	810	810	810	810	810	810
5	7005	Administrative Fees	$4,992	0	992	2,000	0	2,000	0
6	7006	Travel	$16,600	1,383	1,383	1,383	1,383	1,383	1,383
7	7007	Training/Conferences	$75,000	0	15,000	0	20,000	0	0
8	7008	Uniforms	$4,000	0	1,000	0	0	0	1,000
9	7009	Insurance – Disability	$2,586	216	216	216	216	216	216
10	7010	Ins -Worker's Comp	$2,592	199	199	199	299	199	199
11	7011	Insurance – Life	$594	0	0	0	66	66	66
12	7012	Physicals	$2,500	208	208	208	208	208	208
		Total Personnel Costs	$698,151	$53,057	$67,929	$52,937	$71,103	$53,003	$52,003

MANAGEMENT OF FLIGHT DEPARTMENT EXPENSES

During the course of almost every working day, the aviation manager will receive invoices from vendors for services rendered to the department. These invoices will represent work accomplished in a wide variety of areas: fuel changes, handling charges, contract maintenance support, Jepessen subscription fees, lease payments for the hangar forklift, commissary supplies, service fees for maintenance personnel uniforms, monthly service fees for the new scheduling software, etc. Other forms of invoice requiring approval are the expense reports from pilots and maintenance personnel who have been away from home during the course of flight operations, in training, or attending professional seminars. All these items and many more pass through the expense approval process. Large business aviation flight departments have the luxury of staff support for much of this work product, but it is the ultimate responsibility of the aviation manager to confirm the final approval of departmental expenses.

That approval is usually noted with a signature or initials, a date, and the all-important expense code designation. Each invoice should have all three of these approval requirements. The initial of the approval authority assigns responsibility for the action. The date of the approval initiates a timeline that is measured up to the date of eventual payment for the expense. The expense code assigned to the invoice indicates to the finance department where the expense should be applied in the departmental budget. During the course of the year, a business aviation manager will receive hundreds if not thousands of invoices depending upon the size of the flight department. Expense code assignment is the only way to maintain control of this process.

The following chart of accounts, Table 10.4, is offered to demonstrate how a manager would keep track of which code is to be assigned to a particular invoice. The expense code will correspond to the corporation's financial controls system using a unique expense code, often followed by a department code, and an interdepartmental code. At the end of each month, the aviation manager should receive a report from the financial liaison that will indicate how the department's actual monthly expenses compared to the predicted budget for the month. It is important to note any large variances from budgeted figures and be prepared to provide explanations for the difference.

CAPITAL BUDGET

The capital budget consists of a statement of proposed expenditures that is submitted separately from the operational budget. Examples of capital budget items for a corporate aviation department might be engine overhaul,

Table 10.4. Example Coding for Invoice

	Personnel Costs
7001-400-1630	Salaries
7045-400-1630	Contract Personnel Services
7002-400-1630	Insurance—Group Medical
7006-400-1630	Travel
7007-400-1630	Training/Conferences
7008-400-1630	Uniforms
7012-400-1630	Physicals
	Hangar Expenses
7315-400-1615	Ac Spare Parts & Supplies
7100-400-1620	Rent
7120-400-1620	Security
7400-400-1620	Office Expense
7200-400-1620	Insurance—Property
7700-400-1610	Dues & Subscriptions
7410-400-1630	Postage & Delivery
7015-400-1620	Equipment Rental
7905-400-1620	Hangar Utilities
7420-400-1620	Commissary Supplies
7315-400-1615	Hangar Maintenance
8900-400-1620	Other Hangar Expenses
8915-400-1620	Fuel Farm Maintenance
7325-400-1620	Landscaping
	Aircraft Expenses
7115-400-1610	Aircraft Lease
7200-400-1610	Aircraft Insurance
7305-400-1610	Aircraft Detailing
7325-400-1610	Service Contracts
7310-400-1610	Aircraft Supplies
8900-400-1615	Other Aircraft Expenses
	Flight Operation Expense
8901-400-1615	Fuel
7630-400-1615	Crew Expenses
7305-400-1615	Maintenance Parts
7810-400-1615	Landing/Parking/Service Fees
8905-400-1615	Catering
7805-400-1615	Internation Handling Charges
	System Expenses
7505-400-1620	Network
7300-300-1620	Software
7500-300-1620	Telephone

aircraft repainting, interior refurbishing, or other items that are capitalized for tax purposes. Establishing reserve accounts for capital items that are anticipated to be purchased or engine overhauls that can be projected into the future, allows the company to allocate funds on a monthly basis to offset the large outlays when the items are due. Other capital budget items such as a new hangar may require a return on investment (ROI) justification. Table 10.5 is an example of a list of capital budget items.

Capital budgets require a great deal of time to prepare. The aviation manager is not only tasked with running the daily flight operations, but is responsible for looking into the future and properly preparing the flight department to meet the needs of the parent corporation. In consideration of the current assets and personnel and hopefully armed with a forecast of the strategic direction of the corporation, the aviation manager must be able to discuss fleet replacement plans and future capital needs for support equipment.

FINANCIAL CONTROL

The fourth phase in the financial accounting process is controlling and tracking of the budget expenditures as they are made throughout the fiscal year. This phase begins once the budget has been approved and allocated, which normally occurs shortly before the beginning of the fiscal year. Each company has its own unique procedures for budget approval, but in most companies the budget is built and submitted for approval by the person responsible for managing the department where the planned expenditures will occur. This person also serves as the budget manager. Depending on the size of the department, the aviation budget may consist of hundreds of line items and may be very complex. The other extreme is to not have a budget at all. This can occur with smaller companies where the CEO absorbs the aviation department operating expenses within the administrative budget. Most budgets consist of many line items with each line item starting with two important features. These features are a short written description and a numerical code, called an object code. This is usually a four-digit

Table 10.5. Sample Capital Budget Items

June 2012 overhaul two GE aircraft engines	$195,000.00
August 2012 refurbish the cabin interior of N123FR at the at the Savannah overhaul facility	$146,000.00
Resurface hangar roof	$240,000.00
Total 2012 Capital Budget	$581,000.00

code and is needed for the computer to be able to refer to each line item when keeping up with the expenditures. The procedure normally followed after the budget is approved is to spread each line item out over the fiscal year, with planned expenditure amounts shown for each month. This way, the budget manager is able to track the expenditures on a monthly basis and see that the expenditures are being made as planned. The spreading may, or may not, result in an equal amount being spent each month. Some line items, such as dues or fees, may be expended in a single month. Most accounting systems have the capability to produce variance reports, or other reports, which aid the budget manager to keep track of expenditures and variances from the planned budget. A simple spreadsheet may also be used to keep track of the expenditures.

INTERNAL ALLOCATION OF AIRCRAFT COSTS

A basic decision that needs to be made by the company is how the costs of running the corporate aviation department will be allocated within the company. These costs may be allocated internally, or they may be treated as a service and absorbed by all of the divisions within a company. If it is decided to allocate the cost internally, a process should be developed to show how the costs should be charged to the users. The costs may be allocated to all departments within the company, or only to those departments or divisions that use the aircraft. The method chosen will have an impact on the use of the aircraft. A fully loaded chargeback rate incorporating both variable and fixed costs will tend to decrease overall use of the aircraft and encourage its use only at executive levels. Chargeback rates that incorporate only the variable operating costs will tend to encourage overall use of the aircraft at all levels of the company. Either chargeback method may be used depending on the company's preference. Whatever method is chosen, accounting records should reflect clearly how the transportation charges were made due to possible tax implications.

Another chargeback method used by some companies is a flat mileage assessment. A variation of this is to assess amounts that equate to commercial airline airfares between established airline points of service. Under this method, the company normally bears all of the aircraft operating costs in its headquarters account and is compensated in some degree by charges to divisions. An advantage of the flat mileage assessment is that it does not depend on commercial service being available between given points of desired travel. This method also remains constant no matter where the company aircraft goes. The difficulty with assessing flat mileage rates is that no basis may exist for comparison with airline economy fares.

Many corporate aircraft operators make use of the options for cost reimbursement provided by the FAA under Part 91, Subpart F of the Federal Aviation Regulations (FARs). These options include timesharing, interchange, or joint ownership agreements. Precise accounting is very important should the aircraft operate under these types of agreements to give some protection against being taxed as a commercial operation. Flights conducted under these agreements fall under Part 91 of the FARs, meaning that they are considered to be non-commercial for FAA purposes. The IRS is not bound by the FAA's definition of a commercial or non-commercial flight and takes a different view of these operations. This means that even if a flight is conducted under Part 91 of the FARs, it may still be considered commercial by the IRS for federal excise tax (FET) purposes. However, if accurate financial records are maintained it can limit the impact. When determining if a flight is commercial for tax purposes, the IRS first looks at whether or not any compensation changed hands in exchange for the flight. If the entity in possession, command, and control of the aircraft were to receive compensation for a particular flight, the IRS would most likely deem the operation to be commercial. This is why precise records are important. Before discussing each of these types of agreements it is necessary to have an understanding of the three terms as defined by the FAA.

Time sharing (91.501[c][1]) is defined as an arrangement whereby a person or company leases their airplane with flight crew to another person or company, and no charge is made for the flights conducted under that arrangement other than those specified below:

- Charges for fuel, oil, lubricants, and other additives
- Charges for travel expenses of the crew, including food, lodging, and ground transportation
- Hangar and tie-down costs away from the aircraft's base of operation
- Charges for insurance obtained for a specific flight
- Charges for landing fees, airport taxes, and similar assessments
- Charges for Customs, foreign permits, and similar fees directly related to a flight
- Charges for in-flight food and beverages
- Charges for passenger ground transportation
- Charges for flight planning and weather contract services

Through the use of a time-sharing agreement, an aircraft operator is able to seek limited reimbursement for a flight. Under this agreement, a company is permitted to lease its aircraft, with flight crew, to another individual or company. In return, the aircraft operator is permitted to receive reimbursement for a specific list of these out-of-pocket expenses associated with the flight, including an amount equal to twice the cost of fuel used on the flight without incurring a tax liability based on commercial use of the aircraft.

An *interchange agreement* (91.501[c][2]) is defined as an arrangement whereby a person leases an airplane to another person in exchange for equal time, when needed, on the other person's airplane, and no charge, assessment, or fee is made, except that a charge may be made not to exceed the difference between the cost of owning, operating, and maintaining the two airplanes. An interchange arrangement typically benefits two companies, each of which owns an aircraft. It is in effect a time-swap of a corporate asset. The exchange of time must be hour-for-hour, however when the two aircraft are of differing size and capability, a charge is allowed for the aircraft with greater value. The IRS has deemed that interchange agreements constitute commercial transportation due to the fact that one entity typically provides both aircraft and crew. With interchange agreements, the 7.5% federal exercise tax (FET) is computed on the fair market value of the hourly flight time for each aircraft used in the interchange agreement even if no compensation changes hands.

Joint ownership (91.501[c][3]) is defined as an arrangement whereby one of the registered joint owners of an airplane employs and furnishes the flight crew for that airplane and each of the registered joint owners pays a share of the charge specified in the agreement. How the joint ownership arrangement varies in the management and operation of the aircraft is of little concern to the IRA. One owner can provide all services, including crew while the other is permitted to pay their portion of the fixed costs and all of their use through payment of the variable operating costs as specified in the joint ownership agreement. Both owners must be listed on the registration certificate of the aircraft. Joint ownership aircraft are required to be U.S. registered and to operate under FAR Part 91 subpart K guidelines. There are some exemptions for small aircraft, but as a general rule, they must fall into one of the following groups to be able to qualify as non-commercial: (1) must have a maximum takeoff weight of over 12,500 pounds, or (2) must be a multi-engine turbojet aircraft (regardless of size), or (3) must be a fractional program aircraft (regardless of size).

The NBAA website also contains the description of an *Affiliated Group* (91.501[b][5]). "Under certain conditions, use of a business aircraft among affiliated companies may be permitted by the FAA. There must be a proper degree of affiliation between the entities, and the use of the aircraft must be 'within the scope of, and incidental to, the business of the company.' If these conditions are met, the FAA allows for inter-company charges on a fully-allocated basis. For IRS purposes, inter-company charges for affiliated group operations are exempt from FET only if the companies are connected by at least 80% voting stock ownership to a common parent. If this degree of affiliation does not exist, all inter-company charges could be subject to the 7.5% FET."

Charges for use of corporate aircraft may be made to subsidiary companies or by a subsidiary to the parent company or other subdivisions within the corporation. Although business aircraft that operate under Part 91, Subpart F, are classified as noncommercial for transportation furnished within the corporate structure, the IRS may question the appropriateness of certain charges for taxing purposes. During the course of a tax audit, the IRS may disagree with company's aircraft revenue reimbursement methods. For these and other reasons, some companies do not charge individual departments. Chargeback allocations should be charged against the total travel budget of the entity using the aircraft. Company aircraft operating costs seldom equate dollar for dollar to the cost of an individual airline ticket, and it must be recognized that basic costs for transportation do exist. The dollar-for-dollar difference only can be viewed in its proper context when it is related to time and productivity savings gained through using company aircraft, especially when operating with multiple passengers between airports not served directly with commercial airline service.

Some corporations consolidate all of the headquarters service costs, including the company aircraft, and divide those costs among all the operating divisions for a central allocation method. There are a variety of formulas used in this method (e.g., a percentage of net sales or a combination of sales, profits, and payroll). Each formula has its advantages and disadvantages. If the company has established a policy for distributing other central service costs, the aircraft probably would fit into the pattern without difficulty. When a division uses the aircraft, there are no costs allocated for a specific flight. Divisions that may have little need for travel or that are limited in use of the aircraft by company policy may resist this method of cost allocation. The central allocation approach remains a popular alternative with many companies.

HOW TO HANDLE PERSONAL USE OF THE COMPANY AIRCRAFT

The concept of owning and operating a business aircraft, by definition, implies that this viable transportation tool will be used in the course of moving company personnel solely for the purpose of furthering the interests of the corporation. On occasion, a dependant of one of the passengers will be invited to accompany that passenger. Whenever this happens, the company employee is deemed to have incurred personal use of the seat aboard the aircraft that is occupied by their family member. The company employee's income will be imputed (increased) by the value of the seat on that particular flight. This is mandated by the Internal Revenue Service (IRS) and is not to be taken lightly by the corporation in the course of conducting business aviation operations.

As the aviation manager, you are responsible for personal use record-keeping, calculation of the imputed income for each personal seat mile, and proper notification to each company employee that incurs a personal use event when aboard the aircraft. The amount of income is dependent upon whether the company associate is a "control" or "non-control" employee. A control employee is by definition limited to the top 1% of the company officers, or 10 officers, whichever is least, whose compensation is greater than $50,000 per year. A company director is also considered to be a control employee. If the person traveling owns 5% of the equity of the corporation, they are deemed to be a control employee. A non-control employee is logically everyone else in the corporation that does not qualify under the above conditions. The distinction is necessary to understand the level of the multiple that must be applied to the calculation of the value of the seat. Note that the multiples are expressed in percentages in Table 10.6.

The most frequently used method of a passenger's seat valuation of imputed income for personal use of a business aircraft is the standard industry fare level (SIFL) rating. SIFL rates for the six-month period from January 1, 2011, to June 30, 2011, are noted in Table 10.7.

Table 10.6. Control vs Non-Control Employee

Maximum Certified Takeoff Weight	*Control Employee*	*Non-Control Employee*
6,000 pounds or less	62.5 %	15.6 %
6,001–10,000 pounds	125 %	23.4 %
10,001–25,000 pounds	300 %	31.3 %
25,001 pounds or more	400 %	31.3 %

Table 10.7. SIFL Rates

Mileage Range	*Amount Per Mile*
0–500 miles	$ 0.2237
501–1,500 miles	$ 0.1706
over 1,500 miles	$ 0.1640
Terminal Charge	$ 40.90
Mileage Range	*Amount Per Mile*
0–500 miles	$ 0.2237
501–1,500 miles	$ 0.1706
over 1,500 miles	$ 0.1640

Table 10.8. Example Calculation

Number of Statute Miles	2,000
0–500	(500)*($ 0.2237) = $ 111.85
501–1,500	(1,000)*($ 0.1706) = $ 170.60
Over 1,500	(500)*($ 0.1640) = $ 82.00
Subtotal: (a)	$ 364.45
Aircraft Multiples (b)	31.3%
Subtotals: (a) X (b)	$ 114.07
Terminal Charge (c)	$ 40.90
Total: (a) X (b) + (c)	$ 154.97
Number of Statute Miles	2,000
0–500	(500)*($ 0.2237) = $ 111.85
501–1,500	(1,000)*($ 0.1706) = $ 170.60
Over 1,500	(500)*($ 0.1640) = $ 82.00
Subtotal: (a)	$ 364.45
Aircraft Multiples (b)	31.3%
Subtotals: (a) X (b)	$ 114.07
Terminal Charge (c)	$ 40.90
Total: (a) X (b) + (c)	$ 154.97

These rates are expressed in statute miles and are applied as indicated in Table 10.8: Example of a 2,000-statute-mile flight for a non-control employee's guest or a family member, per seat occupied.

Toward the end of the calendar year, the aviation manager is responsible for compiling all of the personal use charges, forwarding them to the finance department, and sending correspondence to each employee who had a personal use event during the year, informing them of the amount of income that was imputed. The employee's W-2 will reflect the increase in income and they are individually liable for paying the tax on the increase in compensation.

If there are bona fide security concerns for certain control employees due to death threats, the possibility of kidnapping, or a history of terrorist activity in the geographic area, IRS Section 1.132-5(m) of the regulations allows for the control employee to be charged at one half the rate stated in Table 10.8. The corporation must have a defined security program for the control employee or employees due to the nature of the business or the notoriety of the individual. The NBAA has published guidance on this subject: *NBAA Personal Use of Employer-Provided Aircraft Handbook,* at www.nbaa.org/member/admin/taxes/personal-use/personal-use-handbook; available to NBAA members. Other means of calculating the valuation of the personal use of a business aircraft can be found in this publication, however, the SIFL rate calculation method is the universally accepted practice of completing this task.

11

Aircraft Acquisition

Learning Objectives: After reading this chapter you should be able to:

- Appreciate the benefits of business aviation aircraft
- Know the purpose of a feasibility study
- Be able to list the steps for conducting a feasibility study
- Be familiar with the *B/CA* charts
- Understand the corporate aircraft selection process
- Draw a business aviation flight department organizational chart
- Be familiar with the process for acquiring a new business aircraft

BENEFITS OF BUSINESS AVIATION

The value of a corporate flight department is well established and widely accepted among many of the most successful U.S. corporations. The fact that over 66% of the largest corporations own and operate a business aircraft validates the benefits offered by this segment of the aviation industry. The growth of the hub-and-spoke airport system after airline deregulation enhanced the use of the company airplane, because of the inconvenience and delay when traveling by the commercial airlines. Additional security requirements instituted after 9/11 have added to the inconvenience of traveling by the commercial airlines and made owning or otherwise using air transportation services even more appealing. The airline industry's decline in service during the past two decades provided the business aviation community with an opportunity to excel. The industry responded with new technology-driven offerings in aircraft, avionics, cabin entertainment systems, onboard data management, as well as an increased focus upon the development of professional management services. While phone, fax, video conferencing, or e-mail obviously are ideal under many circumstances, some critical information sources—such as body language, the strength of a handshake, sequential or lengthy meetings or events, seeing first-hand the whole environment—make "being there" imperative. The greatest benefits to a company from the use of business aviation services are that it can increase management productivity, increase profit margins, and give the company a competitive advantage in the marketplace.

The benefits to a corporation from operation of a corporate flight department, or other air transportation services, fall into two categories: (1) tangible and (2) intangible. Tangible benefits are those that are easily measured and that can be quantified in terms of a dollar value. Intangible benefits are more difficult to quantify; however they may be very important to the success of the company. An example of an intangible benefit is the use of aircraft services in the retention of senior executives. It is difficult to place a dollar value on such a benefit; however, executive productivity is a salient factor in today's business environment. The NBAA has developed 10 general categories of benefits of aircraft ownership to which all others may be related as a subcategory. Table 11.1 contains the 10 major categories of benefits as listed in the NBAA *Business Aviation Fact Book,* published in 1997. They include both tangible and intangible benefits and are listed in order of importance.

Advantages of company use of air transportation services can also be subdivided into two areas, (1) advantages to the passengers and (2) advantages to the company.

Advantages to passengers

1. Time saved by reducing travel and airport waiting time
2. Increased productivity means more time at office
3. Reliability of scheduling and increased flexibility
4. Privacy/quiet, allows work en route
5. Productive private conferences en route
6. Retention of valuable executives
7. Eliminates hassle and delay at airport terminal
8. Improved security and safety
9. Arrive rested and ready to work

Advantages to company

1. Gives competitive advantage over competition
2. Allows the spreading of management talent over a wide area

Table 11.1. Benefits of Using Business Aircraft

Benefits of Using Business Aircraft	
Time Savings	Reduces flight time by providing direct point-to-point service; allows greater productivity while flying
Flexibility	Freedom to set own travel schedule and change schedule as needed
Reliability	Business aircraft are maintained to the highest standard of readiness
Safety	Outstanding safety record on par with large airlines
Improved Marketing Efficiency	Allows sales force to extend area and bring customers to point of sale
Facilities Control	Allows visit to outlying locations
Personal and Industrial Development	Additional mobility allows for companywide training orientation and teamwork
Privacy and Comfort	Allows for confidential communications on board aircraft with cabin configuration as required
Efficiency	Maximizes use of people and time
Security	Allows for control of all aspects of air travel

Adapted from NBAA (1997) *Business Aviation Fact Book*. Washington, DC. Used by permission of NBAA.

3. More frequent trips to remote locations
4. Quick response to market opportunities
5. Accessibility to areas not served by commercial airlines
6. Allows more decentralization of facilities
7. Reduces number of management personnel because of increased mobility
8. Increases revenues
9. Reduces per diem cost, fewer hotel stays
10. Increases overall productivity

OVERVIEW OF FEASIBILITY STUDY

There are two types of studies that may be conducted related to ownership and use of business/corporate aircraft. The first is a feasibility study; this type of study is applicable to a company that does not presently own or operate a corporate flight department. The second type of study is a justification study; this type of study is applicable to a company that already has a corporate flight department and wishes to see if the continued use is justified. Both of these studies are very similar in that they attempt to quantify the benefits so that a cost/benefit analysis may be made. Both of these studies also look at the travel needs of a company and compare the requirements to the capabilities of individual aircraft.

The objective of a feasibility study is to determine whether a company would be well advised to purchase ancillary aviation services or initiate their own business aviation flight department. Appendix B of the *NBAA Management Guide* contains a detailed description of the steps involved in a feasibility study.

Figure 11.1 is a graphical depiction of the overview of these steps. The final step is a decision on the specific type of aircraft to be based on aircraft costs, aircraft characteristics/capabilities, safety, and concern for the environment. As a general rule, if the projected benefits associated with the formation of a flight department exceed the projected costs incurred and the company budget supports the creation of the department, it should be recommended. There are a number of ways to acquire the use of aviation services that should be explored before making a final decision to establish an in-house flight department. Available options include aircraft chartering, aircraft leasing, joint ownership, co-ownership, or fractional ownership. As a first step, it may be advisable to utilize a variety of these services before developing a corporate owned and operated flight department.

Once the decision is made to procure a business aircraft specifically for the corporation, additional factors regarding aircraft selection and the design of the flight department must be considered. Aircraft selection is extremely important, because the aircraft selected must meet the company's travel needs. It's also important to select the most efficient aircraft available to meet these needs. Many experienced aviation managers utilize the *Operations Planning Guide* published each year in the August edition of

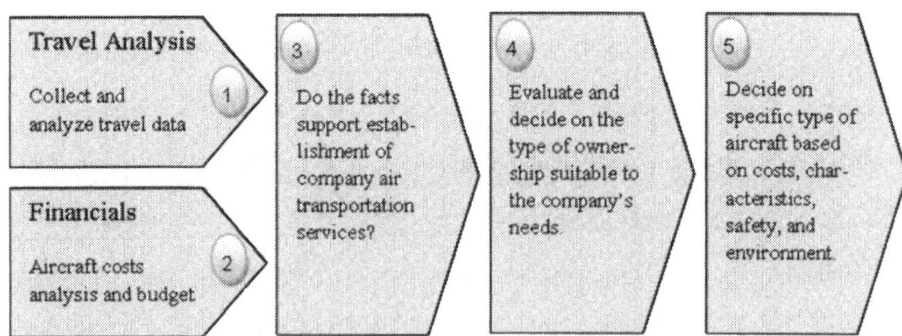

Figure 11.1 Overview of feasibiliy study steps. Developed by the authors.

Business & Commercial Aviation magazine as a starting point for any aircraft comparative analysis. The *B/CA* charts are an excellent source of standardized data with purchase prices based on a standard aircraft configuration. The charts also use a standard NBAA mission profile for each of the aircraft performance characteristics. This allows a more competitive comparison to be accomplished. Referencing the *B/CA* planning charts allows the use of standardized criteria, in order to fine-tune the selection process and arrive at the best aircraft to meet unique mission needs. Once the rough comparative analysis is complete the aviation manager may refine the process of aircraft selection through the use of a detailed cost analysis, break-even analysis, capital recovery analysis, and/or cost-benefit analysis. This methodology is the heart of a feasibility study. A series of practical examples and exercises will be discussed to illustrate how the process works. Completing these practical problems and understanding the concepts behind them is essential to understanding the feasibility study.

Whether or not the corporation already operates a business aircraft, or is considering the purchase of their first aircraft, the use of a feasibility study will enhance the decision-making process. As stated above, the process of determining if business aviation services are justified starts with a travel analysis. This is a simple tabulation of who goes where and when. Costs are considered and totaled and the costs are compared to commercial air travel to determine if company ownership of an aircraft is justified. A cost/benefit analysis is a convenient way to make this determination. A cost/benefit analysis can be either graphical or written, but a graphical depiction is normally used because it shows a side-by-side comparison that is easy to interpret.

ANALYSIS OF TRAVEL NEEDS

The first step in accomplishing a travel analysis is to collect a detailed description of all company travel over a period of time, a tabulation of the official travel record of everyone in the company. The recommended period of time to collect data is at least a year. To be able to complete a valid analysis of the total company travel needs, it is important to collect data on the travel of all company employees from the most senior executives to the lower levels of management. This is not an easy task and involves the collection of a tremendous amount of data, even for a small company. Gormley (1992) recommends the use of a spreadsheet to tabulate the data; List the places people go to (destinations) across the top and from (origin) down the side, with the number of passengers traveling and mileage between the origins and destinations identified in the appropriate cell. The spreadsheet format offers the advantage of being able to tabulate a large volume of data and to be able to add up the sums to unique destinations.

Once the data are collected, they should be transferred to a format similar to that shown in Table 11.2 so that additional analysis may be conducted to match a specific aircraft to these unique projected travel needs. The first column is equal interval distances from the company headquarters to destinations. Any interval can be chosen, but the number of trips in column 2 should match the distances shown in column 1. The third column is the percent in each individual interval and is arrived at by dividing the number of trips in each interval by the total number of trips. The last column is the cumulative percent of the number of trips in each column. The cumulative percent is arrived at by dividing the number of trips in each interval by the total number of trips and tabulating the total for each interval. Once the data is tabulated in the format as shown in Table 11.2, it can be used to construct a travel market graph. The travel market graph is a very useful tool for aircraft selection purposes.

Figure 11.2 is a travel market graph plotted using the data from Table 11.2. Examining the graph, it can be seen that distances are plotted on the x-axis and that both trips and cumulative percentage are plotted on the y-axis. Since it is not practical to purchase an aircraft that has the range to meet all of the company's travel needs 100% of the time, aviation managers use a rule of thumb known as the "85% rule" to help decide what range would be appropriate in order to satisfy company air travel needs. This rule can be explained by examining the travel market graph in Figure 11.2. Looking at this graph it can be seen that there is a red arrow entering the graph on the right side at the 85% mark and moves horizontally until it intercepts the plotted cumulative

Table 11.2. Distribution of Trip (in miles)

Distances	*No. Trips*	*Individual Percent*	*Cumulative Percent*
000–500	0	0.0%	0%
501–600	6	4.3%	4%
601–700	8	5.7%	10%
701–800	10	7.1%	17%
801–900	8	5.7%	23%
901–1000	7	5.0%	28%
1001–1100	5	3.6%	31%
1101–1200	20	14.3%	46%
1201–1300	10	7.1%	53%
1301–1400	0	0.0%	53%
1401–1500	8	5.7%	59%
1501–1600	15	10.7%	69%
1601–1700	20	14.3%	84%
1701–1800	8	5.7%	89%
1801–1900	10	7.1%	96%
1901–2000	5	3.6%	100%

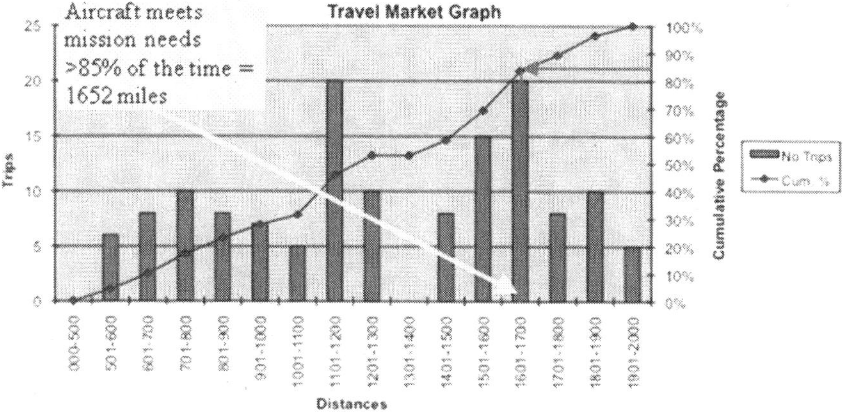

Figure 11.2 Travel market graph. Developed by the authors.

curve. The red arrow then moves vertically until it intercepts a distance shown on the x-axis. This distance is the range of aircraft needed to satisfy this set of travel market needs 85% of the time, without stopping.

The next step is to go into the *B/CA* Charts (see Figure 11.3) and examine each candidate aircraft with this range capability. For every market niche there are usually two or three competing aircraft. An examination of Figure 11.3 shows that the Cessna Citation XLS+ (CE560XL), Bombardier Learjet 45XL, and Hawker Beechcraft Hawker 750 have the capability to meet the range requirement as shown on Figure 11.3. The question is which of these candidate aircraft will best fit the unique travel needs of the company, at the lowest cost? In order to determine the best fit, it is necessary to establish a set of standard selection criteria and use a standardized selection process to arrive at a decision as to which of the three aircraft will meet the company's unique travel needs at the lowest cost.

AIRCRAFT COSTS ANALYSIS

Tabulation of aircraft operating costs as used in the aircraft selection matrix can be accomplished by using the NBAA-recommended template for tabulation of variable and fixed costs in order to arrive at the operational cost per hour and cost per mile as shown on Figure 11.4.

These operational costs are unique to the aircraft and may be used for aircraft selection purposes. Another very important advantage of using this method of tabulating operating costs is that it breaks the costs up into fixed costs and variable costs, which facilitates the use of a break-even analysis.

Business Airplanes

JETS 20,000 LB MTOW OR GREATER

	Manufacturer	Bombardier	Cessna	Bombardier	Hawker Beechcraft	Bombardier	Gulfstream Aero.
	Model	Learjet 40XR Model 45 (Learjet 40)	Citation XLS+ CE-560XL	Learjet 45XR Model 45 (Learjet 45)	Hawker 750	Learjet 60XR Model 60	Gulfstream 150 G150
	B/CA Equipped Price	$10,605,000	$12,450,000	$12,755,000	$13,015,560	$13,860,000	$15,050,000
Characteristics	Seating	2+6/7	2+9/12	2+8/9	2+8/9	2+7/9	2+7/8
	Wing Loading	67.9	54.6	69.0	72.1	88.8	82.3
	Power Loading	3.00	2.46	3.07	2.90	2.56	2.95
	Noise (EPNdB): TO/Sideline/APR	75.5/85.1/93.4	72.2/86.8/92.8	75.5/85.1/93.4	79.3/87.1/93.3	78.8/83.1/[illegible]	80.2/91.2/91.9
External Dimensions (ft)	Length	55.6	52.5	57.6	52.1	58.7	56.8
	Height	14.1	17.3	14.1	18.1	14.6	19.1
	Span	47.8	56.3	47.8	51.3	43.8	55.6
Internal Dimensions (ft)	**Length:** OA/Net	17.7/15.7	18.5/18.5	19.8/19.8	21.3/21.3	17.7/15.8	17.7/17.7
	Height	4.9	5.7	4.9	5.7	5.7	5.8
	Width: Max/Floor	5.1/3.2	5.5/3.9	5.1/3.2	5.8/4.8	5.9/3.8	5.8/4.1
Baggage	**Internal:** Cu ft/lb	15/170	10/100	15/170	47/995	24/350	25/180
	External: Cu ft/lb	50/500	80/700	50/500	32/500	24/300	55/1,100
Power	Engines	2 Hon. TFE731-20BR	2 P&WC PW545C	2 Hon. TFE731-20BR	2 Hon. TFE731-5BR	2 P&WC PW305A	2 Hon. TFE731-40AR-200G
	Output/Flat Rating OAT°C	3,500/ISA+25°C	4,119/ISA+10°C	3,500/ISA+25°C	4,660/ISA+10°C	4,600/ISA+17°C	4,420/ISA+13°C
	Inspection Interval	5,000t	5,000t	5,000t	3,200s	6,500t	6,000c
Weights (lb)	Max Ramp	21,250	20,400	21,750	27,100	23,750	26,250
	Max Takeoff	21,000	20,200	21,500	27,000	23,500	26,100
	Max Landing	19,200	18,700	19,200	23,350	19,500	21,700
	Zero Fuel	16,000	15,100	16,000	18,450	17,000	17,500
	BOW	13,950	12,800	14,140	16,250	14,903	15,200
	Max Payload	2,050	2,300	1,850	2,200	2,098	2,300
	Useful Load	7,300	7,600	7,610	10,700	8,848	11,050
	Executive Payload	1,200	1,800	1,600	1,800	1,400	1,400
	Max Fuel	5,375	6,740	6,062	8,500	7,910	10,300
	Available Payload w/Max Fuel	1,925	860	1,544	2,200	938	750
	Available Fuel w/Max Payload	5,250	5,300	5,760	8,500	6,750	8,750
	Available Fuel w/Executive Payload	5,375	5,800	6,010	8,500	7,448	9,650
Limits	Mmo	0.810	0.750	0.810	0.800	0.810	0.850
	FL/Vmo	FL 270/330	FL 260/305	FL 270/330	FL 290/310	FL 270/330	FL 300/330
	PSI	9.4	9.3	9.4	8.6	9.4	8.8
Airport Performance	TOFL (SL elev., ISA temp.)	4,680	3,560	5,040	4,696	5,450	5,032
	TOFL (5,000-ft elev. @ 25°C)	6,210	5,430	5,824	7,123	8,520	8,120
	Restricted Weight Limit	19,995	20,200	20,876	25,400	23,370	25,105
	NBAA IFR Range	1,590	1,764	1,830	2,160	2,264	2,986
	V2 (SL ISA MTOW)	123	118	130	138	147	135
	Vref w/4 Pax NBAA IFR Res.	113	106	114	119	131	115
	Landing Distance w/4 Pax NBAA IFR Res.	2,355	2,132	2,373	2,245	3,539	2,442
Climb	Time to Climb/Altitude	15/FL 370	15/FL 370	15/FL 370	19/FL 370	13/FL 370	17/FL 370
	FAR 25 Engine Out Rate (fpm)	394	765	589	592	718	438
	FAR 25 Engine Out Gradient (ft/nm)	392	369	272	238	293	201
Ceilings (ft)	Certificated	51,000	45,000	51,000	41,000	51,000	45,000
	All-Engine Service	45,200	46,000	44,700	39,000	42,400	42,400
	Engine Out Service	28,400	26,600	27,900	18,800	24,300	26,400
	Sea Level Cabin	25,700	25,230	25,700	22,200	25,700	23,000
Cruise	TAS	435	353	437	402	423	430
	Fuel Flow	964	861	998	1,214	1,127	1,184
	Altitude	FL 470	FL 450	FL 470	FL 410	FL 430	FL 430
	Specific Range	0.451	0.410	0.438	0.331	0.375	0.363
	TAS	445	431	448	447	446	475
	Fuel Flow	1,077	1,238	1,072	1,824	1,294	1,938
	Altitude	FL 470	FL 410	FL 490	FL 370	FL 410	FL 350
	Specific Range	0.413	0.348	0.418	0.245	0.345	0.245
NBAA IFR Range (200-nm alternate)	Nautical Miles	1,367	1,150	1,357	1,928	1,745	2,335
	Average Speed	421	384	421	392	414	415
	Trip Fuel	3,756	3,663	4,254	6,790	5,250	7,265
	Specific Range/Altitude	0.360/FL 450	0.314/FL 450	0.366/FL 450	0.293/FL 390	0.332/FL 410	0.321/FL 450
	Nautical Miles	1,426	1,746	1,556	1,978	2,264	3,011
	Average Speed	421	386	423	392	416	418
	Trip Fuel	3,687	5,238	4,085	6,750	6,490	8,003
	Specific Range/Altitude	0.367/FL 470	0.333/FL 450	0.372/FL 470	0.293/FL 390	0.346/FL 410	0.338/FL 450
	Nautical Miles	1,590	1,760	1,830	[illegible]	2,293	3,068
	Average Speed	423	396	428	392	415	418
	Trip Fuel	4,074	5,233	4,730	6,856	6,598	8,860
	Specific Range/Altitude	0.390/FL 470	0.333/FL 450	0.385/FL 450	0.307/FL 390	0.348/FL 410	0.338/FL 430
	Nautical Miles	1,884	1,780	1,938	2,168	2,470	3,122
	Average Speed	424	402	425	393	414	419
	Trip Fuel	4,127	6,272	4,797	6,909	6,647	8,945
	Specific Range/Altitude	0.409/FL 490	0.349/FL 450	0.404/FL 490	0.313/FL 390	0.361/FL 410	0.349/FL 450
Missions (4 passengers)	Runway	3,429	2,737	3,578	3,750	3,364	3,623
	Flight Time	0+43	0+46	0+44	0+50	0+43	0+50
	Fuel Used	1,288	1,244	1,258	1,640	1,263	1,230
	Specific Range/Altitude	0.240/FL 370	0.241/FL 300	0.238/FL 370	0.224/FL 430	0.238/FL 370	0.244/FL 450
	Runway	3,860	2,743	3,598	3,824	3,585	3,785
	Flight Time	1+23	1+29	1+24	1+31	1+29	1+32
	Fuel Used	1,625	2,060	1,934	2,372	2,013	1,974
	Specific Range/Altitude	0.312/FL 450	0.287/FL 410	0.310/FL 450	0.263/FL 410	0.298/FL 410	0.304/FL 450
	Runway	3,744	[illegible]	3,384	3,923	4,001	3,971
	Flight Time	2+16	2+26	2+17	2+21	2+17	2+28
	Fuel Used	3,202	3,233	3,500	3,754	3,214	2,998
	Specific Range/Altitude	0.333/FL 450	0.311/FL 430	0.332/FL 450	0.266/FL 410	0.311/FL 410	0.334/FL 450
Remarks	Certification Basis	FAR 25 A-[illegible]/FAR 25 A-13, 1997/03. Opt'l long-range tank increases range by 208 nm	FAR 25, 2008	FAR 25 A-77 FAR 25 A-13	CAR 4b, 1964; FAR 25 Amend. 1984/95/06. Pro Line 21 std. 06 150 APU	FAR 25, 1992/93/06 Pro Line 21 avionics	FAR 25 A108, 2005

Figure 11.3 B/CA charts. Used by permission of B/CA.

Aircraft Operating Costs Form
Date____________

VARIABLE EXPENSE

Fuel, oil, additives, etc. ________
Travel, flight crew ________
Maintenance total ________
Labor, outside general ________
Parts maintenance, replacement, etc ________
Overhaul, engine major ________
Overhaul, airframe major ________
Miscellaneous (catering, landing fees, enroute storage, customs, foreign permits, etc.) ________

Total Variable ________

FIXED EXPENSE, NORMAL

Salaries total ________
Flight crew (No.___) ________
Maintenance (No.___) ________
Administrative/clerical (No.___) ________
Employee benefits ________
Base hangar rent or costs
Hangar and shop equipment cost and supplies ________
Contract training ________
Miscellaneous (office supplies, publications, Manuals memberships, telephone, stc.) ________
Total Fixed, Normal ________
Total Variable plus Fixed Normal ________

FIXED EXPENSE, ADDITIONAL

Insurance total ________
Liability ________
Hull (Rate __%) ________
Major nonrecurring ________
Depreciation (Based upon __ years with __% residual) ________
Total Fixed, Additional ________
Total Operation Expense ________

OPERTIONAL DATA

For Period ________ through ________
Hours flown ________ Miles Flown________ Total Sorties ________

COST PER HOUR		COST PER MILE	
Variable	________	Variable	________
Fixed normal	________	Fixed normal	________
Subtotal	________	Subtotal	________
Fixed additional	________	Fixed additional	________
TOTAL	________	TOTAL	________

Figure 11.4 NBAA annual aircraft operating cost template. Used by permission of the NBAA.

Use of this template can best be illustrated by use of a practical problem. The problem is to compile an Annual Cost of Operation for the Cessna Citation XLS+ (CE560XL), Bombardier Learjet 45XL, and Hawker Beechcraft Hawker 750 using NBAA's "Annual Costs Tabulation Template" and data extracted from the *B/CA* charts with the following assumptions: Assume an average utilization of 600 hours per year. Use a standard NBAA 1000NM IFR mission profile to obtain the fuel usage and block speed for each aircraft. Depreciate all aircraft using the straight-line method for a period of seven years with a residual of 50% at the end of the period. Use typical passenger seating as shown in the *B/CA* charts with a 70% load factor. Assume Jet-A fuel weight of 6.8 lbs/gal and other unique cost data provided in Table 11.3.

The detailed annual operating costs calculation sheets for each of the aircraft are shown as Figures 11.8, 11.9, and 11.10 at the end of this chapter. An explanation for the fuel usage and block speed for the Cessna Citation XLS+ is as follows: Examining the 1000 NM mission, it can be seen that this aircraft took 3 hours and 26 minutes to complete the 1000 NM mission and used 3,211 pounds of fuel. This converts to a block speed of 411 knots and hourly fuel usage rate of 208 gal/hr. These values are used as benchmark inputs to the annual operating cost template to arrive at the costs per

Table 11.3. Conklin & de Decker Supplied Cost Data

	Citation XLS+(CE560-XL)	*Bombardier Learjet LR-45*	*Hawker Beechcraft 750*
Fuel Cost	$2.18	$2.18	$2.18
Crew Travel	$10	$10	$10
Hourly Labor Rate (MH per Flight/Hr)	$44/2.5	$44/2.4	$44/2.3
Parts Cost (per hour)	$50	$55	$60
Engine Overhaul/TBO (hours)	$80,000/4,000	$60,000/4,000	$100,000/5,000
Misc. Flight Expenses (per hour) hrhour)	$12	$12	$12
Captain Salaries (annual) (1)	$72,000	$68,000	$75,000
Copilot Salary (annual) (1)	$48,000	$47,000	$50,000
Flight Attendant (annual) (1)	$20,000	N/A	N/A
Employee Benefits Percent of Salary	10%	10%	10%
Contract Training per Pilot/6 months	$8,000	$7,000	$7,000
Misc. Fixed Expenses	$4,000	$4,000	$4,000
Hangar Rent (annual)	$16,500	$16,500	$16,500
Hull Insurance Percent of Purchase	0.7%	0.7%	0.7%
Liability Insurance (annual)	$48,000	$48,000	$48,000

hour and costs per mile for each aircraft. The same process is used for each of the other two aircraft to compete the calculations. Pertinent decision-making information is extracted from the cost tabulation sheets in Figures 11.8, 11.9, and 11.10 and is shown in Table 11.4 below.

These operational costs figures can be relied upon with a great deal of confidence because they are representative of actual operational costs and were generated by use of a standardized methodology from an independently derived source. The NBAA template separates expenditures into fixed and variable costs. This makes it convenient to conduct a break-even analysis using data from the operational template for each of the three aircraft. In order to construct a break-even chart, a revenue line must first be drawn. A revenue line is somewhat hypothetical unless you are running a charter operation, but may be generated by assuming the charter rate for each aircraft. Charter rates are normally quoted in costs per statute mile and are unique to each aircraft because they are based on actual costs, plus a profit margin. In order to conduct a break-even analysis on these three aircraft, this analysis will assume a charter rate for each aircraft of $15 per statute mile.

A graphical depiction of a break-even analysis is nothing more two lines plotted on a reference chart. In its simplest form, the break-even chart is a graphical representation of costs at various levels of activity shown on the same chart as the variation of income (or sales, revenue) with the same variation in activity. The "break-even point" is represented on the chart below by the intersection of the cost and income lines:

The x-axis is referenced to the number of flight hours and the y-axis is the amount of dollars made in revenue or expended in cost. Fixed cost is a horizontal line intersecting the y-axis at a point corresponding to the value shown on the spreadsheet. The variable cost is represented by a line starting on top of the fixed cost point on the y-axis and sloping up to a value corresponding to the variable cost increase per hour flown, taken from the spreadsheet. The revenue line starts at zero and slopes up to a value of the total expected revenue for the year corresponding to the number of revenue hours flown. The intersection of the variable cost line (total costs) and the total revenue line is the break-even point. Beyond this point the operator starts to make money with each additional revenue flight hour. A simple break-even chart has many uses. It can tell at a glance what the projected profit (or loss) will be

Table 11.4. Operational Costs per Hour and per Mile

	Citation XLS+	*Learjet 45XR*	*Hawker 750*
Costs per hour	$3,029.50	$2,976.95	$3,107.45
Costs per statute mile	$6.40	$5.91	$6.61
Costs per statute seat mile	$.53	$.66	$.73

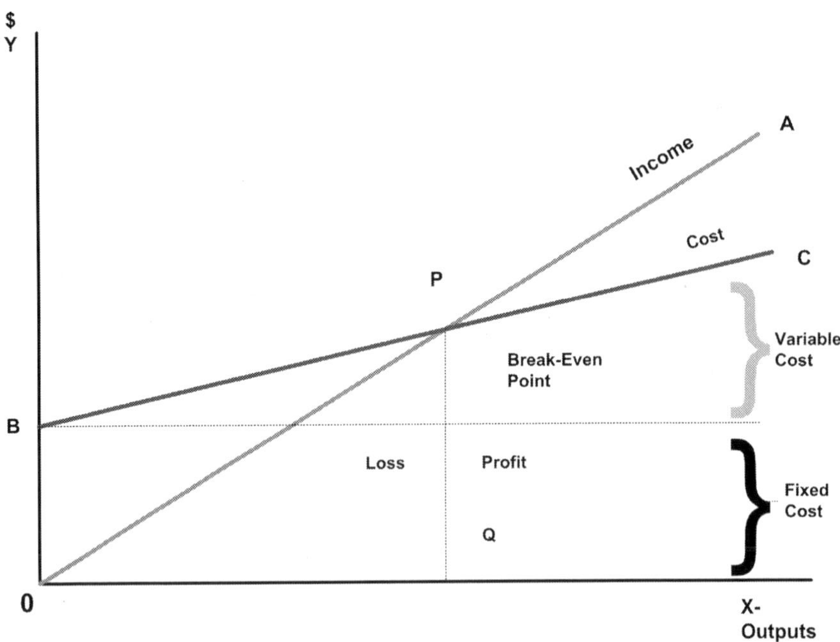

Figure 11.5 Plotted breakeven chart. Developed by the authors.

at any given number of hours flown. It can also be used for aircraft selection purposes. Plotting a break-even for all aircraft under consideration allows a refinement of the selection process by providing a break-even for each aircraft. A comparison of the break-even points for each aircraft can be used to aid in making a decision as to which aircraft is most appropriate.

Plotted below in Figure 11.6 are the break-even charts for each of the three aircraft using the cost data from the NBAA operational costs templates and assuming an income of $15 per statute mile. The break-even analysis is most useful when making a final decision as to the specific aircraft. Once the costs analysis is complete you have the required information needed to move on to the next step and determine if the facts support the need to purchase a selected business aviation aircraft. This critical decision usually involves the most senior levels of management within the company.

DO FACTS SUPPORT THE ADDITION OF AN AIRCRAFT?

With the completion of an aircraft cost analysis for a group of aircraft that will meet travel needs, the aviation manager has all of the information

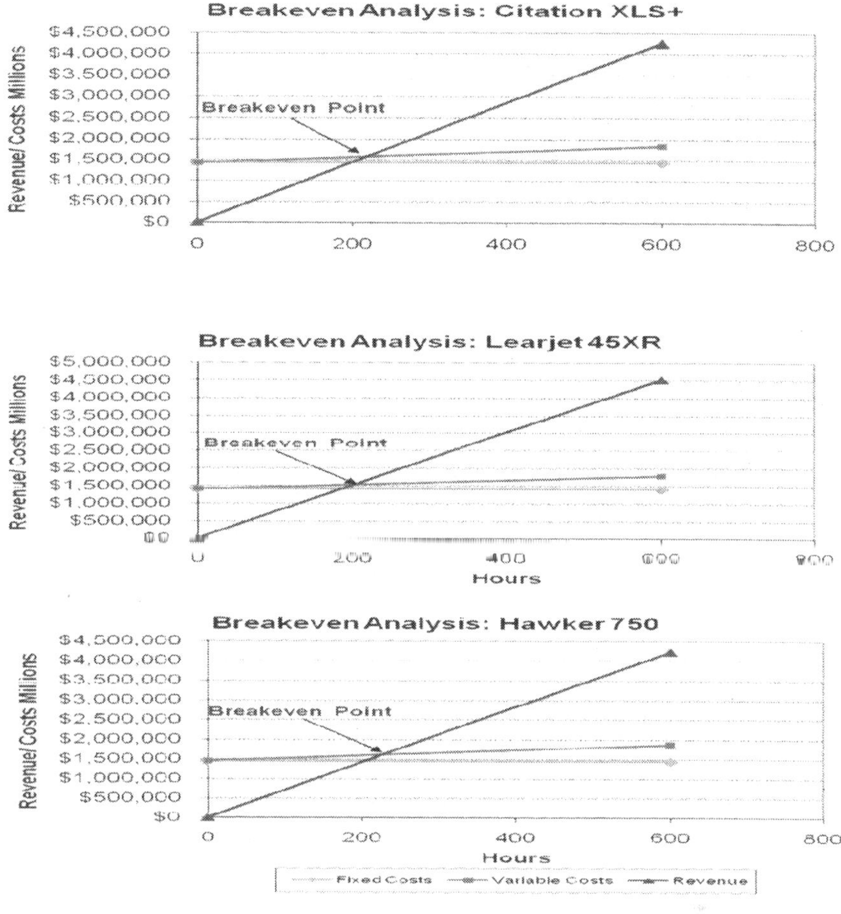

Figure 11.6 Aircraft breakeven analysis. Developed by the authors.

needed to determine if the company's travel needs justify acquisition of a business aircraft. Comparing the cost of the three aircraft previously considered against the cost of commercial aviation requires that a number of additional cost factors which would ordinarily be incurred when traveling on the airlines. First, due to scheduling complications, executives will be forced to overnight more when flying commercially. Extra hotel costs that would not be needed when traveling by corporate aircraft should be taken into account. Time and productivity losses when traveling by commercial air should be considered as well. These costs, along with the airline ticket costs, are tabulated and compared to the cost of operating the aircraft for a year's period of time. A straightforward method used to make such comparisons is to do a cost/benefit analysis. A cost/benefit analysis can be written or graphical; however, a graphical representation typically works better for presentations. Figure 11.7 is an example of how a cost/benefit analysis should look using the actual annual costs of operation of the three previously discussed aircraft under consideration. The commercial airline travel costs in this case are hypothetical; the actual data would come from a tabulation of all company travel costs for a year's period of time.

There are many ways to obtain business aviation services. A corporation or individual may choose to purchase a new or used aircraft and create an in-house flight department. The choice may be made to use one of the many other options such as chartering, leasing, interchange, joint ownership, time-share, or fractional ownership. Another unique option is to use a management company to manage the flight operation, as if it were an in-house department. Each of these options offers advantages and disadvantages under different circumstances. The NBAA maintains an aircraft resourcing options website at www.nbaa.org/admin/options/. This website has a wealth of information available to assist with arriving at the correct decision.

Full aircraft ownership offers the greatest level of flexibility and control over all matters relating to corporate air transportation. Under the FAA regulations, the aircraft owner is responsible for the safety, security, comfort, and cost of operating the aircraft. Aircraft operations can be managed by an in-house flight department or outsourced to an aircraft management company. Most corporations elect to run their own flight department because of the additional flexibility and control that this option offers. Full ownership generally requires a minimum level of utilization to be cost effective. In

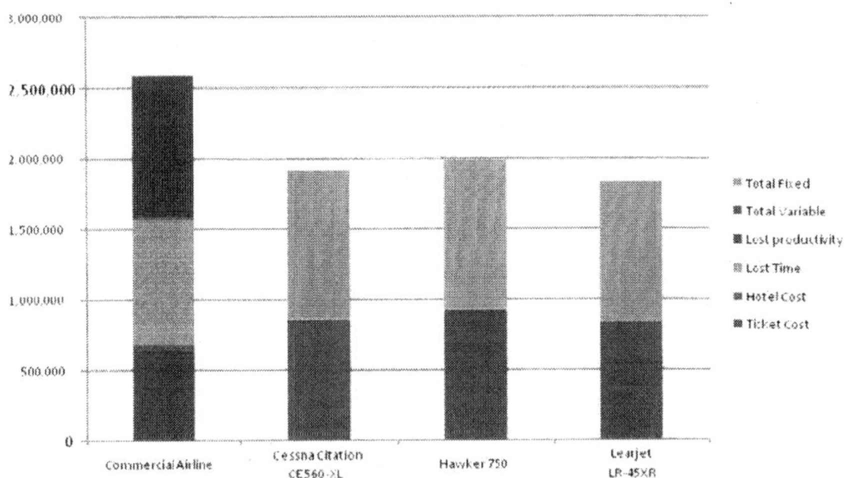

Figure 11.7 Cost/benefit analysis. Developed by the authors.

general, if the company has the need to utilize the aircraft for at least 250 flight hours per year, full ownership is a good option.

STANDARD SELECTION CRITERIA

Except when an aircraft is favored or otherwise chosen for personal reasons, use of the standard aircraft selection matrix is recommended when choosing a specific aircraft. This matrix is suggested by a group of corporate aviation department managers as being representative and valid criteria for corporate aircraft selection purposes. These criteria represent a good mixture of costs and performance. Values for most of the criteria are available directly from the *B/CA* charts; in some cases calculations must be made to fill in the tabular form, but in most cases, it is only necessary to transfer the data directly into the tabular matrix from the *B/CA* charts so that an easy comparison can be made. Table 11.5 contains the recommended aircraft selection matrix with an explanation of what each means.

Table 11.5. Aircraft Selection Matrix

Standard Aircraft Selection Matrix	
Selection Criteria	*Explanation*
Price	This is the B/CA equipped price as taken from the charts.
Monthly Payment	This is the monthly payment assuming a standard down payment, known interest rate and finance period.
Comfort Rating	This rating is based on volume of space available in the cabin per passenger, with dimensions from the B/CA charts.
Runway Requirements	This is the runway length required for takeoff and landing at sea level from the B/CA charts.
Range	This is the nonstop range with IFR reserves and a standard passenger load as taken from the B/CA charts.
Baggage Space	This is the cubic volume of baggage space as taken from the B/CA charts.
Cost of Operation	This is the cost per hour, cost per statue, and cost per seat mile compiled by using the fuel usage as taken from the B/CA charts and operationally supplied costs data.
Safety	This is a subjective safety rating based on certification standards and established safety record of the aircraft, using a scale of 0–10.
Cabin Environment	This is a subjective evaluation of the comfort rating based on air conditioning, pressurization, and other creature comforts using a scale of 0–10.
Maintenance	This is a subjective evaluation based on the ease and cost of maintenance using a scale of 0–10.

APPLICATION OF STANDARD SELECTION CRITERIA

Once the type of ownership is decided, the next step in the process is to decide on a specific type of aircraft based on costs, characteristics, safety, and environmental concerns. Use of the standard selection criteria is an excellent way to examine each candidate aircraft in order to arrive at a final decision on a specific type of aircraft to be used for company air travel needs. Using this process will also assure that the best aircraft is selected to meet unique company air travel needs, at the lowest cost. A good way to tabulate the data is to list the criteria down the left side of the sheet and place the aircraft under consideration in columns as shown in Table 11.6. This allows the decision makers to compare each of the criteria on a side-by-side basis for each aircraft so that a decision can be made.

Tabulating the data in this manner also allows the decision maker to subjectively decide which of the stated criteria are most important to the company. We will now explain where each of the selection criteria as shown in Table 11.6 was derived. The purchase price was taken directly from the *B/CA* table for each aircraft. The monthly payments were computed base on the assumption that 25% was placed as a down payment and the remaining principal was financed over 10 years at 8% annual percentage rate. The monthly payment can easily be computed using the "PMT" function of an Excel spreadsheet and the above assumptions. The comfort rating is a subjective value arrived at by use of the cabin volume for each aircraft as taken from the *B/CA* charts. The sea level takeoff and landing distances come directly from the *B/CA* charts. The aircraft range comes directly from the *B/CA* charts assuming four passengers with available fuel for each aircraft with a standard 200 nm alternate. The baggage space is taken directly from the *B/CA* charts. The cost of operation values was taken directly from the annual cost of operation spreadsheets as shown on Appendices A thru C. Safety is a subjective value based on the individual aircraft accident record. Cabin environment is a subjective value based on pressurization and air conditioning. The maintenance values are subjectively arrived at by how easy the aircraft is to maintain. The cost of operation values come directly from the cost of operation spreadsheets as shown on Appendices A thru C. Fuel cost per year is calculated based on the hourly fuel usage based on a standard 1000 nm profile as taken from the *B/CA* charts and fuel costs of $2.18 per gallon. The payment plus fuel used per year is arrived at by adding the amount of money spent on fuel and aircraft payments for a year's period of time. Assembling the data into a tabular form takes some effort, but the payoff is that it provides all of the data in one place so that an intelligent decision may be made.

Table 11.6 Tabulation of Data

Selection Criteria	*Aircraft #1*	*Aircraft #2*	*Aircraft #3*
Specific Aircraft Name	Citation XLS+ CE-560-XL	Bombardier Learjet LR-45	Hawker Beechcraft Hawker 750
Price (purchase)	$12,450,000	$12,755,000	$13,015,500
Monthly Payments	$113,290	$116,065	$118,435
Comfort Rating	8	6.5	9
Internal Length	18.5 ft	19.8 ft	21.3 ft
Height	5.7 ft	4.9 ft	5.7 ft
Width	3.9 ft	3.2 ft	4.4 ft
Volume	461 cu ft	368 cu ft	604 cu ft
Cubic ft/pax	51.2	40.8	67.1
Runway Requirements			
Takeoff (sea level)	3560 ft	5040 ft	4696 ft
Landing (sea level)	2732 ft	2373 ft	2245 ft
Range			
Non-stop w/IFR reserves	1744 nm	1830 nm	2111 nm
Baggage Space			
Cubic Volume	80 cu ft	50 cu ft	32 cu ft
Weight	700 lbs	500 lbs	500 lbs
Cost of Operation			
Cost per Hour	$3,029.50	$2,976.95	$3,107.45
Cost per Statute Mile	$6.40	$5.91	$6.61
Cost per Seat Mile	$.53	$.66	$.73
Breakeven Point	205 hrs	200 hrs	220 hrs
Safety	6accidents/ 470produced	7accidents/ 342produced	0accidents/ 23produced
General Rating	9	8	9
Cabin Environment	10	10	10
Pressurization	Yes	Yes	Yes
Air-conditioning	Yes	Yes	Yes
Maintenance			
General Rating	9	8	9
Annual Cost of Operation	$1,817,700	$1,789,168	$1,864,468
Fuel Cost/yr	$272,064	$233,752	$294,300
Payment + Fuel Cost/yr	$1,631,544	$1,626,532	$1,715,520

AIRCRAFT COMPLETION PROCESS

I'll relate a personal story that highlights the aviation manager's responsibility when managing the completion of a corporate aircraft. Toward the end of my career I sat, waiting as patiently as possible, to hear the word that the FAA inspector had released the paperwork on the certification of STC Compliance that our new aircraft met FAA regulations. During the previous week, the aircraft had been going through an inspection by several FAA representatives. Their main responsibility was to ascertain whether the 456th model of this particular aircraft was built as per the specifications and engineering drawings. Now, a week after the STC paperwork was promised, we were all still trying to be patient while the exceedingly slow wheel of regulatory process ground. Our new G-IV, I had only recently been informed, was selected for FAA review throughout its entire construction process. The manner in which this is determined has yet to be explained to me, but I was then trying to understand why we were so fortunate, while others, darn it, were spared.

What began a year prior, from contract signing to delivery, had finally been accomplished. The FAA's review and subsequent manufacturer flight tests had been completed. Our acceptance flight and the correction of most of the noted discrepancies were concluded. Our company was now the proud owner of one of the best-built and most reliable business aviation tools in the industry. I was really looking forward to showing my boss, his family and all of our company associates our new aircraft.

Whenever you purchase a new aircraft, one of the most important issues on the mind of the customer is, "when will the new plane arrive?" The date of customer acceptance is a target that the OEM puts out there long before its arrival with a confident expectation of delivery as planned. The aviation manager who represents the customer in this process is under a certain amount of aircraft delivery pressure. How intense that pressure is, is determined by a number of factors. The announced or generally agreed to date of completion is usually one of the pressure points in the life of an aviation manager awaiting the arrival of any new business aircraft, regardless of the type of aircraft or the price being paid. Gulfstream, in this instance, had worked very hard to ensure that our delivery date was met on time. Everything was in place. The contracts with all of the vendors who would provide us the ability to communicate through satellite phone, air-to-ground phone, AFIS, AIRINC, and so on, were set. We had been in touch with our insurance broker to prepare for the appropriate coverage, once the aircraft was delivered. As with most new aircraft purchases, we had negotiated a lease package with a major financial institution to purchase the new aviation asset. That process required more of my time that you can imagine. The insurance documents had been drawn up, the leasing agreement was complete, the registration number was approved, the radio license ready, our specific aircraft MEL was complete and approved, all of the paperwork for MNPS, RNP5 and 10 had been assembled, and the AIRINC representative was scheduled to fly on the acceptance flight to measure the telemetry data required for our RVSM approval.

Every time I have the chance to visit an OEM, I am really impressed with their ability to produce the quality of products they offer. Watching one of these beautiful machines being assembled is similar to watching a new home being built; with of course the exception that the amount of money involved is vastly different. With new construction, the site plan, architectural drawings, and in particular the specification lists of materials normally are assembled prior to the start of any work. Often the price is negotiated after all of these documents have been created. When the excavation is finished, foundation poured, framing compete, and the roof is on, it appears that progress comes to a grinding halt. It seems to remain so until several weeks before the certificate of occupancy is issued. During the last few weeks there appears to be a flurry of activity that has been recently lacking, but finally the project is completed.

I have had the opportunity to be involved in the completion of two new aircraft and the renovation of four others during the previous five years. My main contribution to the process was to coordinate the various efforts into a strategic plan that would provide the best possible aircraft for our company. It is critical to make sure that you are receiving proper counsel during the completion process. If you haven't had the responsibility of purchasing an aircraft before, you may need the advice of those who have. A broker acting on your behalf can help you though the maze of paperwork and process. I was fortunate to have been the beneficiary of the outstanding counsel provided by Boston Jet Search, a buyers-only advocate firm, during the seven aircraft purchases that I have managed in my career. Their style has fit very well with my team process. There are also many outstanding brokers in our industry who also offer purchase and completion assistance.

As well-intentioned as each aircraft manufacturer may be, they will usually only tell you what they think you want to hear as opposed to what you need to hear. This is not meant to cause you a disadvantage as their customer. They all simply believe that they know how to build you the best possible aircraft with little involvement on the part of the customer beyond picking the colors and fabrics to be used. If you haven't had the opportunity to manage the oversight of a completion in the past, it might be advisable to consider hiring a completion consultant. This is especially true if circumstances prevent you from being able to visit the completion facility on a regular basis, at least once a week. If you are not aware of every aspect of the completion, the manufacturer will build the aircraft that they want to build as opposed to the aircraft that you may want to build. They will make their best efforts to adhere to all engineering drawings and the details of the specification that were agreed upon, but there are so many little things that you should be aware of and questions that you should answer during the process.

How many seams will there be in the overhead? Will the solid wood trim used on the edges of the veneer match in tone of color? How large will the exit signs be? Will the placards be tape or silk screened? How will the divan be styled? Will the armrests in the center of the conference group seats stow flush with the seat pans? What are the default settings on all lighting, galley components, and entertainment systems when the aircraft is first powered up? What color options do you have in the cockpit and cockpit seats? What has been designed into your particular cabin layout for maintenance access to components that are behind bulkheads, credenzas, and galley storage? Nothing beats being there when questions arise. What is on the engineering drawings for a particular item may not be exactly what you wanted when you see it being installed. On-site question and review is very important to your overall quality outcome. These questions will be asked if you are there or expected to be on site in a few days, but will not be asked if you or your designated representatives are chronically absent.

The completion process begins with aircraft selection, specification detail, contract negotiation, the purchase process, "green" aircraft delivery (a new aircraft fresh off the assembly line that has yet to be painted; the exterior color of the metallic coating is green), interior completion, paint, completion management process, and final delivery. During the negotiation process there will be numerous opportunities to discuss the aircraft completion. You will be charged for every "work change order" that is not included in the contract that you have negotiated. The hardest work that you will do in the negotiation process is the agreed upon aircraft specification, "spec," and the design package for the interior completion. Make no mistake; the cockpit is the easiest aspect of the design package. If the cabin and galley are not thoroughly discussed to the last detail and then put on paper exactly as you want, your passengers/customers will not be totally satisfied with the results. The cabin fit and finish, the entertainment system, all of the small details of each seat position, that is, your passengers' experience in the seat during taxi, takeoff, and landing, are very important to the level of customer satisfaction you are seeking, the customer in this case being your passengers, the company executives.

The completion is the only time during the buildup of your new aircraft where you can have significant influence as to the quality of the final product. The manufacturer has, for the most part, already finalized all of the production plans and details for the green aircraft. You as the customer, have little to say about the initial airframe construction. The manufacturer and the FAA have already agreed upon the basic process of aircraft design and production. Otherwise, the FAA would not have certified the aircraft in the first place. It is very important for you to visit the green production process of your new aircraft. In particular be aware of major component parts that were designated for the aircraft, their serial numbers and dates of manufacture. Major airframe components should have the same serial number as the aircraft. Those parts were produced to be placed on a particular aircraft. Several years prior to the G-IV project, I had the privilege of managing the purchase and delivery of a beautiful Global Express, manufactured by Bombardier. During the process of inspecting our green serial number 22, Global Express, our completion team discovered that the rudder for serial number 22 had been removed from the aircraft and put on an earlier serial number aircraft that was due off the production line ahead of us. The reason this happened was that the other aircraft's rudder had been "dinged" by a work stand and the completion specialist in charge of that aircraft had insisted that the rudder be replaced. The slightly dented, but repaired, rudder ended up on our aircraft. Once this was discovered, we also insisted on replacing the repaired rudder and Bombardier agreed to comply. This is not meant to cast a disparaging eye toward Bombardier. They build a superior product, as do all business aviation manufacturers. I mention the rudder to emphasize the importance of managing your completion process.

A critical question during the negotiation phase of the purchase process should be, "When does the clock start ticking on life limited parts and calendar inspections?" Is it the date the aircraft receives its green C of A or when the final product is delivered to you, the customer? Back to the question of major component parts, be aware that the flight controls, landing gear, engines, and so on, have serial numbers. It is important to ensure that those match the serial number of the aircraft, or are within a small family of production serial numbers for the series of aircraft being built. This should be discussed prior to and be included in the sales and purchase agreement. The engines should be a matched pair with consecutive serial numbers. If not, you may find your aircraft with an engine that does not have the latest manufacturer modifications. Upon resale, the potential buyer will want to understand why the engines don't have consecutive serial numbers, and will be curious as to whether one or both had been replaced during your ownership. Larger aircraft that have been in production for some time, will require as much as 32 weeks or more to complete. That's seven and one-half months. While you might think that represents far too much time to complete a project of this magnitude, chat with some of your friends in the industry who were involved with the early production numbers of the Gulfstream V or the Global Express.

Bill McBride, director of flight operations for The Home Depot, and I, along with Chris Noblet, our chief pilot, formed a small team in 1999 that monitored the completion of the fifth customer-delivered Global Express. That project was one of the most difficult tasks that I have ever taken on in my aviation career. The folks at Bombardier in Tucson were highly motivated and very talented, but were severely hampered by the process of completing a newly introduced aircraft. Our completion strategy from the customer side was to simply be onsite during the entire project. Chris, Bill, and I rotated shifts of one week at a time. We leased an apartment in the area and purchased a large block of airline tickets in order to save on travel costs. From the induction of the Global in the completion process until the aircraft was delivered to us, what seemed like a lifetime, took only 38 weeks. That, I believe, is still a record for a Global completion. The key elements in our successful completion were the dedication of the technicians involved and our insistence in immersing our completion team in every aspect of the process. Bill's attention to every detail of the completion process and his keen eye for compliance with the drawings and specifications was the number one reason that Bombardier delivered a solid aircraft. I felt like I knew every run of wiring, what was under every floor panel, where all of the access ports were to be located and certainly every element of the design package by the time we flew that beautiful bird home. I also felt like I knew and had bonded with every technician and supervisor that worked on that aircraft. It was a total team effort on the part of the customer and the manufacturer.

The Global Express completion project was also reasonable for us because we had a large flight department, staffed with a great team, that would allow one of the senior managers to be absent on a continual basis for almost ten months. During this time, I also met a number of completion consultants who were monitoring the process for clients whose flight departments were not as large as ours and required a specialist to "babysit" for them. For the most part, I was very impressed with the dedication of the consultants and learned a great deal from them. I would not hesitate to contract with a consultant if I didn't have sufficient time to devote to the monitoring process.

Where will the completion take place? It used to be very common for business aviation manufacturers to only build the green aircraft. During the 1970s and early '80s there were scores of completion centers around the country vying for Canadair, Gulfstream, and Falcon Jet aircraft. Westwinds, Hawkers, and Jet Stars were also completed by outside vendors. Today, due to the large margins involved, new aircraft manufacturers, with few exceptions, complete their own aircraft. Over and above that, there are some excellent independent completion centers that will pick up a manufacturer's overload and are well positioned to renovate older aircraft that have just changed owners.

A mature aircraft is a lot of fun to complete. All of the completion engineering has been accomplished. You do not have to suffer the pains of waiting for innumerable engineering dispositions to be completed prior to the installation of a major interior detail such as a new and improved water system compressor, or the latest version of the vacuum toilet that promises to cure all previous shortcomings. Managing the completion process of an early serial number aircraft also means that you have to accept the fact that regardless of the thrill of being one of the fortunate few who will fly the newest version of aviation technology, you will eventually be disappointed that your bird will not have the latest production modifications when you take delivery. The OEMs, original equipment manufacturers, are so stimulated by their senior management to get the product in the hands of customers, or should I say, make sales, that they push new innovation to the point that what they want to deliver and what they are capable of delivering are two different things. The 1990s were a perfect example of this phenomenon. Remember the advertising wars between Gulfstream and Bombardier as to whose new ultra-long-range aircraft could fly 6,500 nautical miles? Both the GV and the Global Express are fabulous aircraft and a pilot's dream to fly. Both aircraft suffered the pangs of initial delivery disappointments. Eventually, with nerves worn painfully thin and patience all but gone on the part of some early delivery customers, both aircraft began to be completed on schedule and with a very high level of quality.

Negotiate the right to fly the green aircraft and conduct the same tests that the factory pilots have performed in order to gain the C of A. That flight, with one of the test pilots, is a great confidence builder for you and the eventual customer. As an experienced pilot you should fly the same acceptance flight profile from the left seat that was conducted by the factory test pilots several days before. This will afford you the opportunity to put the green aircraft through the majority of the paces that the test pilots accomplished during the certification flight.

Negotiate the expectation of a completion schedule. Some manufacturers are happy to provide the customer with a timeline that will indicate the major milestones in the completion process—milestones such as final wiring installed, floor panels down and secured, power on, ground power checks completed, seats built, cabinetry completed, the date the aircraft will be painted, and the dates of the first flight out of completion as well as the scheduled customer acceptance date. Other manufacturers will be very hesitant to release that information. Whether they do or don't, none of them are likely to provide the customer with a document that will for the most part cause disappointment. The reason is, no matter how many of a particular aircraft have been completed, there are always glitches that arise. During the many months of completion, the manufacturer can often overcome the snags from the various stages in the process and still produce the completed product on time. Agree upon a reasonable design due date. Agree upon when critical items or decisions have to be made. Each completion is unique in the lead times for decisions concerning cabin layout design, fabrics, wood veneers, paint scheme, registration number design, cockpit layout options, entertainment systems, and galley layout design. The OEM will need to specify critical dates by which these decisions need to be made in order to obtain the necessary materials to build your aircraft on time. You will then be responsible to ensure that the customer decisions are made in time to comply with those critical dates.

When will it be completed? That is always the number one question on everyone's mind. The boss certainly wants to know when the new aircraft will arrive and be put into service. All of your aviation department associates are curious. Every industry rumor, whether it applies or not to your particular type of aircraft, will be magnified during the completion process. It is best to set a conservative date, based on the completion center's prediction, and never change it, as far as your customer is concerned. If you tell your customer that the aircraft will be ready ahead of schedule and it isn't, your customer will be disappointed even if it comes in at the original date on the contract. That disappointment is short-lived, once the aircraft has arrived, unless it was way past the promised completion date.

During the initial negotiations, you should be cognizant of two significant dates. If possible, you should attempt to have both the green delivery date and the "completed" aircraft delivery dates specified in the contract. The first will certainly affect the second, although the new aircraft manufacturer may suggest that that won't happen. If the aircraft is late on the production line, it will be late out of completion. If penalties can be imposed for a late green delivery, it is in your best interests to have them as part of your sales agreement. I feel that you are at a disadvantage if you do not have late delivery fees as part of your contract. This will have to be negotiated up front and will be difficult if not impossible to enact after the sales agreement is signed. You should consider what steps will be taken if the completed aircraft is late by a significant amount of time. An out clause that will return all monies paid to date with a negotiated interest rider should be part of any sales agreement. That sounds good up front, but no one wants that to be the final outcome. The OEM should be liable financially to the customer when the aircraft is unreasonably late. That penalty should be in the form of a daily fee to be subtracted from the final purchase price.

Meet and be completely satisfied with the person in the completion process that is designated as your completion liaison with the manufacturer. This customer service representative can make or break the completion. These "customer service program managers" are specifically assigned to customers from the beginning of the process. Our representative with Gulfstream provided the flight department with weekly progress reports that included digital pictures of any detail that was requested. Weekly updates allow you to better understand where you are in the process and thus you will be better prepared to ask appropriate questions during the times when you are on site. It is important to note that all deliveries will be accompanied with a list of items that are to be repaired, improved, or replaced in the immediate future. This "exceptions" list should become part of the delivery paperwork with the signatures of both parties. These are snags or discrepancies that are agreed to by everyone, but due to the time constraints of the delivery, the manufacturer could not complete.

In retrospect it is important to remember certain critical items when you are involved with the completion of a new aircraft. The contract drives the process. What you are able to gain in negotiation will pay off in the long run. A well-written agreement will ultimately provide the best possible outcome for your company. The specification and design package drives the completion. Your direct involvement and your ability to partner with the manufacturer will drive the quality of the eventual product.

CORPORATE AIRCRAFT Annual Operating Costs for (CE-560-XL) Utilization: 600 Hours			
		Costs:	$12,450,000
VARIABLE EXPENSES:			
Fuel, oil, additives, etc	208×$2.18×600		$272,064
Travel, flight crew	$10×600		$6,000
Maintenance total			$120,000
Labor, outside general	2.5×$44×600	$66,000	
Parts, maintenance, replacement, etc	$50×600	$30,000	
Overhaul, engine major	2×($80,000/4000)×600	$24,000	
Miscellaneous (landing fees, customs, permits, etc.)			$7,200
Total Variable			$405,264
FIXED EXPENSES:			
NORMAL:			
Salaries total			$140,000
Flight crew	$72,000+$48,000	$120,000	
Flight Attendants		$20,000	
Employee benefits			$14,000
Hangar or tiedown cost			$198,000
Flightcrew training	$8,000x2		$32,000
Miscellaneous (Office supplies, publications, manuals, telephone, etc.)			$4,000
Total Fixed Normal			$388,000
Total Variable plus Fixed Normal			$793,264.00
FIXED EXPENSES ADDITIONAL:			
Insurance total			$135,150
Liability		$48,000	
Hull (Rate .7%)	.007×$12,450,000	$87,150	
Depreciation (SL, based on 7 yrs with 50 % residual)			$889,286
Total Fixed, Additional			$1,024,436
Total Fixed			$1,412,436
Total Operational Expenses			$1,817,700
OPERATIONAL DATA:			
Hours flown/Block Speed		600	411
NM/sm flown	600×411	246600	284083
		per hour	**per statute mile**
Cost variable		$675.44	$1.43
Cost fixed normal		$646.67	$1.37
Sub total		$1,322.11	$2.79
Cost additional		$1,707.39	$3.61
Total		$3,029.50	$6.40
Cost per statute seat mile		6.40/12	$0.53
Cost per Passenger statute seat mile (cost per statute seat mile / load factor)			$0.76

Figure 11.8 Annual operating costs (CE-560-XL). Developed by the authors.

CORPORATE AIRCRAFT Annual Operating Costs for (LR-45XR) Utilization: 600 Hours			
		Costs	$12,755,000
VARIABLE EXPENSES:			
Fuel, oil, additives, etc	194x$2.18x600		$253,752
Travel, flight crew	$10x600		$6,000
Maintenance total			$114,360
Labor, outside general	2.4x$44x600	$63,360	
Parts, maintenance, replacement, etc	$55x600	$33,000	
Overhaul, engine major	2x($60,000/4000)x600	$18,000	
Miscellaneous (landing fees, customs, permits, etc.)			$7,200
Total Variable			$381,312
FIXED EXPENSES:			
NORMAL			
Salaries total			$115,000
Flight crew	$68,000+$47,000	$115,000	
Flight Attendants		$0	
Employee benefits			$11,500
Hangar or tiedown cost			$198,000
Flightcrew training	$7,000x2		$28,000
Miscellaneous (Office supplies, publications, manuals, telephone, etc.)			$4,000
Total Fixed Normal			$356,500
Total Variable plus Fixed Normal			$737,812.00
FIXED EXPENSES ADDITIONAL:			
Insurance total			$137,285
Liability		$48,000	
Hull (Rate .7%)	.007x$12,755,000	$89,285	
Depreciation (SL, based on 7 yrs with 50 % residual)			$911,071
Total Fixed, Additional			$1,048,356
Total Fixed			$1,404,856
Total Operational Expenses			$1,786,168
OPERATIONAL DATA:			
Hours flown/Block Speed		600	437
NM/sm flown	600x437	262200	302054
		per hour	**per statute mile**
Cost variable		$635.52	$1.26
Cost fixed normal		$594.17	$1.18
Sub total		$1,229.69	$2.44
Cost additional		$1,747.26	$3.47
Total		$2,976.95	$5.91
Cost per statute seat mile		5.91/9	$0.66
Cost per Passenger statute seat mile (cost per statute seat mile / load factor)			$0.94

Figure 11.9 Annual operating costs (LR-45-XR). Developed by the authors.

CORPORATE AIRCRAFT Annual Operating Costs for (Hawker 750) Utilization: 600 Hours			
		Costs	$13,015,000
VARIABLE EXPENSES:			
Fuel, oil, additives, etc	225x$2.18x600		$294,300
Travel, flight crew	$10x600		$6,000
Maintenance total			$120,720
Labor, outside general	2.3x$44x600	$60,720	
Parts, maintenance, replacement, etc	$60x600	$36,000	
Overhaul, engine major	2x($100,000/5000)x600	$24,000	
Miscellaneous (landing fees, customs, permits, etc.)			$7,200
Total Variable			$428,220
FIXED EXPENSES:			
NORMAL:			
Salaries total			$125,000
Flight crew	$68,000+$47,000	$125,000	
Flight Attendants		$0	
Employee benefits			$12,500
Hangar or tiedown cost			$198,000
Flightcrew training	$7,000x2		$28,000
Miscellaneous (Office supplies, publications, manuals, telephone, etc.)			$4,000
Total Fixed, Normal			$367,500
Total Variable plus Fixed Normal			$795,720.00
FIXED EXPENSES ADDITIONAL:			
Insurance total			$139,105
Liability		$48,000	
Hull (Rate .7%)	.007x$13,015,500	$91,105	
Depreciation (SL, based on 7 yrs with 50 % residual)			$929,643
Total Fixed, Additional			$1,068,748
Total Fixed			$1,436,248
Total Operational Expenses			$1,864,468
OPERATIONAL DATA:			
Hours flown/Block Speed		600	408
NM/sm flown	600x408	244800	282010
		per hour	**per statute mile**
Cost variable		$713.70	$1.52
Cost fixed normal		$612.50	$1.30
Sub total		$1,326.20	$2.82
Cost additional		$1,781.25	$3.79
Total		$3,107.45	$6.61
Cost per statute seat mile		6.61/9	$0.73
Cost per Passenger statute seat mile (cost per statute seat mile / load factor)			$1.05

Figure 11.10 Annual operating costs (Hawker 750). Developed by the authors.

REFERENCES

Cannon, Jim. (2002, Jun). Managing your aircraft's completion. *Business & Commercial Aviation*, 90–92.

Gromley, M. (1992, January). Justifying the business aircraft: the analysis. *Business & Commercial Aviation* 54–61.

National Business Aircraft Association. (1997a). *Business Aviation Fact Book 1997*. Washington, DC.

_______. (2007). *NBAA Management Guide*. Washington, DC.

12

Safety Management Systems

Learning Objectives: After reading this chapter you should be able to:

- Prioritize the importance of safety to the operation of a business aviation department
- Explain why a systemic approach such as safety management system (SMS) is the preferred aviation safety system of the future
- List the steps necessary to develop a safety management system for a business aviation department
- Propose the process needed to establish a business aviation flight department SMS

Business aviation can trace its roots back to the dawn of flight. The first recorded use of an aircraft as a promotional tool was the 1910 flight by the Wright Brothers from Dayton to Columbus, Ohio (Searles 1997). The Wright Flyer transported two packages of silk for Max Morehouse, the president of a dry goods store in Columbus, and then ". . . conducted flying exhibitions after the goods were delivered" (Searles 1997, p. 2). Two years prior to this event, the first recorded death from an aircraft accident occurred when a similar Wright Flyer experienced a failure of one of its propellers (Brady 2000). The Wrights and other pioneers of the fledgling aviation industry had learned a valuable lesson from that tragic event. Rudimentary as it was, safety management from the beginning of flight and for a long time to follow was forensic in nature (Stolzer 2008, p. 43). Charles Lindbergh completed his historic flight across the Atlantic Ocean on May 20–21, 1927 to claim the Raymond Orteig $25,000 prize for the first nonstop aircraft flight between New York and Paris. Raymond Orteig was a French immigrant who had become the owner of two New York hotels before making the prize offer in 1919. Lindbergh was a 24-year-old airmail pilot in 1926 when he heard of the offer and convinced a group of St. Louis businessmen to back him financially in the attempt to fly across the Atlantic. As a successful airmail pilot, Lindbergh had always been safety-conscious and had developed a hazard identification process that he used to help him avoid aircraft accidents while flying the airmail routes. This hazard identification process was a rudimentary safety system that worked well for him in the environment in which he operated. He used this hazard identification process for the flight across the Atlantic, but overlooked one thing. He nearly failed in the attempt for the historic flight due to lack of sleep the night before the takeoff. When he touched down at the Le Bourget Aerodrome, Paris, France on May 21, 1927, at 10:22 PM local time he had flown a total of 33 hours, 30 minutes, 29.8 seconds; he had not slept in 55 hours. Had everything else not been working in his favor, he may have failed in this attempt due to the lack-of-sleep hazard, which he had overlooked.

During the Golden Age of flight, weather was very much an issue with most pilots. Visibility was a persistent hazard to safe flight. Low ceilings and the lack of a horizon were real hazards in un-instrumented aircraft. "In 1929 Doolittle made the first ever completely blind flight. Glued to a crude panel of rudimentary instruments that he'd helped develop, he crouched in a cockpit under a black hood, flying blinder than if it were night" (Perret 1993, p. 40). Jimmy Doolittle became a business aviation executive with Shell Oil the year after he made that historic flight. The flight was an extension of the research that he was conducting to gain his PhD from the Massachusetts Institute of Technology (Hoppes 2005).

SMS AND BUSINESS AVIATION

Safety management systems (SMS) in business aviation began with the first efforts by aviation professionals to join together to share information for the good of the overall community. It was and still is a community of dedicated pilots, mechanics, dispatchers, flight attendants, and administrative personnel who share a common goal: safety of flight. By their very nature, business aviation flight departments in the past were reticent to share company information. That stemmed from their individual corporate cultures of competition and the security of intellectual property. Initially, this culture of not sharing information presented a barrier to implementation of an SMS system in the business aviation community, because sharing data is an important part of the SMS concept. There are many other aspects of SMS, as will be discussed later, but sharing is one of the most important concepts.

Fortunately, this barrier of not sharing has been largely overcome and today most aviation department managers are aware of the importance of sharing data in the interest of flight safety.

To illustrate how things have changed, I will relate a story based on my personal experience. When my tour of duty as a naval aviator ended in 1973, I accepted a copilot position with W. R. Grace in New York. The first document that I was given was the aviation department policy and procedure manual. That was the standard procedure at the time. From the instructions that were given, it was very clear that you were expected to operate within those guidelines. I was based at Westchester County Airport (HPN). HPN was considered at the time to be the hub of business aviation. Many New York corporations housed their aircraft at HPN. Each flight operation had a policy and procedure manual. Each was slightly different, reflecting the personality and aviation background of their respective chief pilot. Within every flight department, however, once a flight was underway, the trip captain would dictate how the flight was to be conducted; "I know this is what the book says, but we will do it this way on my flight deck." I heard that comment many times in my early days in business aviation. Much of this stemmed from the fact that the chief pilot did not solicit operational input from the troops (the other pilots); he simply dictated how it was to be done. In a large flight department, you had to remember how each captain operated in order to do your job well and get along; there was no systematic approach where safety information was shared between the flight departments and used to prevent accidents. What little information these early pioneers in this segment of the aviation industry did share was operational best practices. However, there was very little exchange of information as it was and not applied in a systematic way to prevent accidents. During the 1930s in large corporations such as Texaco and Mobil Oil, operational practices were dictated by the experience level of the most senior pilot. Cockpit resource management in the early days of business aviation was very dictatorial in nature. The captain made the rules and that was final. Cockpit resource management (CRM) had not yet come of age.

The first step in bringing the fledgling business aviation community together following World War II was the formation of the Corporate Aircraft Owners Association (CAOA), which was incorporated on February 13, 1947 (Searles 1997, p. 31). Six years later, the CAOA evolved into what is known today as the National Business Aviation Association (NBAA). The fledgling association fulfilled a critical need "to protect [business aviation] interests from discriminatory legislation by federal, state, and municipal agencies...to enable corporation aircraft owners to be represented as a united front...[to foster] improvements in aircraft, equipment, and service...and to further the cause of safety and economy of operation" (Searles, p. 30). Since its beginning in 1947, the NBAA has become a strategic force in the development of the business aviation industry. Not only does the NBAA provide a voice for the industry on Capitol Hill, it has matured into a provider of educational products that aid in the enhancement of aviation safety.

In 1979, Bill Mack, the aviation director at National Distillers, and Don Baldwin, a captain with Texaco Air Transport, initiated a grassroots effort in the formation of the Northeast Corporate Aircraft Association (NECAA). This organization was founded to share safety-related data and conduct seminars for the promotion of best practices. A majority of the large business aviation flight departments in the New York metropolitan area joined NECAA. This was the first organized effort in the U.S. business aviation community by operators to form a regional association. NECAA was also an early advocate for professional development in the industry. NECAA was eventually folded into NBAA.

The NBAA published its first *Management Guideline* in the early 1980s. Within that document there was an attempt to establish a best practices standard. Most business aviation operators by then were training their crews at Flight Safety International (FSI) training centers around the country. FSI worked very hard to produce standardized operational learning. FSI established many standard operating procedures that were gained from the best practices of their clients. Chief pilots became more inclusive and began to delegate responsibilities for safety and standards.

On December 10, 2001, under the auspices of the International Civil Aviation Organization (ICAO), the International Business Aviation Council (IBAC) developed the International Standard for Business Aviation Operations (IS-BAO) standard. This standard is the vehicle that is used by the business aviation community for the implementation of SMS, not only in the United States, but around the world.

The IBAC, a division of ICAO based in Montreal, met on December 15, 2001, to certify the formal process of SMS for business aviation operations worldwide: the IS-BAO. This effort to formalize best practices was commendable. Through the IS-BAO process, ICAO was asking business operators to step up and measure their individual policies and practices against an international standard that was being proposed as "The Standard." The audit component of IS-BAO, which provides certification and periodic review and renewal, added credibility to the process. This effort mandates that operations have to "walk the talk" vs. "talk the talk." The audit process measures the integration of the standard throughout each organization that wishes to become IS-BAO certified. Growth of this effort was very slow in the beginning, but it has certainly taken flight in the past few years.

IS-BAO has, for the first time, gathered together operators from a segment of the aviation industry that was, for all intents and purposes, self-regulated (FAR Part 91) and infused each one with quality management principles.

Each associate within an IS-BAO certified operation is responsible for quality and safety, not just the chief pilot. This is a standard that will be around for a long time. In order to operate within the European theater beginning in November of 2010, any operator, airline, or corporation must have a formal SMS program in place. That program will have a certification element and must have an audit function as part of the process. The FAA has delayed implementation of similar requirements, but I predict that comparable regulations will be adopted in the near future.

SMS—THE FUTURE OF AVIATION SAFETY

The term "safety management," as used by ICAO, includes two key concepts. First, the concept of a state safety program (SSP), which is an integrated set of regulations and activities aimed at improving safety. Second, the concept of safety management systems (SMS), which is a systematic approach to managing safety, including the necessary organizational structures, accountabilities, policies, and procedures (ICAO 2011).

BUSINESS AVIATION SAFETY MANAGEMENT SYSTEM

The concept for the safety management system used within the business aviation community is illustrated in Figure 12.1. This illustration is consistent with the SMS concept as explained in FAA publications and is built on four components. The first component is safety policy, which is spelled out in various publications as shown in Figure 12.1. The second component is safety risk management where hazards are identified and analyzed. The third component is safety assurance, where continous improvement is made by use of reviews, measurement, and monitoring. The final component is safety promotion; here safety awareness is maintained by a campaign of training and communications programs. It is important to realize that a successful business aviation safety management system must have support from the highest levels of the corporate structure.

POLICY MANUAL

The first, and most important, task of putting together an effective SMS program is the creation of a policy manual. This document will become the operational "how to" tool for the flight department. In order for a policy manual to be effective, it should have approval from top management within the corporation. That approval should be noted in the form of an endorsement

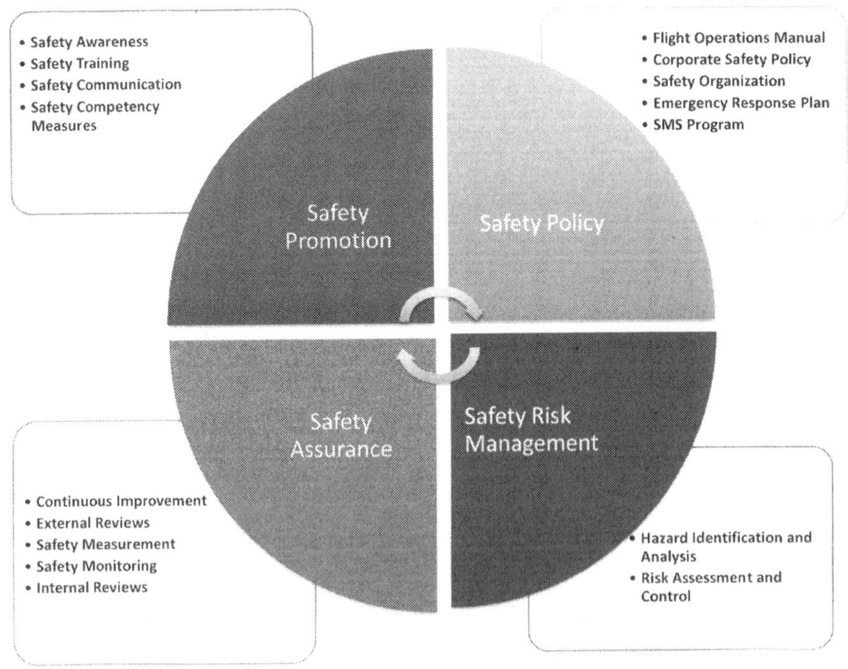

Figure 12.1 The SMS concept. Developed by the authors.

contained within the manual. "While all members of the organization must know their responsibilities and be both empowered and involved with respect to safety, the ultimate responsibility for the safety of the system cannot be delegated from top management" (Stolzer 2000, p. 25).

It is very important that the policy manual is written with the opportunity for input from every associate in the flight department. Empowerment begins with a sense of participation. While it is unreasonable to input every idea or opinion, it is very important to allow members of the department to have a voice in the creation of policy and/or the possibility of submitting suggestions for amendments. In a large business aviation department, a policy or standards committee, consisting of members of all functional groups, ensures that meaningful input is a continuing process. A standards committee forms the foundation for the enhancement of safety policy. Buy-in from the personnel who work within its guidelines is a critical aspect to the functionality of a policy manual.

As discussed in Chapter 1, the majority of business aviation flight departments are single-aircraft operations. As such, there is little if any manpower available to take on a project like the creation of an effective policy manual, let alone a comprehensive SMS. Many of these aviation entities are flown single-pilot. The task is daunting. There are, however, a number of sources available that make the job less cumbersome. The NBAA website contains valuable information that will assist in the formulation of or updating of the flight department policy manual. The URL: (www.nbaa.org/member/admin/management-guide/mgmt-guide-spr2009-fullset.pdf) (available to NBAA members) provides access to the 199-page *NBAA Management Guide*. The document presents a sound foundation upon which a safe and effective business aviation department can be built. It contains an outline for an operations manual, with suggested topics (*NBAA Management Guide* 2009, p. 1–3). This outline highlights the three major sections of any business aviation organization: administration, operations, and maintenance. Within each section, the guide reveals topics that should be included in the policy manual under consideration.

Chapter 10 of the IS-BAO standard, *Company Operations Manual*, specifies, "The operations manual shall be amended or revised as is necessary to ensure that the information contained therein is kept up to date. All such amendments or revisions shall be issued to all personnel that are required to use this manual. It shall contain at least the following:" (IS-BAO 2010, p. 10-1).

- table of contents
- amendment control page and list of effective pages; each page has an effective date on it
- duties, responsibilities and succession of management and operating personnel
- operator safety management system
- operational control system
- MEL procedures
- normal flight operations
- standard operating procedures
- weather limitations
- flight and duty time limitations
- emergency operations
- accidents/incidents consideration
- personnel qualifications and training
- recordkeeping
- a description of the maintenance control system
- security procedures
- performance operating limitation
- use/protection of flight data recorder (FDR)/cockpit voice recorder (CVR) records
- handling of dangerous goods

The IS-BAO process is a goal as well as a means to achieve an effective safety management system for a business aviation flight department. The foundation for any effort toward an overall safety system is the development of a sound flight operations policy manual. The illustration in Figure 12.1 represents the steps necessary to prepare for IS-BAO certification.

RISK MANAGEMENT

Once a set of standards and guidelines exist for the flight operation, the next fundamental function of an SMS program is the safety risk management (SRM) process. This function is the heart of any SMS program because it identifies the hazards and sets a plan for controlling them. Both the FAA and ICAO recognize the need for SRM. "They...describe a three-step process: identify hazards; assess risk; and control risk" (Stolzer 2008, p. 112). Similarities abound within the business aviation industry. Individual flight departments are more alike than they are dissimilar. The vast majority of hazards in business aviation have been identified; risks have been assessed and controlled. Although flight departments are quite similar in operational style, equipment, structure, and mission, they do differ widely in the type of industry they serve, unique destinations frequently visited, experience level of personnel, and operational philosophy. Within these differing styles and operational dissimilarities lay unique hazards that need to be identified.

The basic tenant of SRM, stated above, is that once identified, hazards must be thoroughly vetted to reveal risks that must be managed. Notice that the last sentence didn't include the words "shall" or "should." The ICAO Safety Management Manual is available at URL: http://www.icao.int/anb/safetymanagement/Documents.html, and provides an extremely detailed resource on the subject of aviation safety management. On pages 5–13 of the ICAO document, a summary is provided outlining the five fundamentals of safety risk management:

- There is no such thing as absolute safety—in aviation it is not possible to eliminate all safety risks.
- Safety risks must be managed to a level "as low as reasonably practicable" (ALARP).
- Safety risk mitigation must be balanced against time, cost, and the difficulty of taking measures to reduce or eliminate the safety risk.
- Effective safety risk management seeks to maximize the benefits of accepting a safety risk while minimizing the safety risk itself.
- The rationale for safety risk decisions must be communicated to the stakeholders affected by them to gain their acceptance.

The introduction to the 2009 FAA *Risk Management Handbook* is available at URL: www.faa.gov/library/manuals/aviation/media/FAA-H-8083-2.pdf. This handbook emphasizes the fact that risks involved with flying are quite different from those experienced in daily activities. Managing these risks requires a conscious effort and established standards. Pilots who practice effective risk management have predetermined personal standards and have formed habit patterns and checklists to incorporate them.

Let's take a look at the three elements of risk management: hazards, risk, and control. By looking at these three elements, the business aviation professional can employ an effective and efficient strategy in which to employ the risk management leg of the SMS process. We will now discuss each of these elements and see how they are applied.

HAZARD IDENTIFICATION

If a risk management system is to be supportive of an effective SMS, it must be based "upon an accurate and consistent method of hazard identification" (Stolzer 2008, p. 113). Hazards can be classified as an action or circumstance that has the potential of causing damage, loss, or harm to personnel or equipment. The operative word in that definition is "potential." An adverse weather condition is an example of a hazard. Hazards are preconditions that the ICAO delineates into three categories: natural (weather, geophysical, geographical, environmental); technical (aircraft components, facilities, support equipment); and economic (growth, recession, cost of equipment) (ICAO-SMM 2009, p. 4-3).

Recognition of hazards comes with experience. The recognition of a hazard that has the potential to cause an adverse event is normally realized by the more senior of two pilots in a multi-crew cockpit. The ability to recognize hazards has been shown to be heavily influenced by experience and training. As mentioned above, hazards can be uncovered within all facets of a flight operation. Within the flight department undetected hazards may be found within the operations/administration or maintenance functions, as well as the aircraft and flight crew. The key to hazard recognition is the system or process that is used for detection. This is not centered on the aircraft, but the entire flight department. Hazards are as prevalent in the "technical" category as in the "natural" category. The work environment is replete with examples of potential hazards:

- Fall protection
- Hazardous waste
- Equipment operations (tug, forklift)

- Spills
- Tool inventory
- Hearing protection
- Ladder/stair/platform
- Aircraft on jacks
- Walking paths in the hangar

RISK

"Safety risk is defined as the assessment, expressed in terms of predicted probability and severity, of the consequences of a hazard" (ICAO 2009, p. 5-2). We face risks every day. How well we manage risk is dependent upon our judgment, experience, skills, and importantly what the risk is. As mentioned earlier, the more robust the hazard identification process within an active SMS, the better the opportunity there is to mitigate an associated risk. Stolzer, Halford, and Goglia stipulate in *Safety Management Systems in Aviation* that risk is "an estimate of the effectiveness (or lack thereof) of hazard controls in preserving the value of an asset in a given scenario" (Stolzer 2008, p. 131). Whereas hazards have the potential to cause damage, risk analysis, in part, measures the probability of an event occurring. Table 12.1 depicts a safety risk probability with a numerical value.

Safety risk probability is a scheme that assigns a numerical value to a likelihood or probability of occurrence (ICAO 2009, pp. 5–6). Table 12.2 depicts a safety risk severity scheme that assigns a letter value to the severity of occurrence (ICAO 2009, p. 5–7).

Table 12.3 ties these two concepts together into a logical safety risk management matrix that can be used to measure the acceptable level of risk associated with different aspects of flight operations.

The safety risk assessment matrix, Table 12.3, is a useful tool to measure the acceptable level of risk with an aspect of the flight operation. It represents a blend of risk probability (likelihood) and risk severity. If, in the judgment of the risk evaluator, the combination of risk factors falls into the

Table 12.1. Safety Risk Probability Table

Likelihood or Probability	*Meaning*	*Value*
Frequent	Likely to occur many times (has occurred frequently)	5
Occasional	Likely to occur sometimes (has occurred infrequently)	4
Remote	Unlikely to occur, but possible (has occurred rarely)	3
Improbable	Very unlikely to occur (not known to have occurred)	2

Table 12.2. Safety Risk Severity Table

Severity	*Meaning*	*Value*
Catastrophic	• Equipment destroyed • Multiple deaths	A
Hazardous	• A large reduction in safety margins, physical distress, or a workload such that the operators cannot be relied upon to perform their tasks accurately or completely • Serious injury • Major equipment damage	B
Major	• A significant reduction in safety margins, a reduction in the ability of the operators to cope with adverse operating conditions as a result of increase in workload, or as a result of conditions impairing their efficiency • Serious incident • Injury to persons	C
Minor	• Nuisance • Operating limitations • Use of emergency procedures • Minor incident	D
Negligible	• Few consequences	E

Table 12.3. Safety Risk Assessment Matrix

Risk Probability	*Catastrophic A*	*Hazardous B*	*Major C*	*Minor D*	*Negligible E*
Frequent 5	5A	5B	5C	5D	5E
Occasional 4	4A	4B	4C	4D	4E
Remote 3	3A	3B	3C	3D	3E
Improbable 2	2A	2B	2C	2D	2E
Extremely Improbable 1	1A	1B	1C	1D	1E

red area (values 5A, 5B, 5C, 4A, 4B, and 4C), the risk is deemed to be intolerable and is unacceptable under the existing circumstances. If the value falls into the yellow area (values 5D, 5E, 4C, 4D, 4E, 3B, 3C, 3D, 2A, 2B, and 2C), the risk is deemed to be tolerable but may require management input in order to allow the risk. In the green region (values 3E, 2D, 2E, and 1A–1E), the risk is deemed to be acceptable.

Following the identification of hazards and the evaluation of the potential for risk, it is necessary to take steps to mitigate the risk. Mitigation of risk is accomplished by the implementation of appropriate control measures. The following categorization schemes, ranked from most to least effective, are utilized by safety managers to evaluate hazard controls (Stolzer 2009, p. 157):

- Eliminate the hazard—get rid of it; don't go there.
- Reduce the hazard level—lower the severity or the likelihood (probability), or both.
- Provide safety devices—prevent exposure; TCAS, for example.
- Provide warnings or advisories—both visual and aural.
- Provide safety procedures—checklists, emergency procedures.

It's a fairly simple process to make lists. It's another to actually design control mechanisms to mitigate risks. In aviation, we have an advantage that has been built up over a century of time. We have a forensic storehouse of knowledge concerning hazards, risks, and controls. From the first recorded heavier-than-air fixed wing accident in 1908 involving a *Wright Flyer*, to the most recent article reviewing the factors involved in a contemporary aircraft accident, the lessons of how not to operate an aircraft are well established. The airlines and corporate aviation both enjoy well-deserved safety records. The reason that these impressive safety records have been built over the years is that the mission of the safety professional is to make aviation as safe as possible and they have contributed greatly to this safety record.

If an accident occurs tomorrow, it will likely be due to human error. More than 80% of aviation accidents in the past several decades have been caused by human error. In order to make the aviation environment even safer, safety management systems are designed to continue to look for hazards involving people and their relationship with each other, hardware, software, and the environment. Figure 12.2 depicts a hazard control model that is easy to understand and places emphasis on the aforementioned relationships, the SHELL model (Stolzer 2009, p. 159).

The SHELL model looks at relationships between people (L = liveware) and software (S), hardware (H), the environment (E), and other people (L). Understanding these relationships is key to the control of potential hazards and risks.

Figure 12.2 Shell model. Developed by the authors.

SAFETY ASSURANCE

The third and somewhat critical aspect in its own right in the safety management system hierarchy of construct is safety assurance. This building component of SMS is akin to the quality improvement segment process within a robust quality management system, found in many aspects of manufacturing. Quality improvement and safety assurance each play a critical role in their respective management systems. Each represents the process of review, reflection, reaction, and retooling. When W. Edwards Deming took on the challenge of assisting Japan in their post-war recovery, he blended the concept of management by objectives with the Plan-Do-Check-Act (PDCA) cycle (Carson 1993). Dr. Deming is considered by many to be the father of total quality management (TQM) systems (Redmond 2008). One of the tenets of his work was the repeated evaluation of the effectiveness of each process in order to ensure a continuation of the improvement in quality. Dr. Deming took quality control out of the hands of the inspector and gave it to the worker who produced the product (Redmond 2008, p. 435).

Safety management systems (SMS) and quality management systems (QMS) represent refinements of TQM over time. Several principles of both SMS and QMS can be compared and contrasted; SMS is after all a derivative of QMS. In the ISO 9000 standard, one of the eight principles (tenets) of QMS is "continual improvement process" (CIP) (Martínez-Lorente 2004). In QMS, customer outcomes or satisfaction is considered to be a primary indicator of effectiveness. CIP relies upon data collected, measured, and analyzed against a predetermined baseline to enhance its impact on quality (Battles 1998).

Safety management systems in aviation were created using "safety assurance" (SA) as one of the four pillars of SMS. "The safety assurance functions in SMS have their origins in the international quality management standard, ISO 9000" (Stolzer 2008, p. 27). In this regard, both QMS and SMS share a common purpose as well as a common heritage. Safety assurance, however, differs from continual improvement in the manner in which data is collected for review and analysis. While CIP relies on systematic data sampling, SA is more periodic in nature. Safety assurance is management driven. Audits, both internal and external, are typically scheduled in advance. Because SMS is not attempting to tweak a machine tolerance specification to improve throughput quality, it is unnecessary to conduct repetitive inspections or audits over a short span of time. Once the procedural policy has been written and the risk management program has been adopted by the organization, a successful SMS program relies on its process of internal review and assessment to continually verify its relevance (Stolzer 2008, p. 27). Aviation is a high-reliability industry. "High-reliability organizations are those that operate in an environment of high hazard but, from a statistical standpoint, do not have mishaps where these hazards cause a tragedy" (Bagian 2006, p. 288). Sound policy development coupled with an effective risk management system does not require constant inspection. What SMS does effectively accomplish through the implementation of a robust safety assurance program is the occasional discovery of hidden nuances of current policy or the revelation of a hazard created by the introduction of a new piece of technology.

Safety management systems are only as effective as the personnel functioning within the system will allow. It is very important in any form of SMS to take into account the vulnerabilities of people who will be working within that system: "Both the strengths and the weaknesses of the human are appropriately accounted for" (Bagian 2006, p. 288). The acceptance of SMS by flight crews, maintenance technicians, schedulers, ticket agents, cabin service, and ground support personnel is vital to its overall mission. Employee buy-in is very important to the success of any new management initiative. Within an aviation organization, customer service and safety of flight will both be enhanced with the integration of a continual improvement process (QMS) and the adoption of a safety assurance protocol (SMS). They each have a role to play.

FLIGHT RISK ANALYSIS TOOL

Within the operational environment of business aviation, one of the constant pressures that flight crews experience is balancing safety of flight with the needs of the passenger-customer. Long before engine start, the pilot-in-command (PIC) accepts a trip request from the corporate office and begins flight planning. During planning, questions arise as the pilot investigates the destination airport, considers the weather forecast, estimates the fuel required, reviews the routing, and contemplates the proposed time of departure and arrival. Whenever performance issues are noted (runway length on departure or arrival, field elevation, restrictive meteorological conditions, etc.), the decision to continue in the "go" mode becomes even more burdensome. Most business aviation flight departments have written policies and procedures to guide their pilots in decision-making, but typically the burden falls to the PIC to accept trip assignments as they are requested. As the number of mitigating factors that add to a flight's complexity continue to build—weather, duty day, destination runway length, and so on—the PIC is forced to make a complicated series of judgment calls. The Flight Risk Analysis Tool (FRAT) offers a welcome aid to this decision process. Safety is the number one priority of business aviation pilots—as demonstrated by its low accident rate. Corporations purchase business jets to provide the ultimate in flexibility and customer service. Pilots employed by these corporations work very hard to give them what they pay for.

FRAT is an excellent pre-flight review document that completely analyzes each flight leg during the planning phase and highlights potential hazards. These pre-flight identified hazards alert the pilot and scheduler to the possibility of impending risk. FRAT is similar in construct to the Controlled Flight into Terrain (CFIT) checklist developed by the Flight Safety Foundation, which has proven to be an effective tool that aids pilots in go/no-go decisions (Sheehan 2003, pp. 8–11). The unique aspect of FRAT is the multi-level review and flight release criterion that removes the go/no-go pressure from the flight crew. The underlying principles of FRAT are based on the policy manual and the aviation department's risk management procedures (RMP). Upper level management has endorsed this product as an enhancement of SMS. It is web-based and has become an integral part of the operational dispatch and safety policy of the flight department (McBride 2010).

Potential hazard information is categorized by functional groups. Each hazard has an assigned value. The operation/scheduling department enters some of the information on the form when the flight request is received. The PIC for the flight is responsible for completing the document, on line, prior to departure. At any point during the scoring process, if the total value of the sum of the individual hazards rises above a predetermined value, the chief pilot has to be contacted and must approve the trip. An even higher value brings the aviation director into the decision making process. In most cases, when the total falls below the first alert level, the trip is released. This method takes the burden of pre-departure decision making off the shoulders of the PIC and provides an excellent safety review for everyone involved. The flight crew can then concentrate on its flight duties and not worry about whether the decision to go was a good one or not (McBride 2010).

When each flight leg is completed, it is the responsibility of the PIC to enter flight log information into a handheld electronic device (i.e., Blackberry), and forward the document to the operation/scheduling department. In the post-flight form contained within the electronic device, there is a section for additional information. This can be used to alert maintenance to an informational anomaly, relay passenger requests, inform operations of any changes to the schedule, and identify any hazard information that was discovered during the flight. Several large corporate flight departments have adopted FRAT. This tool may prove to be an excellent source for future SMS safety assurance initiatives, especially with single aircraft operations.

SAFETY PROMOTION

The primary concern of any business aviation organization is to provide accident-free flying through a proactive safety management system aimed at reducing the risks of operating and maintaining aircraft to the lowest possible level. The fourth component of SMS is safety promotion. "One of the most challenging elements of SMS is the creation and nurturing of a safety culture in which every person from CEO to new-hire understands his or her role in maintaining a safe operation, and actively participates in controlling and minimizing risk" (Stolzer 2008b, p. 28). This commitment speaks to the heart of any active SMS program. Everyone needs to buy into the safety culture in order for it to be successful. SMS isn't a directive from the top that, take it or leave it, you must conform to. SMS institutes a cultural shift that provides an opportunity for each associate to participate in the shaping of a proactive work environment based on the principles of safety. Open communication is vital to the success of safety promotion. Each member of the organization needs to feel included in the process. Communication through membership in a working group, the safety committee, or a safety council should be spread throughout each discipline within the flight department. Individual suggestions should be solicited from those department members who are not currently part of a working group or committee. Rotation in and out of working groups and committees is encouraged to facilitate proper communication and involvement.

As the SMS program for a business aviation flight department gains maturity, many lessons are learned by the organization. Improvements to the system will become apparent as SMS becomes more ingrained into the flight department's culture. Learning can be fostered from the parent corporation as well as other flight departments on the airport employing similar disciplines. Consideration should be given to continue educational pursuits in safety-related subjects by those individuals who express an interest. At a minimum, members of the aviation management team will find it necessary to attend IS-BAO refresher courses. If someone in the department is willing to take the time, perhaps becoming an IS-BAO auditor would serve the department's needs for an internal auditor. During audits, the department has the opportunity to learn a great deal from the audit staff. There are always areas that can be improved or tweaked. The follow-up report from the audit team will provide a great summary that can be reviewed by all committees and working groups. Incorporation of these lessons will strengthen the department's safety management system.

SAFETY THROUGH ENHANCED PROCEDURAL STANDARDS—STEPS

In order to break down the barriers to entry that block many business aviation flight departments from considering an SMS initiative, perhaps a simpler more stepwise approach is needed. Figure 12.3 outlines such an approach. Building an SMS process, especially for a single-aircraft operator with limited resources, becomes manageable when approached one step at a time. Reaching level 5 IS-BAO commitment can always be a goal, but not necessarily an achievable one. If the business aviation flight department can manage to reach level 3, its safety program will have been greatly enhanced. Often when the goal is the sole focus, the journey or steps along the path tend to lose their importance. In safety management, each step is an integral piece of the SMS puzzle.

STEPS—A METHODOLOGY FOR SINGLE-AIRCRAFT OPERATIONS

Implementation of a SMS initiative leading to IS-BAO registration can be somewhat overwhelming at first glance. For a single aircraft flight operation, obstacles on the IS-BAO implementation horizon are perceived to be so large that the process is doomed even before it begins. Most if not all business aviation flight operations want to enhance safety through the use of best practices, but appear to be lacking in the people and process power to achieve that objective. Many of these believe their size limits their ability to achieve the goal of SMS implementation.

Taking on the task of SMS development one step at a time provides a paced solution to the overall question of "How do we get there from here." If an operation is allowed to proceed in a methodical fashion, they will be able to show measured progress toward the ultimate prize. The building

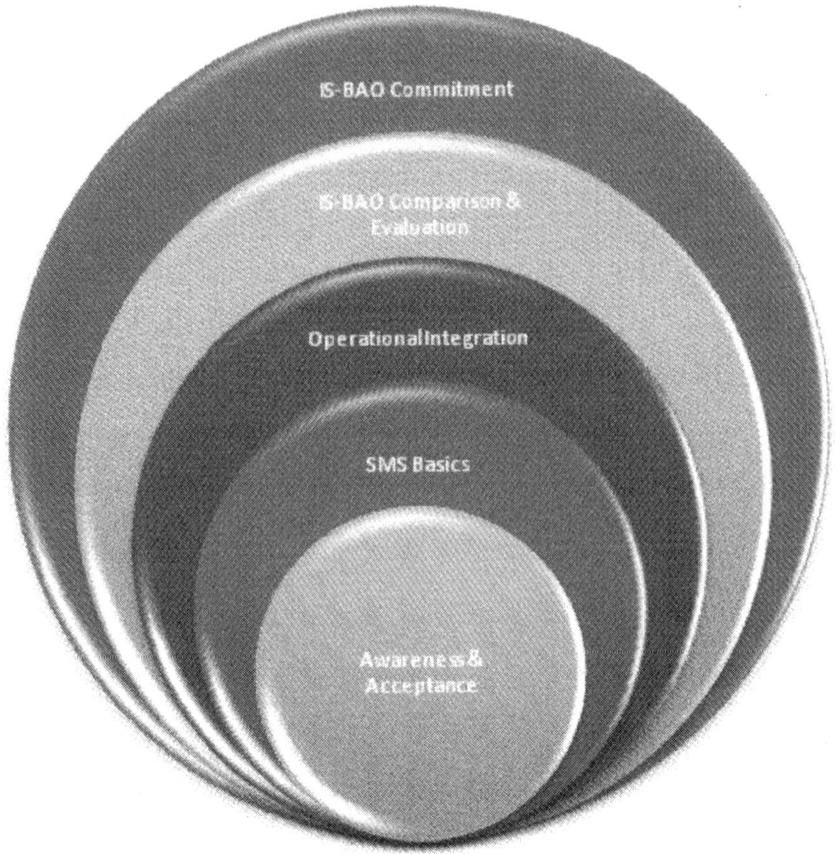

Figure 12.3 Continous SMS improvement: STEPS. Developed by the authors.

blocks of SMS remain intact: safety policy, safety risk management, safety assurance, and safety promotion. Building an SMS program using a step criterion demonstrates the flight department's commitment to the enhancement of safety, even if the eventual goal of IS-BAO registration is beyond its current capacity.

Level 1

It is impossible to build an effective and long-lasting safety program without the acceptance of the need for such a program by everyone in the flight department. Acceptance and endorsement from the top of the corporate organization is as important as the acknowledgement of the need by those who provide the day-to-day services (Stolzer 2008). This principle is especially critical to the initiation and development of SMS in a small business aviation flight department. Within the structure of a small company that operates a business aircraft, the aviation professional responsible for the day-to-day operations will not be very far removed from the senior management group. The intimacy created within a small corporate environment is evident when discussing the subject with chief pilots of single aircraft operations. "Our CEO was fully aware of the quality of our flight operation, but we wanted to take it to the next level" (Moore 2010). Scott Moore, chief pilot of Luck Stone, who operates a King Air 350 out of a company-owned airstrip near Richmond, Virginia, also revealed that the first step for his operation began as an exercise to update the existing operations manual. Luck Stone has owned and operated a company aircraft for 38 years. "Our old manual was out of date and just didn't fit the way [we] were flying the aircraft" (*NBAA Insider* 2010, p. 1).

Another long-term business aviation owner is Thomas & Betts Corporation. For the past 20 years, Thomas & Betts has flown a variety of business aircraft. "We had complete cooperation from our CEO to upgrade our safety process to become eligible for IS-BAO registration" (Wesson 2010). Wesson also shared that his infrastructure consisted of himself, a second pilot, and a chief of maintenance. All the administrative and operational requirements for the department are handled by these three positions. Commitment to safety and buy-in from the aviation associates is fairly straightforward in such a small group environment.

Level 2

In order to take the next step following awareness and acceptance, it is necessary to examine the basic principles of SMS. Figure 12.1 illustrates the four building blocks of SMS. Safety begins with a foundational safety policy. The need to have an effective set of operational guidelines cannot be overemphasized. Prior to any consideration of an initiative resulting in IS-BAO registration, a single-aircraft operator must have a solid set of policy and procedure guidelines. No safety program can function without a set of guidelines. The NBAA usually conducts flight operations manual (FOM) workshops five to six times during the calendar year. The schedule of these two-day seminars can be found on the NBAA website, www.nbaa.org. FOM workshops are designed to provide the aviation manager with all the tools necessary to construct a company aviation policy and procedure manual. In today's electronic cockpits, it is essential to have a set of operational standards. "In the case of computerized control systems, the possibility that humans will misunderstand the operational logic of the system clearly jeopardizes safety" (Lawrence 2007, p. 718).

Many business aviation flight departments are more than willing to share information with others. Excluding company proprietary data, it is not uncommon to find a more mature or well-established department on the airport mentoring a new business aviation entity in policy construction, regulatory compliance, training strategies, and so on. For those flight departments that lack the resources to produce a safety policy manual, outside consulting services are available. One such firm, Baldwin Aviation, specializes in single-aircraft SMS implementation. "The core of Baldwin's program is the operations manual and a validating safety-management program" (Anonymous 2006, p. 66). "We lacked the staff to initiate our SMS initiative and turned to Baldwin Aviation for assistance. They provided us with the direction we needed to merge our procedures into a sound policy manual" (Hyland 2010). Policy and procedure manual construction or reconstruction, whichever comes next, should incorporate the vision of SMS. A final draft of the new policy manual should be reviewed against the IS-BAO standard. The IS-BAO guide can be purchased from IBAC; go to www.ibac.org. Among the publications that are included with the complete IS-BAO guide is a "Generic Company Operations Manual." This is an excellent document that provides the user with the necessary structure and language to build a business aviation policy manual. It is imperative that this exercise be completed before moving on to safety risk management, hazard identification, and risk assessment. Traditional risk management is guided by known facts. It lacks the capability of effectively preventing unpredictable events (Bergeon 2009, p. 50).

At level 2, initial and recurrent training programs that meet IS-BAO guidelines should be established for those who operate and maintain the aircraft. Level 2 provides an excellent opportunity to network with the parent corporation's safety and risk management departments. Many functions within the SMS program have already been established at the corporate level. An SMS toolkit is part of the information available to IBAC and NBAA members. The toolkit contains (IS-BAO 2010):

- Step by step process to develop and implement a SMS
- A CD containing SMS reference documents
- SMS maintenance tools
- Current operators' best practices

Safety assurance (SA) and safety promotion (SP) can be developed in concert with the safety risk management (SRM) segment of SMS (see Figure 12.1). It is important to remember, however, the order of incorporation of these basic concepts when organizing an SMS effort. As previously mentioned, a risk analysis tool similar to FRAT is an excellent tool that integrates SRM and SA.

Level 3

Safety promotion (SP) provides a natural bridge to the expansion of the safety culture though adoption of SMS and integration with company process and practices. As previously stated on page 310 and included here for emphasis, the primary concern of any business aviation organization is to provide accident-free flying through a proactive safety management system aimed at reducing the risks of operating and maintaining aircraft to the lowest possible level. "One of the most challenging elements of SMS is the creation and nurturing of a safety culture in which every person from CEO to new-hire understands his or her role in maintaining a safe operation, and actively participates in controlling and minimizing risk" (Stolzer 2008b, p. 28). This commitment speaks to the heart of any active SMS program. Everyone needs to buy into the safety culture in order for it to be successful. SMS is not a directive from the top that, take it or leave it, you must conform to. SMS institutes a cultural shift that provides an opportunity for each associate to participate in the shaping of a proactive work environment based on the principles of safety. Open communication is vital to the success of safety promotion. Each member of your organization must feel included in the process.

Communication through membership in a working group, the safety committee, or a safety council should be spread throughout each discipline within the flight department. In a single-aircraft operation, formation of working groups or a safety committee will necessitate the inclusion of several non-aviation members from the company. Volunteers should be solicited from company associates who are not currently part of a working group or committee. Rotation in and out of working groups and committees is encouraged to facilitate proper communication. If possible, initial and recurrent training programs in safety management will assist in compliance with future regulatory requirements.

Level 4

As the SMS program for a business aviation flight department gains maturity and migrates towards IS-BAO preparation, many lessons are learned by the organization. Improvements to the system will become apparent as SMS becomes more ingrained into the flight department's culture. Learning can be fostered from the parent corporation as well as other flight departments on the airport employing similar disciplines. At this point, the organization stands on the foundation of a solid policy manual. Risk management processes are in place that measures the inherent personality of the flight operation and how criteria-based formats, like FRAT, allow the flight crew to manage safety issues more succinctly. Links to safety initiatives with the parent corporation have been established. As small as the flight department is, safety is now discussed more frequently in informal settings. The focus becomes more of what impact the introduction of a new piece of technology will bring on the safety culture, than the addition of the technology itself. Consideration should be given to continue educational pursuits in safety-related subjects by those individuals who express an interest. At least one member of a single-aircraft flight department should attend an IS-BAO workshop. Such an initiative will serve to identify who is willing to be responsible for the next step in the process. If the company wishes to move toward IS-BAO registration, having an individual in the flight department who has attended a workshop is critical to success in Level 5.

Level 5

When a flight operation chooses to apply for IS-BAO registration, the process is straightforward. Attendance is mandatory by a department representative in an IS-BAO workshop. These workshops are scheduled often in various locations in the United States and on occasion overseas. Information on the IS-BAO program can be found at URL: www.ibac.org/is_bao.php. During the one-day session, each attendee receives the IS-BAO guide that outlines the certification process. The workshop is designed to aid the attendee with the requirements and steps necessary to prepare and apply for recognition as an IS-BAO–registered flight department. The next and somewhat critical step in the process of the implementation of the IS-BAO doctrine into a flight department is the use of a gap analysis. From the guidelines and worktables included in the SMS toolkit, a systematic comparison of "many of the elements of an SMS already in place, however, they may not be documented and linkages may be lacking" (IBAC 2010, p. 1). An existing flight department can take its policy and procedures manual and compare its contents with the IS-BAO standard. Using this step-by-step development tool, the department may discover that it is operating within a very high percentage of the overall goals of IS-BAO. This requirement points to the importance of the existence of a well-constructed flight operations manual (FOM). Supplementing the gap analysis tool, the IS-BAO manual contains a section titled "Acceptable Means of Compliance (AMC)." This is a very useful document in review of the multiple facets necessary for the construction of an IS-BAO compliant manual.

Following the completion of levels 1–5, the single-aircraft operator applies for IS-BAO registration. This process is outlined in detail in the IS-BAO manual (IS-BAO 2010). The operator may elect to have a pre-audit review conducted by an IS-BAO accredited auditor. If an outside consultant was used in the SMS building process, a pre-audit review should not be necessary. An accredited auditor can be selected from an extensive list found on the IS-BAO website. It is important to note that ethical auditing principles dictate that the same auditor may not be used in preparation for an audit and then subsequently perform the registration audit on the same entity. The auditor should be capable of spending one day on site, having previously reviewed the single-aircraft operations policy manual. Registration follows the auditor's approval and is valid for two years from the inspection date.

BUSINESS AVIATION FLIGHT DEPARTMENT SAFETY MANAGEMENT SYSTEM INTEGRATION

SMS integration into any existing business aviation department regardless of size is a time-consuming and introspective process. The current ICAO regulatory mandate aside, the opportunity to enhance the overall safety culture of an organization by implementing a SMS in a phased-based manner is invaluable. Figure 12.4 illustrates how SMS may be implemented into an

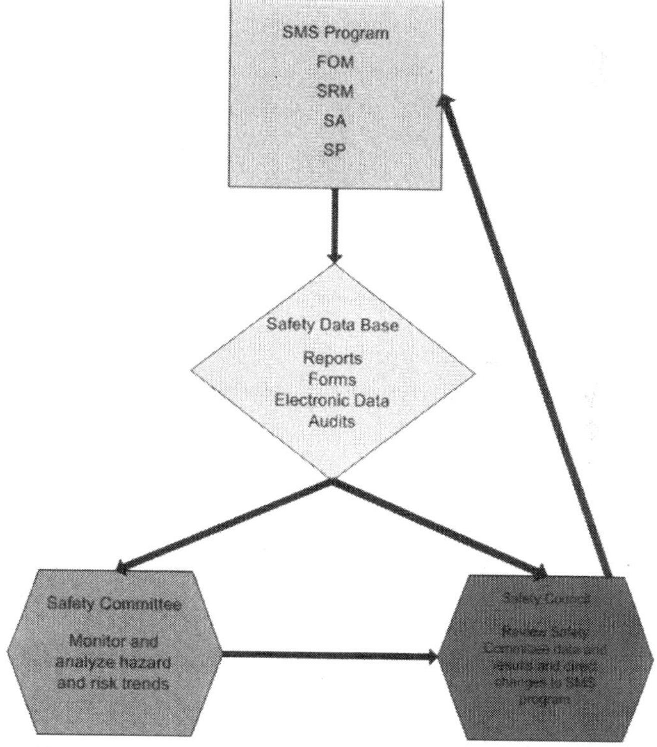

Figure 12.4 Steps for integration of SMS into a business aviation department. Developed by the authors

existing business aviation structure in a phased-based manner. Since SMS is fundamentally a data-driven decision-making process, collecting data into an electronic safety database is essential to allow examination and analysis of the data in an orderly manner. Audits are also important to make sure the data are correct and used properly. Oversight committees are needed to monitor risk trends and direct changes to the SMS program. Typically, documentation of the SMS Program in a business aviation department is contained in the flight operations manual. Other documents of importance are the safety risk management (SRM) plan, Safety Analysis (SA) plan and Safety Promotion (SP) plan as shown on Figure 12.4. Not only is the safety of the flight operation elevated by implementation of an SMS program for a business aviation department, but the bond with the parent corporation gains added strength as a result of the increased emphasis on safety. As safe as business aviation has been in the past, acceptance of SMS will result in elevation of the safety bar to new heights, and is a must in today's aviation culture.

REFERENCES

(2010, March/April). *Business Aviation Insider*, 1. Retrieved from www.nbaa.org/news/insider/2010/0310/

Bagian, J. P. (2006). Patient safety: Lessons learned. *Pediatric Radiology 36*(4): 287.

Battles, J. B., Kaplan, H. S., Van der Schaaf, T. W., and Shea, C. E. (1998). The attributes of medical event-reporting systems: Experience with a prototype medical event-reporting system for transfusion medicine. *Archives of Pathology & Laboratory Medicine 122*(3): 231.

Bergeon, F., Hensley, M. (2009). Swiss cheese and the PRiMA model: What can information technology learn from aviation accidents? *The Journal of Operational Risk 4*(3): 47.

Brady, T. (2000). Advancements in powered flight before World War I. *The American Aviation Experience: A History*. Carbondale, IL: Southern Illinois University Press, 67–97.

Carson, P. P., & Carson, K. D. (1993). Deming versus traditional management theorists on goal setting: Can both be right? *Business Horizons 36*(5): 79.

Federal Aviation Administration. (2009). *Risk Management Handbook*. Washington, DC: U.S. Department of Transportation.

Help is on the way. (2006). *Business & Commercial Aviation 99*(5): 66.

Hoppes, J. D. 2005. *Calculated Risk: The Extraordinary Life of Jimmy Doolittle, Aviation Pioneer and World War II Hero.*. Santa Monica, CA: Santa Monica Press, 177.

Hyland, M. D. (2010, July 1). Personal communication.

IBAC Gap Analysis Tool. (2010, January). (pp. 1-10, A-1-3, B-1-8).

International Civil Aviation Organization. (2011). Safety management publications and resources. Retrieved from http://www.icao.int/anb/safetymanagement/Documents.html

International Standard for Business Aircraft Operations (IS-BAO). (2010). Montreal, Canada: International Business Aviation Council.

Lawrence, P., Gill, S. (2007). Human hazard analysis. *Disaster Prevention and Management 16*(5): 718.

Martínez-Lorente, A. R., & Martínez-Costa, M. (2004). ISO 9000 and TQM: Substitutes or complementaries? An empirical study in industrial companies. *The International Journal of Quality & Reliability Management 21*(3): 260.

McBride, W. T. (2010, May 18). Personal communication.

Moore, S. A. (2010, May 13). Personal communication.

National Business Aviation Association. (2009). *NBAA Management Guide.*

Perret, G. (1993). *Winged Victory: The Army Air Forces in World War II.* New York: Random House.

Reason, J. (1997). Reducing the impact of human error on the worldwide aviation system. Paper presented at the *Ninth International Symposium on Aviation Psychology,* Columbus, OH; Apr 27–May 1,1997.

Redmond, R., Curtis, E., Noone, T., & Keenan, P. (2008). Quality in higher education. *The International Journal of Educational Management 22*(5), 432.

Searles, R., Parke, R. (1997). A new business tool takes wing. *NBAA's Tribute to Business Aviation.* Washington, DC: National Business Aviation Association, 1–15

Sheehan, John J. (2003). *Business and Corporate Aviation Management: On-Demand Air Travel.* New York: McGraw Hill.

Stolzer, A., Halford, C., Goglia, J. (2008a). History and evolution of safety. *Safety Management Systems in Aviation.* Burlington, VT: Ashgate Publishing, 39–62.

______. (2008b). Introduction to SMS. *Safety Management Systems in Aviation.* Burlington, VT: Ashgate Publishing, 13–38.

Twombly, M. (1998). High fidelity: Safety training for pilots. *Risk Management, 45*(6), 46.

Ueltschi, A.L. (1997). *The History and Future of FlightSafety International.* (Ed. Garvey, W.). New York: FlightSafety International.

Wall, S. (2007). Technology improving small-plane safety. *Knight Ridder Tribune Business News,* A.1.

Wesson, D. R. (2010, June 28). Personal communication.

13

Security

Learning Objectives: After reading this chapter you should be able to:

- Assess the security threat to business aviation under various operational scenarios
- Outline security responsibilities within a business aviation department
- Judge the importance of baggage and hazardous cargo to the overall security plan
- List the requirements for aircraft accident/incident reporting
- Appreciate the importance of dealing with the media during an emergency situation
- Assess the aircraft hijack threat to business aircraft

Worldwide terrorism dramatically changed the focus on corporate security and has resulted in extensive precautionary measures at U.S. airport terminals and at major international locations. However, these actions normally do not extend into the general-aviation areas of most airports, and security for corporate and private aircraft may be minimal at best. The drug trade has made the theft of aircraft an ever-increasing risk. Measures aimed at reducing the threat of terrorism, crime, and drug trafficking point to the importance of protecting personnel, facilities, high-value equipment, and personal property. This chapter will discuss the various aspects of security for a business aircraft and its associated company personnel.

Within the organizational structure of a corporate aviation department the overall authority for security of company personnel, flight department associates, facilities, aircraft, equipment, supplies and other items falls to the corporate security manager/officer. Aviation security now commands a greater role in the overall management responsibility of the aviation department manager (ADM). That responsibility is delegated to the ADM by the person most accountable for the welfare of personnel and company assets, the CEO. Security of a business aviation department is sufficiently unique to require close coordination between the security manager/officer and the ADM. Safety and security is in reality the overall responsibility of the most senior officer in the corporation. Chapter 12 discussed how important that relationship is to the adoption and integration the aviation department's safety management system.

The pilot-in-command (PIC) of each trip has overall authority for the safety and security of the aircraft, crew and passengers for the duration of the trip. He and other members of the crew are responsible for protecting information about the identity and affiliations of passengers and any planned movement of the company aircraft. Responsibility for security of the aircraft at home base is delegated to the manager of maintenance as a part of his normal supervisory duties.

The scheduler/dispatcher/operations assistant is accountable for protecting all passenger information and any planned movement of company aircraft. Specific information pertaining to the schedule should be released only to those with a need to know. Every associate within the flight department should be aware of the need to protect information concerning the corporation, its personnel, and property. That is especially important when it comes to the company aircraft and its passengers.

Department personnel who observe a potential threat to security should notify the ADM and the security officer immediately and assist, if necessary, in minimizing or eliminating the threat. Any passenger who expresses a security concern should make that concern known to the pilot-in-command, who will respond accordingly. Corrective actions taken to minimize or eliminate the perceived threat should be communicated back to the concerned passenger as soon as possible.

SCHEDULING INFORMATION—SECURITY

The security of information concerning the movement of any business aircraft, including who the passengers are, where the aircraft departed from, where the aircraft is going next, and up to and including who owns the aircraft, should be held within the purview of aviation department personnel. An important part of the internal security of passenger and aircraft information is the passenger manifest. This document clearly designates who is allowed to board the company aircraft. In order to reduce the possibility of unauthorized individuals gaining access to company aircraft, the flight crew must limit access to aircraft boarding when away from the department's domicile. The PIC will ensure that only authorized passengers are permitted to board the aircraft and that their names correspond to the passenger manifest. If there is any doubt, the pilot should politely ask for a form of identification, preferably one with a photograph. Nonscheduled passengers must be fully identified, including name, affiliation, and the name of the associate sponsoring their travel. All information will be entered on the trip log for recordkeeping purposes. The ADM must approve the addition of any unscheduled passenger before that person is allowed to board the aircraft. No information about trip itineraries, destinations, departure or arrival times, or the identity or affiliation of passengers will be given to any person who is not positively identified or has not demonstrated a need to know.

Printed copies of the flight schedule should have a limited distribution. Associates receiving printed schedules should be periodically reminded to protect the information and to dispose of the forms in an appropriate manner. Electronic receipt of the flight schedule and passenger manifest should be restricted to a limited audience and protected through collaboration with company management information systems personnel. The scheduler/dispatcher/operations assistant should maintain a personal profile on file for each passenger, including their home address and phone number, the name, relationship and phone number of next-of-kin, and other profile information for use in the event of an accident or security incident. For passengers on international trips, the information should include birth dates and passport numbers.

FACILITY SECURITY

At the home base hangar, it is ideal to have a dedicated parking lot for associates and passengers. Entry to the lot should be controlled through an electronic gate. Parked cars in the hangar should be kept to a minimum. However, when it is necessary, cars should be parked so they do not block work areas or interfere with security sensors. Keys to all vehicles must be available to flight department personnel to allow for moving them to make room for parking aircraft or maintenance-related work activity. Keys may be left in a vehicle at the owner's risk, but it is recommended they be placed in the lock box, typically in the maintenance office. Entrances to the hangar and maintenance facility should be closed, locked, and alarmed whenever the work areas are not occupied.

Visitors to the aviation department should be directed to a reception area in the facility and wait until they can be greeted and escorted by a flight department associate. Unescorted visitors in the hangar, on the ramp, or inside any work area should be greeted and politely asked for identification. They should then be personally shown to the reception area or, if they have no business with the company, escorted off the property. If any person is observed performing an unlawful act, immediately notify airport security and keep the person under surveillance. It is never advisable to use force to detain a suspicious person. All personnel assigned to the flight department must be familiar with the use of security systems, to include arming and disarming warnings systems, responding to alarms, and initiating emergency notification procedures. The best rule to always follow is to have the last person leaving the facility each day ensure that all entrances are secured and locked and that all alarm systems are armed and functioning properly.

AIRCRAFT SECURITY AT HOME BASE

All aircraft entrances and compartments should be kept closed and locked whenever the aircraft is left unattended in the hangar or on the ramp. Typically the only times the aircraft should be left open in the hangar or on the ramp is when a departure preparation is underway, an arrival has just occurred, during maintenance, cleaning, or servicing of the aircraft. When positioned for departure, the aircraft may be left open for the arrival of passengers, provided it is kept in clear view by a crew member or the scheduler/dispatcher/operations assistant from the passenger lounge area. A business aviation aircraft is a curiosity to most people. As such, when the opportunity arises, the flight crew will always be confronted with the question of, "Can I look inside your aircraft?" Not wanting to be disrespectful or rude, more often than not, one of the pilots will relent and allow a cursory tour to take place. This is a lapse of judgment that could have dire ramifications. A corporate aircraft is not a toy or a lounge to be inspected by non-company personnel. The integrity of the overall security effort for any business/corporate aviation department begins with the aircraft. As impersonal as it may seem, a company aircraft is an extremely expensive asset that is tasked with the ultimate safety of its crew and passengers. Therefore, sightseers should not be allowed in or near the aircraft or hangar facilities. Any unauthorized person loitering in the area should be challenged and escorted politely off company property. During pre-flight inspections, crew members should be alert for any suspicious objects or packages, indications of tampering, or evidence of unauthorized entry into the aircraft. If an object is found that warrants investigation, proper authorities should be contacted.

SECURITY OF AIRCRAFT—AWAY FROM HOME BASE

Whenever the schedule dictates that a company aircraft remains on a ramp, other than home base, for an extended period of time, all doors should be secured and locked. Ramp personnel should provide chocks for all three landing gear. The gear should also be secured with appropriate pins, under the recommendations of the manufacturer. Interior shades need to be closed during the day. The aircraft should be parked in a well-lighted area that is easily visible to airport authorities. Extended stays with the crew absent from the aircraft can raise additional security issues; parking brake set or off, security tape attached, towing instructions arranged with line personnel, and the possible need for transient hangar space. In a hangar or on the ramp, appropriate security measures dictate that aircraft entrances and compartments be kept closed unless maintenance, servicing, or cleaning is being performed. If work is performed on the aircraft away from home base, it is recommended that a crew member remain with the aircraft during servicing. All refueling procedures should be supervised by a crew member. Whenever there is the slightest doubt as to the quality of the fuel, a fuel test kit should be used to investigate contaminates or the presence of water in suspension. On random occasions at familiar fixed-base operations (FBO), it is recommended that fuel testing be initiated through a documented process of internal evaluation.

If the aircraft is scheduled to be left in a high-risk area, consideration should be given to repositioning it to a more secure airport or location on the airfield that is less exposed. It is the responsibility of the PIC to take all necessary measures to protect the aircraft. If security officers are needed to guard the aircraft, the crew should follow a series of predetermined procedures outlined in the company security manual. This document should outline the procedures utilized in obtaining the services of a local interpreter, briefing the local security guards as to points of contact, and the duties expected of the security detail. Other sources to be considered include the local police or a private security firm, but arrangements should be made in advance. Crew members must leave instructions with the FBO for contacting them while away from the airport. As mentioned previously visitors and sightseers will be discouraged from approaching or entering the aircraft. Any person loitering near the aircraft shall be considered suspicious and will be politely asked to state his reasons for being there. If a visitor is permitted on board, under special circumstances, a crew member must escort that person at all times. Passengers should not be allowed to conduct tours of the aircraft by themselves.

Crew members should instruct the FBO to refrain from posting the identity, departure time, or destination of the aircraft on any status board visible to visitors. They should give out no information over the phone as to the identity or movement of the aircraft. During pre-flight inspections, crew members should be alert for any suspicious objects or packages, indications of tampering, or unauthorized entry into the aircraft. Be particularly aware of attempts to conceal drugs aboard the aircraft. If an object is found that warrants investigation, do not attempt to move or open it. Contact a representative of the FBO and ask that the appropriate agency or civil authority be notified.

PASSENGER SECURITY

During the planning phase of each trip, awareness of passenger security must always be in the forefront of each arranged event. Flights to familiar destinations where the aviation department is well known can become routine for the scheduler and the crew. Typically the atmosphere is much more relaxed. Perhaps the staff at the local fixed-based operation (FBO) has become so used to seeing your aircraft and crew that they feel as though they are an extension of your operation. Familiarity with passengers leads to the occasional exchange of social discourse concerning not only the passengers, but the flight operation as well. The issue to manage in this instance is the balance of customer service and passenger security. As the aviation manager, you implement policy that is designed to enhance security within your organization, but you have little if any control or influence in the conduct of security within the service companies that are utilized on a daily basis.

It is certainly proper to emphasize the importance of informational security to company personnel, but it is improbable that that effort can be extended to outside vendors. The points of communication become the best opportunity to manage passenger security away from home. First contact concerning the need for external services is typically established by the flight department scheduler. Details such as expected arrival time, ground transportation, special handling requests, crew hotel, and anticipated departure are often shared with the FBO. Once en route, the scheduler will follow up with a verification of the availability of services and an expected time of arrival. Upon arrival, the flight crew takes over the point of communication of the passenger and aircraft servicing. A delicate balance of security policy and effective working relationships is necessary.

The old saying, "Familiarity Breeds Contempt," is attributed to one of Aesop's fable, concerning a lion and a fox. The point is to not allow familiarity to influence the need to maintain vigilance. During operations within the confines of an unfamiliar destination, especially during international operations, a heightened level of security is certainly necessary. It is the responsibility of the pilot-in-command to deplane passengers in an area that is secure. Upon arrival, the aircraft will be directed to a parking spot. The flight crew will not have an option to opt out of the designated parking spot for another more desirable position. Spots are assigned by the airport authority. Once the passengers have deplaned and are on their way, a more secure parking spot can be negotiated.

If passengers are picked up by car or greeted by a company representative, a crew member should approach the driver or official and confirm their identities before allowing passengers to deplane. In an unfamiliar area or one that is potentially hazardous, a crew member should escort the passengers until reaching a secure area. If a driver or escort is not waiting for the passengers, a crew member will escort them to the FBO passenger lounge and assist them, as required, in making contact with their party. Caution is advised when making arrangements for ground transportation, however. This is often a method used by terrorists or kidnappers to gain access to their victims.

Although the normal duties of the flight crew do not include making lodging and ground transportation arrangements for passengers, there may be occasions when these services will be required. If the aircraft is required to divert to an alternate, for example, the crew becomes responsible to assist the passengers in making necessary arrangements for travel and accommodations. At international destinations, the names of English-speaking medical personnel should be available in the event of passenger or crew member becoming sick or injured. It may be necessary to contact the American embassy or consulate while in a foreign country. The pilot-in-command will ensure that the telephone numbers for key diplomatic offices are available.

BAGGAGE HANDLING

Business aviation passengers typically have their luggage with them in their personal vehicle when they arrive at the airport for a planned departure. It is not unusual for the passengers to remove their luggage from their automobile and carry it into the FBO or company aviation facility. From there, ground support and flight crew can stage the baggage for loading aboard the company aircraft. Staging the luggage provides several advantages for the crew; stowing logistics, weight and balance verification, any hazmat identification issues, and ultimately the security of the passenger bags. Staging typically takes place in or adjacent to the baggage compartment in the aircraft, depending on ramp and weather conditions.

When luggage is sent to the aircraft separate from the passengers, the bags must be positively identified by the respective passenger before being loaded onto the aircraft. Unidentified packages or unmarked bags must never be carried aboard a company aircraft. This particular mandate in conjunction with the positive identification of each passenger as a company associate or guest of the company are two of the most important safeguards in any sound business aviation security program. It is the responsibility of the flight crew to ensure that all bags placed aboard the aircraft are identified and counted for each passenger. The crew is also responsible to ensure that each passenger has his or her proper bags and the off load count matches the on load count. A passenger bag is that was supposedly loaded onto the aircraft before departure and now is missing upon arrival, can be one of the most aggravating issues that a flight crew faces in regard to customer service. The bag could still be in the trunk of the passenger's car, parked at the departure facility. It could also still be onboard the aircraft. Either way, the image that is portrayed to the passenger is lack of operational control, and therefore a lack of attention to detail.

Whenever possible, if a crew member meets the passengers when they arrive, they should ensure that all baggage is out of the automobile. Utilizing the flexibility of a private ramp that allows automobile access to a position adjacent to the aircraft, it is imperative that a flight crew member be positioned to meet the vehicle at the aircraft. If the passengers of the vehicle are not recognized by the crew member and they are not listed on the manifest, they should be escorted off the ramp in their automobile and provided access to a passenger lounge until their identification can be verified. Skill is required to handle situations that may pose an inconvenience to passengers. It is vital that the passengers understand that their safety and security are the most important aspects of the impending trip.

Do not allow a hired or personal car to be driven away from the aircraft or drop-off area without checking that all appropriate bags are out of the vehicle. If the crew is meeting passengers at an international departure point and the passengers are carrying their bags, it is safe to assume that they have already accounted for all of their bags. More often than not however, during international operations, the passenger's baggage will be brought to the aircraft in a separate van from the passenger van, by the handling agency that you have contracted with for ground support. If you can afford the loss of a member of the crew during an international departure, have that crew member and an agent meet the passengers at the terminal when they arrive at the departure airport. Keep in contact via cell phone or other communication devices. If the bags arrive prior to the passengers, it is imperative that an accurate bag count was conducted at the passenger ground arrival point and that it match the bag count at the aircraft. Although the temptation to leave as soon as possible or the impending approach of a slot time is looming, it is imperative that passengers identify their baggage before it is loaded aboard the aircraft. If the bag count is accurate and each bag has a passenger identification tag that is recognized by the crew member at the aircraft, prior to passenger arrival at the aircraft, it is safe to commence baggage loading.

Upon reaching a destination that requires deplaning of passengers and baggage, it is imperative that one crew member ensure that the cabin is completely clear of all documents, bags, and any personal items belonging to passengers that are departing the aircraft. Following engine shut down on the ramp, a designated crew member will enter the baggage compartment and off-load the appropriate bags for that particular destination. The responsibility for the security of passenger baggage is shared by all crew. All passenger bags should be stored in a separate area in the baggage compartment from the crew bags. All associated bags should be off-loaded at the appropriate stopping point for each passenger or group of passengers. If possible, confirm that each deplaning passenger has the correct baggage before leaving the airport area.

If a passenger bag is inadvertently left on board the aircraft, it is the pilot in command's responsibility to ensure the bag or bags are forwarded to the passenger via the most expeditious means available. The passenger should be contacted prior to forwarding the baggage in order to coordinate the transfer. It is not deemed appropriate to leave a passenger bag at the FBO for the passenger to pick up. Customer service and passenger security mandate that a crew member coordinate all passenger baggage arrangements. Passengers should, however, be responsible for ensuring a proper baggage count. It is the responsibility of each passenger to watch over their own individual luggage whenever a crew member is not available to watch over it. If a bag is left in the rental car or in the limo upon arrival at the hotel, it should be the passenger's individual responsibility to retrieve the missing baggage without the assistance of the flight crew.

The crew may accept unaccompanied baggage, but only with advance notification and suitable means to identify it. Crew members should not accept "special mail" or hand deliveries unless they are fully aware of the package's contents and the circumstances surrounding its delivery. The pilot-in-command is the final authority on accepting unaccompanied packages.

HAZARDOUS CARGO

Business aviation departments principally transport company personnel and are not authorized to carry hazardous materials. Hazardous cargo transport is regulated under the auspice of Hazardous Material Regulations (HMR), Title 49, Code of Federal Regulations, and is limited to cargo operators, restricted to non-passenger flights. The International Civil Aviation Organization (ICAO)—188 signatory states, under the United Nations, the United States is represented by the FAA—ICAO 49 CFR 171.11 outlines the rules under which hazardous material can be flown internationally. It is important to become familiar with these regulations, even though the reader may never be involved in a hazardous material transport flight.

It is recommended that all business aviation flight departments, unless specifically authorized by the FAA and ICAO, strictly prohibit the transportation of materials classified as hazardous materials aboard the company aircraft. Shipping containers containing hazardous materials are normally easy to identify because they are required to have a "Hazardous Materials" warning label or marking. However, if the crew has any doubts concerning the contents of a package or container or its classification as a dangerous material, it should not be loaded on the aircraft. The PIC has the authority to question passengers about the contents of luggage and cargo.

The following is taken from the Federal Register concerning hazardous materials handling:

When a package reaches high altitudes during transport, it experiences low pressure on its exterior. This results in a pressure differential between the interior and exterior of the package since the pressure inside remains at the higher ground-level pressure. Higher altitudes create lower external pressures and, therefore, larger pressure differentials. This condition is especially problematic for combination packagings containing liquids. When an inner packaging, such as a glass bottle or plastic receptacle, is initially filled and sealed, the cap must be tightened to a certain torque to obtain sealing forces sufficient to contain the liquids in the packaging. This will require certain forces to be placed upon the bottle and cap threads as well as the sealing surface of the cap or cap liner to ensure the packaging remains sealed. Once at altitude, due to the internal pressure of the liquid acting upon the closure combined with the reduced external air pressure, the forces acting on the threads and the forces acting on the sealing surfaces will not be the same as when the packaging was initially closed. Under normal conditions encountered in air transport (26 kPa reduction in pressure at 8000 ft), the pressure differentials are not overly severe. However, if the compartment is depressurized at altitude or if the compartment is not pressurized at all, such as on certain "feeder" aircraft, the pressure differential may be severe enough to cause package failure and release of the hazardous materials in the aircraft. High-altitude stresses are encountered when cargo and feeder aircraft transport packages in non-pressurized or partially-pressurized cargo holds.

A seemingly "minor" incident can quickly escalate and result in irreversible, possibly catastrophic, consequences. For example, a closure failure of an inner container could cause an outer package to fail, resulting in fumes, smoke or flammable liquid acting as a catalyst to a more serious incident. The interaction of events occurring on aircraft, such as electrical fires, static electricity or other materials interacting with the leaking material, could result in a catastrophic event. The successful testing of inner packaging designs may lower the likelihood of such an event. Taking a systems-safety approach that includes multiple safety processes and redundancies can prevent a minor incident from becoming potentially much worse.

HMR Part 173 defines hazardous materials under the following categories:

a. Explosives
b. Flammable liquids and solids
c. Oxidizing materials
d. Corrosive liquids
e. Compressed gases
f. Poisons
g. Organic peroxides
h. Radioactive materials
i. Magnetic materials

A complete list of prohibited materials is contained in HMR 175.10. If a hazardous material is inadvertently loaded or transported on a company aircraft and an accident occurs, such as the spilling or leaking of a container, a crew member on site should immediately call CHEMTREC at 1-800-424-9300 for guidance and assistance.

WEAPONS

Passengers should not be allowed to carry a weapon on board an aircraft. If firearms are to be transported, they must be unloaded, put into a "safe" condition, placed in a container or carrying case, and checked in with the crew before the flight. It is imperative that passengers who are transporting firearms aboard company aircraft notify the ADM prior to the scheduled flight in order to coordinate the proper disposition of the weapon. All weapons should be stored in an area that is not accessible while in flight. If the aircraft has a baggage compartment that is accessible during flight, the PIC must ensure that adequate control measures are used to prohibit access to the weapon.

INTERNATIONAL SECURITY

Flight crew passports and ID cards should be renewed at least six months before their expiration date. This measure prevents a document currency requirement from affecting the availability of a crew member for international travel. A crew member's ID card should have a photograph that clearly shows how the person looks at the current time. The International Business Aviation Council (IBAC) crew identification card is recognized by ICAO and universally accepted by customs and security officials. Security measures at major airports in Europe, the Far East, Asia, and South America, post–September 11, 2001, have been bolstered. Enhanced security measures are in place. Identification cards will be checked carefully and crews and passengers can expect to be escorted to and from the aircraft.

When an international flight is scheduled to a country or an international destination that the department has not visited previously, the security manager/officer in coordination with the ADM should perform a threat-assessment report (TRA). This report should include the date(s) of the trip; cities and countries to be visited; airports, including planned alternates; and special considerations, i.e. high-profile passengers, visits to prominent locations, or anything to cause press coverage or other special notice. Additional guidance for international operations is found in Chapter 6.

DEALING WITH THE TSA

The Transportation Security Administration (TSA) has been in the forefront of every American's thought since the September 11 attacks in New York, Washington, D.C. and Pennsylvania. Commercial airport security changed dramatically. The TSA continues to evolve and expand with each new public attempt to disrupt the operation of and/or destroy a commercial aircraft. The American public has accepted the inconvenience of longer security lines and the enhanced scrutiny, in exchange for the perception of an increased level of safety that the system provides. One initial reaction from the TSA that had an instant effect on business aviation was the restriction imposed on the industry of operating in and out of Ronald Reagan National airport—DCA. Business jets were banned from utilizing DCA due to its proximity to so many government facilities, just across the river. Washington Dulles International airport—IAD—became the destination airport for business aviation traffic in and out of our nation's capital.

Another restriction quickly imposed by the TSA, post 9/11, was the requirement for foreign registered business aircraft to obtain an international waiver to enter the country. This process was initially quite cumbersome. In order to expedite the procedure and provide the same level of scrutiny, the TSA has partnered with the Customs and Border Protection (CBP), to gather required data through CBP's Electronic Advance Passenger Information System (e-APIS). The target date for implementation of e-APIS was September 1, 2010. Introduced in early 2009, the e-APIS program has proven to be highly effective in gathering various data points: aircraft ownership, registered operator, passenger information, and intended destination within the United States. ("NBAA welcomes TSA's move" 2010).

In an attempt to bring business aircraft into compliance with commercial aviation security regulations, an FAA Notice of Proposed Rule Making

(NPRM) was issued in October of 2008, asking for industry comment on what was termed Large Aircraft Security Program (LASP). The proposed regulation would cover all aircraft with a maximum certified takeoff weight (MTOW) above 12,500 pounds (12-5), and the general aviation (GA) airports that serve these larger aircraft. LASP is a TSA plan that includes security training for flight crews, periodic security audits for operators, and requirements for GA and other airports that service large aircraft ("New TSA proposal" (2008)). Industry reaction to LASP was overwhelmingly negative. The NPRM spelled out the requirement for business jets to restrict over 100 items of personal and business nature that are commercially banned for carriage by passengers; the requirement to carry law enforcement officers aboard business aviation flights; audits by third parties into the operational aspects of business aviation departments; and the arbitrary limitation imposed with the 12-5 rule that did not apply to lighter aircraft with similar performance characteristics.

The endeavor to regulate private and business aviation security within the same TSA structure, LASP, was put on hold in the latter part of 2009, when the original proposal was withdrawn. The nature of non-commercial business aviation is such that the access to and use of company aircraft is a restricted entity. When corporate security guidelines are in place that dictate who, what, when and where business aircraft operate, the potential for misuse of that asset is greatly diminished.

ACCIDENT AND INCIDENT

Annex 13 of the Convention on International Civil Aviation defines an aircraft accident as "an occurrence associated with the operation of an aircraft which takes place between the time any person boards the aircraft with the intention of flight and all such persons have disembarked, in which a person is fatally or seriously injured, the aircraft sustains damage or structural failure, or the aircraft is missing or is completely inaccessible." The definition of an aircraft incident from the same governing body: "An occurrence other than an accident, associated with the operation of an aircraft, which affects or could affect the safety of operations." The definitions of an aircraft accident or incident are slightly different under the U.S. regulatory system, in that the definitions are more precise than the ICAO definition. There are also very strict reporting requirements as described below.

The Code of Federal Regulations, Volume 3, Title 49—Part 830 defines an aircraft accident as "an occurrence associated with the operation of an aircraft which takes place between the time any person boards the aircraft with the intention of flight and all such persons have disembarked, and in which any person suffers death or serious injury, or in which the aircraft receives substantial damage." An aircraft incident means "an occurrence other than an accident, associated with the operation of an aircraft, which affects or could affect the safety of operations." Fatal injury means "any injury which results in death within 30 days of the accident." Serious injury is further defined as "any injury which: (1) Requires hospitalization for more than 48 hours, commencing within 7 days from the date of the injury was received; (2) results in a fracture of any bone (except simple fractures of fingers, toes, or nose); (3) causes severe hemorrhages, nerve, muscle, or tendon damage; (4) involves any internal organ; or (5) involves second- or third-degree burns, or any burns affecting more than 5% of the body surface." Substantial damage means "damage or failure which adversely affects the structural strength, performance, or flight characteristics of the aircraft, and which would normally require major repair or replacement of the affected component. Engine failure or damage limited to an engine if only one engine fails or is damaged, bent fairings or cowling, dented skin, small punctured holes in the skin or fabric, ground damage to rotor or propeller blades, and damage to landing gear, wheels, tires, flaps, engine accessories, brakes, or wingtips are not considered 'substantial damage' for the purpose of this part."

The Independent Safety Board Act of 1974, as amended and codified in the Code of Federal Regulations (NTSB Part 830) requires the immediate notification by the operator of any civil aircraft of U.S. registry involved in an aircraft accident or *serious* incident as defined below, or when an aircraft is overdue. This notification is to be given "by the most expeditious means available" to the nearest National Transportation Safety Board (NTSB) Office. Contact information for the NTSB offices is available at www.ntsb.gov. The following 12 items are defined as serious incidents: (1) Flight control system malfunction or failure; (2) Inability of any required flight crewmember to perform normal flight duties as a result of injury or illness; (3) Failure of any internal turbine engine component that results in the escape of debris other than out the exhaust path; (4) In-flight fire; (5) Aircraft collision in flight; (6) Damage to property, other than the aircraft, estimated to exceed $25,000 for repair (including materials and labor) or fair market value in the event of total loss, whichever is less. (7) For large multiengine aircraft (more than 12,500 pounds maximum certificated takeoff weight): (i) In-flight failure of electrical systems which requires the sustained use of an emergency bus powered by a back-up source such as a battery, auxiliary power unit, or air-driven generator to retain flight control or essential instruments; (ii) In-flight failure of hydraulic systems that results in sustained reliance on the sole remaining hydraulic or mechanical system for movement of flight control surfaces; (iii) Sustained loss of the power or thrust produced by two or more engines; and (iv) An evacuation of an aircraft in which an emergency egress system is utilized. (8) Release of all or a portion of a propeller blade from an aircraft, excluding release caused solely by ground contact; (9) A complete loss of information, excluding flickering, from more than 50% of an aircraft's cockpit displays known as: (i) electronic flight instrument system (EFIS) displays; (ii) engine indication and crew alerting system (EICAS) displays; (iii) electronic centralized aircraft monitor (ECAM) displays; or (iv) Other displays of this type, which generally include a primary flight display (PFD), primary navigation display (PND), and other integrated displays; (10) airborne collision avoidance system (ACAS) resolution advisories issued either: (i) When an aircraft is being operated on an instrument flight rules flight plan and compliance with the advisory is necessary to avert a substantial risk of collision between two or more aircraft; or (ii) To an aircraft operating in class A airspace. (11) Damage to helicopter tail or main rotor blades, including ground damage, that requires major repair or replacement of the blade(s); (12) Any event in which an operator, when operating an airplane as an air carrier at a public-use airport on land: (i) Lands or departs on a taxiway, incorrect runway, or other area not designed as a runway; or (ii) Experiences a runway incursion that requires the operator or the crew of another aircraft or vehicle to take immediate corrective action to avoid a collision. (iii) An aircraft is overdue and is believed to have been involved in an accident.

EMERGENCY RESPONSE PLAN

An important underpinning of any sound safety and security program is an effective emergency response plan (ERP). Although viewed by many as negative in nature, being properly prepared to deal with a crisis that has just occurred has a far-reaching positive effect on the corporation's image and potential viability. Few events have a more latent impact on the perception of a corporation than how the management team is able to handle a threat, incident, or accident involving the company aircraft. Every ounce of effort expended by the aviation department to provide safe, efficient, and viable transportation services is placed under a microscope whenever (if ever) an accident occurs. Building an ERP, specifically tailored to aviation and yet tied directly to the corporate safety department, is a must in today's environment of instant communication. How to react, who to call, who not to talk to, what information is needed, and what regulatory requirements have just been initiated, can all be scripted through the construction of an ERP.

A corporate ERP does not have to be an exhaustive document, but it must be functional. This is an instance where the aviation manager will need to consult with the corporate director of safety and the corporate general council. The ERP is a legal document that will come under very meticulous scrutiny if it is ever utilized in the event of a real-time situation. In most corporations, the master copy of the ERP is held by the company legal department. Copies of the document should be limited and reside at key communication points within the purview of those responsible for initiating action.

The ERP should, as most control documents do, begin with a statement of purpose by the CEO. There should also be a notice from the legal and safety departments within the corporation. Following the usual control/revision pages and table of contents, there should be a stand-alone page containing the Emergency Notification List (names and cell phones) of the key managers who must be alerted in case of a corporate emergency involving an aircraft. The next page should contain a list of the members of the Go-Team (those persons who are expected to be the first company responders to the scene) and their contact information. Members of the security committee should be included on the Go-Team page.

A list of agencies and their contact information should be listed next:

- FAA—FSDO
- NTSB field office
- Tower
- Fire
- Ambulance
- Airport manager
- County sheriff
- Bomb squad
- FBI
- State police

It is important to remember that, if an incident or accident should occur and the ERP is to be exercised, the nature of such notification is very political in nature. Only those agencies deemed critical to the orderly management of the situation should be initially notified. At no time should information concerning a company incident or accident be released to a third party without the consent of the CEO.

The ERP should contain a stand-alone page that can be duplicated, laminated, and placed in a separate folder residing next to a telephone nearest each key point of communication within the aviation department. This page outlines specific information that must be gathered initially in the event of an accident notification call:

- Brief description of the call
- Time
- Location

- Number of persons; crew/passengers
- Description of injuries
- Registration number of the aircraft
- Type of aircraft
- Aircraft damage
- Property damage
- Local hospital responding and phone number

If an aviation department employee is on the scene of an incident or accident involving a company aircraft, it is very important that they attempt to secure the site within the limits of their capability, given the circumstances, and locate the aircraft flight data recorder (FDR) and cockpit voice recorder (CVR). The NTSB should be the only agency that is authorized to receive custody of the FDR and CVR. Obtain the name, address, and agency of the person taking possession of the FDR and CVR. NTSB agents are required to have identification available at all times.

The aviation department manager (ADM), or a qualified representative appointed by the ADM, should immediately travel to the scene of a company aircraft accident/incident if the on-scene crew members are incapacitated or need assistance. Upon arrival, the ADM will serve as the company representative to the NTSB, the FAA, or any other agency responsible for investigating the accident/incident. The ADM must collect and impound all records relating to the flight crew, the aircraft, and the mission. The ADM should personally make contact with the following:

- National Transportation Safety Board (See 49 CFR, Part 830.15)
- Legal counsel for the company
- Aircraft insurance carrier

In addition, the chief of maintenance/maintenance manager should travel to the scene of the accident/incident and assume responsibility for movement, storage, and repair of the aircraft. Each crew member associated with the accident/incident will be required to prepare a statement setting forth the facts, conditions, and circumstances relating to the accident/incident. The statements should be submitted to the ADM in a timely manner and will be forwarded to NTSB.

A company ERP is only as good as the ability of the organization to exercise the document's contents. It is therefore critical to the overall success of the process to, on occasion, hold an emergency drill, announced, so that key members of the company can take out the ERP and use it. An ERP is not only a critical aspect of a business aviation department's security program; it is an integral part of the department's overall aviation safety management system (see Chapter 12).

AUTHORITY OF THE PILOT-IN-COMMAND

The pilot-in-command (PIC) will remain in command of the aircraft during and after any emergency until the aircraft has been safely landed. In the event of a forced landing, the PIC will remain in command of the situation until relieved by appropriate emergency-response and/or medical personnel. The PIC's authority consists of:

Maintaining control of the aircraft and landing it as soon as practicable, taking into consideration all factors that would affect the safety of the personnel on board.

Alerting appropriate controlling agencies and notifying them of the situation, location, and intentions.

If practicable, notifying the aviation department of the pending emergency.

After landing, evacuating the aircraft and taking necessary immediate actions to prevent additional injury or loss of life.

In the event of an incident or accident, alerting scheduling/dispatch and or operations in order to initiate the ERP.

Treating injuries and provide for the continued safety and welfare of survivors.

Establish contact, through any means available, with emergency-response personnel.

If the PIC is incapacitated, the second-in-command (SIC) will assume the duties and responsibilities of the PIC. If neither pilot is available, the flight attendant or highest-ranking passenger should assume the proper authority.

In addition to the above, the senior crew member who is capable of lending assistance following an accident or incident should seek the assistance of uninjured crew and passengers in order to:

- Remove all passengers and survival equipment to a safe distance. No one should be allowed to return to the aircraft if there is a danger of fire or explosion.
- Administer first aid, as necessary, and request medical assistance. Monitor the condition of all persons and provide necessary assistance until help arrives.
- Assist fire fighters, rescue teams, or law enforcement officers in performing emergency actions by providing information on trapped or missing persons, survivors, nature of injuries, etc.
- Arrange for a medical examination of all passengers and crew members, whether or not they appear to be injured. Request a written doctor's report on each person.
- Notify all appropriate emergency, control, and regulatory agencies by any means available, as time and circumstances permit.

- Arrange for security of the accident scene and the protection of the aircraft and its contents from theft or further damage. Ask for the assistance of law enforcement officials or an airport representative.
- Survey the scene, noting the weather, the location and extent of damage to the aircraft and other property, and any other conditions pertinent to the situation. Gather and record information from crew members, passengers, and witnesses. Record names and phone numbers of witnesses and other contacts, if possible. If anyone is taking photographs, ask for copies of the photos.
- Notify a flight department associate or an appropriate corporate representative as soon as possible. Report on the condition of personnel, the status of the aircraft, and intentions. Report your location and how you can be reached.

DEALING WITH THE MEDIA

If the reader takes away only one thought concerning aviation and the media it is this: never, under any circumstances, make any statement to news media representatives at the scene. It is also never a good idea to speculate on the circumstances of any accident or incident, either verbally or in writing. "When microphones and cameras are pointed at you, you need to be certain that you keep the agenda focused on aviation and not on the company you fly for" (Cannon 2006, p. 85). If you are involved in an accident or incident, do not discuss the situation with anyone at the scene other than fire fighters, rescue teams, or law enforcement officers. Official statements should only be made to representatives of the FAA or NTSB, with valid identification. As a crew member, you have the right to legal counsel before making official statements, and are not required to make any statement that could be incriminating.

The following is taken from an article, "The New Candid Cameras," written for *Business & Commercial Aviation Magazine* in February of 2006:

> Think that something like this won't happen to you? Think again. As I was sitting at my desk putting the initial words together for this article, CNN news flash. A Gulfstream V owned and operated by Nike flew across the television in my office. Right main not down and locked with the other gear fully extended. Local media in a helicopter, I assume a weather reporter and camera crew, were hovering over Hillsboro, Oregon (KHIO) shooting the initial visual flyby by the G-V crew. As most of you who are familiar with Gulfstreams know, the emergency extension procedure is almost foolproof, but certain processes need to be adhered to prior to using the emergency extension procedure. The Nike crew, in the air and I'm certain on the ground, did a magnificent job. It gives you a real since of pride, regardless of your corporate affiliation, to see

a beautiful aircraft like the G-V on TV coming in for a landing, knowing that the outcome will be successful, despite the reservations and doubt in the voice of the television commentator. Following a beautiful landing and rollout, the aircraft taxied up to and halfway into Nike's corporate hangar at HIO.

In this instance, Nike was able to control all aspects of the incident up to and including the press conference that followed. They were not able to control the so-called "experts" whom CNN lined up on the phone to discuss the emergency. This process was best described to me as the "Billy Bob" show. More often than not some retired airline pilot will offer as much insight into what a business aviation aircraft is about to do, as a flight instructor in a 172 would pointing out the finer aspects of how the United 777 crew will bring in their crippled bird for a safe landing (Cannon 2006, p. 85).

BOMB THREAT

Any threat of a bomb, directed against a business aviation facility or aircraft, should be treated as real. The first priority of the company associate receiving the call is to remain calm and collect as much information as possible from the person making the threat. A bomb-threat checklist, see Figure 13.1, should be utilized to record all information. This checklist should be located and easily accessed at all aviation department key communication points. The associate who receives the call must attempt to remember the exact words of the caller, and write them down. Attention should be paid to background noises or conversations. Carefully listen to the tone and other qualities of the caller's voice to aid in identification.

Facility Threat

If a bomb threat is directed against the flight department office or hangar facility, associates should accomplish the following:

- Sound the alarm to evacuate the building. Assemble at a pre-designated area and account for all personnel.
- As you leave, be alert for any unknown or suspicious package. NOTE ITS POSITION, BUT DO NOT MOVE OR TOUCH IT.
- Go to a nearby telephone and call 911. Inform the emergency dispatcher of the bomb threat and provide as much information as possible. Give the dispatcher your name, location, and phone number. Stay near the phone to provide additional information and directions, if needed.
- Keep everyone at least 300 feet away from the building. Do not allow anyone to approach or reenter the building until police or fire department officials have arrived and have assumed on-scene control.

Figure 13.1 Bomb Threat Checklist

Stay Calm. **Listen Carefully.** **Ask Questions.** **Write It Down.**
Be Friendly. **Keep The Caller On The Line As Long As Possible.**

Date: ______________________ Time: ______________________ a.m. p.m.
Exact words of the caller: ______________________

____

____

QUESTIONS TO ASK:

1. Where is the bomb right now? ______________________
2. When is the bomb going to explode? ______________________
3. What will make it explode? Timer? __ Movement? __ Altitude sensor? __ Other? __
4. What kind of bomb is it? ______________________
5. What does the bomb look like? ______________________
6. Why did you plant a bomb? ______________________
7. Will you call me again? ______________________
8. Where are you calling from? ______________________
9. What is your name? ______________________
10. What is your phone number so I can ask more questions?

    ____

TRY TO DETERMINE THE FOLLOWING: (Circle or fill in)

IDENTITY: Male __ Female __ Adult __ Teen __ Child __ Age? ______________

VOICE: Loud Soft Whisper High Deep Fast Slow Disguised? ____Other? _______

ACCENT: Local? _______ Region of U.S.? ______ Foreign? _______ Race? ________

LANGUAGE: Literate Slang Foul Distinct Slurred Stutter Other? _________

EMOTION: Calm Angry Excited Depressed Laughing Crying Intoxicated Sober Rational Irrational Other: ________________

BACKGROUND NOISE: Office Factory Bar Voices Music Party Traffic Aircraft Children Animals Other: __________________

BOMB THREAT - SUPPLEMENTAL INFORMATION

What phone number did the caller use to call you? ______________________

How long did the call last?

Did the caller know much about the Company? Did he/she mention any executives?

Did the caller know much about the Flight Department? Did he/she mention any associates?

Did the caller know much about the aircraft? Did he/she specifically mention our aircraft?

Did the caller seem to know anything about bombs or explosives? Any technical terms?

(*Continued*)

Figure 13.1 Continued

Your full name and position: ____________________

Your address and home phone number: ____________________

Who did you notify? When? ____________________

____

Other Information: ____________________

____

____

Note: It is vital that this information remain confidential. The recipient of this call should not discuss the nature of the threat or other information about the call except when questioned by company security or an official investigator. If you recall additional information after you have turned in this report, notify the Director of Flight Operations.

Provide information and assistance, as required, when requested by the on-scene controller (police or fire department).

- Contact key company personnel. Give them your name, location, and phone number.

Threats to Aircraft

If a bomb threat is directed against a business aircraft, the associate receiving the call must:

- Contact the PIC of the aircraft by any means available. Full information about a threat to an aircraft in flight must be communicated to the PIC, so he can make informed decisions and take appropriate action.
- If the aircraft is operating on the airport, attempt contact through the tower or FBO. If the aircraft is airborne, ATC should be contacted for assistance in warning the crew of the threat.
- ARINC (Aeronautical Radio, Inc.) can be used if the aircraft is being operated within an area of ARINC control.
  - ARINC, New York—(516) 589-7224
  - ARINC, San Francisco—(415) 349-2725
  - ARINC, Honolulu—(808) 836-3463
  - ARINC, San Juan—(809) 791-3280
  - ARINC, Fort Worth—(214) 267-5761
  - ARINC, Houston—(713) 443-0424
- If the aircraft is operating in an international area not in ARINC control, request assistance from the FAA Security Department in Washington, D.C., by calling (202) 426-3391.

- After warning the crew, notify airport authorities and/or law enforcement officials at the site of intended landing. If the aircraft will be landing at home station, dial 911 and report the bomb threat to the emergency dispatcher. In addition, contact the nearest FBI office.

What to Do as a Flight Crew Member

When a report of a bomb threat is received by the crew, the following actions are recommended:

Prior to takeoff or following the landing:

- Stay calm and make an announcement to the passengers that there is a need to evacuate the aircraft. If a flight attendant or flight attendant is aboard, direct him or her to prepare the cabin and instruct the passengers on evacuation procedures.
- Stop the aircraft in a safe area, shut down the engines, and quickly evacuate the passengers and crew. Keep everyone a safe distance from the aircraft and do not go back inside.
- Wait for the arrival of emergency response personnel (fire department, bomb squad, etc.) and follow the directions of the on-scene controller.

While airborne:

- Declare an emergency, inform ATC that you have received a bomb threat, and ask for clearance to the nearest suitable airport. Set transponder code to 7700. Request emergency equipment to standby. Ask for the advice of an FAA bomb expert.
- Make an announcement to the passengers that there is a need to land as soon as possible and to evacuate the aircraft. If a cabin attendant is on board, direct him or her to prepare the cabin and instruct the passengers on evacuation procedures.
- Decrease airspeed to reduce stress on the aircraft. Consider lowering the landing gear, if performance parameters permit, to minimize damage to the gear in the event of an explosion.
- Maintain cabin pressure altitude to minimize the possibility of triggering an altitude-sensitive device. Descend to same altitude as the cabin, and then maintain zero differential for the remainder of the descent. This will minimize the blast effects to a pressurized cabin.
- Instruct the cabin attendant or designate a passenger to conduct a search of the cabin for any package that could contain an explosive device. Do not allow anyone to touch it. Move passengers to seats as far away as possible from a suspected bomb and have them put on their seat belts and shoulder harnesses.

- Prepare the passengers for an emergency landing and brief them on procedures.
- After landing, stop the aircraft in a safe area, shut down the engines, and evacuate. Account for all passengers and crew members. Keep everyone at least 300 feet from the aircraft and do not allow anyone to go back inside.
- Wait for the arrival of emergency response personnel (fire department, bomb squad, etc.) and follow the directions of the on-scene controller.
- The PIC will be responsible for securing the aircraft after the departure of emergency personnel and determining if the aircraft will be needed as part of an official investigation.

AIRCRAFT HIJACK THREAT

Due to the events surrounding the September 11, 2001, terrorist attacks, normal TSA hijacking procedures do not necessarily apply in business aviation operations. The best point of prevention of an attempted hijacking is on the ramp. If approached by someone threatening to hijack the aircraft, the crew is cautioned that they may face dire circumstances when airborne and may be better served confronting the situation on the ramp. The circumstances surrounding an attempted or actual hijacking of a business aircraft cannot be predicted. A calm and cooperative attitude, tempered by good judgment, is the best protection in the event of a hijacking incident. Keep the following general principles in mind:

- The safety of the passengers and crew members is paramount. The aircraft shall be considered expendable, but every effort shall be made to protect the lives of the people on board.
- A hijacker must be considered dangerous. He or she is likely to be desperate or unbalanced, which can lead to unpredictable or irrational acts. Use all means at your disposal to keep the hijacker calm.
- Comply with the demands of a hijacker to the extent possible. If you are told to do something that would jeopardize safety, explain to the hijacker the reasons why it would be and, if possible, suggest an alternative.
- Attempt to maintain communications with the outside. Keep ATC informed of the situation and your intentions.

If a hijacking occurs, attempt to notify the air traffic control agency by transmitting, "We are being hijacked," and setting the transponder code to 7500. If the crew is unable to change the transponder setting or when not under radar control, transmit a radio message which includes the phrase,

"(Aircraft call sign), Transponder Seven Five Zero Zero." Air traffic control (ATC) should acknowledge receipt of the code 7500 signal and ask for confirmation of the situation. If the crew reaffirms that a hijack of the aircraft is underway, ATC will notify the appropriate authorities. If the PIC or crew member in communication with ATC deems that the situation has become desperate and wishes to have armed intervention, it is procedurally correct to transmit code 7500 for at least three minutes and then change to code 7700. Again, ATC should acknowledge receipt of the change in code.

Once the aircraft has landed, the use of flaps as a means of communication has been established to signal authorities who may be standing by to offer assistance. If the flaps are retracted after landing, the crew is communicating that they do not want armed intervention to take place. The crew must change the transponder code back to 7500 from 7700. The pilot may emphasize the fact that intervention is no longer desired by transmitting a radio message, ""(Aircraft call sign), Back on Seven Five Zero Zero." If the crew determines that armed intervention is necessary after landing, remaining on transponder code 7700 and leaving the flaps in the full down position is a universally accepted means of communicating to ground personnel that intervention is needed.

If the normal communications procedure of the aviation department is use of cockpit speakers during flight operations, both pilots should don headsets out of sight of the hijacker. Turn the first officer's cockpit speaker on with the volume up. Use the #1 radio for normal communications and give the hijacker the impression that he/she is hearing all communications. Turn the captain's cockpit speaker off. Use the #2 radio tuned to an emergency frequency for discreet communications through the headset. The captain should talk in low tones with his face turned away, and should attempt communications only when the hijacker's attention is diverted or when conversation is masked by the cockpit speaker. The captain can also discreetly press the microphone transmitter button when talking to the hijacker or the first officer to communicate information to the outside agency.

HANGAR/FACILITY FIRE

The aircraft should always be positioned within a hangar in a manner that would allow an expeditious extrication in the event of a fire within the facility. While the first priority in an emergency of this type is the safety of all personnel, all steps that will ensure the safety of company associates and assist in the removal of the company aircraft should be planned for in advance.

Remember "R.A.C.E.," the four steps to respond to a fire (www.uic.edu/depts/envh/HSS/Fire.html):

R. **RESCUE** anyone who has been injured or who is in physical danger. Get them safely away from the location of the fire. Use the team approach (minimum of two persons) if attempting a rescue. Don't risk becoming an additional victim.

A. **ACTIVATE** the nearest alarm. Alert other people in the building about the fire. Avoid creating panic. Designate one person to report the fire by dialing 911. Others should check offices, lavatories, and storage rooms to make sure everyone has been alerted and is safely out.

C. **CONFINE** the fire by closing doors (do not lock) and windows to keep it from spreading. If the fire is small, you may be able to put it out. Fire extinguishers are stationed at various locations in the hangar and office spaces. Don't attempt to fight a rapidly spreading fire.

E. **EVACUATE** the building using any available exit. Provide assistance to anyone who needs help in getting out. If caught in heavy smoke, stay low and crawl along a wall or corridor to an exit. Never go up, unless you are below grade. Always down and out. Cover your nose and mouth with a handkerchief (wet, if possible) and take shallow breaths. Assemble a safe distance from the building and account for other members of the organization.

SEVERE WEATHER

During periods of severe weather, monitor a local radio or television station for a National Weather Service tornado watch or warning. Online weather services or vendor services under contract within the corporate hangar or offices may be the most accurate and timely resources as to impending storms and cell movement. The Civil Defense Warning System will use emergency sirens to sound a tornado warning. A public warning will be issued using a five-minute steady blast of the siren. Upon receipt of a tornado warning, move away from exterior office areas and hangar bays and toward enclosed interior areas of the building. If you are outside, immediately proceed inside and take cover. Stay away from windows and be careful of broken or falling glass. Ensure that the threat has passed before exiting the facility.

OTHER EMERGENCIES

By their nature, emergencies vary greatly and are unexpected. Response procedures cannot be outlined for every contingency. Remaining calm and exercising good judgment are essential when dealing with any emergency.

Refer to the list of emergency contacts and communicate with them promptly to report an emergency and get the advice and assistance needed to respond appropriately.

DISASTER RECOVERY PROCEDURES

If a disaster results in the loss of or damage to flight department facilities, arrangements must be made to resume normal flight operations as quickly as possible. While the specific circumstances of a disaster will dictate the actual course of action, the following procedures may be used as a guide to establishing a temporary base of operations.

If a company aircraft is stolen, damaged, or destroyed, other owned/leased or chartered aircraft will be used to fulfill trip requirements to the extent possible. Certainly a short-term option is the use of airline flights that coincide with travel requests to destinations served by commercial air service. The senior passenger for a trip must be notified whenever a charter aircraft is being considered for a trip, and he or she should be given an estimate of charter costs before confirming the flight. Repairs or replacement of a damaged or destroyed aircraft should be coordinated, with input from the insurance carrier and appropriate members of the corporate staff to assist in financial planning.

If a company owned hangar is damaged or destroyed, aircraft will be parked in a transient aircraft hangar owned by a local FBO until a longer-term arrangement can be made with the FBO or another flight department. Maintenance will be performed, to the extent possible, at the temporary location, but assistance may be required from the FBO maintenance facility if company personnel shop tools and equipment are not available for use. Major inspections should be contracted out to a licensed repair station whenever the corporate hangar is not available.

OSHA RESPONSE TO CATASTROPHE

OSHA (Occupational Safety and Health Agency) will respond to a workplace catastrophe resulting in multiple fatalities, extensive injuries, massive toxic exposures, or extensive property damage. OSHA will dedicate resources to investigate and uncover the cause of the event. Their intended actions are outlined in OSHA Instruction CPL 2.94. A toll-free emergency hotline is available for reporting fire hazards, imminent dangers, or other workplace safety and health emergencies to OSHA. The number is 1-800-321-OSHA, and it is to be used for emergency purposes only.

REFERENCES

Cannon, Jim. (2006, Feb). The new candid cameras. *Business & Commercial Aviation.*

International Civil Aviation Organization. (2004). Use of ICAO technical instructions (49 CFR Ch 1-171.11). Retrieved from http://edocket.access.gpo.gov/cfr_2002/octqtr/pdf/49cfr171.11.pdf

NBAA welcomes TSA's move to eliminate burdensome international waiver requirements. (2010, July 26). NBAA press release. Washington, DC.

New TSA proposal must balance security with mobility. (2008, October 9). NBAA press release. Washington, DC.

Occupational Safety and Health Administration. (1991). OSHA response to significant events of potentially catastrophic consequences (OSHA Instruction CPL 2.94). Retrieved from http://www.osha.gov/Firm_osha_data/100001.html

U.S. Government. (1998). Title 49—Transportation, Chapter VIII—National Transportation Safety Board (Part 830). Code of Federal Regulations. Retrieved from http://www.access.gpo.gov/nara/cfr/waisidx/49cfr830.html

———. (2002). The hazardous materials regulations (HMR; 49 CFR Parts 171-180). Code of Federal Regulations. Retrieved from https://hazmatonline.phmsa.dot.gov/services/Pub_Free.aspx

14

Working with Senior Management

Learning Objectives: After reading this chapter you should be able to:

- Assess the importance of working harmoniously with senior management
- Evaluate the role of the aviation department manager when acting as the representative of the aviation department
- Realize the need to use discipline in the interest of safety when acting as pilot-in-command of a business aircraft
- Be aware of the broader need to represent business aviation at the national level

As aviation professionals, we are expected to consistently offer the very best in safety and comfort to our passengers. It is recommended that you view the executives and their guests who fly aboard your aircraft as customers. Your job as a manager is to provide excellent customer service. This is what aviation managers do. This is what you signed up for when you decided to make business aviation your avocation. As hard as you try to satisfy your customer's needs, they always seem to have questions about the art and science of maintaining and operating aircraft. The folks you fly simply don't have the time or the inclination to fully understand what, or how, you and your colleagues do what you do. Often a question may arise concerning why the ride was bumpy, or why the arrival was ten minutes later than scheduled, or what that noise was during some portion of the trip. We've all had to explain a wide variety of causes for an untold number of tiny issues that may arise at some stage in a flight. The more perfect the trip, the less questions or concerns from the passengers. You and your crews control the outcome. There is a direct correlation between the amount of effort expended by your professional staff and the level of customer satisfaction that results from those efforts.

What do you do when instances occur beyond your span of control or outside of your influence? One morning you pick up the *USA Today* that was under your hotel door and right on the front page, the headline is shouting that there has been an aviation accident. As horrible as it is for you to read about the misfortune of another crew and their passengers, it has a profound effect on your customers who are possibly reading the same article. You may quickly form an opinion about the cause of the announced incident or accident, but your customers won't. They will only hear what the media is saying or read the opinion of the author of the article in the paper. Many of them will want to talk to you, to be reassured by you. Your passengers live in an uninformed world when it comes to aviation. They have to fly in order to conduct business. In the back of their thoughts is the nagging misconception as to the level of safety every time they take off or land. You and the professionals you work with must constantly support the perception of safety in the minds of your passengers.

Every casual conversation your principals have with friends not conversant about aviation, each article they read about an incident and every time they drive to the airport in bad weather, small doubts creep into the trust that you have established with them that they will in fact be safe. There are steps that you can take as an aviation manager to alleviate those fears and diminish those doubts. The best approach is to proactively communicate your philosophy of safety to each of your customers. Respond to the customers you serve. Whenever you see or read about an aircraft incident, try to gather all of the pertinent facts and attempt to interpret what procedures you have in place that would possibly aid in the avoidance of something similar happening to your flight department. Most aviation accidents are caused by people not following established procedures. Training, procedures, diligence, and lack of complacency are all watch words that you should constantly use to emphasize your flight department's dedication to safe operations.

Immediately following any negative news concerning business or commercial aviation, act by responding to all of your senior executives and their respective administrative assistants, via e-mail or memorandum. E-mail is a very effective and efficient means of getting your safety message across to the audience you are attempting to influence. Explain that an incident has occurred and briefly outline the known circumstances. Then follow up with a description of what your flight department is doing or will do in order to minimize the possibility of an occurrence of such an event. It is advisable to close the e-mail with an open invitation to discuss the matter further.

Share the correspondence you have just sent to the corporate office with all of the members of your aviation team. Promote the attributes of your fellow crew members and maintenance professionals in memorandum or e-mails to your boss. Personally tell your fellow aviation associates that they are doing a good job. Tell your customers about any promotions, advancement in professional credentials or any major contributions that your fellow team members have made recently. Keep it up. Constantly reinforce your dedication to safety to your passengers as well as to the members of your flight department.

Share your thoughts and concerns with other managers in your area. Seek the advice and counsel of friends in the industry. Those collective ideas can benefit everyone, especially your passengers. It is very important to them that you are connected to other managers in business aviation. Your assessment is always enhanced whenever you seek the opinion of others before making important decisions. If you are fortunate to have a local association in your area, become part of the group. It will take some of your valuable time to actively participate in local association activities, but in the end, you will find that the dividends received for you and your department far outweigh the initial efforts.

It is critical that your customers understand that you are participating in the process of increased safety and security. Make them aware that the aviation department has the personnel and skill sets to handle their safety and security when they have the need to fly. It is becoming an old cliché, but it is very important to your department that you, the manager, become more proactive than reactive. Be proactive with your safety program (Chapter12). Constantly seek ways to improve. When forced to be reactive, when events dictate, visit, call, or write to your senior management team.

WHAT LEVEL ARE YOU REPORTING TO?

As the corporate/business aviation manager, you will have many occasions to interact with the senior management team of your parent corporation. You get to know these executives very well. If you joined the company as a junior pilot, years ago, you perhaps first met many of the executives as you began to fly trips. These were after all your passengers and they would be interested in meeting a new pilot who was assigned to their flight. Business aviation is far more intimate in nature than the airlines, when considering the physical proximity of the crew to the passengers onboard the aircraft. Air carriers, for reasons of security, have been forced to lock their cockpit doors. Corporate executives on a small to medium size business jet can see and hear the cockpit crew during a flight. Many business jets and turboprops do not have doors between the cabin and the cockpit and simply have a curtain installed just aft of the pilots' workplace to provide some means of privacy for the passengers. Business aviation cockpits are, therefore, not access-limited and it is not unusual for a passenger to unfasten his or her seatbelt and walk a few steps up into the cockpit to pass information or to engage the crew in a conversation. This practice is of course to be discouraged during climb and descent, but if the boss feels compelled to let you know that a change in the itinerary has just happened, you may be tapped on the shoulder.

John Sheehan, author of *Business and Corporate Aviation Management*, and a seasoned consultant in the business aviation community, opines:

> First, who's the boss? Certainly, your reporting senior qualifies for this title, but in most companies there is a near-familial bond between the chairman and/or CEO and the flight department. This bond is forged over many hours of enjoying the peace and quiet of a magic carpet that provides additional productive time and quiet interludes with which to collect one's thoughts and plan for the future. Yes, there usually is a special link between the big boss and the flight department, regardless of what the organizational chart says.
>
> Other bosses? Sure; frequent flyers assume the mantle of boss, again because of the special affinity they develop for a service that benefits them in many ways. How about those who control the flight department's destiny, the CFO, the CEP secretary, and chairman's wife? Yup, they are pretenders to the title, too, just because of the special relationships developed over time. The truth is that all of these, and perhaps others, should be treated with deference and understanding if the flight department is to remain healthy and viable. Treat them like bosses and you will be rewarded with loyal support for some time to come. (Sheehan 2003)

It is this personal level of familiarity that can make or break a career in business aviation management. While they may treat the entire crew, and especially the aviation manager, as if they were all close personal friends, you and your colleagues will be better served to understand from the outset that you are, in fact, not best friends of the passengers. This is not to say that you shouldn't treat them with the utmost respect and courtesy, but it is critical to understand that you are employed to provide a deliverable: safe and efficient transportation services. The reality of the nature of the job is that you will spend most of your working hours with many of the senior executives of the corporation, while the vast majority of the employees of the company have never met or in some cases never seen the top echelon of managers. The president of the company will call you by your first name and ask how the family is doing. You will be introduced as "our pilot" to guests and family members. You may on occasion crew a trip to a company outing or family vacation site and be asked to stop by for a meal.

As a company employee, you should feel at ease to participate in corporate events. You may be invited to do so because you flew passengers to the event site. You may be invited to do so because you manage the aviation function. The distinction to keep in mind from the outset is, if you do attend, don't become overly familiar with or feel free to partake in activities as if you were privileged to be or entitled to be there. Not to lessen the spirit of the offer from a senior passenger to take part, but it is important to understand the need for caution.

They are your customers and as has been emphasized throughout this text, you are in the business of customer relationships. Ray Kroc, the founder of McDonalds, once said, "Look after the customers and the business will take care of itself." Another of his famous quotes, "We're not in the food industry, we're in people industry; we just happen to sell hamburgers." Mr. Kroc has also been credited with the notion that McDonalds was in the real estate business and just happened to be selling hamburgers. As an aviation manager, you need to recognize that in fact you and your colleagues are in the customer service industry and just happen to be operating airplanes. Not to diminish the importance of safety and standardization, but given the fact that your organization is professionally managed and maintained, the deliverable that you are offering to the executive staff your parent corporation is the ultimate in customer service.

The main opportunity to have influence with senior management and/or your boss is during formal meetings that are regularly scheduled. If you do not have regularly scheduled meetings and most of the communication has been on an informal basis, it is imperative that you work toward regularly scheduled meetings with your boss. As the manager, you will have a limited amount of time to discuss issues concerning how you manage the flight department. That is what you have been hired for and how you will be evaluated by senior management. Your performance as a financial manager (see Chapter 10) will be closely scrutinized. You will be asked to justify the use of capital for major projects, the current and future staffing levels, expense account policy, and budget variances. The manner in which you create and manage the annual budget is more critical to your success that how well you can fly or maintain an aircraft. You are being paid to manage, not necessarily to operate the flight department. Investigate the possibility to further your managerial skills through company sponsored training programs. It is a great way to gain knowledge and at the same time network with other executives within the company.

In the absence of communicated access to senior management, they are going to form their own and often inaccurate opinions of how the aviation department functions. When you discuss your philosophy of how the aviation department functions, you must be clear and easily understood. You will not have the luxury to lapse into stories about your past experiences in aviation. As mentioned previously, you should avoid at all costs discussing anything of substance during the course of flying a trip.

Communication, either written or verbal, should take place between you and your boss at least once a month. As the manager of the aviation department, you need to project a constant message to your boss and the senior officers of the company that you are constantly working on process and personnel improvements. A monthly written report generated from your office is one means of communication. Such a report should include departmental statistics: hours flown, miles covered, passenger load, destinations visited, any significant milestones met during the month and especially any special recognition of departmental personnel. It is also important to include financial data that show how the department is doing on a monthly and yearly basis as it relates to the approved budget. Not much attention is paid to these reports, other than to provide the comfort that things are being looked after. If your boss has a question concerning the flight department, it will more often center on an expectation of service that was not fulfilled. The inquiry will often come from a passenger who observed an instance or was dissatisfied with some level of service. That concern will be passed to your boss and subsequently will land upon your desk. Your aviation team, no matter how hard they try, will not be able to avoid questions as to why a particular decision was made. It is human nature to ask why the flight was delayed, or why the crew had to miss the approach, or why the coffee was not as good as on the last trip, and so on.

What is important to you as a manager and subsequently to your team in general is that you cannot become consumed with questions, concerns, or criticisms from your boss or other executives. Corrections should be made to assuage any issues. Communication to your boss that the problem is solved, a policy has been changed, or the department crew member has been counseled, should be face to face or in written form and in a timely manner.

Whenever you are scheduled for meetings with your boss they will almost always take place in his or her office. On occasion, it would be nice to have them out to the airport for a meeting. Timing meetings with your direct report should on occasion coincide with a departmental meeting of your entire staff following your meeting with the boss at the airport. That offers the opportunity for your staff to interact with your manager. Attempt to hold monthly meetings with your boss in order to exchange information on the status and vibrancy of the aviation department. Put together a brief agenda and ensure that it is circulated several days prior to the scheduled meeting. It is important for effective communication and to build trust between you and your boss that you do not bring surprises to a scheduled meeting. Let them know ahead of time what you are going to talk about. Any last minute additions should be conveyed via email prior to the get together.

The least productive spot to have a meeting with your boss is in the cabin of your company's business jet. That is especially true if you are functioning as pilot-in-command and your boss is the chief executive officer of the company. The time afforded to the CEO onboard the company plane is often the only minutes or hours that he or she has to relax and reflect. They are out of the office, away from the phone and e-mail and many other necessary distractions that occur during the normal course of a business day. It is perhaps the only personal time that the principal and his wife have had together in days or weeks. If you walk back and surprise them with concerns or questions, they will not be as receptive to discussing issues as you would like for them to be. You may have them captive and therefore command their attention, but it will be difficult to make an effective presentation during an impromptu meeting in the cabin of a business jet you are in command of. Simply showing up in the cabin with a brief agenda and catching the chairman or any other executive off guard is one of the biggest mistakes you can make as a manager. Your passengers scheduled the trip in order to save time. It is certain that while on board, they will be working on issues relating to the meeting or site visit that will take place at your destination. There may be an occasion where the chairman has invited you come along on a scheduled trip as a passenger. If this occurs, you will generally be afforded the opportunity to have some quality time with the boss. Indirectly related to the makeup of your passenger list and the size of the company aircraft, will be the level of privacy that you will have for your meeting.

Executives want to be prepared for every meeting they attend. The foundation for that preparation is an understanding of what subjects will be covered during the meeting. Each participant should be provided the courtesy of an agenda in advance of any meeting. Agendas are tools for the preparation of effective communication. Any reports or statistics that will be discussed during the meeting should be sent to each person attending, days or even weeks prior. They need to be informed in order to make informed decisions. As aviation managers, we often are called upon to make decisions on the fly. We thrive in this atmosphere, because that's how we have been trained as aviators. As we mature in our professional lives, most of us learn the sound logic of planning and briefing, but it is a necessary part of our professional makeup that we are able to make split second decisions in the event of a fault or emergency with the aircraft. It is very important, however as the aviation manager, not be viewed as someone who shoots from the hip: ready, fire, aim. Executives who fly in the back of our aircraft are not attuned to making snap judgments, especially when it comes to expending large amounts of capital. Always be prepared to speak about your department in a statistical format. You will often be approached by senior executives, who have a high curiosity about the cost and utilization of the company aircraft.

DISTRACTIONS FROM THE BACK

The lead passenger on your flight walks up to the cockpit one morning on the way to Denver and asks how the weather looks. He wants an update from his earlier CNBC briefing. Having just received a recent update on the destination current and forecast, you respond that current conditions indicate that you will be shooting an instrument approach. He asks if you think you will be able to land on time and you respond that the chances are very good, given the current forecast. He then emphasizes how important this meeting is to the company and that they really need to land on time at the destination airport. Prior to takeoff, one of your passengers mentions that he is prone to motion sickness and forgot to take the medication that has been prescribed for him. How many times have you been asked at a critical phase of flight if something could be fixed or if something could be arranged or another fact, important to the questioner, but distracting to you? We all deal with standard forms of distraction every day. Aircraft mechanical discrepancies, destination weather, onboard entertainment systems not operating properly are operational forms of distraction.

Business aviation has enjoyed a stellar safety record during the past two decades, but regardless of how hard the men and women in this vibrant industry work to maintain a safe environment, incidents will happen. There is no guarantee of a zero accident rate. There have been some noteworthy incidents within our community during the past several years: accidents that have been caused because of lack of attention to detail and carelessness of the flight crew. When the pilots become focused on factors other than the functional operation of the aircraft, items on a checklist may be skipped. There have been some tragic accidents in years past that are examples of a distraction becoming a part of the series of events leading up to a mishap. Pilots are often distracted before a flight even begins by one or more late arriving passengers. A late departure for a destination that is considered to be a day-only airport with a passenger load anxious to make a scheduled event, may not have been found to be the cause of an accident that occurred after sunset, but it certainly had to be a contributing factor. This can especially be disconcerting when there are slots involved. All the hard work that is involved in planning a trip to airports or through airspace that require reservations, can go awry when you miss a slot time because a passenger is not there at the scheduled time. This can set the tone for a "hurry up" pace in the cockpit. As we all know from experience, whenever the pace quickens beyond the normal flow, often something can be overlooked. Veteran pilots will all tell you that if you feel like things are going too fast, they probably are. One tried and true method of delaying distractions is to adopt a special rule called the "10,000-foot rule." The rule is that below 10,000 feet during departure or arrival, the cockpit conversation is limited to checklist and appropriate departure and arrival briefings.

Drew Callen, Boston Jet Search, who has consulted with numerous Fortune 100 companies and many high-net-worth individuals on a variety of business aviation issues, observed, when asked how he viewed the subject, "Distractions from the back are rarely heard by the flight crew, but often felt." What Mr. Callen is alluding to is a long-established fact that once the boss puts something in the heads of subordinates, regardless of their station within the organization, it does make a difference in their decision-making process (Cannon 2005).

Examples of distractions that can lead to accidents are: failure to properly deice due to timing or the exorbitant cost of modern deicing fluids, failure to pay attention to the appropriate loading of passengers and cargo in combination with minimum fuel considerations, tinkering, and so on. These examples can be the result of distractions caused by informal company policies. Distractions can come at any time and from any direction. Within your department has anyone asked whether the policies and procedures you have in your departmental manual are setting your flight crews up for possible distractions at the wrong time during a flight? If you have a minimum runway requirement in your operations manual and a clear understanding throughout your organization that this is an absolute minimum, then you should not have passengers pressuring your captains to land at an airport where there is less than the stated FAA approved landing minimum.

The chief financial officer of a corporation with five business jets, whom the aviation manager reports to, emphasized the need to establish a set of guidelines that make passengers aware of the importance of the go/no-go decision being in the hands of the flight crew. "Our operations manual stresses the supportive nature of our chairman's commitment to safety. Our captains have the final say in all matters relating to the safe conduct of a flight. While customer service is always in the forefront, critical decisions relating to safety are made without influence from the back of the aircraft." One tried and true method of delaying distractions is to adopt the 10,000-foot rule mentioned previously.

All the great work accomplished by the Flight Safety Foundation in the 1980s and '90s with CFIT (Controlled Flight Into Terrain) is a great example of how our collective consciousness was raised by pointing out the many variables that, combined, could lead up to a possible accident. Cockpit distractions, whether they began as a casual hint to the captain prior to engine start, while en route, a matter of informal policy, or any other unintended way, can become a factor at a critical time during a flight. Just because something is subtle and lying in the back of the minds of the flight crew doesn't mean that it can't be a very dangerous thing. While you may not eliminate distractions during the normal evolution of any particular flight, you can work to minimize them by creating a solid base of operational understanding within the department and the ranks of senior management, your customers. Another very important way to minimize the effect of distractions on flight crews is to emphasize the fact that they need to be able to recognize the distraction, discuss the fact that it happened, and to put it in its proper place with all of the other cockpit tasks that are being accomplished at the time. A clear understanding by all crew members as well as senior management that knowledge of the limitations of the operational use of the business aircraft is critical to the safe conduct of each flight.

Within the hierarchy of the corporate organizational structure the need to have a thorough understanding of the process of trip approval, trip acceptance, trip planning, and trip implementation is vital to the overall mission of the flight department. When looking for aviation topics to brief your boss or an executive group, choose from the following list and construct some brief presentation materials: the fueling process, winter operations process, hazardous materials process, maintenance process, importance of senior commitment to the operation and safety, function of scheduling/dispatch, communications, flight and duty time discussion, number of aircraft qualified on, what an MEL is all about, and the importance of training.

A FRAGILE INDUSTRY

Business aviation had been enjoying a decade of unprecedented growth until the gavel fell in November of 2008 opening the congressional hearings on the U.S. automakers' request for federal funds to stay afloat. When confronted as to how they had traveled from Detroit to Washington D.C., the heads of GM, Ford, and Chrysler meekly revealed that they had flown in on their respective company jets. The politicians and media pundits leapt upon that revelation like vultures on a fresh kill. Not one of the CEOs made any attempt to rebut the onslaught. They simply joined the ranks of the "fat cat privileged," and the subsequent folklore among the uninformed populace, based on the abuse by a few.

The result? Some companies, afraid of the bad press associated with ownership of a company aircraft, cancelled new aircraft orders, placed existing aircraft on the market, terminated personnel, and in a few instances, closed entire flight departments. Used aircraft inventories soared and market values dramatically fell. Business leaders by the dozens instantly became sensitive to how they and their companies were perceived by others and—in spite of how efficiently and reliably their aviation departments had been managed for years—downsized, cut back and stayed away from using the most effective tool in their business for the sake of saving a few dollars.

To be fair, the economy is certainly to blame for decisions to reduce staff and equipment in light of dwindling revenues, but as anyone who has built or annually defended an aviation budget will point out, you are either in the game or not. Cutting back on the amount of flying doesn't really save significant dollars. The fixed cost of ownership of an aviation asset far outweighs the variable cost of pushing the engine start button to begin a trip.

Many older hands remember what it was like in the late 1960s and '70s. Corporate jets were looked upon by everyone as the "royal barge," the "chairman's chariot." This was back when a new G-II cost $4.5 million and a fresh-off-the-assembly Beech Bonanza was $85,000. Use of the company aircraft was reserved for the fortunate few. How the industry has changed. Business use today far outweighs personal use. Richard Santuli, founder of NetJets, said to CNBC on June 3, 2009, "Seventy-five percent of the trips flown do not involve the CEO or senior executives." Richard emphasized, "Today's corporate jet is an effective business tool. . . . Most trips consist of four to five passengers eating box lunches and visiting three city pairs in one day." The opportunity to fly to 5,000 airports within the United States alone provides the flexibility that American companies need to assess, compete, and deliver services in a cutthroat technology driven economy. Combating the misconceptions, even within your own corporate structure, is more of a challenge today than ever before. Some aviation managers take this position: "They don't ask me for anything and I certainly don't volunteer anything." That approach may work in good times, but a "head in the sand" mentality will allow others less knowledgeable to make judgments about the future of your department. The Fractional providers cancelled new deliveries in 2009 to combat the economic downturn. New customers for fractional services are trending towards 10- to 25-hour cards versus purchasing a quarter share in an aircraft. "The Marquis Card program has been a wonderful addition for NetJets," Mr. Santuli shared. With traditional hours down and fractional operations in neutral, charter demand is on the upswing.

Management companies are feeling the pinch as well. "Many of my clients are combining trips within the company, eliminating deadheads and just being more operationally efficient," offered a senior executive with Jet Aviation. That strategy appears to be in consort with almost everyone on the Part 91 side of the house. Eliminating deadheads to the bare minimum has saved significant operational costs. During Masters Week in April 2009, some corporations who wished to avoid any media scrutiny, chartered aircraft to attend the Masters with customers. Some had their company jet drop them off at an outlying field and drove further that they would have ordinarily traveled by car. However, a number of companies chose to continue to do business as usual and had their company aircraft fly their executives and customers to Augusta for the opportunity to entertain and influence. Whatever the strategy, the ramp at Bush Field was not as crowded as in years past. If you are doing business on a global scale today, the business jet is still an invaluable tool in providing safe, efficient, and secure transport. Flying to Europe today is like flying to Chicago. Trips to Asia and the Middle East still take place on a regular basis for international corporations. Security and efficient use of time are still the most important aspects of using the business jet.

"Go to Andrews Air Force Base and inquire as to how many jets are taking government officials to and from Washington," challenged a director of aviation in the Northeast operating five business jets. Who is flying aboard all those military/business jets? When President Obama flew to Europe for the G20 meeting, 500 people accompanied him. The entourage did not use commercial aviation for that trip. Aircraft manufacturer's OEM demonstration aircraft are very busy. "To schedule an opportunity to fly using a demo from any manufacturer you need to still book out 30 to 60 days."

Bill Munroe, retired sales director for Bombardier, reflected that whenever an industry is under attack the initial reaction to panic should be strongly avoided. "Don't panic; look for opportunities," Bill insisted. "Instead of being overly defensive, this is a good time for personal reflection." How can a flight department become more efficient? Where is the department adding value within the corporation? As managers, you must be able to quantify these answers.

How well does your boss listen when you provide critical data on cost and operational issues? How serious are you taken when you offer constructive alternatives and proposals for your department's future? If you believe that your efforts are not given the same level of visibility as other managers within the corporation, the answer is to work on ways to increase that visibility. Managers who have won the trust of senior officers within the company as to their professional judgment and business knowledge will carry much more weight during crisis periods than those who are simply viewed as good people who just fly aircraft.

Business aviation has an excellent safety record. However, that emphasis on safety is but a small part of the overall customer service effort put forth by industry mechanics and pilots every day. It is assumed that operations will be conducted professionally with safety of flight as the goal of each and every trip. It is the intangible things that distinguish business aviation from other endeavors. It is the subtle customer service issues that make a difference in difficult economic times. The entire team has to speak with one voice and provide the best customer service possible. It is very important that the aviation manager work toward fostering support throughout the entire corporate structure. The job of aviation manager involves more diversity than ever. The need for financial knowledge, the ability to promote business aircraft within the company, and the continued educational component make the responsibility for corporate aircraft services more challenging than ever.

Once the challenge is understood, what can a manager do to combat the seemingly ever-increasing hazards that are placed in way of the path to success? The answer may lie with becoming more involved within the corporation than merely managing the aviation department. Attending corporate activities and meetings whenever possible; work with your boss and ask for sponsorship to learn more about what manner of contribution that you and your flight department can make to the future success of the company. Search for opportunities to add value. Every effort on your part will be appreciated and will enhance the value of the aviation group. If you don't think effort in this regard is noticed, think again. The proactive approach is very progressive. It is very important that the entire aviation team gets onboard with a unified goal of contributing to the success of the corporation.

As the aviation manager, your relationship with the senior management group is understandably significant. On par with that importance is your department's relationship with the administrative staff at corporate headquarters that works directly for the senior management group. All travel and special needs are directed through the executive administrative assistants. The rapport between your scheduling function and the executive support staff is critical to the flight department's overall mission of customer service. The job of administrative assistant to a highly-placed executive is quite hectic. One of the major demands of the assistant's time is the coordination of business and personal travel for their boss. The aviation department can unload a great deal of that burden. This is an area that allows the aviation manager to act as liaison in the establishment of meaningful customer service. In order to accomplish that connection, the administrative assistants need to understand exactly how your department functions.

As part of an overall campaign to engage the entire company in your effort to promote the aviation department, invite the administrative staff out to the airport for a visit. This could take the form of an organized presentation to several small groups of assistants or simply a one-at-a-time appointment. Understanding that an administrative assistant has very little time during the workweek, it is difficult to manage hangar tours. An alternative would be for you and or several of your staff to make a presentation at corporate headquarters over lunch for the administrative staff. Variations on this theme will depend upon the location of the aviation department, the personality of the corporation, and the amount of time available. Regardless of the manner in which your flight department establishes a positive working relationship with corporate headquarters, the need to do so should not be overlooked.

One creative extension of the effort to promote and communicate with the parent corporation on a regularly scheduled basis is explained by a very proactive aviation manager in the southeastern United States:

> We have followed with a continued effort to engage as many of the corporate headquarters staff as possible. We currently publish a quarterly newsletter which is sent electronically to more than 150 officers and assistants at our company headquarters....We report news that relates to our audience, and constantly tell our own story, which focuses on company values and innovations....I realized a long time ago that what we do is appreciated, but our challenge is to ensure that our executives realize the value we bring every day, reinforcing corporate initiatives and behaviors and establishing our image as a vital tool within the enterprise.

This particular aviation group has a portal on the parent company's website in order to provide details on process and function when utilizing the department's transportation services. When a new senior executive joins the company, it behooves the aviation manager to schedule a brief face-to-face meeting to further extend the message of a safe and cost-efficient aviation group.

If you are shy about meeting senior officers and engaging in conversation concerning the effectiveness of the aviation department to the parent company, you may be in the wrong job. As clearly stated by another proactive aviation manager in the Pacific Northwest: "Get out ahead of the wave if at all possible. Drive the change. If you fill the moat around the hangar and pull up the drawbridge, you will be excluded from discussions pertaining to the future of your flight operation and thus have no say in the potential outcome." You will suffer a loss of credibility unless you remain engaged and this could harm the aviation department.

Another aviation manager in the Southwest shared, "We are always looking for the least-cost solution that will continue to provide the professional standard of travel which our executives count on every day." Some additional ways to lower departmental expenses are: cutting the training budget to reflect once a year vs. every six months for pilots; reducing outside travel for seminars and meetings; shelving decisions to repaint or refurbish existing aircraft; freezing pay increases; and revising travel expense policies.

Aviation managers must spend a lot of time on missionary work in order to promote business aviation within the company. One seasoned aviation manager with two large jets and a staff of ten based in the Northeast, admits, "Throughout my career, the most frustrating aspect of my job is having to defend business aviation....We use Travel Sense, created by the NBAA Staff....The statistics from Travel Sense provide me with data that I can use in the justification discussions....My monthly reports are reviewed by all of our senior officers. Our flights are strictly oriented to business use. We have a real understanding of time management when the aircraft is being used." Developed in the mid '90s by the Operations Staff of NBAA, the program interfaces with various links, Travelocity as an example, and compares seat costs of airline city pairs to the company aircrafts seat cost.

The value of executive time is a critical factor in the analysis that Travel Sense produces. The cost is $600 for the program for NBAA members. With no annual fee, updates are free when issued. The next step, according to Scott O'Brien, project manager, Operations Services Group of the NBAA, is to make Travel Sense web-based. "We aren't there yet, but hope when the funding is available that this valuable operational tool will be available through the website."

Public corporations, especially those that have been assisted by federal funds, find themselves under an increased level of scrutiny. Those who have been the targets of media and political criticism because of a combination of financial woes and large corporate fleets, certainly represent a small minority of our industry. So, do the abusers of privilege represent a small number of business leaders who own business aircraft? That aside, the number of privately-held aircraft has been on the rise for quite some time.

REFERENCES

Cannon, Jim. (2005, Nov). Distractions from the back. *Business & Commercial Aviation*, 146.

Santuli, Richard. (2009, June 3). Statement on CNBC.

Sheehan, John J. (2003). *Business and Corporate Aviation Management: On-Demand Air Travel.* New York: McGraw-Hill.

Appendix A

Abbreviations and Acronyms

AAIP	Approved Aircraft Inspection Program
AC	Advisory Circular
ACAS	Airborne Collision Avoidance System
ACSF	Air Charter Safety Foundation
AD	Airworthiness Directive
AFM	Aircraft Flight Manual
AMC	Acceptable Means of Compliance
AMO	Approved Maintenance Organization
ASAP	Aviation Safety Action Program
AOC	Air Operator Certificate
APU	Auxiliary Power Unit
ASR	Air Safety Report
ASRS	Aviation Safety Reporting System (NASA)
ATC	Air Traffic Control
CAMP	Continuous Airworthiness Maintenance Program
CAP	Corrective Action Plan
CAR	Corrective Action Record
CASE	Coordinating Agency for Supplier Evaluation
CASS	Continuing Analysis and Surveillance System
CDL	Configuration Deviation List
CEO	Chief Executive Officer
CFR	Code of Federal Regulations (U.S.)
CFIT	Controlled Flight into Terrain
CHDO	Certificate Holding District Office (FAA)
CMO	Certificate Management Office (FAA)

CRM	Crew Resource Management
CVR	Cockpit Voice Recorder
DAR	Designated Airworthiness Representative
DER	Designated Engineering Representative
DG	Dangerous Goods
EASA	European Aviation Safety Agency
EGPWS	Enhanced Ground Proximity Warning System
ELT	Emergency Locator Transmitter
EPA	Environmental Protection Agency
ERP	Emergency Response Plan
EU	European Union
FAA	Federal Aviation Administration (U.S.)
FAR	Federal Aviation Regulation (U.S.)
FBO	Fixed Base Operator
FDR	Flight Data Recorder
FMS	Flight Management System
FOD	Foreign Object Damage
FOM	Flight Operations Manual
FOQA	Flight Operational Quality Assurance
FSDO	Flight Standards District Office (FAA)
GMM	General Maintenance Manual
GOM	General Operations Manual
GPS	Global Positioning System
GPWS	Ground Proximity Warning System
HFACS	Human Factors Analysis and Classification System
IBAC	International Business Aviation Council
ICAO	International Civil Aviation Organization
IEP	Internal Evaluation Program
INFO	Information for Operators
IPM	Inspection Procedures Manual
IS-BAO	International Standard for Business Aviation Operations
ISO	International Organization for Standardization
JAA	Joint Aviation Authorities
JAR	Joint Aviation Requirement
JHA	Job Hazard Analysis
LOSA	Line Operations Safety Audit
MEL	Minimum Equipment List
MISR	Maintenance Interruption Summary Report
MMEL	Master Minimum Equipment List
MNPS	Minimum Navigation Performance Specifications
MRB	Maintenance Review Board

MRM	Maintenance Resource Management
MRO	Maintenance Repair Organization
MRR	Maintenance Reliability Report
MSAW	Minimum Safe Altitude Warning
MSDS	Material Safety Data Sheet
NAA	National Aviation Authority
NASA	National Aeronautics and Space Administration (U.S.)
NM	Nautical Mile
NTSB	National Transportation Safety Board (U.S.)
OEM	Original Equipment Manufacturer
OM	Operations Manual
OSHA	Occupational Safety and Health Administration
PBE	Personal Breathing Equipment
PIC	Pilot-in-Command
PPE	Personal Protective Equipment
QAR	Quick Access Recorder
QAS	Quality Assurance System
RA	Resolution Advisory
RII	Required Inspection Item
RNP	Required Navigation Performance
RSM	Repair Station Manual
RVSM	Reduced Vertical Separation Minimum
SARPs	Standards and Recommended Practices (ICAO)
SAFO	Safety Alert for Operators
SB	Service Bulletin
SDR	Service Difficulty Report
SIC	Second-in-Command
SID	Standard Instrument Departure
SIDA	Security Identification Display Area
SM	Safety Manager
SMM	Safety Management Manual
SMS	Safety Management System
SOPs	Standard Operating Procedures
SUPS	Suspected Unapproved Parts
STC	Supplemental Type Certificate
TAWS	Terrain Awareness and Warning System
TCAS	Traffic Alert and Collision Avoidance System
TCDS	Type Certificate Data Sheet
TEM	Threat and Error Management
TSA	Transportation Security Administration (U.S.)
U.S.	United States

Appendix B

Operations Definitions

AGENT—The significance of the words "agent" and "agents" as used in operations specifications is that the certificate holder is the principal and that the certificate holder is accountable and liable for the acts or omissions of each of its agent or agents.

AIR AMBULANCE AIRCRAFT—An aircraft used in air ambulance operations. The aircraft must be equipped with at least medical oxygen, suction, and a stretcher or other approved patient restraint/containment device. The aircraft need not be used exclusively as an air ambulance aircraft and the equipment need not be permanently installed.

AIR AMBULANCE OPERATIONS—A.) Air transportation of a person with a health condition that requires medical personnel as determined by a health care provider; or B.) Holding out to the public as willing to provide air transportation to a person with a health condition that requires medical personnel as determined by a health care provider including, but not limited to, advertising, solicitation, or association with a hospital or medical provider.

AIRCRAFT FLIGHT CAN—Binder or similar folder kept in each aircraft during all flights, in which the aircraft performance, maintenance and flight log, trip paperwork, deferred maintenance log, NEF log, and other flight-related paperwork and material is kept.

AIRWAYS NAVIGATION FACILITIES—Airways navigation facilities are those ICAO Standard Navigation Aids (VOR, VOR/DME, and/or NDB) that are used to establish the en route airway structure within the sovereign airspace of ICAO member states. These facilities are also used to establish the degree of navigation accuracy required for air traffic control and Class I navigation within that airspace.

AUTHORITY—A power that a person is vested with.

AUTO FLIGHT GUIDANCE SYSTEM (AFGS)—Aircraft systems, such as autopilot, auto throttles, displays, and controls, that are interconnected, in such a manner so as to allow the crew to automatically control the aircraft's lateral and vertical flight path and speed. A flight management system is sometimes associated with an AFGS.

AVAILABLE LANDING DISTANCE (ALD)—ALD is that portion of a runway available for landing and rollout for aircraft cleared for land and hold short operations (LAHSO). This distance is measured from the landing threshold to the hold-short point. Air traffic is responsible for providing this data for each LAHSO runway throughout U.S. Terminal Procedures Publications, Airport/Facility Directory, and from the tower when requested.

CATEGORY I INSTRUMENT APPROACH—A Category I instrument approach is any authorized precision or non-precision instrument approach that is conducted with a minimum height for IFR flight not less than 200 feet (60 meters) above the touchdown zone and a minimum visibility/RVV not less than one-half statute mile or RVR 1800 (for helicopters, one-fourth statute mile or RVR 1600).

CERTIFICATE HOLDER—In a charter department's operations specification the term "certificate holder" means the holder of the certificate described in Part A Paragraph A001 and any of its officers, employees, or agents used in the conduct of operations.

CLASS I NAVIGATION—Class I navigation is any en route flight operation or portion of an operation that is conducted entirely within the designated Operational Service Volumes (or ICAO equivalents) of ICAO standard airway navigation facilities (VOR, VOR/DME, NDB). Class I navigation also includes en route flight operations over routes designated with an "MEA GAP" (or ICAO equivalent). En route flight operations conducted within these areas are defined as "Class I navigation" operations irrespective of the navigation means used. Class I navigation includes operations within these areas using a pilot or any other means of navigation that does not rely on the use of VOR, VOR/DME, or NDB.

CLASS II NAVIGATION—Class II navigation is any en route flight operation that is not defined as Class I navigation. Class II navigation is any en route flight operation or portion of an en route operation (irrespective of the means of navigation) that takes place outside (beyond) the designated Operational Service Volume (or ICAO equivalents) of ICAO standard airway navigation facilities (VOR, VOR/DME, NDB). However, Class II navigation does not include en route flight operations over routes designated with an "MEA GAP" (or ICAO equivalent).

COCKPIT DISPLAY OF TRAFFIC INFORMATION (CDTI)—A CDTI is a generic display that provides a flight crew with surveillance information about other aircraft including their position. Traffic information for a CDTI may be obtained from one or multiple sources (including ADS-B, TCAS, and traffic information services) to provide improved awareness of proximate aircraft and as an aid to visual acquisition as part of the normal see-and-avoid operations both in the air and on the ground.

DECISION ALTITUDE (Height)—DA(H) is specified minimum altitude in an instrument approach procedure by which a missed approach must be initiated if the required visual reference to continue the approach has not been established. The altitude value is typically measured by a barometric altimeter; the height value (H) is typically a radio altitude equivalent height above the touchdown zone (HAT) used only for advisory reference and does not necessarily reflect actual height above underlying terrain.

DUTY—A task or function a person must do.

FAULT DETECTION AND EXCLUSION (FDE)—FDE technology allows onboard GPS equipment to automatically detect a satellite failure that effects navigation and to exclude that satellite from the navigation solution.

FLIGHT MANAGEMENT SYSTEM (FMS)—An integrated system used by flight crews for flight planning, navigation, performance management, aircraft guidance, and flight progress monitoring. (Heritage GOM)

FREE FLIGHT—A safe and efficient flight operating capability under instrument flight rules in which the operators have the freedom to select a path and speed in real time. Air traffic restrictions are imposed only to ensure separation, to preclude exceeding airport capacity, to prevent unauthorized flight through special use airspace, and to ensure safety of flight. Restrictions are limited in extent and duration to correct the identified problem. Any activity that removes restrictions represents a move toward free flight. (Heritage GOM)

GENERAL OPERATIONS MANUAL—Within the United States, any published instrument flight procedure (victor**[AU: OK?]** or jet airway, SID, STAR, SIAPS, or instrument departure. Outside the United States, any designated signal coverage or published instrument flight procedure equivalent to U.S. standards.

GLOBAL POSITION SYSTEM (GPS) LANDING SYSTEM (GLS)—GLS is a differential GPS-based landing system providing both vertical and lateral position fixing capability. The term GLS may also be applied to any GNSS-based differential corrected landing system.

LARGE-CABIN AIRCRAFT—Challenger, Gulfstream (II, III, IV, V), Global express, Falcon (900, 1000, 9000)

LEASE—A lease is where an aircraft owner transfers possession and use of a specific aircraft to a lessee for a fixed period. In a lease, as opposed to other types of custody/use agreements, the lessee has the right to possess and use the aircraft even if the aircraft owner needs the aircraft returned, assuming the lessee has made timely payments and is properly maintaining the aircraft. In accordance with Section 119.53(b), the certificate holder may not wet lease from or enter into any wet leasing arrangement with any person not authorized by the FAA to engage in common carriage operations under 14 CFR Parts 121 or 135 (as appropriate), whereby that other person provides an aircraft and at least one crewmember to the certificate holder. (Heritage GOM)

LIFE VEST, NON-QUICK-DONNING—A non-quick-donning life vest is one which must be removed from its container, placed over the wearer's head, and/or requires steps beyond inflation to make it ready to use for its intended purpose. (Heritage GOM)

MAJOR CONTRACT TRAINING—Any flight training, flight testing, or flight checking leading to and maintaining certification and qualification of air carrier flight crew members in accordance with the requirements (maneuvers and procedures) explicitly stated in 14CFR Parts 61, 121, or 135; or in SFAR 58 Advanced Qualification Program (AQP), as applicable. (Heritage GOM)

MEDICAL PERSONNEL—A person with medical training who is assigned to provide medical care during flight. (Heritage GOM)

MINIMUM DESCENT ALTITUDE (HEIGHT)—MDA(H) is the lowest altitude in an instrument approach procedure to which a descent is authorized on final approach or during circle-to-land maneuvering. The "altitude" value is typically measured by a barometric altimeter. The "height" value (H) is typically a radio altitude equivalent height above the touchdown zone (HAT) or height above airport (HAA) published elevation. The (H) is used only for advisory reference and does not necessarily reflect actual height above underlying terrain. [This definition is consistent with both current U.S. operator usage and ICAO international agreements.] (Heritage GOM)

OPERATIONAL SERVICE VOLUME—The Operational Service Volume is that volume of airspace surrounding a NAVAID that is available for operational use and within which a signal of usable strength exists and where that signal is not operationally limited by co-channel interference. Operational Service Volume includes all of the following: (1) The officially designated Standard Service Volume excluding any portion of the Standard Service Volume that has been restricted. (2) The Expanded Service Volume (3) Within the United States, any published instrument flight procedure (victor or jet airway, SID, STAR, SIAP, or instrument departure). (4) Outside the United States, any designated signal coverage or published instrument flight procedure equivalent to U.S. standards. (Heritage GOM)

OUTSOURCED TRAINING—Any training, testing, or checking activity that a certificate holder provides by way of a contract arrangement with another party. (Heritage GOM)

POLAR AREA (NORTH)—The north polar area of operations is that area that lies north of latitude N 78 00. (Heritage GOM)

QUALIFIED LOCAL OBSERVER—A person who provides weather, landing area, and other information as required by the operator and has been trained by the operator under a training program approved by the Principal Operations Inspector.

RAW TERRAIN—Raw terrain is devoid of any person, structure, vehicle, or vessel.

RELIABLE FIX—A "reliable fix" means station passage of a VOR, VORTAC, or NDB. A reliable fix includes a VOR/DME fix, an NDB/DME fix, a VOR intersection, an NDB intersection, and a VOR/NDB intersection provided course guidance is available from one of the facilities and the fix lies within the designated operational service volumes of both facilities that define the fix. (Heritage GOM)

REQUIRED NAVIGATION PERFORMANCE (RNP)—A statement of navigation performance necessary for operations with a defined airspace.

REQUIRED NAVIGATION PERFORMANCE (RNP) TIME LIMIT—Applies to aircraft equipped with INS or IRU systems where those systems provide the means of navigation to navigate to the degree of accuracy required by ATC. The FAA-approved time in hours—after the system is placed in navigation mode or is updated enroute—that the specific INS or IRU make/model can meet a specific RNP type on a 95% probability basis. It is used to establish the area of operations or routes on which the aircraft navigation system is qualified to operate.

REQUIRED NAVIGATION PERFORMANCE (RNP) TYPE—A value typically expressed as a distance in nautical miles from the intended position within which an aircraft would be at least 95% of the total flying time. For example, RNP-4 represents a lateral and longitudinal navigation accuracy of 4 nautical miles on a 95% basis. Note: Applications of RNP to terminal area and other operations may also include a vertical component.

RESPONSIBILITY—Something a person is accountable for. (Heritage GOM)

RUNWAY—In these operations specifications the term "runway" in the case of land airports, water airports and heliports, and helipads shall mean that portion of the surface intended for the takeoff and landing of land airplanes, seaplanes, or rotorcraft, as appropriate. (Heritage GOM)

VFR STATION-REFERENCED CLASS I NAVIGATION—VFR station-referenced Class I navigation is any operation conducted within the operational service volumes of ICAO standard navigation aids under visual flight rules (VFR) which uses non-visual navigation aids (stations), such as VOR, VOR/DME, or NDB as the primary navigation reference. VFR station-referenced Class I navigation includes Class I navigation conducted on-airways and off-airway routings predicated on airways navigation facilities. These operations also include Class I navigation using an area navigation system that is certificated for IFR flights over the routes being flown. (Heritage GOM)

Appendix C

Maintenance Definitions

ABORT—To terminate prematurely.

ACCESSORY—A part, subassembly, or assembly designed for use in conjunction with or to supplement another assembly or unit.

ACCIDENTAL DAMAGE—Shall mean a physical degradation of an item caused by contact or impact with an object or influence that is not a part of the aircraft or by improper manufacturing or maintenance practices.

ACCOMPLISHED BY—Shall mean a term usually found on work sheets and in the MIP Manual that identifies a person, generally in maintenance, designated to sign for the completion of items on the work sheets.

AIRCRAFT DISCREPANCY LOG—Is a document that is used to record discrepancies and certain maintenance events and is kept as part of the aircraft maintenance records.

AIRCRAFT MAINTENANCE LOG—Is a document that is used to record maintenance events and is kept as part of the aircraft maintenance records.

AIRWORTHY—Shall mean the condition of an item (aircraft, aircraft system, or part) that meets its type design or properly altered condition and the item operates in a safe manner to accomplish its intended purpose. Aircraft with MEL items are still considered airworthy and in compliance with its type design.

AIRWORTHINESS DIRECTIVE (AD)—Is a safety directive issued by the FAA. An Airworthiness Directive begins with an Airworthiness Directive worksheet prepared by an aviation safety engineer in the accountable aircraft certification office or directorate. The directorate then assigns a docket number to that worksheet. The docket number is the primary tracking number for both a Notice of Proposed Rulemaking and for the Final Rule

Airworthiness Directive. The Final Rule Airworthiness Directive will have a number and a 14 CFR Part 39 amendment number assigned when it is issued and sent to the Federal Register for publication.

EMERGENCY AD—An AD that has an immediate effect on safety and may require the immediate grounding of aircraft, so that the AD can be complied with before the aircraft is flown again.

ALTERNATIVE METHOD OF COMPLIANCE (AMOC)—Providing the AD allows for an AMOC you can use a different way of dealing with the unsafe condition if (1) it has the equivalent level of safety as that prescribed in the Airworthiness Directive and (2) the different (alternative) method has been approved by the aircraft certification office or directorate responsible for that Airworthiness Directive.

AUDIT—A methodical examination and review to examine and verify compliance to a standard.

BENCH CHECK—Shall mean the removal of the unit from stock or from the aircraft or engine for a thorough check of its performance as prescribed for in applicable maintenance, overhaul, or service manuals for all its functions. It may include minor adjustment, markings or lubrication but will in no way affect its service time limit status.

BENCH SERVICE—Shall mean a functional or visual check of an item in the appropriate shop to determine whether or not the item may be returned to service, or whether it requires adjustment, repair, or overhaul; and the accomplishment of any such adjustment, repair or overhaul.

BLOCK HOURS—Shall mean the number of hours incurred by an airplane from the moment it first moves under its own power with the intention of flight until it comes to rest in the blocks at the point of landing.

BUY-BACK PROCEDURE—Shall mean the process in which an RII inspector has found that an " RII inspection item" performed is unsatisfactory. A new discrepancy as an "RII inspection item" is required to be accomplished prior to clearing the original RII inspection.

"C" CHECK—A group of inspection and scheduled maintenance items with intervals as defined and identified in an inspection program. Some aircraft have "C" checks and some do not. Some have "A" and "B" checks, but no "C" checks. Some have mixed time intervals, such as 300/600/1200 hour checks with and without a "C" check. A "D" check is a heavy, major inspection on large aircraft.

CALENDAR DAY—A 24-hour period from one minute after midnight to midnight the same day determined by aircraft geographic location and local time.

CALENDAR MONTH (C/M)—Used for tracking maintenance tasks that are scheduled by calendar time. All maintenance tasks scheduled by calendar time will be due by the last day of the month in which they fall due.

CALIBRATION—Is the application of a specifically known and accurately measured input to ensure that an item will produce a specifically known output that is accurately measured and/or indicated. Calibration includes adjustment or recording of corrections, as appropriate.

CAMPAIGN ITEM—Shall mean an item created by a need to check an aircraft fleet or sub-fleet, aircraft equipment, ground equipment, etc., to ensure reliability or to add/remove a part.

(Usually determines condition of airworthiness for aircraft.)

CANCELLATION—Is a planned flight, or flight leg that is not flown.

CERTIFY—Shall mean to physically verify and attest that the work scope intent was accomplished.

CHANGE—Shall mean to remove a component, check the area exposed by unit removal and install a serviceable appliance. Check condition of installed appliance, lines and connections. Check operation when applicable.

CHECK—Shall mean the examination necessary to determine the operation condition of mechanisms, components, systems and engines; performed in accordance with the aircraft and engine maintenance manuals.

CHECK INTERVAL—Is a defined interval such as flight hours, cycles, or calendar time between checks. The intervals between scheduled maintenance inspections on our aircraft are defined in the aircraft specific inspection program.

CHECK/REPAIR—When found in the instruction for "Accomplished By" shall mean that the mechanic will check the unit or area and perform such work as is necessary to bring the unit or area up to the company standard of reliability and/or appearance.

CLOSE VISUAL INSPECTION—Is an intensive visual check of a specified detail, assembly, or installation. The inspection searches for evidence of structural irregularity using adequate lighting and, where necessary, inspection aids such as mirrors, hand lens, etc. Surface cleaning and elaborate access procedures may be required.

COMPONENT—Is any self-contained part, combination of parts, subassemblies, or units that perform a distinctive function necessary to the operation of a system. In this manual, it is a part that is tracked by time, cycles or has a life limit.

COMPONENT FAILURE—Shall mean the failure of a component to perform its intended function.

COMPUTERIZED MAINTENANCE PROGRAM—A computerized used to trace all maintenance requirements on the aircraft.

CONDITION INSPECTION—Shall mean, inspection of engine components or assemblies for the purpose of determining condition.

CONDITION MONITORED—Shall mean a maintenance monitoring process under which data on a significant population of specified items in service is analyzed to indicate whether some allocation of technical resources is required. Not a preventative process, conditioned monitored maintenance allows failures to occur and relies upon analysis of operating experience to indicate the need for appropriate action.

CONFIGURATION DEVIATION LIST (CDL)—Shall mean the CDL document that is used in conjunction with an aircraft MEL. Many general aviation aircraft do not use a CDL document.

CONFIRMED FAILURES—The inability of an item to perform within previously specified limits that are verified by shop examination.

CORRECTIVE ACTION—Shall mean a description of work performed with enough information to be understood by individuals familiar with maintenance actions.

CORROSION—The partial or complete deterioration away, dissolving, or softening of any substance by chemical or electrochemical reaction with its environment.

CORROSION PREVENTION AND CONTROL DOCUMENT (CPCD)—A document to provide guidance in the evaluation, effectiveness and improvements in an operator's corrosion prevention and control program.

CRACK—A rupture or flaw; an incomplete separation of a part.

CYCLE—Aircraft Operating: Is described by the manufacturer. Engine Operating: Shall mean a thermal cycle, including the application of takeoff power, for an engine. APU: Related to aircraft operation and recorded independently of hourly meters.

DAILY UTILIZATION—The average daily flying hours for each individual aircraft. It is computed by dividing the total flying hours accumulated by the aircraft in a reporting period by the number of in-service aircraft days during the same period.

DAMAGE TOLERANT—A qualification standard for aircraft structure. An item is judged to be damage tolerant if it can sustain damage and the remaining structure can withstand reasonable loads without structural failure or excessive structural deformation until the damage is detected.

DEFERRED WORK ITEM—From time-to-time it may be necessary to defer inspector recorded or pilot recorded discrepancies. Such items may be deferred provided they comply with the minimum equipment list procedures published in the General Operations Manual (GOM).

DEFERRED MAINTENANCE ITEM (DMI)—Reported aircraft discrepancies that have not been corrected and are being controlled by Maintenance Control. Only items that do not impact safety or airworthiness may be deferred, except a provided for in the MEL.

DELAY—The failure of an originating flight to depart at the scheduled time plus one hour, or, when a through service or turnaround flight remains on the ground longer than the allocated ground time plus one hour, the resulting late departure is called a delay.

DELETED ITEM—A term that identifies an obsolete or "not applicable" item on a worksheet and that has been properly authenticated by a qualified person.

DEPARTURE—Each time an aircraft leaves the blocks for a flight leg and completes a takeoff.

DURING FLIGHT—The period from the moment the aircraft leaves the surface of the earth on takeoff until it touches down on landing.

ENGINE CHANGE—The removal of an installed engine, and its subsequent replacement, by a serviceable engine.

ENGINE POSITION—The numerical designation assigned to an engine based upon its installed location on the aircraft. The left-most engine of the airplane is designated No. 1 and increases left to right consecutively in ascending order.

FERRY FLIGHT—The repositioning of an aircraft, either for operational or maintenance reasons that generally do not involve any regulated flight activity other than compliance with FAR 91.

FLEET—The number of aircraft under the management of a flight operation. Commercial operations will list this number in their Operations Specifications (D085).

FLEET LEADER CONCEPT—Shall mean inspections on specific aircraft selected from those which have the highest operating age/usage in order to identify the first evidence of deterioration in their condition caused by fatigue damage.

FLIGHT HOURS—Is the accumulated time interval between wheels-off and wheels-on.

FUNCTIONAL CHECK—Is a check of one or more functions of a part or parts of a unit or system without removal from the aircraft nacelle, assembly, or system. These checks will be carried out in accordance with the manufacturer's functional check procedure or other approved methods using any specified equipment that may be required.

HARD TIME—A prescribed interval for overhaul, restoration, or other maintenance action—such as check of life-limited parts. This is used to denote those intervals or maintenance programs that are controlled by the FAA.

HIDDEN FUNCTION—(1) A function which is normally active and whose cessation will not be evident to the operating crew during performance of normal duties. (2) A function which is normally inactive and whose readiness to perform, prior to it being needed, will not be evident to the operating crew during performance of normal duties.

INSPECTED BY—A term found on maintenance work documents that identifies maintenance functions that must be attested to.

INSPECTION CHECK—Is a visual examination to determine the airworthiness condition of an aircraft, engine, system or appliance or any component part thereof, unless other special techniques or tools are specified.

INSPECTION–DETAILED (STRUCTURAL)—A close intensive visual inspection of highly defined structural details or locations searching for evidence of structural irregularity (using adequate lighting and, where necessary, inspection aids such as mirrors, etc. Surface cleaning and access procedures may be required to gain proximity).

INSPECTION–EXTERNAL (POWERPLANT)—Is a visual check of the exposed portion of an item or assembly without disturbing its operational condition.

INSPECTION–EXTERNAL SURVEILLANCE (ZONAL)—Is a visual check that will detect obvious unsatisfactory conditions/discrepancies in externally visible structure or system/powerplant items. It may also include internal structure or installations that are visible through quick-opening access panels/doors. Work stands, ladders, etc. may be required to gain proximity.

INSPECTION–SURVEILLANCE (STRUCTURAL)—Shall mean a visual examination of defined internal or external structural areas from a distance considered necessary to carry out an adequate check. External includes structure that is visible through quick opening panels/doors. Internal applies to obscured structure requiring removal of fillets, fairings, access panels, doors, etc., for visibility (using adequate lighting and where necessary, inspection aids such as mirrors, etc. Surface cleaning and access procedures may be required to gain proximity).

INSPECTION–INTERNAL SURVEILLANCE (ZONAL)—Shall mean a visual check that will detect obvious unsatisfactory conditions/discrepancies in internal structural and system/power plant installations. This type of inspection applies to obscured structure and installations that require removal of fillets, fairings, access panels/door, etc.

INTERIM REPAIR—A rework, replacement, reinforcement, or adjustment of a part or parts of an aircraft, engine, or appliance to restore the parts to an airworthy condition for a prescribed period.

LINE STATIONS—Stations manned by company maintenance personnel or authorized by the company as a station to perform service for the aircraft.

LUBRICATION AND SERVICING—Any act of lubricating or servicing an item for the purpose of maintaining its inherent design operating capabilities.

MAINTENANCE—Shall mean those actions required for restoring or maintaining an item in serviceable condition, including servicing, repair, modification, overhaul, inspection, and determination of condition.

MAINTENANCE CONTROL—A focal point for communications and coordination with operations for the maintenance department. This function is accomplished through the manager/director of maintenance or his delegate.

MAINTENANCE AND INSPECTION PROGRAM MANUAL (MIP)—The document that contains the specifications for the maintenance program.

MAINTENANCE PLANNING DOCUMENT (MPD)—Used on many large aircraft as the source of manufacturer's recommend times for repair, service, overhaul, and time and cycle limitations. Unless line-item extensions are approved for the operator by the FAA, these are the times and cycles used to determine maintenance events and limitations.

MAINTENANCE REVIEW BOARD (MRB)—Is a group consisting of representatives from the manufacturer, the FAA, industry and operator groups that work to determine maintenance requirements or changes to the MPDs.

MAINTENANCE PROGRAM—Shall mean a program that defines a logical sequence of maintenance actions to be performed as events of pieces of a whole that, when performed collectively, result in achievement of the desired maintenance standards.

MAINTENANCE SIGNIFICANT ITEMS (MSI)—Shall mean items identified by the manufacturer whose failure:

- Could affect safety (ground or flight),
- Is undetectable during operations,
- Could have significant operational economic impact, or
- Could have significant non-operational economic impact.

MAJOR ALTERATION—(Ref. FAR Part 43 and FAR Part 1 Definition) Shall mean an alteration not listed in the aircraft or aircraft engine specifications that might appreciably affect weight, balance, structural strength, performance, powerplant operation, flight characteristics, or other qualities affecting airworthiness.

MAJOR REPAIR—(Ref. FAR Part 43 and FAR Part I Definition) Shall mean, a repair that, if improperly done, might appreciably affect weight, balance, structural strength, performance, powerplant operation, flight characteristics, or other qualities affecting airworthiness.

MINIMUM EQUIPMENT LIST (MEL)—Shall mean the list of the airworthiness related items that may be inoperative and still allow release of the aircraft on a revenue flight. The MEL also includes the conditions under which some items may be inoperative and some items must be operative.

MASTER MINIMUM EQUIPMENT LIST (MMEL)—This is the FAA's master planning document, aircraft type specific, for construction of an operator's minimum equipment list (MEL). The document is revised either as a numbered change (usually requires updating an operator's MEL) or a lettered change, such as Rev 7a to 7b, which contains minor changes and is usually not a mandatory update requirement unless there are changed items which are specific to the operator's MEL.

MODIFICATION—Shall mean alteration to the physical design of the aircraft, systems, engines, or components.

MAXIMUM PERMITTED LIFE—Shall mean the time specified by an appropriate authority after which a particular item must be removed from service. It may also be termed life-limited.

NON-AIRWORTHY—Shall mean a condition that renders the affected unit unsafe or unsuitable for service.

NON-DESTRUCTIVE TEST—A technique developed to assist in the evaluation of condition and security performed with the aid of specific methods and supplementary devices; such as x-ray, eddy current, ultrasonic, magnetic particles, liquid penetrates, etc.

NON-ROUTINE INSPECTION ITEM—Shall mean maintenance items generated during periodic checks as a result of inspection and scheduled (routine) mechanical work. These items are coded to the appropriate ATA system.

NON-ESSENTIAL EQUIPMENT AND FURNISHINGS—Those items installed on the aircraft as part of the original certification, supplemental type certificate, or engineering order that have no effect on the safe operation of flight and would not be required by the applicable certification or operational rules.

NOT APPLICABLE (N/A)—A term used in conjunction with a signature to indicate that a step or item on a work document does not apply to a job being accomplished or the aircraft being worked. NOTE: N/A determination should be made only by an authorized representative of the manager/director of maintenance.

ON CONDITION (OC)—Shall mean a term used to identify items in the maintenance program that are maintained in a continuously airworthy condition and checked at periodic intervals, progressive inspections, checks, services, repair, and/or preventive maintenance against a physical standard by visual means, measurements, tests, or other means without teardown to determine their continued airworthiness. The purpose of an on-condition maintenance program is to remove the unit from service before failure occurs and while the unit is operating normally. This involves the use of the maintenance program to assess the ability of the component to remain serviceable until the next scheduled inspection within the limits of the relevant maintenance manual reference. The periodic check must be able to verify the continued airworthiness of the component and may consist of one or more of the following tasks:

- Functional Check
- Internal/External Leak Check
- Operational Check
- Filter Check/Change
- Condition/Security Check

OPERATIONAL CHECK—The check of a system or component after replacement, repair, or change of the system.

OPERATIONAL CHECK FLIGHT—A flight check of a system or component after replacement, repair, or change of the system.

OVERHAUL—The disassembly, inspection, and repair of a component, engine, appliance, or structure as necessary to be in compliance with the overhaul limits established by the manufacturer. In addition, it has been tested in accordance with approved standards and technical data acceptable to the FAA. Limits other than the manufacturer's limits may be used if such limits have been approved by the FAA.

OVER WEIGHT LANDING—A landing that was done, either under normal or emergency conditions, that was done at a weight known to be in excess of the aircraft's maximum landing weight, as determined by the aircraft type data sheet.

PARAMETER—A characteristic element.

PERIODIC CHECKS—Checks performed at regular intervals.

PILOT-IN-COMMAND (PIC)—The pilot designated by the operator as the person responsible for the safe and compliant operation of the aircraft on any given flight.

QUALIFIED PERSONNEL—Those who have received adequate training, instruction, or check-out to perform and/or accept the work to which they are assigned and, when required, hold appropriate FAA certificates.

REPAIR—The restoration of an airframe, powerplant, or appliance to an airworthy condition.

REQUIRED INSPECTION ITEM (RII)—A maintenance event, such as control rigging, or any repair or service so designated by the operator that requires additional inspection by a second trained and qualified technician before the aircraft is returned to service.

SCHEDULED ITEM—An item assigned to a specific interval as per our approved maintenance program.

SERVICE (Servicing)—The replenishing of fuel, oil, lubricants, supplies, cleaning, and the completion of all work items covered in the applicable service forms.

STRUCTURAL SIGNIFICANT ITEM (SSI)—A structural detail, structural element, or structural assembly that is judged significant because of the reduction in aircraft residual strength or loss of structural function, which are consequences of its failure.

SUPPLEMENTAL INSPECTION PROGRAM (SID)—An extended service life program for the aircraft in response to FAA advisory circulars. An inspection is established for each principal structural element (PSE).

SUPPLEMENTAL TYPE CERTIFICATE (STC)—A supplemental type certificate (STC) is a type certificate issued when an applicant has received FAA approval to modify an aircraft from its original design. The supplemental type certificate, which incorporates by reference the related type certificate, approves not only the modification but how that modification affects the original design.

TASKS–MAINTENANCE—An action or set of actions required to achieve a desired outcome that restores an item to or maintains an item in serviceable condition, including inspection and determination of condition.

THE BOOK—This is a binder found in each aircraft containing various forms and items required for crew members and maintenance. The aircraft inspection status sheet and aircraft discrepancy logs will found in this binder. Additional operations forms will also be found in this binder.

TECHNICAL REPRESENTATIVE—A person designated by Heritage Flight to act on their behalf to oversee maintenance being performed by outside agencies.

TEMPORARY REPAIR—Is the repair of a system or component in a manner that will be airworthy for a specific period, as listed in the maintenance manual or approved by engineering, until a permanent repair can be accomplished.

TIME BETWEEN OVERHAUL (TBO)—Is the defined interval between overhaul such as flight hours, cycles, or calendar time.

VISUAL CHECK—Is a check for condition and security using work standards to gain proximity to the areas being checked but performed visually without the use of supplementary visual aids or devices other than a light.

ZONE—Is an aircraft location in a system of identification to facilitate the grouping of system and structural items for servicing and maintenance checks.

ZONE CHECK—Shall mean a defined area of an aircraft to be inspected. Typically this will be defined per a manufacturer's procedure.

Index

About the Authors

James R. Cannon is the director of the International Standard for Business Aircraft Operations (IS-BAO) Program, where he is responsible to the International Business Aviation Council for maintaining the IS-BAO Standard, audit process, and workshops. As a former naval aviator, Jim has extensive flight and managerial experience, accumulating over 14,200 flight hours, with type ratings in seven different business aircraft. His managerial experience includes 25 years of senior management experience in business aviation, with six years of service on the NBAA board of directors. He has authored over 50 articles in aviation management for international publications and served as an IS-BAO auditor. His educational credentials include a BS degree in industrial management from the University of Tennessee and an MBA from the University of Connecticut.

Dr. Franklin D. Richey is the associate dean for the College of Aviation at the Daytona Beach Campus of Embry-Riddle Aeronautical University, where he is responsible for assisting with the administration of 10 degree programs to over 2,400 students. These degree programs range from the associate of science to the PhD in aviation. Before joining Embry-Riddle in 1982, Dr. Richey completed a career as a naval aviator in the U.S. Marine Corps where he accumulated over 10,000 hours of flight time. Since joining Embry-Riddle, he has been active in encouraging young students to seek a career in business aviation. He presently serves as advisor to the "Official NBAA Student Group" and teaches a course in the PhD in aviation degree. His educational credentials include a BS in meteorology from the Naval Postgraduate School, an MBA from Pepperdine University, and a DBA from Nova Southeastern University.